The Child's Theory of Mind

The MIT Press Series in Learning, Development, and Conceptual Change

Lila Gleitman, Susan Carey, Elissa Newport, and Elizabeth Spelke, editors

Names for Things: A Study in Human Learning, John Macnamara, 1982

Conceptual Change in Childhood, Susan Carey, 1985

"Gavagai!" or the Future History of the Animal Language Controversy, David Premack, 1986

Systems That Learn: An Introduction to Learning Theory for Cognitive and Computer Scientists, Daniel N. Osherson, 1986

From Simple Input to Complex Grammar, James L. Morgan, 1986

Concepts, Kinds, and Cognitive Development, Frank C. Keil, 1988

Learnability and Cognition: The Acquisition of Argument Structure, Steven Pinker, 1989

Mind Bugs: The Origins of Procedural Misconception, Kurt VanLehn, 1989

Categorization and Naming in Children: Problems of Induction, Ellen M. Markman, 1989

The Child's Theory of Mind, Henry M. Wellman, 1990

The Child's Theory of Mind

Henry M. Wellman

A Bradford Book
The MIT Press
Cambridge, Massachusetts
London, England

First MIT Press paperback edition, 1992
1990 Massachusetts Institute of Technology

This book was set in Palatino by Compset, Inc. and printed and bound in the United States of America.

Library of Congress Cataloging-in-Publication Data

Wellman, Henry M.
 The child's theory of mind / Henry M. Wellman.

    p.   cm.—(Learning, development, and conceptual change)
 "A Bradford book."
 Includes bibliographical references.
 ISBN 0-262-23153-0 (hb), 0-262-73099-5 (pb)
 1. Cognition in children. 2. Philosophy of mind. 3. Children—
Attitudes. I. Title. II. Series.
BF723.C5W45   1990
155.4′13—dc20   89-49578
                                                                      CIP

For my parents, Hank and Martha, and my wife, Karen

Contents

Series Foreword

This series in learning, development, and conceptual change will include state-of-the-art reference works, seminal book-length monographs, and texts on the development of concepts and mental structures. It will span learning in all domains of knowledge, from syntax to geometry to the social world, and will be concerned with all phases of development, from infancy through adulthood.

The series intends to engage such fundamental questions as

The nature and limits of learning and maturation: the influence of the environment, of initial structures, and of maturational changes in the nervous system on human development; learnability theory; the problem of induction; domain specific constraints on development.

The nature of conceptual change: conceptual organization and conceptual change in child development, in the acquisition of expertise, and in the history of science.

Lila Gleitman
Susan Carey
Elissa Newport
Elizabeth Spelke

Acknowledgments

In the mid-1970s I collaborated with John Flavell in research on me-tamemory, that is, people's knowledge or beliefs about their memo-ries. But I found that my basic interest in this research encompassed a broader topic: people's, and specifically children's, understanding of the mind—their developing knowledge and beliefs about the men-tal world and mental phenomena, for example, knowledge about everyday activities such as remembering, thinking, and dreaming, and about more exotic topics such as neuroanatomy and mind-brain relations. Hence, borrowing a phrase from Premack and Woodruff (1978), I began to term my interests the child's "theory of mind."

My aim in writing this book has been to craft a story about chil-dren's developing theories of mind that is reasonably valid and com-prehensive. This story must be compiled out of bits and pieces of my own and others' research. My own research encompasses several in-vestigations, some recently published in other sources, some only just completed, some in progress. My prior publications, because they do not include the most recent work, and because of their mod-est length in comparison to the scope of the topic, do not provide an integrated description of the research program or a comprehensive story of children's development. These are the virtues of the present book, I hope. To achieve the needed comprehensive exposition I have made free use of work that is available in other recent articles. This is not unusual but it requires proper acknowledgment. In this regard, I note:

1. My article "First steps in the child's theorizing about the mind" (Wellman, 1988a) is an expanded version of the last part of chapter 1 of this book.
2. The report of the three studies reviewed in chapter 2 parallels that of Estes, Wellman, and Woolley (1989).
3. Chapter 3 includes a reprise of two of the three studies pub-lished in Wellman and Bartsch (1988) as well as some new research.

4. Several of the studies reported in chapter 6 are published in Bartsch and Wellman (1989) and Wellman and Bartsch (1988).
5. Chapter 7 includes research reported in Wellman and Woolley (in press).

In general, and especially in those cases where an alternate publication exists, I have avoided journal-like presentation of inferential statistics. I believe that, given precise experimental designs and methods, the main results of many studies can be precisely presented in graphs. For this reason, and for readability, I have relied primarily on graphical presentation of the findings. The results are unambiguously statistically significant where expected. Statistical tests are presented in the cited alternate publications and occasionally in a note when that seems helpful.

Because I wish to present my own research in an integrated fashion as well as to depict children's developing theories of mind more generally, this book is admittedly egocentric and personalized. I rely heavily on others' research but I organize that research around my own. I believe that by the end of the book I have made it clear that a great deal of clever research exists due to the efforts of a great many researchers; telling the tale of the child's theory of mind is a cooperative enterprise, by no means simply my own. I ask these other researchers to forgive my personalistic style of presentation.

Many persons and organizations have contributed to advancing my interests and work, beginning with John Flavell and Carl Johnson. I am indebted and grateful to them both. More recently, I have been aided and inspired by discussion with other colleagues now interested in these topics. Of special note here are Heinz Wimmer, Josef Perner, Paul Harris, Alison Gopnik, Michael Chandler, Susan Gelman, Susan Carey, and Marilyn Shatz whose researches have spurred and informed me. It is exciting to join forces with such excellent colleagues in tackling overlapping and in some cases identical questions. My ideas have been shaped by my reading of several philosophers and psychologists, but it is not easy for me to identify all the influences on my thinking and thus acknowledge the appropriate sources. I am indebted, at the very least, to my reading of Churchland, Lewis, Laudan, Davidson, Stitch, and Morton among philosophers and Piaget, Heider, Carey, Lakoff, and Medin among psychologists and linguists.

Even the research presented in this book that I claim as my own is largely collaborative, engendered by discussion with and executed by the efforts of several excellent students. Most notably I wish to acknowledge and thank David Estes, Karen Bartsch, and Jacqui

Woolley, without whose efforts and ideas this book could not have been written. Others have provided crucial assistance: Mita Banerjee, Catherine Givens, Bill Bacon.

Much of the research summarized here was supported by a research grant (HD-22149) and a career development award (HD-00525), both from the National Institute of Child Health and Human Development. The writing of this book was supported by a sabbatical from the University of Michigan and by an award from the James McKeen Cattell Foundation. I gratefully acknowledge the help of these institutions along with my home units at the University of Michigan: the Department of Psychology and the Center for Human Growth and Development. My own skills and ideas have prospered because of the support of these units specifically and the university generally. In this context I especially wish to thank my colleague Harold Stevenson for his expert advice and his friendship.

Finally, I have dedicated this book to my parents and to my wife. I am constantly aware of how much support, encouragement, and sustenance I unfailingly receive from these sources. Heart and mind are closely tied together for me, and never more so than with these individuals.

The Child's Theory of Mind

Chapter 1
Children, Theories, and the Mind:
An Introduction

The title for this book encompasses my three themes: theories, theories of mind, and the child's developing theories of mind. I am interested in charting children's knowledge of an intriguing topic, the mind, and in pursuing a particular characterization of that knowledge: that it constitutes a coherent commonsense theory. I am not alone in this interest or in my choice of terminology (see, for example, Astington, Harris, and Olson, 1988).

Arriving at some sort of understanding of mind is an important accomplishment of childhood. It is important, I believe, because knowledge of the mind is central to several larger conceptual achievements. For example, an understanding of mental phenomena illuminates our understanding of the physical world because immaterial things such as dreams contrast with material objects. Thus, understanding the mind is part of children's and adults' ontological knowledge (Keil, 1979)—their understanding of what sorts of things there are. In this regard, children's efforts parallel the more developed and articulated efforts of philosophers of mind. Both undertake a fundamental cognitive endeavor: "I see philosophy as a field which has certain central questions, for example, the relation between thought and reality" (Putnam, 1975, p. xvii).

An understanding of the mind is also fundamental to an understanding of the social world. Children come to understand that the overt actions of self and others are the products of internal mental states such as beliefs and desires. They thus come to distinguish between accidental and intended behavior, between wishes and reality, between plans and outcomes, between truth and deception. In this respect, our understanding of the mind is part of our larger understanding of human action, our everyday or commonsense psychology:

> In everyday life we form ideas about other people and about social situations. We interpret other people's actions and we predict what they will do under certain circumstances. Though these

ideas are usually not formulated, they often function adequately. They achieve in some measure what a science is supposed to achieve: an adequate description of the subject matter which makes prediction possible. In the same way one talks about a naive physics . . . one can talk about a "naive psychology" which gives us the principles we use to build up our picture of the social environment and which guides our reactions to it. . . . [We] must deal with common-sense psychology regardless of whether its assumptions and principles prove valid under scientific scrutiny. If a person believes that the lines in his palm foretell his future, this belief must be taken into account in explaining certain of his expectations and actions. (Heider, 1958, p. 5)

In this book I focus primarily on one aspect of our commonsense psychology, specifically our naive understanding of the mind. But the notion of mind is central to commonsense psychology generally. In our everyday psychology we explain and understand human behavior mentalistically.

The questions that motivate this book, then, are, when and how children acquire a commonsense mentalism and consequently a commonsense mentalistic psychology. Or, what is our everyday understanding of mind like, especially what is it like in childhood? To answer these questions requires careful study of children. Heider analyzed adult conceptions by appealing primarily to common adult intuitions. But children's understandings might be different from our own, and indeed they seem likely to be quite different at younger ages. Thus, I take part of my task to be empirically researching the nature of children's conceptions. The empirical enterprise here is somewhat akin to cultural anthropology; the aim is to understand a worldview that might prove different from our own. Achieving this aim requires data from child informants.

Heider embedded his analysis of naive psychology in a larger theory of interpersonal relations—Lewin's life-space theory. His explication was not derived from that theory but was framed by it. I hope to frame my analyses within a different larger theory. In brief, I contend that our naive understanding of mind, our mentalistic psychology, is a theory. It is a naive theory but not unlike a scientific theory. Following Morton (1980) I will term this contention the theory-theory. Thus, I favor a strong and intriguing rendition of Heider's hint that our commonsense ideas in this realm "achieve in some measure what a science is supposed to achieve." A general theory-theory is obviously not a new position (see also Churchland, 1981; Fodor, 1987; Stitch, 1983). However, I claim that children's knowledge in this domain is theorylike at an early age. Indeed, part of the intrigue in studying children's theory of mind is that it may constitute their first commonsense theory.

Recently, developmental psychologists (Carey, 1985a), educators (Champagne, Klopfer, and Gunstone, 1982), and cognitive psychologists (Murphy and Medin, 1985) have become increasingly intrigued with the possibility that much human knowledge is organized around naive theories that encompass substantial domains (naive psychology, biology, physics). These everyday theories develop and change, and they constrain derivative concepts. Everyday theories provide meaning and organization to individuals' understanding of the world and color attempts to learn and infer more. The interrelated claims that naive knowledge inheres in theories, that this is true for children as well as adults, and that conceptual change is a kind of theory change provide a promising perspective on some fundamental concerns about cognition and cognitive development. However, the key notion, that of everyday theories, is in need of serious development. In part what is needed is precise description of some examples of commonsense theories and their development. Also needed is conceptual analysis and clarification of the theory construct itself. A focus on commonsense theories of mind provides a useful vehicle for undertaking both of these tasks and thus for advancing our understanding of everyday theories more generally.

The Phenomena

What sorts of understandings do we have about the mind? What concepts are generated and organized by underlying commonsense theories of mind? Here are some obvious examples shared by most adults:

1. Thoughts are different from things. A thought about a dog is distinctly different from a dog. One is mental and immaterial, the other physical and concrete.
2. Beliefs are different from actuality. Thus beliefs can be false; one can believe the earth is flat, although it is actually spherical.
3. Desires are different from outcomes; plans are different from acts. I can desire to visit Australia and even plan to go, but actually going to Australia is a different matter altogether, one not necessarily arising from my desires and plans. I may never go because I lack the money; or I may be hijacked to Australia when I do not want to go. In this sense mental activities are different from actions themselves.

4. Fantasy is unconstrained by factuality. One can imagine impossible, not-real, or simply hypothetical objects and states of affairs: unicorns, perfect vacuums, eternal youth, life after death.
5. Mind is private and mind is individual. My mind is not yours. My thoughts, desires, consciousness are not directly public. Consequently, mental states or attitudes can be quite different from one person to another. I can think of myself as handsome; you can think of me as quite plain.
6. Mind is not body. My body may be chained, but my thoughts can be free. My mind may be tired when my body is rested and energetic.
7. Reasoning about mind is different from reasoning about facts or physical states. Factually, if Reagan is the president, and Reagan is a retired actor, then the president is a retired actor. But even if Jill thinks that Reagan is president, she does not necessarily think the president is a retired actor.

These examples suggest that for adults at least there is a mental world of thoughts, beliefs, desires, fantasies, mental entities, and private selves—a world that we know and understand but one quite different from the physical, public, factual, material world.

Acknowledgment of this mental world seems pervasive, entrenched in many everyday presumptions and understandings. This can be made clear by a thought experiment. Imagine the worldview of a creature, an alien, say, with no conception of mind. Such an alien might be able to remember, to know, to learn but would posses no constructs such as memory, knowledge, and mind to frame its understanding of behavior and cognition. For such a creature, persons would be seen and heard, but they would not be understood as possessing a backlog of ideas or beliefs organizing their actions and lives. Indeed for such a creature, no one would be construed as possessing private persona underlying public behavior. Ubiquitous concepts such as illusions, interpretations, mistakes, deceptions, and impressions, not to mention beliefs, guesses, hopes, and wishes, would be absent from the alien's conceptual repertoire because those concepts hinge on an understanding of the potential noncorrespondence between mental states and external events.

It is difficult to imagine such an alien worldview but not impossible. A quintessential behaviorist, for example, who explains behavior purely on the basis of functional relations between observable stimuli and observable responses, adopts such a nonmental perspective. Still, this thought experiment shows just how different a nonmental worldview is from the everyday view we typically take for granted.

From this brief reconnaissance into our everyday mentalism, fascinating questions arise concerning the ideas of children. Is an understanding of mind inborn? Or are children at some early age like the alien described and then develop an understanding of mind? If so, when and how are such notions acquired? A classic hypothesis is that indeed children initially do not share adult notions of mind, that they have instead a nonmental perspective on events we construe so mentalistically. This hypothesis was early and forcibly argued by Piaget:

> Let us imagine a being, knowing nothing of the distinction between mind and body. . . . His notions of self would undoubtedly be much less clear than ours. Compared with us he would experience much less the sensation of the thinking self within him, the feeling of a being independent of the external world. . . . The psychological perceptions of such a being would be entirely different from our own. Dreams, for example, would appear to him as a disturbance breaking in from without. . . . We shall try to prove that such is the case with the child. The child knows nothing of the nature of thought, even at the stage when he is being influenced by adult talk concerning "mind", "brain", "intelligence." (Piaget, 1929, p. 37)

Piaget's term for this early nonmentalism was *childhood realism*. More recent investigators have also endorsed childhood realism, as we shall see. In this book I advance an alternative developmental hypothesis. I do not propose that an understanding of mind is innately given (as does Fodor, 1987); it is not available at birth, nor does it simply emerge by maturation. An understanding of mind is constructed by the child in the course of development. But at the same time I do not think that past developmental accounts are correct; accounts such as Piaget's have gotten the developmental story wrong and quite young children are mentalists. Importantly, however, I wish not just to refute prior claims but to replace them; I wish to craft a more accurate story of early knowledge, its nature and development. To me, the new, improved developmental story is as fascinating as the old. The fascination of the topic itself and the intrigue of an important development remain the same, but the story is different.

Overview

In this book I argue that while infants do not have a theory of mind, young preschoolers do. Acquisition of such a theory is a momentous achievement. Initially I focus on the knowledge of mind possessed by three-year-olds. This age manifests a very early chapter, if not the first, in the story of the development of a mature theory of mind. It is important to capture adequately this early step. If we are off the mark initially, then subsequent chapters are thrown off as well because later developments build on earlier ones.

My proposal as to the status of young children's knowledge of the mind is sufficiently complex that it requires several chapters to develop adequately. The proposal is sufficiently broad that it encompasses a great variety of topics, issues, and data. In this section I give an overview of the topics and issues and explain the layout of the rest of the book, focusing on my three themes: theories, theories of mind, and children's theories of mind.

Theories

What constitutes a theory is a deep and unresolved question in the philosophy of science (see, for example, Suppe, 1974). Nonetheless, three features seem central to whether some body of knowledge is a theory. These features are not definitive, but they provide an initial framework for discussion. In chapter 5, I characterize theories in greater detail.

Imagine a continuum of the sorts of knowledge a person might possess. At one end are discrete, minimally connected facts about some set of things—for example, since I am mythologically naive, my knowledge of mythical creatures such as dragons, gryphons, and unicorns, or my (impoverished) knowledge of the vice-presidents of the United States. At the other end of the continuum might be a scientific theory about some domain of phenomena. For example, consider the knowledge of astronomy possessed by an expert astronomer. What features characterize knowledge at the theorylike end of this continuum?

First, as you progress along this continuum toward the theory end, knowledge gets more coherent. By coherent I mean that the concepts and terms of interest become embedded in one another, each providing necessary support for the rest. Indeed, in theories it becomes impossible to consider a single concept in isolation because its meaning and significance are determined by its role in an interrelated web of other constructs and terms. The notion of a planet, for example, is a concept entrenched in a larger understanding of the solar system, comets, and asteroids and how bodies revolve around others because of differing mass and gravitational forces. In the extreme, concepts within a theory—theoretical terms—get their meaning through their interconnections with other terms in the theory, by virtue of their place in a context of cohesive propositions.

A second characteristic feature of many theories is that they rest upon specific ontological distinctions or commitments. Theories carve phenomena into different kinds of entities and processes; they specify, directly or indirectly, the kinds of things that are in the relevant domain. Current understanding of astronomy, for example, specifies that stars are not pinpoints of light on a heavenly spherical screen at fixed distance from us but massive bodies each similar to the sun, coexisting and interrelating within an extended space-time continuum of immense extent. Scholars with very different philosophies of science agree that a theory is held together in part by an accepted conception of its objects (Carey, 1985; Morton, 1980; Churchland, 1984).

Third, a theory provides a causal-explanatory framework to account for, make understandable, and make predictable phenomena in its domain. Celestial mechanics, for example, provides explanations for days, seasons, tides, eclipses, and the observed movements of stars and planets, to name just a few. What counts as an explanation differs across theories; consider, for example, the differences between astronomy and economics. However, that a theory revolves around a causal-explanatory scheme seems essential.

In total, then, subscribers to a theory share a basic conception of the phenomena encompassed by the theory, a sense of how propositions about these phenomena are interdependent, and consequently what counts as a relevant and informative explanation of changes and relationships among the various phenomena. To use an example somewhat closer to home, consider the similarities and differences between behavioristic and Piagetian theories of behavior and development. Both offer coherent, causal-explanatory schemes based on distinctive ways for conceptualizing the domain of human action; they are cogent theoretical accounts. Of course, the ontological commitments (such as their respective foci on behavior versus mental structures) and causal-explanatory workings of these two theories are quite different.

Theory of Mind

An obvious question, given this analysis, is whether our everyday understanding of mind constitutes a theory. This is an intriguing question, indeed, a controversial one in philosophy of mind (Stitch, 1983; Morton, 1980). An answer requires a detailed characterization of our adult knowledge of the mind. I provide such a characterization in chapter 4. For now, I will offer two preliminary justifications for assuming that the adult's understanding of mind is something theorylike. First, in current philosophy of mind, a strong contender as a model for everyday adult understanding of the mind is what Morton (1980) calls the theory-theory. The theory-theory is the contention that our knowledge of the mental world—the realm of beliefs, desires, intentions, thoughts, and so forth—is a theory (see also Churchland, 1981, 1984). It is a naive theory, not a developed or disciplined scientific theory, but a theory nonetheless.

Second, intuitively adults' knowledge of the mind can be characterized by the three theory-relevant features outlined. Thus, with respect to coherence, adults' understanding of mental terms and their related concepts seems like a coherent, mutually defining body of knowledge. If I must try to define what dreams are, for example, I will refer to thoughts and mental images. If I try to define thoughts, I will mention dreams, memories, imagination, fantasies, and the like.

With respect to ontology, adults' knowledge of the mind is based on a basic and relevant ontological distinction: that between internal mental entities and processes on the one hand and physical objects and events on the other. In our everyday conception, mental entities and processes, such as thoughts and dreaming, are categorically different sorts of things from external physical objects and events, such as rocks and thunderstorms, and from manifest observable actions, such as running. The presence of this ontological divide in adult thinking is evident in many natural language distinctions: idea-thing, psychological-physical, fantasy-reality, mind-body, mental-real.

Finally, with respect to casual-explanatory frameworks, adults' understanding of the mind is part and parcel of such a framework. Indeed, a coherent conception of the mind is central to everyday explanation and prediction of human behavior. We explain our own and others' actions mentalistically, that is, in terms of the wishes, hopes, beliefs, plans, and intentions of the actor. A shorthand description for this causal explanatory system is that it is a belief-desire construal of action. John's going to the store to buy groceries, for example, is explained by John's desire to eat and his belief that he can buy food at the grocery store. Similarly, I may decide to go to the grocery store rather than to the drugstore because I desire to get food, not pharmaceuticals, and I believe that food is found at the grocery store.

In sum, adults seem to possess a theory of mind, manifest in a naive psychology. The notions invoked there—thoughts, dreams, beliefs, and desires—form an interconnected coherent body of concepts;

they rest on, or indeed define, basic ontological conceptions; and the theory provides a causal-explanatory account of a domain of phenomena: human action and thought.

The Child's Early Theory of Mind

I believe that children also have a theorylike understanding of the mind by three years of age. What sort of data would support such a claim? From the preceding discussion it follows that we need data as to children's understanding of the coherence, the ontology, and the causal-explanatory framework of the theory. In chapter 2, therefore, I provide data with regard to whether three-year-old children appreciate the necessary ontological distinction between mental and physical entities. On this topic, my collaborators and I have investigated, for example, children's understanding of the distinction between a thought about a chair versus a chair. In chapter 3 I tackle whether three-year-olds understand the key causal-explanatory notion of our theory of mind—that is, whether and when children understand that actor's mental states, specifically their beliefs and desires, cause their overt actions. Finally, what about coherence? In chapter 4 I describe the coherence of the adult theory of mind, as I see it. Following that depiction, in chapter 6, I present data as to three-year-olds' initial understanding of this coherent theory.

After describing three-year-olds' initial belief-desire psychology and concomitant theory of mind, I move in two directions. In one direction I consider younger children still. Here the question is, Where does the child's initial theory of mind come from? In chapter 8 I propose some answers to this question. One is that younger children have a still earlier theory; specifically, I argue that the three-year-old's initial belief-desire psychology arises, in part, as a theory change from the two-year-old's earlier psychology. The two-year-old's naive psychology, I propose, is based on an understanding of simple desires; it includes no understanding of belief, that is, no understanding that persons possess internal mental representations—convictions—as to how the world is.

In the other direction I consider how three-year-olds' theory of mind changes substantially in the course of subsequent development. In essence in chapters 9, 10, and 11, I contend that three-year-olds' early understanding contrasts with that of older children's and adults' in two respects.

First, I argue that although three-year-olds are committed adherents to our folk psychological theory of mind, they are only novice theorists, mastering the theory's central tenets and grasping its most obvious implications but not fluent yet in the theory's workings, applications, and nuances. Many of us have encountered different levels of mastery of a theory—for example, when we have taught students about behaviorism or about Piaget's theory. It is easy to imagine, then, a person who upon exposure to the theory accepts it—considers himself a behaviorist, for example—and understands the basic workings of the theory but has not yet mastered the theory. Consider, for example, an apprentice behaviorist who has not yet confronted the construct of secondary reinforcement and thus believes that all conditioned behavior is a product of primary reinforcers such as food. Or consider a novice behaviorist who is as yet unaware of the theoretical relationship of conditioning, pseudoconditioning, and habituation. In short, there can obviously be persons ignorant of a great deal of the theory who would mistakenly attribute to the theory simplistic predictions but nonetheless whose understanding of the domain in question reflects the general theoretical position. Such a novice could still appreciate many of the theory's essential distinctions—that between classical and instrumental conditioning, for example. He or she could articulate a coherent understanding of the basic set of theoretical terms and descriptions of the theory—for example, conditioned and unconditioned stimuli, conditioned and unconditioned responses, shaping, and extinction. And he or she could appreciate in principle, if not in detail, the explanatory heart of the theory: the acquisition of new behaviors from a prior behavioral repertoire and a specific conditioning history. Thus it is easy to image persons who have a sensible theoretical understanding of a domain of inquiry and yet are limited and even faulty in their predictions and explanations from the theory. Something like this, I claim, is the extent of three-year-olds' knowledge with respect to our everyday psychology. The three-year-old's theoretical commitment is clear, and a basic grasp of the theory's coherence, ontology, and explanatory system is in place, but little more is understood. I describe children's growing expertise, beyond three, in chapters 10 and 11.

Second, it is important to consider the notion of mind that characterizes the young child's theorizing. In this regard, I claim that children's theory of mind changes in an important and qualitative way during the preschool years because their notion of mind itself changes. Consider two different senses for the term *mind*. One is the notion of mind required for a rudimentary but coherent mentalistic theory of human action. Notice that the primary object of theoretical consideration here is human action. The phenomena of interest are not behaviors—forming the hand like so or moving the body thusly—but actions described with respect to an actor's beliefs and desires—

going to the store. The mentalism entrenched in such a theory is of critical importance, but the notion of mind itself need not be fleshed out in any detail. In fact, it seems to me that the young child could explain and predict much about human action by treating the mind itself as something like a simple container. To understand that persons "hold" beliefs, for example, does not require an elaborated notion of the mind and its workings; the requisite notion need be nothing more than the repository or the sum of a person's mental attitudes and contents.

Contrast that concept of mind with a second one—one more like that underlying contemporary cognitive psychology. In this case the mind itself and its organized collection of processes becomes more focal. The mind not only holds beliefs; it perceives, construes, and interprets information about the world and then hypothesizes, conjectures, and reasons about this information. This results at times in decisions, beliefs, and knowledge and at other times in confusion, wonder, and misunderstandings. In this second sense, the mind is an intermediary that interprets and directs all perception and action; it is, in current terms, a central information processor.

I think that young preschoolers have a theory of mind in the first sense but not in the second. They have yet to achieve an understanding of the mind as an interpretive, executive, mediating entity. These two notions of the mind—mind as the sum of one's thoughts versus mind as a processor and interpreter—are similar in at least one fundamental respect: both honor the ontological distinction between thoughts and things, ideas and acts. Very young children grasp the distinction between thoughts and beliefs versus what is so; older children move beyond this to achieve a conception of a mind that actively mediates and construes. I detail this distinction and developmental description in chapter 9.

In this initial chapter I have reviewed a series of interrelated claims and outlined the story I will tell. Serious questions begin to emerge from this brief outline. Precise conceptual analyses as well as empirical research are needed to tell the story fully and convincingly. In this book I undertake to provide some of the requisite theoretical and empirical analyses.

Chapter 2

Understanding the Basic Distinction between Mental and Physical Phenomena

Theories carve phenomena into different classes and kinds. Our everyday understanding of mind achieves this as well. For example, our understanding of mind encompasses distinctions among various mental states, such as the difference between dreaming and day-dreaming or between knowing and guessing. At a more basic level of analysis, however, our everyday understanding of mind rests on a fundamental, ontological distinction: that between internal mental phenomena on the one hand and external physical and behavioral phenomena on the other. This is the bedrock on which a theory of mind is built. In this chapter I examine when children recognize this ontological distinction central to our everyday understanding of mind. To this end, my collaborators and I have examined children's understanding of the subjective, nonphysical status of mental entities, and hence whether or in what way children might be realists. I begin by clarifying these notions: ontological distinctions, childhood realism, and mental entities.

Ontological Distinctions

By terming a distinction an ontological one, I mean only that it deals with our most basic conceptions of what sorts of "things" there are in the world. I do not have a theory of ontological knowledge to present nor do I intend to resolve deep philosophical issues. I wish only to characterize briefly what makes a distinction ontological and why such distinctions are so important to our conceptions and theories. In my discussion here I will rely substantially on Frank Keil's analysis (Keil, 1979, chapter 3).

Ontological types are distinguishable, in principle, because they engender category mistakes rather than falsehoods. If I say that "that brick is lighter than air," I may be incorrect; the statement would be false if, for example, the brick is an ordinary heavy one. If, however, I say literally that "that idea is lighter than air" I am not simply incorrect; instead I have made a category mistake. This is a category mistake because ideas are not the kind of thing that can be literally heavy or light. In our everyday understanding it is neither true nor false to attribute to mental entities (an idea) spatiophysical properties (is heavy or is not, is at home or is away). Rather than true or false, such attributions are anomalous. In this fashion it is possible to appreciate that some categories differ in ontological status (bricks versus ideas) and others do not (bricks versus balloons). Theories encompass both sorts of category distinctions—those evident in falsehoods and those evident in category mistakes. But the essential character of a theory is dependent in the first instance on its ontological distinctions. Recall in this regard that a radical behaviorist would claim that our everyday category of mental things is empty. There are no such things, really, behaviorism asserts; there are only varieties of stimuli and responses, that is, varieties of physical and behavioral events. In contrast, our everyday mentalism divides the world into two ontologically different categories: mind versus matter. An essential question for understanding children's development of a theory of mind, then, is whether and when they appreciate this ontological distinction.

Childhood Realism

The term *childhood realism*, coined by Piaget, has been used widely as a description of young children's thinking, meaning roughly an inability to distinguish mental from real, physical phenomena. For example, Flavell (1970a) states that realism describes young children's tendency to "substantiate" or "physicalize" psychological phenomena: "Thus, for instance, dreams are initially conceived as external, palpable realities, potentially visible to others" (p. 1023).

Discussions of childhood realism can prove difficult and complex. The complexity is partly a result of the enthusiasm with which Piaget's initial analysis has been appropriated and expanded by others. In addition, there is a potential confusion between childhood realism and the realism commonly discussed in philosophy.

In philosophical discourse, one sense of realism refers to the view that the everyday objects of our perception (rocks, other people) exist independently of our thinking of them, occupying portions of an external space encompassing them and us. This sort of realism affirms the commonsense notion of a world of real objects presenting themselves for our perception. Realism in this sense can be contrasted with idealism, which encompasses a variety of views holding that we have no true knowledge of the existence of such a real world (because we can access only our own subjective perceptions) or even that an objective world does not exist and "external objects" are nothing but our own ideas. Realism in this sense appeals to the fundamental ontological distinction between ideas and independently existing physical objects: physical objects are material, external, public, and objective, whereas ideas are mental, internal, private, and subjective. Even idealist philosophers use this everyday distinction as a starting point for their arguments; their claim, however, is that we are mistaken in our commonsense belief that physical objects have an objective existence. Thus, realism and idealism both recognize a potent naive dualism between thought and objects. Childhood realism, in contrast, ignores such a distinction, or more accurately it precedes this dualism. Childhood realists, the claim goes, construe ideas as physical objects.

The construct of childhood realism as used by Piaget and subsequently by others confounds two notions. I will term these notions ontological (childhood) realism and epistemological (childhood) realism. This terminology is a bit strained, but the distinction is an important one. Piaget failed to distinguish clearly between these two notions because he believed young children are afflicted with both.

By ontological realism, I mean a belief that mental phenomena are real physical phenomena, for example, that dreams are external pictures observable by others. As Keil (1979) expressed it, young children "apparently think that all things are types of physical objects" (p. 128). Piaget spoke directly about this sort of conceptual adualism and at times was willing to attribute a strong form of this confusion to young children: "The child cannot distinguish a real house, for example, from the concept or mental image or name of the house" (Piaget, 1929, p. 55).

Epistemological realism is more concerned with the acquisition of knowledge or how ideas and objects are related. For example, if for children ideas are literally physical things (the ontological issue), then they could be acquired (an epistemological issue) in the same way that physical things are acquired. That is, we might collect them from the available objects we find in the world, or they might seek us out and attach themselves to us like stray dogs, or we might even build them up out of other available things and materials. Although this example shows that ontological and epistemological realism can be intimately connected, they are distinct notions. One refers to the existential status of ideas; the other refers to the origins and nature of ideas. The distinction between these two sorts of realism can be made clear by envisioning a person who is an ontological dualist—that is, who conceives of ideas and physical things as fundamentally different—but who is at the same time an epistemological realist. Such a person might firmly distinguish between thoughts and objects as types of things but nonetheless believe that ideas are directly, physically caused by objects and correspond exactly to objective situations. For example, such persons might "proceed as though they believe objects to transmit, in a direct-line-of-sight fashion, faint copies of themselves, upon anyone anyone who happens in the path of such objective knowledge. Within such a view projectile firings from things themselves bombard and actively victimize individuals who function as passive recorders and simply bear the scars of information which has been imbossed upon them" (Chandler and Boyes, 1982, p. 391).

Epistemological realism of this sort is to be contrasted with epistemological constructivism. From a constructivist perspective, ideas and even perceptions do not directly impress themselves on us and therefore do not directly correspond to reality. Instead, the person actively construes sensory information, forming imperfect representations. As a result, for example, different persons can have very different subjective impressions, thoughts, and even perceptions of the same situation.

Piaget did not distinguish between the ontological and epistemological aspects of childhood realism and thus did not consider the possibility that children might be afflicted with one form of realism but not the other. I claim that young children are not ontological realists, but they may still be epistemological realists. Given this claim, an obvious first question to address is whether young children are ever ontological realists. That is the focus of the research described in this chapter.

Mental Entities

In order to assess children's understanding of the ontological distinction between ideas and things, my collaborators and I have questioned them about mental entities. I therefore need to define mental entities and specify their place among other mental and physical phenomena. Again, my aim is not to resolve deep and persistent philosophical controversies but simply to clarify my terminology. An important preliminary point is that in everyday (and scientific) usage, we employ the language of the external physical world to talk about mental phenomena. Ideas are "rough" or "clear"; someone's thinking is "sharp" or "fuzzy." By analogy, just as the physical world includes physical entities (rocks and houses), physical events (rainstorms and recitals), and physical-chemical-biological activities or processes (respiration and combustion), so too the mental world is describable as encompassing mental entities (specific thoughts and beliefs), mental events (dreams and fantasies), and mental activities or processes (re-membering, thinking, free associating). This imperfect analogy high-lights some useful distinctions within the mental realm. For instance, a conversation about dreams might focus on dreaming as a process (rapid eye movement sleep), or on dreams as events (with a story line that unfolds in time), or on dream entities (a dream-monster).

Much talk about the mental world involves such mental verbs as *remember, guess, believe, think, know, dream*. Statements using such verbs typically identify one sort of mental activity out of many—dreaming versus remembering—and identify some content. Thus, I dream *about a dog*; I guess *what you will say*; I imagine *a unicorn*. I have used the term *mental entities* to refer to the mental contents or prod-ucts of such everyday mental activities and statements (Wellman and Estes, 1986). Mental entities therefore include the dream-dog in the statement, "I had a dream about a large dog." Mental entities (a dream-dog or a thought-of-a-dog) are distinctly different from corre-sponding real entities (a dog), and this difference is a central instance of the general difference between thought and object, mental and physical, mind and reality.

As is clear in these examples, mental entities are representational entities. The actual contents or specifics of some mental entity rep-resents and refers to something, its referent. A memory of a particular large black dog known in childhood is not the same as the dog, but it represents, or mentions, or refers to it. Thus, I need to highlight some aspects of the representational relationship between thoughts and things. Again, I do not aim to resolve thorny issues about refer-ence, but it is useful to distinguish three possibilities. First, the refer-ent of a mental entity may really exist (or have once existed). Or the referent may be hypothetical—perhaps existing and perhaps not, as, for example, when a bachelor fantasizes about his future wife. Fi-nally, the referent may be mythical—clearly nonexistent or fictional—as, for example, when we think about a unicorn. In all these cases, however, even in the case of a thought about an existing physical object, the mental entity itself is mental and not physical. It is important to note that mental entities are not unique in being repre-sentational. Photographs and drawings, for example, are also repre-sentations. In this regard mental entities, such as a thought-of-a-dog, can be understood as the mental parallel to something like a picture-of-a-dog. Of course, thoughts are not necessarily graphical like pic-tures, and thoughts are mental, insubstantial, and nonphysical whereas pictures are physical objects. Still, both are similarly repre-sentational entities.

Finally, a distinction can be drawn between a particular mental entity and mental representations and processes generically. This is the distinction between a thought-of-a-dog and thoughts, between a particular idea and ideas in general. Thoughts, ideas, and dreams in unspecified general terms have been termed "abstract objects" by Keil (1979). In our research, we have questioned children about specific mental entities, but children's responses across a variety of specific instances evidence an understanding of the mental realm more generally.

Initial Studies

Consider first the sorts of intuitive criteria that adults invoke to distinguish mental entities—such as a thought about a chair—from everyday physical objects—a chair. At least three such criteria are immediately obvious (Wellman, 1985b). First, physical objects, as opposed to their mental counterparts (a chair versus a thought about a chair), afford behavioral-sensory evidence. You can see a chair, touch it, sit on it, break it up, and burn it, but you cannot do these things to an idea or to an image of a chair. Second, physical things such as my furniture or the rooms of my house have a public existence. Other people can see and touch the walls, stand on the floor, sit on the bedroom chair. In contrast, for example, consider a mental entity such as a dream-of-a-room or a dream-of-a-chair. It might seem to me that I can see and touch such a dream-chair while dreaming, but no one else experiences these things similarly. In general, mental entities lack the sort of public existence that physical objects possess. Third, a physical object, for example, my bedroom, has a consistent existence. Each morning when I wake up, there it is. Mental entities are not similarly consistent. Each night when I go to sleep, I have different dreams; my image of a chair can come and go simply by willing it, quite unlike an actual chair.

In our initial research (Wellman and Estes, 1986), we asked whether young children judge physical and mental entities to be different in terms of these three criteria. The first study involved a series of brief presentations, each of which contrasted two characters. One presentation contrasted a boy who had a cookie with a boy who thought about a cookie. The chid was asked which of these entities—the cookie or the thought-cookie—could be seen, touched, and manipulated (behavioral sensory contact), which could be seen by someone else (publicness), and which could be manipulated in the future (consistency). Different types of mental-physical contrasts were included involving four different verbs: *think, dream, remember,* and *pretend*.

Three-, four- and five-year-olds were very good at these judgments. Even three-year-olds were correct in ascribing behavioral-sensory, public, and consistent status to physical objects but not mental entities 75% of the time, greatly in excess of chance. In addition, when children did make errors, they were as likely to ascribe not-real status to physical items as they were to ascribe physical status to not-real, mental items. Thus, even in the errors they made, young children did not display any systematic tendency toward ontological realism—that is, to interpret mental entities as physical and real.

There was a problem with this first experiment, however. Suppose children tend to misinterpret presentations about mental entities to be merely specifying nonpossession. That is, they do not understand "thinking about a cookie" to specify a mental experience, but they nevertheless at times come up with a reasonable interpretation of such descriptions. Specifically, "This boy is thinking about a cookie" might be translated into "This boy hasn't got a cookie." Young children's interpretation of mental terms in this fashion would constitute a subtle but convincing form of realism.

This concern shaped the next study we conducted (Wellman and Estes, 1986, experiment 2). We again presented mental entities as well as physical objects and had the child judge them on the basis of the three reality criteria. This time each item was a simple story about a single character. Sometimes the story depicted simple mental entities—such as a thought about a dog—sometimes a mental entity coupled with explicit mention of nonpossession of the real object, and for control purposes there were simple possession and simple nonpossession items as well. We reasoned that if young children tend to translate descriptions of mental entities into descriptions of real but absent objects, then they should do so more frequently when explicit mention of nonpossession was made along with use of the mental term. That is, such children should be even more correct on mental plus nonpossession items than they are on mental items.

Children saw a picture of the character (with no objects depicted) as that character's experience was described: "Judy doesn't have a kitty, but right now she is thinking about a kitty." Following each presentation children were asked behavioral-sensory, publicness, and consistency questions about each character's experience. Correct responses in this study are shown in figure 2.1. Consider first the top of the figure where three hypothetical patterns of results are displayed. On the left is the case where children are ontological realists in some strong and obvious sense. That is, children believe mental

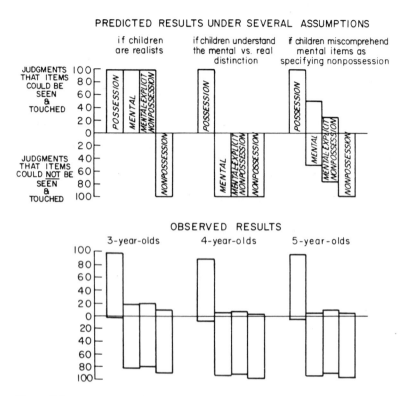

Figure 2.1
Predicted and observed responses to the judgment items in experiment 2 of Well-man and Estes (1986). From Wellman and Estes (1986).

entities to be real physical objects. If they do, then only nonpossessed items should be judged as not visible, intangible, and so on, since possessed physical objects and mental entities are equally real. What about the subtle realism case where children at times judge mental entities correctly but only when they interpret talk about such items as talk about nonpossessed objects? If this occurs, then results something like those in the upper right would obtain. Children would distinguish mental from possessed items but would do so more and more clearly to the extent that the items specify nonpossession. Thus, some decreasing stair-step pattern should be apparent for their judgments of mental, mental-explicit nonpossession, and nonpossessed entities. Finally, as presented in the middle of the figure, what if children understand the mental-physical distinction? Then only possessed items should be judged visible and tangible. As is clear from the data at the bottom of the figure, children at all ages correctly distinguished the real and mental items.

In these studies, children's ability to distinguish between mental and physical entities was also quite clear in their explanations. For example, when children were asked to say why they could not touch a thought about a dog versus why they could not touch a dog that had run away, their explanations typically fell into one of four categories:

1. Mental identity: Children said that the item is mental by using terms such as *dream, thought, imagination, pretend,* and *mind* or *brain.*

2. Reality status: Children appealed to the item's reality: "It's real"; "It's not real"; "It's not really anything."

3. Location-possession: Children talked about the object's location—here or away—or the character's possession or loss of the item: "It ran away"; "He has one."

4. Physical ability–moral constraint: Children talked about their physical ability or about moral and social constraints on action: "I'm big enough"; "My mom won't let me"; "It's not too hard."

Other sorts of explanations, and incomprehensible explanations, occurred, but these four broad categories encompassed 85% of children's explanations.

We have compared children's explanations across different item types by means of star graphs (Anderson, 1960). Figure 2.2 shows nine such graphs. Consider the upper left-hand graph. The star has four arms; each arm corresponds to one of the four categories of explanation and is marked off in percentages. The distance along an arm thus corresponds to the percentage of the children's total explanations of that one type. The plots along each arm are then connected to form a graphical figure. The upper left-hand graph shows explanations from the three-year-olds observed in Wellman and Estes (1986, experiment 2) when asked to explain their judgments for real, physical items. When asked, for example, why they say a character can touch a real ball that is physically present, three-year-olds typically say, "Because it's there." They almost never mention mental terms. The data for the other item types and for the other age groups are shown in the remainder of figure 2.2.

Note, first, the similarity in explanations across the ages, that is, for the three-, four- and five-year-olds. Note next that the explanations characteristically and appropriately differ across the item-types: real objects, mental entities, and real but absent or nonpossessed ob-

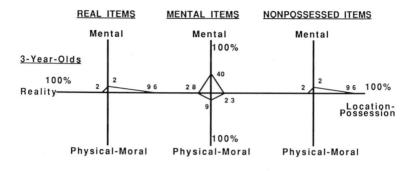

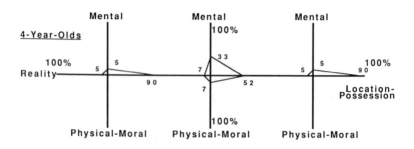

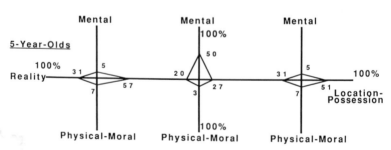

Figure 2.2
Star graphs for children's explanations in experiment 2 of Wellman and Estes (1986).
Each star presents percentages of the four different explanation types given for a
single item type by one of the three age groups.

jects. Recall that children say that both mental and nonpossessed items cannot be touched. But why? Look at the graphs. Mental entities cannot be touched in part because they are not there, they are not real, and, essentially, mental entities cannot be touched because they are mental—just a dream, only pretend, only in the story character's mind. In contrast, absent, not-possessed physical objects cannot be touched simply because they are "gone away"; they are "not there."

The data thus far show that children make appropriate distinctions between physical and mental entities in their judgments and in their extended explanations. Three-year-olds are nearly as clear about this fundamental distinction as four- and five-year-olds, who are essentially at ceiling. In fact, natural language research suggests that children understand some appropriate distinctions between mental and physical entities and events toward the end of the third year of life. Shortly after their second birthday, children begin to use mental terms such as *think, know,* and *remember* in their speech (Bretherton and Beeghley, 1982; Limber, 1973). Of course, it is possible that children could use such terms in a limited or inappropriate fashion that does not rest on an appropriate conceptual distinction between the mental and physical worlds. For example, they could use mental terms only in conceptually empty, conversational ways, as when adults say "know what?" or ". . . , you know." Or children could use mental terms merely for objective reference. Piaget (1929) claimed that children use the term *think* but believe that "thinking is with the mouth" and that "there is nothing subjective in the act of thinking" (p. 38). Similarly, Misciones et al. (1978) claimed that "limited to thinking in terms of the external appearance of things, children initially hypothesize that *know* and *guess* refer to external perceivable aspects of situations" (p. 1113). However, careful analysis of young children's speech suggests that children honor a mental-physical distinction in their everyday use of mental items.

We addressed these possibilities in a study of one child's everyday utterances,[1] corroborated by an analysis of smaller speech samples from thirty other children (Shatz, Wellman, and Silber, 1983). We coded children's use of mental verbs—essentially *know, think, mean, forget, remember, guess* and *pretend,* which account for 95% of children's first mental terms. First we coded such uses into those involving (1) probable mental reference (reference to a distinctively mental state or process), (2) objective reference, (3) empty conversational uses, and (4) residual, uninterpretable productions. Intercoder reliabilities for these codings averaged 85%. These codings revealed that the first use of mental terms for probable mental reference, carefully distinguished from conversational uses and objective reference, occurred late in the third year at about two years, nine or ten months of age. I refer to these uses as "probable" mental references because the possibility of facile but still objective use of mental terms is hard to discount completely in unconstrained natural utterances and situations. However, corroboration of mental reference at this young age comes from a further analysis of specifically contrastive uses of mental terms. If one possesses a sufficient sample of utterances, it is possible to uncover times when the child uses mental verbs in a strikingly contrastive way. For example:

Child: I thought there wasn't any socks [in the drawer], 'cept when I looked I saw them. I didn't know you got 'em.

Child: They're not real. I was pretending.

Child: I thought it was an alligator. Now I know it's a crocodile.

Child: I was teasing you. I was pretending 'cept you didn't know that.

Father: I made it up.

Child: Then it's not true.

Father: Why?

Child: Because you said you made it up. I know when you make something up it's not true.

In such contrastives, the child spontaneously contrasts reality and mentality, the objective and the subjective, fact and belief. The child distinctly rules out for the listener certain objective misinterpretations of his or her utterances ("It's not real, I was just pretending"; "I thought it was there 'cept it wasn't"). Such contrastive uses indicate that the child recognizes some distinction between mental entities and states and external objective ones and that he or she means the former, not the latter.

Contrastives of this sort occur in children's speech just before the age of three years. In our study (Shatz et al. 1983) contrastive uses emerged at exactly the same time as mental verbs used for mental reference, that is, at about two years, nine months or so in our sample of children. Such contrastives accounted for approximately 20% of the focal child's probable mental references from age two and a half to four years. This early contrastive use of mental verbs strongly suggests that, at least at times, quite young children distinguish the mental from the physical in their use of mental terms.

These results from Wellman and Estes (1986) and from Shatz et al. (1983) make clear that young children are not ontological realists in the strong sense of equating mental entities with their corresponding physical referents. Thus, the strong sense of realism, evoked by Piaget's (1929) claim that "the child cannot distinguish a real house . . . from the concept or mental image or name of the house" (p. 55), seems untenable. The possibility remains, however, that children might hold some more subtle realistic misconception. Wellman and Estes (1986) provided evidence against one such misconception—construing mental entities as simply absent or nonpossessed physical entities. Other sorts of realistic misconceptions are clearly possible, however. For example, ideas and dreams may indeed be conceived of as physical things but as special, seemingly insubstantial types of physical things, perhaps equivalent in naive conception to such real substances as smoke or shadows or air. Piaget (1929) quoted older preschoolers as saying that thoughts are smoke, air, shadows, lights, or sounds. Keil (1979) made a similar point:

> Five-year-olds apparently think that all things are types of physical objects and therefore find it perfectly appropriate for physical object predicates to span events and abstract objects. This finding does not necessarily mean that ideas and dreams must have the properties of the things thought or dreamt about, but only that children attribute to them some physical properties and have great difficulty thinking of them as nonphysical entities. . . . Since children are forced to make such abstract entities physical, it is not surprising that one of their strategies is to give abstract things the properties of the physical objects that those abstract things denote. The point is that there are many other possible strategies that children can use, and they are not bound to make an entity such as a dream physical by attributing to it the properties of the dreamed-of object. Some children in the preschool study made dreams physical by thinking of them as rocks, while others thought of them as clouds, and in neither case were the dreams about rocks or clouds. (Keil, 1979, p. 128)

A number of less substantial physical entities exist with which mental entities might be confused. For adults, however, mental entities contrast with even these "close impostors," as they can be called. The following list provides some contrasting examples:

(1) Real external objects: material, public, external things.

(2) Absent real objects: like (1) but outside sensory range.

(3) Insubstantial objects (air, smoke): like (1) but seemingly intangible and/or invisible.

(4) Physical representations (drawings, pictures): material, public objects but representing some other object with very different physical features.

(5) Internal sensations (such as a stomachache): private and internal but localizable and still physically real experiences.

(6) Mental entities (ideas, dreams): immaterial, private, and symbolic cognitive representations.

Given the subtle features of mental entities (6), a young child might plausibly identify them with something like smoke, shadows, pains, or pictures (3–5) even if he or she does not identify them with prototypic external objects (1) or with absent objects (2).

   The sorts of entities listed above populate one region of a larger conceptual space. This space is an ontological one, encompassing different kinds of possible things. I do not believe (as claimed by Keil, 1979) that ontological knowledge is strictly hierarchically organized. But this space can be partitioned reasonably, and fundamentally different sorts of things can be contrasted with one another. In the research that I present next, my collaborators and I have been generally interested in children's understanding of this larger conceptual space, but our specific interest is whether children recognize one basic division within this space—that between mental (6) and physical (1–4) entities.

An Experiment with Close Impostors

To begin to assess whether young children differentiate mental entities from close impostors, Jacqui Woolley and I (Estes, Wellman, and Woolley, 1989) asked children simple judgment questions like those used by Wellman and Estes (1986), for example, "Can you touch a dreamed tree with your hand?" But in this case we were interested primarily in children's explanations for such judgments. We especially wished to examine whether children distinguished between mental and physical items designed to elicit identical judgments regarding various physical acts. One cannot touch the shadow of a tree nor can one touch a dream-tree, but adults explain their physical inability in the two cases quite differently.

Method

Fifty-nine preschool children were tested: 19 three-year-olds (range 2–11 to 3–11), 20 four-year-olds (range 4–0 to 4–11), and 20 five-year-olds (range 5–3 to 6–6); 32 girls and 27 boys. Each child heard 18 brief stories of two to three sentences each and responded to three behavioral-sensory questions after each story. Each story was accompanied by a simple black-and-white line drawing of a child character. The objects in the stories were not depicted in the drawings.

Three general types of stories were used, involving mental entities, solid physical objects, and close impostor entities. All the entities are shown in table 2.1. The alignment of the rows in this table shows our attempt to include comparable contents across the different item types. Thus, every mental X can be contrasted with a similar solid physical X, and many of the solid physical items can be contrasted with close impostor items.

An example of the stories is: "See this boy. He always wanted a bicycle. Sometimes when he is asleep, he dreams about a bicycle." Following each story the child was asked three judgment questions: whether the story character (1) could see the entity referred to in the story with his or her eyes, (2) could touch the entity with his or her hands, and (3) could hide the entity under his or her bed. Each question was prefaced by a simple clause that reiterated the gist of the story ("*Now that this boy is dreaming about a bicycle,* can he touch that bicycle with his hands?"). Each judgment answer was followed by an

Table 2.1
Items Used in the Close Impostor Experiment

Mental Entities	Solid Physical Objects	Close impostors
1. Thought: Ball	4. Real ball	
2. Dream: Bike	5. Real bike	
3. Memory: Baby food	6. Real baby food	
	7. Real tree	12. Shadow of a tree
	8. Real toothpaste	13. Used-up toothpaste
	9. Real lion	14. Photograph of a lion
	10. Real leaves	15. Burned-up leaves
	11. Real sand	16. Smoke
		17. Pain: Tummy-ache
		18. Sound: Beep

explanation question solicited, for example, by asking, "Why can't the boy see it with his eyes?"[2]

Results

Children's explanations were our primary interest. Nevertheless, some of children's judgment answers could sensibly differentiate mental from solid physical entities. Indeed, children's judgments of the mental versus solid physical items for the see and touch questions replicated the findings of Wellman and Estes (1986). When the children were asked if someone could see or touch prototypic physical objects such as a ball, 90% of their responses were *yes*, as was appropriate. When asked if mental entities could be seen or touched, 75% of the responses were appropriately *no*.

Given that children demonstrated a discernable grasp of behavioral-sensory differences between mental entities and solid physical ones, did they appropriately distinguish mental entities versus close impostors? While both smoke and thoughts are intangible, for example, they are by no means identical kinds of things, and adults can allude to appropriate differences between them in their explanations.

Across children ($N = 55$), items (18), and questions (3), we collected 2,970 explanations. Children's explanations typically fell into one of four superordinate substantive categories, or into a residual category including "I don't know," incomprehensible replies, and refusals to answer. The four focal categories are those outlined earlier: (1) mental descriptions ("He's just imagining it"), (2) reality status considerations ("It's not real"), (3) location-possession explanations ("It's not there"), and (4) physical ability/moral constraint considerations ("It's too big," or "Her mom doesn't let her"). This categorization scheme is presented in more detail in Estes, Wellman, and Woolley (1990). These four categories captured 82% of children's explanations. Intercoder reliability between two independent coders was 90%.

Because we wished to show that children recognize mental entities as different from other kinds of entities that also fail simple behavioral-sensory tests, we focused on children's explanations of their negative judgments (that something cannot be seen, touched, or hidden). Negative judgments comprised 62% of the total judgments and 77% of all judgments of mental entities and close impostors.

Star graphs (Anderson, 1960) again provide an informative means of representing children's explanations. Nine different star graphs are presented in figure 2.3; each of the four arms of each star corresponds to one category of explanation. The graphs reveal first and foremost

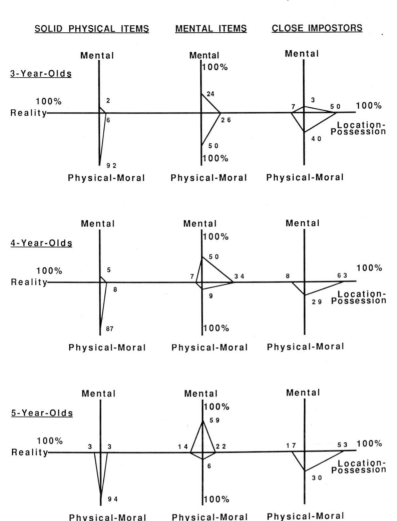

Figure 2.3
Star graphs for children's explanations for items in the close impostor experiment.
From Estes, Wellman, and Woolley (1989).

that children at all ages used distinctively different patterns of explanation for the different item types. When children said that solid physical items cannot be seen, touched, or hidden, it was for physical or moral reasons. In most cases, the negative judgments for solid physical items occurred for the "hide under the bed" question. For example, *It can't be hidden under the bed*, "because it's messy" (baby food), "because it's too big" (bike), or "because her mom will get mad" (toothpaste). Comparing children's explanations for these physical objects and for mental entities shows that young children have different conceptions of mental and physical entities. In contrast to the physical-moral explanations given for solid physical items, mental items elicited predominantly mental explanations. Even for three-year-olds, mental items elicited more mental explanations and fewer physical explanations than did physical items.

More focally for this experiment, children gave very different sorts of explanations for close impostor items in comparison to mental items. For close impostor items children gave predominantly location-possession explanations—they said the item in question was unavailable or gone—along with some physical ability explanations—they said the actor could not accomplish the specified act (touch the smoke). Table 2.2 presents some typical examples of these explanations. Such explanations seem to be sensible (if not always accurate) attempts to deal with the close impostor items' peculiar physical statuses. In contrast, mental items received predominantly mental explanations. This is striking for four- and five-year-olds, but even three-year-olds' mental explanations were almost never given for close impostor items and were significantly more frequent for mental items.

Since these mental explanations for mental items are of special interest, table 2.3 presents some examples of such explanations. Of the mental explanations given, 20% simply but appropriately repeated the mental term used in the story presentation (in answer to why a boy thinking of a ball could not touch it, "he's just thinking of it"). Table 2.3 presents five mental explanations at each age randomly sampled from those in which the child did not just reiterate the presented mental term. This random sample gives a flavor of children's typical mental explanations. In addition, table 2.3 presents three additional explanations at each age, chosen to provide an indication of the sophisticated responses that many children at times achieved.

Table 2.2
Examples of Children's Physical Ability and Location-Possession
Explanations for Close Impostor Items

Three-year-olds

(Can't touch a shadow): The shadow doesn't get in his hands.

(Can't touch smoke): It's air.

(Can't hide smoke under bed): It's too thin.
                              The smoke can't come inside her hands.

(Can't touch used-up toothpaste): It's all gone.

(Can't touch pictured lion): She can just touch the picture.

(Can't see burned-up leaves): It's not there, it's all burned up.

Four-year-olds

(Can't see used-up toothpaste): 'Cause when it's all gone, you can't see it.

(Can't touch a shadow): 'Cause it would just be something he wouldn't
                        feel.
                        'Cause it's invisible.

(Can't see a beep): It's just a noise.

(Can't touch burned-up leaves): Because they're only crumbs.

(Can't hide burned-up leaves): Because they're all gone.

(Can't touch a beep): Because it's just air that makes a sound.

Five-year-olds

(Can't hide used-up toothpaste): 'Cause there's no more left.

(Can't touch smoke): 'Cause it floats up, the hand would be in-between the
                     smokes.

(Can't touch burned-up leaves): No, only the ashes.

(Can't touch a pictured lion): Well no, but she *can* touch the *picture*.

(Can't hide a beep): Because it's invisible, they're not there, you can't see
                     them.

(Can't touch a shadow): No, can't see them, it's air.

Table 2.3
Mental Explanations from the Close Impostor Study

Randomly Sampled Mental Explanations[a]	Other Informative Explanations[b]
Three-year-olds	*Three-year-olds*
—'Cause it's her imagination. Because he's just remembering it in his brain.	—It's just in his head; he's imagining a bicycle; a dream of a bicycle.
—'Cause it's in his mind.	—Because he is only imagining it.
—Because he's thinking it and he can't see it.	—Because he's just dreaming about it.
—Because it's in his imagination.	*Four-year-olds*
Four-year-olds	—No, because it's only a dream; but he could touch it with his mind-hands.
—Because it's in his head.	
—'Cause it's just baby food and he's not eating it, he's thinking about it.	—'Cause it's invisible; 'cause you just imagine it.
—'Cause it's in his mind.	—'Cause it's inside his head, he's just thinking about it.
—'Cause he's just thinking about it.	*Five-year-olds*
—'Cause her hand can't fit in her head.	—Because if you're blind or not you can still see things in your imagination.
Five-year-olds	
—Because it's imaginary.	—Because it's in his head, or in his eyes, or wherever it is.
—Because it's not there; it's in his head.	
—Not real; it's in his mind.	—Because he's just looking at it in his imagination.
—Because it's not real; he just sees it in his imagination.	

a. Five randomly sampled mental explanations that do not simply repeat the mental verb used in the story.
b. Three mental explanations, from three different children, that seem especially clear or informative.

Discussion

At all ages children were able to distinguish mental from physical entities appropriately—even from invisible and intangible physical entities. These data replicate those of Wellman and Estes (1986) in showing that young children are not realists in the sense of equating mental entities with the physical objects to which they refer. More important the data begin to confirm that young children also are not realists in the more subtle sense of confusing mental entities with physical but intangible entities such as smoke, shadows, or sounds, nor do they seem to confuse mental entities with physical representational entities such as photographs. Our hypothesis was that if children did pass through a stage of subtle realism in which mental entities were confused with things like shadows or air, then during this stage they should say that mental entities have exactly the same properties as these close impostors. No evidence from our research supports this view. In this respect, even three-year-olds demonstrated some knowledge of the categorically mental quality of mental entities.

Our data also show, however, that three-year-olds, while significantly distinguishing mental entities from physical ones, do not do so as consistently as four- or five-year-olds. In particular, three-year-olds often used physical-moral explanations ("You can't touch it because you'll get too dirty") to explain their judgments of mental entities. One possible explanation of these findings is that such young children are displaying remnants of a realistic conception of mental entities. If such a description characterizes three-year-olds, then perhaps children younger than three are firm realists, and the basic developmental sequence from ontological realism to subjectivism, as Piaget described, is correct but occurs earlier in childhood than he believed.

I favor an alternate interpretation of three-year-olds' errors, however. When this kind of error occurred, children's comments often suggested that they were talking about the object referred to (a thought about a *ball*), not the mental entity itself (a *thought* about a ball). Mental entities are representational entities and thus involve both a representation (a thought) and a referent (about a ball). Young children at times may confuse representation and referent, replying to questions about the representation with answers about the referent. Often questions about a person's thoughts ("tell me about your dream") are requests to talk about referents ("there was a big white dog coming to get me"). The developmental trend may indicate that three-year-olds, while largely correct, are more likely than older children to answer questions by talking about the referent rather than the mental entity.

David Estes and I addressed this issue and provided a richer, more comprehensive test of children's ability to distinguish mental entities from closely parallel physical impostors by conducting two studies of children's conception of another mental phenomenon, mental imagery (Estes, Wellman, and Woolley, 1989).

First Experiment on Children's Understanding of Mental Images

Studying children's understanding of mental images allowed us to address several important issues. First, in our prior studies we had children make judgments about the mental entities of another person. Examining their conceptions of their own mental entities, such as their own mental images, would extend our findings from others to self.

Second, given our prior findings, which are inconsistent with ontological realism, we wanted to devise a strong, even decisive test of that position. Mental images are a useful vehicle for such a test. They share several properties with concrete pictures or photographs. Thus, if children were going to confuse some mental entity with a physical object, a confusion between mental images and photographs is very likely. Further, in our mental imagery studies we termed mental images "pictures in your head" when talking about them to children. This terminology was intended to be an open invitation for children to indulge in mistaken realistic conceptions. Such phrasing encourages the child to conceive of images as real physical pictures. We hoped to show that children's understanding of the crucial distinction between physical objects and mental entities is clear and compelling even in a case that seems ripe for realistic confusions.

Finally, we wanted to probe further into children's understanding of the distinctive features and properties of mental phenomena. In this regard, the judgments made by children of mental entities that I have discussed so far are consistently negative. Mental entities are not real, cannot be touched, *cannot* be seen. But mental phenomena have important positive features as well. For example, one can imagine a mental light bulb turning on simply by thinking of its doing so. Simply thinking will not turn on a real light bulb. Mental entities, unlike physical entities, can be manipulated and transformed by mental effort and attention alone. Are children aware of this property?

Focusing on the transformational properties of mental images has a methodological advantage. In asking children about their ability to

transform mental images, we devised a question about mental entities that required a positive response. This procedure allowed us to
rule out any sort of negative response bias as an explanation for some
of our prior results.

The top portion of figure 2.4 shows how we incorporated all of
these aims into the design of our first study on images. Shown is an
idealized pattern of correct responses to questions about three contrasting sorts of entities: (1) real objects, such as a deflated balloon;
(2) real hidden objects, unseen and inaccessible, such as a deflated
balloon hidden in a box; and (3) mental images of real objects, such
as a mental image of a deflated balloon. For the mental image question, we first showed the children the balloon, asked them to close
their eyes and make a "picture of it in your head," and then questioned them about "that balloon in your head." The questions we
asked are shown along the horizontal axis in figure 2.4: "That balloon
in your head, can you *see* it with your eyes"? and "Can you *touch* it
with your hands"? (the two behavioral-sensory questions), "Can I see
it with my eyes"? (a publicness question), and "Just by thinking about

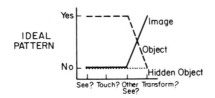

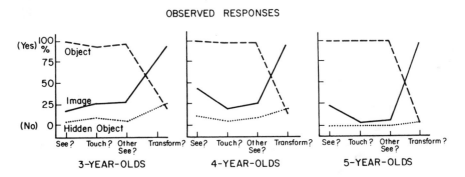

Figure 2.4
Responses to the four questions for each type of entity in the first mental image
experiment. The top portion shows an idealized pattern of correct responses. The
bottom figures show actual performances by each age group. From Estes et al.
(1989).

it, can you make it stretch out long and skinny?" (a transformation question).

This design permits evaluation of several alternative hypotheses, each of which would result in patterns of response different from the ideal one. If children mistakenly think that images are real external objects like pictures, they should answer about images just as they do about visible objects. More plausibly, if children think that images are real but inaccessible objects—literally pictures inside the head— then they should answer about images as they do about the hidden objects—objects inside a box. Finally, if children simply have some sort of negative response bias with respect to questions about mental entities, they should respond negatively to all image questions.

The correct response pattern is simplistic in one respect. We did not necessarily expect children (or adults for that matter) to deny consistently that they see their images, because "seeing" an image is an acceptable, even common way of talking. Note, however, that we phrased the see question as, "Can you see [the item] *with your eyes*?" Given that phrasing, we did expect children to affirm less often that they see their images with their eyes than that they see real objects with their eyes.

Method

Seventy-two preschoolers participated: 24 three-year-olds (3–1 to 4–0); 24 four-year-olds (range 4–1 to 4–9); and 24 five-year-olds (range 5–0 to 5–10); 33 were girls.

As is clear in the top portion of figure 2.4, the transformation question is crucial to the logic of this experiment. That mental images, but not physical objects, can be transformed mentally creates the desired case in which a positive response is correct for a mental entity and a negative response is correct for a physical object. We had to have a sensitive measure of children's knowledge of this property of mental images because of its importance, but it was difficult to be certain that the question about transformational imagery was unambiguous for preschool children. Therefore, if children at first claimed to be unable to transform a mental image, they were interviewed further. In this probe, children were asked to try to transform the image, and then were queried as to their success or failure. Of course, interviewing children in this fashion might make them change their original response (without an awareness of the transformation of mental images), so an appropriate control was necessary. The same probe was therefore used after responses to transformation questions on hidden object items. If the probe itself simply induced children to change their initial answers, they should have changed their answers on these hidden object items as well as on the mental image items.

Procedure

We began with a warm-up task to familiarize children with the mental image terminology. Children were shown a drawing of a "smile," a simple crescent with upwardly oriented ends, and were told, "Close your eyes and think about this happy smile. Try to make a picture of that happy smile in your head." After this, they watched as the picture was rotated 180 degrees. The experimenter said, "See how I can make it turn into a sad frown? Think real hard, and try to turn that happy smile upside down in your head until it's a sad frown."

For the primary task, three objects were used—a cup, a pair of scissors, and an uninflated balloon. Each child was thus questioned about nine entities—a mental image of each of the three objects and the objects themselves when visible and the objects when hidden. These entities were referred to as "the [object] in your head," "the [object] on the table," and "the [object] under the box," respectively. On mental image presentations, after the object was shown to the child and he or she had been asked to form a mental image of it, the object was placed out of sight in a box on the floor.

The four questions in figure 2.4 were asked about all nine entities. In its general form, the transformation question was, "Just by thinking real hard, without moving your hands, can you . . . ?" The transformations were, for the cup, "make it turn upside down," for the scissors, "make them open and close," and for the balloon, "make it long and skinny." When children denied being able to transform a mental image, the probe procedure was used: the child was asked to try to form the mental image ("make a picture of the cup in your head") and then to try to make the transformation. The child was then asked whether he or she had made the transformation. This probe procedure was also used after at least one hidden object transformation question per child.

Results

The bottom portion of figure 2.4 indicates the correspondence of each age group's performance to the ideal pattern. The obvious primary conclusion from these data is that although overall correspondence to the ideal pattern improved somewhat with age, even the three-year-olds' answers corresponded in essence to the ideal. These young children judged mental images differently from both visible and hidden objects. Most important all age groups exhibited the appropriate crossover from negative to positive responses on the image transformation question and from positive to negative responses for the visible object transformation question. As expected, the largest deviation from the ideal pattern was on the *see* question for mental images. Finally, as in the close impostor experiment, in spite of generally good performance, the younger children also at times answered that they could touch their mental images and that they could be seen by someone else.

The data in figure 2.4 are based on children's final response to the transformation questions when the probe was used. That is, children were credited with judging that the image (or some other object) could be transformed if they said so initially of if they said so after the probe. Figure 2.5 compares initial and final answers to the transformation question (before and after the probe) for both mental images and hidden objects. Consider the mental image items first. If initial responses alone are considered, children often answered *no* to the transformation question. After the probe procedure, performance by each age group improved, and final responses approached ceiling (93%, 93%, and 96% *yes* responses for the three-, four-, and five-year-olds, respectively).

For comparison, the pattern of initial to final responses on the transformation question for hidden objects is shown in the right half

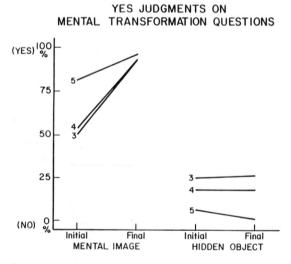

Figure 2.5
Performance on the transformation question in the first mental image experiment, both before (initial) and after (final) the probe question. From Estes et al. (1989).

of figure 2.5. In this case, children rarely changed their answers; initial and final responses did not differ for any age group. Thus, children were not simply changing their answers in response to probing questions by an adult. They did so only, appropriately, with respect to mental image transformations.

Each child was asked 12 questions on the three mental image items. Above-chance performance consisted of answering correctly 9 or more of the 12 questions ($p < .05$, one-tailed). For the image items, 71% of three-year-olds, 67% of four-year-olds, and 92% of five-year-olds achieved this level of performance. Thus, the majority of children at all ages were consistently correct in their responses.

As is evident in figure 2.4, negative judgments were correct for see, touch, and publicness questions on both mental image and hidden object items. Thus, as in the close impostor study, appropriate differences in children's explanations for their identical judgments were especially revealing. Explanations were coded into one of four mutually exclusive categories (or into a residual category that included "I don't know," incomprehensible replies, and refusals to answer): (1) mental: the child alludes to the mental status of the entity by using a mental term in the explanation ("It's just imagination"; "I'm just thinking in my mind"); (2) not real: the child says that the entity cannot be seen, touched, or seen by someone else because it is not real; (3) inaccessible: the child invokes the entity's inaccessibility to justify a negative response ("It's inside my head"; "It's under the box"; "I can't put my hand through the box"); (4) impossible: the child states without further elaboration that he or she cannot perform the action in question ("Nobody could do that"; "I couldn't if I tried"). These four categories captured 82% of the explanations, and intercoder reliability was 92%.

For hidden objects, children gave essentially only one type of explanation. In 80% of the cases, they explicitly invoked the inaccessibility of the object. Though inaccessibility explanations were also the most frequent type of explanation for mental image items (43%), they occurred only about half as often as on hidden object items (80%). Moreover, of the inaccessibility explanations for mental images, 59% were of the form "because it's in my head" or "brain." This sort of explanation was never given on hidden object items. Most revealing was the fact that children invoked types of explanations on mental items that they never used for hidden objects. In 15% of their explanations about mental images, they either referred to the mental status of images or claimed that images are not real.

Discussion

The overall correspondence of judgments to the ideal pattern strongly suggests that children of preschool age do not systematically attribute to mental images the properties of physical objects. The deviations from the ideal pattern that did occur generally support the conclusion that most children were in fact comprehending the questions about mental images and answering appropriately. For example, one deviation was a tendency to say that mental images could be seen. Inspecting a mental image is a quasi-visual experience and sufficiently like visual perception that the metaphor of seeing is universal (Shepard, 1984). The fact that deviations from the ideal pattern of responses on mental image items were considerably greater on the see question than on the touch and publicness questions suggests that children were undergoing the experience that is the basis for this metaphor.

Performance on the transformation questions and probes also suggests that these preschoolers were forming and transforming mental images in response to the instructions and that they understood that thoughts but not physical objects can be manipulated by mental effort alone.

Second Experiment on Mental Images: Mental Images versus Photographs

Despite the generally high level of performance in the preceding study, the youngest children still gave some apparently realistic responses. Three-year-olds and some four-year-olds at times said that they could touch their mental images and that another person could see their mental images. When children made this kind of error, their comments often suggested that they were referring to the object they had been asked to imagine ("Yes, I could touch it because it's right over there on the floor where you put it"). Occasionally, their explanations of correct judgments about mental images also indicated that they might have been answering about the object itself ("I can't touch it because you took it away"). Such comments may indicate that young children at times interpret questions about mental entities to be about the object represented—the referent, not the representation.

This error seems to be of the same general kind as those that Piaget (1929) observed when he questioned children about words. He found that young children will answer yes to questions such as, "Is the word *needle* sharp?" This finding led Piaget to claim that young children believe words have the properties of the things to which they refer, a symptom of the child's deficient ontology he termed *nominal realism*. Markman (1976), however, questioned whether errors of this kind should be taken as evidence that children have such an exotic notion. According to Markman, a more plausible interpretation of these findings is that children have difficulty interpreting such questions correctly. In her research, she found that, consistent with Piaget's results, seven-, and eight-year-olds agreed that "the word *car* has wheels." When given a choice, however, ("What has wheels—a car or the word *car*?"), they consistently answered correctly, recognizing the distinction between word and referent. Rather than being nominal realists, young children may simply have an understandable tendency to construe questions about words to be about their referents.

My claim is that this tendency to interpret questions about representations to be about referents is a general one that occurs not only with words but with other representational entities as well, including mental images. In a third experiment, we examined this possibility directly in two ways. First, we added a choice procedure similar to Markman's. Second, we directly compared children's conceptions of mental and physical representations by asking them to make judgments about both a mental image of an object and the object's photograph in a closed container. An inaccessible physical representation (a photograph in a box) was the closest close impostor for a mental image we could devise. Both are representations in that they depict something else, and neither affords behavioral or sensory contact. Furthermore, we referred to them in similar terms as "the picture in your head" and "the picture in the box." If children were subtle ontological realists, then they might well conceive of mental images as literally inaccessible physical representations, as real "pictures in the head." Forcing children to make judgments and provide explanations about the differences between images and hidden pictures might reveal misconceptions not yet revealed or it might reveal further sophistication in children's understanding of these fundamentally different entities.

A second extension beyond the first experiment on mental images involved the elimination of all mental terms from the procedure. In this third experiment, no common mental terms were used by the adult at any time during the session. In the prior study, the terms *think* and *thinking* were used in the instructions and in the questions about mental images ("Close your eyes and think about the cup; try to make a picture of the cup in your head"). It is unlikely that children's performance in our prior studies can be explained by attributing to them some subtle miscomprehension of ordinary mental terms, one that would allow them to answer our questions appropriately even without a reasonable conception of the mental phenomena to which those terms refer. Nevertheless, it is remotely possible that appropriate use and apparent comprehension of mental terms could mask a failure to understand that such terms refer to immaterial, subjective mental states or processes. Piaget, in fact, argued explicitly that the appearance of mental terms such as *think* in the speech of the child at around three years of age does not mean that "children themselves are conscious of the duality" between thought and things (1929, p. 43). By eliminating use of any mental terms at all in our procedures, we hoped to provide direct evidence against the general claim that correct performance on our tasks could represent some sort of facile but incorrect comprehension of everyday mental terms.

Method

Sixty preschoolers participated: 12 three-year-olds (3–5 to 3–11); 24 four-year-olds (4–1 to 4–11); and 24 five-year-olds (5–0 to 5–11); 37 were boys and 23 were girls.

The top portion of figure 2.6 shows the overall design of the study. Two kinds of representational entities were contrasted: a mental image and a photograph in a closed container. Five questions were asked about each of these entities. Four of the questions were the same as those asked in the prior study; there was also one question about the possibility of using the representation (either the image or the photograph) for some function for which the actual object could be used (termed the function question in figure 2.6). As is clear in the figure, mental images and inaccessible photographs are alike in that neither can be used in the same way as the objects they represent, and neither can be seen, touched, or seen by someone else. They differ in that mental images can be mentally transformed but inaccessible photographs cannot. If preschool children understand how mental and physical representations differ, then their judgments should conform to this ideal pattern.

Procedure

The "happy smile" warm-up task preceded the substantive items but with the term *think* eliminated. Each child was questioned about both a mental image of and a photograph of two familiar objects (a cup and a pencil), for a total of four items. The instructions used to get the children to generate mental images were the same as in the prior study except that mention of thinking was eliminated. Similarly, the transformation question was the same as before but with mention of

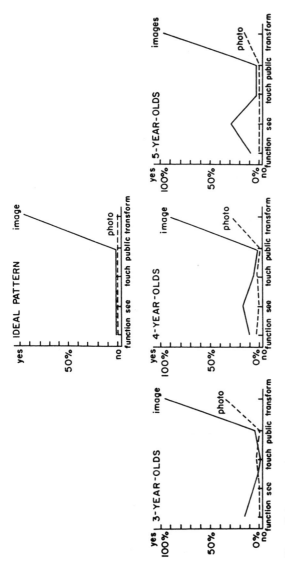

Figure 2.6
Responses to the five questions for the two types of entity in the second mental image experiment. The top portion shows an idealized pattern of correct responses. The bottom figures show actual performances by each age group. From Estes et al. (1989).

thinking eliminated ("Without moving your hands, can you make that picture of the cup in your head turn upside down?").

The function questions were, for the cup, "use it to get a drink of water," and for the pencil, "use it to draw something with." The transformations for the transformation questions were, for the cup, "make it turn upside down," and for the pencil, "make it move up and down."

On both mental image and photograph items, the actual object was always present on the table in front of the child during questioning. This procedure makes the mental image items different from those in the prior study, in which the actual object was removed before questioning children about the image. On photograph items, the function question was always asked before the photograph was placed in the box so that children would not answer negatively simply because the picture was inaccessible.

Finally, two sorts of probe procedures were used to follow up initial responses. First, as in the prior study, children who denied being able to transform a mental image were asked to try to do so. And to assess whether the probe itself induced children to change their answers, this probe was also used after the transformation question on one image and one photograph item per child.

Second, errors on the other four questions (see, touch, publicness, and function) on both mental image and photograph items were followed by a clarification-choice procedure. In this procedure, children in effect were asked to state whether it was the object or its representation they were referring to in their answers. For example, if a child said she could touch the picture in her head, she was asked, "Is it the cup on the table or the picture of the cup in your head that you can touch with your hands?" To test the effect of this clarification-choice procedure, it was also used following one image question and one photograph question when the child's response was correct.

Results

As can be seen in the bottom part of figure 2.6, correspondence to the ideal pattern was generally very good. Young children do not believe that a mental image of an object is simply an inaccessible picture of the object. Thus, despite some deviations from the ideal pattern (especially for the photograph transformation question), the main result is consistently correct performance at all ages. Each child answered 10 questions about mental images and 10 questions about photographs. Above-chance performance requires answering correctly 8 or more of the 10 questions ($p < .05$, one-tailed). On the image items, 56 of 60 children reached this level of performance when final answers were taken into account. On the picture items, 59 of 60 got 8 or more correct when their final answers were taken into consideration.

These analyses were performed on children's final answers. They take into account responses to both the probe on the transformation question and to the clarification-choice procedure on the other questions. We also examined the effects of these two probe procedures on children's answers. Figure 2.7 compares initial and final performance on each question (both with and without the transformation probe and clarification-choice procedure). Initial and final responses mirror one another closely; differences were always in the direction of greater accuracy on the final responses. Thus, for example, probing on the image transformation question appropriately yielded more *yes* responses, but probing photograph transformation responses appropriately yielded more *no* responses. More important, the clarification-choice probe clarified children's initial errors on both photograph and image items. In both cases, for example, children at times judged that the representation could function as the referent (an image or a photo of a cup could be used to get a cup of water). In both cases, however, when asked to clarify whether it was the representation or the real object that could be so used, children indicated it was the referent, not the representation. Thus, the probe procedures did not simply induce children to change their initial responses; instead children discriminately corrected initial mistakes.

Children in this study made the same kinds of explanations as in the prior study, and analyses of these explanations replicated the central findings in that study. However, one type of explanation oc-

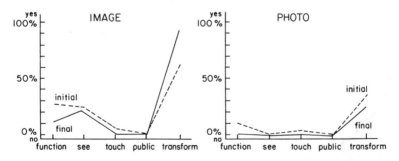

Figure 2.7
Performance in the second mental image experiment before (initial) and after (final) the transformation question probes and the clarification-choice probes. From Estes et al. (1989).

curred in this study that did not earlier. On photograph items children frequently (16%) justified their negative answers by simply noting that the entity in question was "just a picture." Only two explanations of this kind (0.6%) were ever used in answer to questions about mental images in spite of the fact that mental images were explicitly termed "pictures in your head."

The quantitative data presented thus far do not do justice to the sophistication of some of the explanations these young children provided. Table 2.4 presents some examples of children's mental explanations in this and in the prior study. Across the two experiments, only 4 of 36 of the three-, 10 of 48 of the four-, and 24 of 48 five-year-olds gave mental explanations. Thus, mental explanations were less common than in the initial experiment on smoke, shadows, and so on, but there is a good reason for this difference. In that initial experiment, we counted explanations of the type "it's only in his head" or "brain" as mental explanations. In both of the mental image experiments, we did not. In the mental image experiments, the experimenter used the phrase "picture in your head" to present the task; therefore, to be conservative, we did not count explanations of this sort as mental. Though less frequent, children's mental explanations were still informative. The examples in table 2.4 give a flavor for children's typical mental explanations.

Discussion

The results of this image versus photograph experiment confirm and extend those of the prior studies. Preschoolers distinguished between mental images and inaccessible physical representations in their judgments (and explanations), although the two were described to them in similar terms. The results reflect a solid understanding of the distinction between mental and physical representations. This high level of performance was achieved even though the adult used no conventional mental terms during the procedure. This contradicts the possibility that preschoolers' knowledge of mental phenomena might be limited to some deceptively useful miscomprehension of common mental terms.

The results of the two mental image studies fit together nicely. Children in these studies consistently judged that mental images cannot be seen, touched, seen by someone else, or used in the way a real object can be used, but they can be mentally transformed. Their judgments about mental images differed appropriately from their judgments about inaccessible physical representations and about actual objects. The overall pattern of their judgments for these different

Table 2.4
Sample Explanations from the Mental Image Studies

Randomly Sampled Mental Explanations[a]	Other Informative Explanations[b]
Three-year-olds	*Three-year-olds*
—(Transform image?) Yes, because my head thinks.	—(Image public?) No, but you could see a cup in *your* head.
—(Touch image?) No, because it's my imagination.	—(Transform image?) Yes, because brains can do that.
—(Image public?) No, people can't see my imagination.	—(Touch image?) No, because it's not real.
—(Touch image?) No, imagination is imagination.	*Four-year-olds*
—(Transform image?) yes; can't really do it, but I can pretend to do it.	—(Transform image?) Yes, your mind is for moving things and looking at things when there's not a movie or a TV around.
Four-year-olds	—(Image public) No, because it's only in *my* head, but you could make it in your head.
—(See image?) No, because it's imaginary.	—(See image?) People can't see my imagination.
—(Image public?) No, cause you can only think about it.	*Five-year-olds*
—(Image public?) No, because it's *my* imagination.	—(Transform real scissors?) No, because that doesn't respond to my head. I could think and they wouldn't open because my head doesn't connect to that.
—(Transform image?) Yes, because I have dream-hands.	—(Touch image?) How can you reach inside your head? Besides it's not even there.
—(See image?) No, cause you're just thinking about them.	—(Transform image?) I think a special way. I can make things come true in my head.
Five-year-olds	
—(Transform image?) Yes, I just could; I could think it right now.	
—(See image?) No, because you just think about it in your mind.	
—(Touch image?) No, not in your head; cause you can only think.	
—(Transform image?) Yes, because I would imagine it going up and down.	
—(Image public?) No, 'cause *I'm* thinking about them.	

a. Five randomly sampled mental explanations.
b. Three explanations, from three different children, that clearly capture the mental, nonphysical character of thought.

kinds of entities conformed closely to an ideal pattern of judgments. Importantly, errors that might be taken as evidence of Piagetian realism often disappeared in the last study when children were allowed to choose whether it was the mental image or the object itself that had the property in question. These corrections showed that children understood the essential differences between images and objects, although they at times confused talk about the former to be about the latter. Equally important, the clarification-choice procedure improved performance on photograph questions. This strongly suggests that when they do occur, errors on questions about mental images specifically and representations generally are due to children's mistaking questions about representations to be about their referents. Such errors do not index a lingering realistic misconception about the nature of mental entities but instead reflect a general difficulty in talking about representations.

General Discussion

Preschool children in these studies consistently judged that mental phenomena—thoughts, memories, dreams, and mental images—differed in fundamental ways from physical phenomena, even from potentially confusing impostors, such as smoke, shadows, and "pictures in a box." These preschool children also often gave cogent and appropriate explanations for their correct responses. Let me outline the range of evidence on these matters.

1. Children appeal to the commonsense criteria of behavioral sensory evidence (visibility, tangibility) to distinguish mental entities—such as a thought about a dog—from prototypic physical objects—a dog.

2. However, children do not mistake such characteristic features to be essential. Therefore, like adults, children distinguish mental entities from "close impostors," that is, from physical entities that themselves are intangible or invisible (smoke, sounds). In making these more precise distinctions, children argue that mental entities are "not real," are "just mental" (just imagination, just a thought), and are, figuratively, just in the head or mind. In addition, children contend that mental entities—mental images, for example—can be transformed just by mental effort, which is insufficient to transform parallel physical entities.

3. Young children understand that mental entities are peculiarly private. In our first studies (Wellman and Estes, 1986) comparing the publicness of mental entities with physical objects, we simply asked

whether a second person could see a first person's mental entity (a thought about a dog). Children uniformly said no. But they also uniformly said that the first person could not see his or her own mental entities. Thus, their answers could have just reflected an understanding that mental entities are invisible, not necessarily an understanding that mental states and entities are subjectively private. In the mental imagery studies, however, children often said that they could see their own images. This is a reasonable response given the quasipictorial nature of images; adults commonly say they "see" their images. However, when young children said that they could see their own image, they denied such visual experience of their image to someone else. Over the two mental imagery experiments, children provided 77 instances in which they differed on their answers to the see ("can you see . . .") and publicness ("can I see . . .") questions. In 60 of these instances (78%), they said they could see their image but someone else could not, attesting to their knowledge of the subjective privacy of mental entities and experiences. As one child put it "[You can't see my image] because it's only in *my* head, but you could make it in *your* head."

4. Children judged mental entities such as images (one sort of representational entity) as quite different from photographs (another sort of representational entity). At times children were confused as to whether talk about representations is about the representation or the referent. But this confusion was apparent for both mental and concrete representations. In both cases, children understood that the representation itself, the image or the photo of a cup, say, was different from the referent, a cup itself. Thus, children answered the function question appropriately (figure 2.6), affirming that they could not get a drink of water with a picture or an image of a cup but that they could with a cup.

5. Children responded correctly to questions about mental entities with unspecified real referents (a thought about a dog), as well as about mental entities with specified referents (a mental image of this cup). With respect to the latter, children's responses were correct both when the referent itself was removed from view (in the first imagery study) and when it was left in plain sight (in the second imagery study). Thus children do not think mental entities are merely hypothetical entities about nonexistent, unavailable, or unspecified things. Even when judging mental entities about present, existent things (a mental image of *this* real cup), children are able to distinguish the coexisting mental and physical entities.

6. At the same time, these young children recognize that mental entities can be about nonexistent, nonreal states of affairs. This is best

demonstrated in experiment 3 of the Wellman and Estes (1986) studies. Here, three-year-olds (as well as four- and five-year-olds) consistently judged that certain objects—for example, spoons that sing—do not exist and have never been seen by them. Nonetheless, children consistently affirmed that they could think and dream of such things.

All of these understandings were apparent in three-year-old children, as well as in four- and five-year-olds. This early understanding of mental phenomena was not confined to some facile but superficial interpretation of common mental terms. Our findings thus warrant some strong conclusions. A primary conclusion is that children's understanding differs diametrically from the traditional Piagetian view.

Comparison to Piaget's Position

I wish to compare our findings with Piaget's to clarify my position by contrasting it with a very serious competitor. Certainly the two positions do contrast. Recall Piaget's description of young children's ignorance of the mind. According to the traditional Piagetian view, it is as if young children live in an exotic, alien world, one in which the distinction between the mental and the physical is nonexistent. However, preschool children in our studies responded as though they and we inhabit the same world and divide it into the mental and the physical realms along the same boundary.

My position is that young children are dualists: knowledgeable of mental states and entities as ontologically different from physical objects and real events. Piaget claims that they are "adualistic," confusing these two primary domains of thought. Piaget's proposal is not a straw man; it is sensible and coherent. Moreover it was based on supportive empirical findings. When Piaget asked such questions as, "What do you think with?" and "What are thoughts?" young children responded that thinking is done with the mouth and that thinking is overt speech or one's breath (1929, pp. 33–60). Thus Piaget concluded: "We have traced three distinct stages. . . . [In the first] children believe that thinking is 'with the mouth'. Thoughts are identified with the voice. Nothing takes place in the head. . . . There is nothing subjective in the act of thinking. The average age for children of this stage is 6" (Piaget, 1929, p. 38). Similarly, when Piaget asked young children such questions as, "Where do dreams come from?" and "Can you see your dreams?" children answered that dreams come from outside us, from "the sky" or "the air"; they answered that we see dreams "with our eyes" and that dreams occur outside us "against the wall" or as "lights which are in the room" (pp. 88–122). Thus: "The answers obtained can be classified as belonging in three distinct stages. During the first (approximately 5–6 years) the child believes the dreams to come from outside and to take place within the room and he thus dreams with his eyes" (p. 90) or alternatively, dreams are speech and one dreams "with the mouth" (p. 93).

According to Piaget, children's confusion of the two primary domains of entities and causation—the physical and mental worlds—is apparent in two different sorts of thinking. On the one hand, young children conceive of physical events, such as rivers' flowing and the sun's rising, as the result of personal psychological causes. For example, nighttime comes because the clouds get together to cover the sun and they do it "on purpose" because "we ought to go to sleep" (Piaget, 1929, p. 294). This is animism, a sort of thinking that confuses the physical and the psychological by attributing apparently psychological attributes and causes to physical phenomena. At the same time the opposite confusion obtains: human thoughts are physical things. This is childhood realism; any sense the child has of the psychological realm is actually a distorted sort of physicalism. Thus, Piaget notes that some children say dreams are thoughts; however, for them, "thought is voice, that is to say is composed of air and smoke" (Piaget, 1929, p. 102). Thus dreams, albeit termed thoughts by the child, are seen as made of physical components: "the dream, insofar as it is thought, being held to consist in speaking, in air and in the breath from respiration" (p. 107). It is important to note just how deep and complete this confusion of mind and matter is for the child, according to this story. Because the child thinks that words, for example, are physical properties of objects in the real world and speech is the physical voice, then even if the child offers a psychological-seeming explanation for an action—a cloud moves "because it was told to"—this does not count as a psychological explanation in any adult-sensible fashion. Similarly, when the child says the clouds move "because they feel cold, so they walk" (Piaget, 1930, p.67), the child is incorrectly designating a sort of animistic causation, but the child is not really appealing to such explanatory mental constructs as feelings, desires, or beliefs. The child is not because he or she does not understand feelings or desires or beliefs in the requisite sense of internal mental states. Because children's worldview is so different from that of adults, it is possible for both ontological realism and animism equally to characterize the young child's thought. Ontological realism and animism might seem contradictory, but to the child they are part and parcel of the same adualistic point of view.

This description of Piaget's work inspires an important question: how are the findings presented in this chapter and Piaget's apparently contradictory ones to be reconciled? One possible reconciliation is to conclude that Piaget is right and we are wrong. Piaget's findings, after all, have been replicated by other investigators; perhaps our data constitute an atypical failure to replicate. An alternative possibility is that Piaget's subjects and our own are providing similar data; it is the two interpretations, not the two data sets, that differ so dramatically.

I believe that we have not simply failed to replicate Piaget's prior findings or those of other investigators such as Laurendeau and Pinard (1962), who replicated Piaget directly. Instead I believe that these earlier findings are replicable but misinterpreted. It would be helpful to show, therefore, that the children we tested and the children tested by Piaget or by Laurendeau and Pinard are in fact giving similar responses.

My demonstration of this state of affairs involved taking the responses of children in our studies and classifying them according to Laurendeau and Pinard's coding system. If our findings are atypical, then our findings and Laurendeau and Pinard's should still look substantially different even if coded according to an equivalent scoring system. If, however, the two sets of data look quite similar when children's responses are evaluated with a comparable method, then it is the interpretation of those responses that is at issue. I used Laurendeau and Pinard's (1962) system of analyzing children's responses because they spelled out their coding system more precisely and in more detail than did Piaget (1929), yet their results replicated Piaget's.

Laurendeau and Pinard (1962) interviewed children about only one sort of mental phenomena, dreams. Here are some of their questions:

> "Where does a dream come from?" "Where are dreams made, where do they come from? . . . Do they come from inside of you, or outside of you?" "Who makes the dream come? . . . Is it you or someone else?"
>
> "When you dream that you are playing in the street, where is your dream? In the street, or in your room?"
>
> "When your mother is in your room, can she also see your dream? And I, if I were in your room, could I see your dream?"
>
> "When, during the night, you dream that you are playing, are you really playing? . . . Is it the same as when you play for real? Then, are your dreams true?" (pp. 63–65)

From my perspective these kinds of questions, like those Piaget himself asked, are objectionable in several ways: some are unclear; others seem to presuppose that dreams actually are substantial entities that are made of something and come from somewhere. But the primary focus for the current analysis concerns Laurendeau and

Pinard's system for categorizing and interpreting children's responses. What they did, following Piaget, was to evaluate the overall quality of children's responses to all questions by classifying each child's pattern of responses into one of four categories:

1. Incomprehension or refusal: The child provides no comprehensible answers. This is evident in answers such as "I don't know" or "Because."

2. Integral realism: The child describes dreams in terms suitable for external concrete physical objects. For example, "The dream is in the room," "on the wall," "in front of me" (Laurendeau & Pinard, 1962, p. 107). Dreams can be seen by others; thus "Mother can see my dream" or "Mother can't see it" because the room is too dark (p. 108). Dreams are made up of physical substances like "cloth," "wood," "skin" (p. 109). And dreams can be touched (p. 109).

3. Mitigated realism: The hallmark of mitigated realism is that sometimes the child gives integral realism answers and sometimes subjectivist answers. In addition, dreams may be described as internal or as intangible but in ways one would use to describe internal or intangible physical entities, such as internal organs or moving pictures. Thus, the dream is "in the heart" (p. 114) or "in the tummy," "in the eyes" (p. 113). Children might describe dreams as in the head but still, "they will uphold the possibility that others can see the dream inside the head" (p. 114). Or, if dreams are described as events or even as pictures, they take place "outside" (p. 116) or "in front of ourself" (p. 117) and "the dreamer is not the only one who can look at the spectacle" (p. 119).

4. Subjectivism: Dreams are described as subjective, private, mental experiences. For example, "it's in the mind," "it's in the imagination" (p. 121), "it's inside of me, in my thinking" (p. 125).

Laurendeau and Pinard's data are shown on the left side of table 2.5. Incomprehension was fairly common, especially at the younger ages. Excluding incomprehensible replies, in the preschool years the responses were split between the two sorts of realism, with mitigated realism predominating as children get older. Subjectivism appeared only late in this age range, at about six years.

In order to compare our data with theirs, an independent rater, uninformed about our hypotheses, coded children's responses in two of our studies according to Laurendeau and Pinard's coding system. Since our studies are so different from the open-ended interviews of Piaget and of Laurendeau and Pinard, coding the data into their cat-

Table 2.5
Percentages of Children in Each Laurendeau and Pinard Category

| | Laurendeau and Pinard (1962) | | | | | Close impostor experiment and Wellman and Estes (1986) | | | | |
Age	N	Incompre-hension	Integral Realism	Mitigated Realism	Subjectivism	N	Incompre-hension	Integral Realism	Mitigated Realism	Subjectivism
6	49	10	10	38	41	—	—	—	—	—
5½	—	—	—	—	—	31	0	8	53	39
5	46	24	24	38	13	—	—	—	—	—
4½	50	46	26	28	0	36	6	22	55	17
4	49	55	20	24	0	—	—	—	—	—
3½	—	—	—	—	—	36	16	39	29	16

egories required some adjustments and extrapolations. Recall that Laurendeau and Pinard's system is a system for coding explanations. Therefore, we focused on the explanations collected about mental entities in the close impostor experiment of this chapter (nine explanations per child) and the explanations about mental entities in study 2 of Wellman and Estes (1986) (eight explanations per child). These are the two studies in which we have collected children's explanations most thoroughly. In addition, Laurendeau and Pinard's system is a system for coding the overall quality of a child's responses across an extended set of replies. To arrive at this sort of overall evaluation from our data, we began by coding each of the eight or nine explanations per child as individually representing one of the four Laurendeau and Pinard categories. Then children were assigned to one of these same four categories on the basis of their overall responses. Each child was assigned to the category of the majority of his or her individual explanations, except that if a child showed a mixture of responses in categories 2 and 4, 3 and 4, or 2, 3 and 4, he or she was assigned to the category of mitigated realism. This procedure is in accord with Laurendeau and Pinard's description of mitigated realists as evidencing some ʼsubjectivism answers coupled with realism responses. Therefore, in our procedure, three-fourths or more of a child's individual responses (six of eight or seven of nine) had to be subjectivist before a child was considered as evidencing subjectivism overall. The responses of 55 children were coded by two coders and agreement was .89.

Applying this coding system produces the data presented in the right-hand portion of table 2.5. Some differences are apparent across the two data sets. For example, we got much less incomprehension and refusal to reply in our data than did Laurendeau and Pinard, probably because our questions are more straightforward and less open-ended. But excluding incomprehension, our children's responses were very similar to Laurendeau and Pinard's. Our data, as theirs, yield essentially a split between the two sorts of realism in the younger children, with mitigated realism predominating as children get older. Only in the oldest children do we find much subjectivism according to this scoring system.

My conclusion from these closely comparable findings is that the difference between our estimation of children's knowledge of mental phenomena and that of Laurendeau and Pinard cannot be simply a failure to replicate. Instead we have come to quite different interpretations of similar data. Given this conclusion, I now wish to argue that my interpretation is correct and Piaget's and Laurendeau and Pinard's is wrong. I believe that my interpretation of young children's

understanding should override Piaget's because I offer not only findings similar to Piaget's but additional findings as well. In the light of
this more comprehensive data base, it now seems clear that children
understand the basic distinction between mental and physical entities
and realms. More specifically, interview studies such as Piaget's and
Laurendeau and Pinard's include only half of the needed experimental design. If we wish to determine whether someone distinguishes
or confuses two sorts of things, we need to compare his or her responses to both things. For this reason, the studies reported in this
chapter included a variety of informative contrasts. Children's answers to questions about mental entities were compared directly to
their answers about various kinds of physical entities. Our use of this
procedure clearly reveals that children can make the appropriate, at
times quite subtle, distinctions. Their judgments and explanations are
sensibly different for these different sorts of entities.

Why, then, do children seem so realistic when coded by Piaget's
and Laurendeau and Pinard's methods? The problem, I believe, is
that in the absence of directly comparable responses about both mental and physical entities, these prior investigators were encouraged to
interpret quite literally young children's explanations of mental entities alone. Young children's statements that "dreams are smoke" or
"dreams are pictures" were coded as meaning dreams actually are
smoke or are concrete photographs rather than that dreams are like
smoke or akin to pictures. Such literal interpretations are incorrect;
children's statements should instead be seen as attempts to point out
some informative analogies and similarities, not as literal attempts to
specify identities.

For two reasons, such statements on the part of children should be
taken as nonliteral but informative attempts to talk about difficult topics. First and more decisive, our complete data show that young children are aware of the appropriate differences. They know that mental
entities are not literally smoke, shadows, physical objects, pictures,
or even inaccessible pictures of objects. The second reason is that in
speaking nonliterally about the mind, young children are only engaging in common adult practice for talking about mental phenomena.
Adults say that dreams are like pictures and we "see" our images.
We use the language of the external world to refer to the mental
world. That we do so does not mean that we are ontological realists.
The same is true for young children.

It is important to note that given either our methods or Laurendeau
and Pinard's, young children do at times say that they can touch or
see their dreams or thoughts. Such errors, however, seem best interpreted as revealing a tendency of young children to interpret ques-

tions about mental representations (a dream about a ball) to be about their referents (the ball). These responses, although interesting, should not be taken as evidence of ontological realism because young children make similar errors about concrete external representations such as photographs, and as we have shown, they can correct such errors when asked to do so.

Comparison to Keil's Position

I have referred to Keil's position several times, so it is important to discuss briefly the difference between his findings and ours. Childhood realism, according to Keil (1979), is a manifestation of the fact that ontological categories develop out of other ontological categories. Keil concluded that most five-year-olds conceive of all things as types of physical objects. The evidence for this conclusion came from tasks requiring children to judge certain sentences as anomalous (to state that both "an idea is heavy" and its opposite, "an idea is light," are "silly"). Keil found that preschoolers and kindergartners accepted physical predicates such as "is heavy," "is red," and "is tall" for dreams and ideas, as well as for trees and dogs.

The fit between our findings and Keil's hinges on two points: the sorts of entities about which children were questioned and the sensitivity of the methods used. We queried children about particular mental entities (a thought about a dog); Keil questioned them about ideas and thoughts in themselves. There is an obvious difference between a particular dream entity (a dream-dog) and a dream as a thing in itself. Thus, there are at least three sorts of entities the child must sort out: real physical objects (a dog), specific mental entities (a thought of a dog), and thoughts as things in themselves (abstract objects, as Keil terms them). It seems clear from our data that young children categorically distinguish real objects from mental entities. This implies, I think, that they know quite a bit about the mental status of thoughts versus the physical status of material objects. Even if they understand this underlying ontological distinction, however, children might still be confused about abstract objects. In this regard it seems likely that Keil's methods did confuse young children. Specifically, although Keil wanted to ask children about dreams and ideas in the sense of abstract objects (dreams and ideas as things in themselves), young children probably responded in terms of dreams and ideas about particular referents. For example, suppose a child is asked whether the statement "a dream is tall" is OK or silly. In Keil's data young children answer that such statements are OK rather than silly. Keil concluded from these responses that the child attributes physical predicates (is tall) to abstract objects (a dream). However, it seems more likely that the child simply interprets these questions to be about possible dream content rather than about dreams themselves. That is, children may search for instances where a dream (content) could be tall (a dream about a giant) and answer accordingly. That children might focus on specific ideas or dreams rather than ideas or dreams as abstract objects is not surprising since ideas and dreams specifically, and thoughts generically, are never contentless; they are always "about" something. These entities are difficult to talk about in themselves, removed from their contents, even for adults.

In short, as noted with respect to Piaget, errors on Keil's task seem best interpreted as children answering questions about mental representational entities (a dream) as if they were questions about representational referents (a dream about a *giant*). Our data on children's understanding of specific mental entities show that young children have this tendency. But the data also show that in spite of this tendency, young children grasp the basic ontological distinction requisite to a theory of mind.

Conclusions

In arguing that young children are firm about the distinction between mental entities and real objects, I am not claiming that they will correctly classify every example of these things. We must distinguish children's understanding of the distinction in question from their understanding of individual instances. Children (or adults) can know full well the essential distinctions between real objects and events versus mental entities and still not know where a specific instance is best placed. Waking from a powerful and realistic dream, a child (or even an adult) may be slow to realize that that specific experience was a mental rather than a real experience, yet he or she fully appreciates the distinction. Similarly children might not know that dragons are mythical whereas dinosaurs are real (extinct) animals (Morison and Gardner, 1978) but still be clear that there could be two such different sorts of things. I am not claiming that by three years of age children have acquired an adult knowledge about the mentality or reality of all entities. Indeed, I think that much acquisition of this specific knowledge is acquired in later childhood. But I am claiming that children understand the essential distinction.

In sum, our findings indicate that children's first understanding of mind is characterized by ontological dualism. It may still be the case, however, that this dualism is coupled with epistemological realism. Young children understand the fundamental distinction between thought and objects, but they may assume that external objects directly generate thoughts, which objectively mirror reality. Suppose, for example, that at first young children are ignorant as to how thoughts originate from and correspond to things. They simply appreciate that thoughts can originate from encounters with things (you see it; you know it's there) or from mental effort (you think it up, imagine it), but they have no specific understanding of how this works. If children simply assume an unspecified direct connection between thoughts and things, then part of Piaget's original description would be apt: children might well be epistemological realists, albeit not ontological ones. In fact, young children's putative epistemological realism consumed a large part of Piaget's attention. For this reason, many of his interview questions dealt with the origins of thoughts: "Where do dreams come from?" "Where does thought come from?" "Where do names come from?"

When disentangled in this fashion, some of Piaget's descriptions ring true, as when he described young children's beliefs that thoughts come from things in the world. He (1929) claimed, for example, that young children assume a direct origination of thought from things, even in the case of dreams known to be fictional. "Whilst regarding the dream [of a person] as false, that is to say as an image displayed in front of us in order to deceive us, the child nevertheless adheres to the suggestion that the image *is part* of the person it represents and is a material emanation" (p. 102). "He has not yet the capacity to regard the image of a person that he has actually seen [the dream of the person] as something internal that has been produced by thought. The immediate source of this image is regarded as the person" (p. 103).

In these discussions, Piaget claimed that young children believe that thoughts generally, and even dreams specifically, are caused by thing-produced emanations. The heart of the claim concerns the child's ignorance of constructivism. The constructed, indirect nature of thought is held to be unknown to young children, who assume a much more direct connection between things and thoughts.

Young children's confusion as to the origins of thoughts does not imply a parallel confusion as to the ontological status of thoughts. Our data argue clearly that the first understanding of mind is one of ontological dualism, perhaps combined with some form of epistemological realism. These conclusions are based on findings concerning young children's reflection on and conception of their own and others' mental experiences, their awareness, understanding, and control of imagery, as well as their conceptions of other kinds of things such as photographs, smoke, and shadows. This interwoven set of findings seems fitting; mental phenomena themselves are complex, multifaceted, and interrelated. Philosophy of mind and cognitive science take as their domain a host of related phenomena and processes. Young children's conceptions seem to mirror this complexity in scope, if not in sophistication; even very young children are beginning to recognize and think about a variety of mental phenomena. Furthermore, young children demonstrate at least one firm foothold in this complex and potentially confusing domain: a solid and articulate understanding of the fundamental distinction between mental entities and physical objects.

Chapter 3

Young Children's Understanding of Belief

Suppose I say, "Joe believes his uncle's car is green." In the terminology of chapter 2, I would be referring, in part, to a mental entity (a thought of a car, in the form of a belief). However, I also would be specifying a particular mental state or attitude, namely that of believing; not dreaming of a green car, or imagining a green car, or even thinking of a green car, but believing that car is green. Believing is a mental attitude of conviction, the thought that something is true. It is the attitude that takes a description ("the car is green") as corresponding (to some degree) to a state of affairs in the world. Beliefs, considered generically, encompass a variety of states of conviction: knowing, being sure, suspecting, surmising, even some sorts of guessing. But, in essence, beliefs are mental states or attitudes about world states. In this way, beliefs are different from mental states such as fantasy in being reality directed.

Beliefs therefore are a special sort of hybrid construct, spanning mind and world in a particular fashion. Beliefs describe both a mental state and the world; beliefs are thoughts about (potentially) actual states of affairs. Beliefs are representations intended to capture something real. This special hybrid quality of belief has made its analysis problematic for philosophers, but it also makes beliefs especially suited to the task of providing mental explanations for actions in the world. This is the typical job description of belief statements and attributions; in our everyday psychology, beliefs constitute mental causes for actual behaviors.

Of course, a person's beliefs may be wrong. I may believe I put out the trash this morning when I never did so. Beliefs do not necessarily correspond to actual states of affairs; representations do not necessarily faithfully capture reality, even representations intended to do so. When we say that someone "believes" something rather than "knows" something, we are acknowledging this potential lack of correspondence. In this sense, beliefs, like all other mental states or entities, rest on the independence of the mental and physical worlds.

The believer, however, is in the state of crediting (to some degree) a correspondence between mental content and physical reality. This double-sided nature of belief is especially clear in the case of a false belief. If we say Bill has a false belief, we are noting both Bill's conviction (his posited correspondence between world and mind) and at the same time a world-to-mind noncorrespondence.

From the research reviewed in chapter 2 it seems clear that even young children understand the independence of mental entities from the physical world. But it is not clear whether children understand the peculiar nature of mental attitudes of conviction. If children understand the mental nature of mental entities but not the attitude of believing, then they might construe themselves and others as possessors of mental states and experiences (dreams, ideas, thoughts) but not understand that some thoughts are meant to represent the world and hence not understand how mental states can cause actions. That is, there might exist in young children a severe quarantining of mind and world and of mind and behavior. If so, young children could have an early theory of mind, but it would not be at all like our adult theory, which centrally incorporates a mentalistic explanation of action by a construct of belief. The focus of this chapter, then, is children's understanding of belief and whether they, like us, construe human actions as resulting from internal states of belief. The question is not whether young children themselves possess beliefs. I assume that children themselves are cognitive representational organisms. Similarly, the question is not whether an everyday construct like belief can form the basis of a good or valid scientific psychology (Churchland, 1981; Stitch, 1983). My focus is on the development in children of such everyday concepts in the first place. The question is how and when children employ a construct like belief to understand their own and others' everyday behavior.

I will assume, as a point for departure, that adult naive psychological explanation encompasses something like a system of reasoning about beliefs and desires as introduced in chapter 1. This accounts, among other things, for such everyday explanations as:

(1)   Why did Mary go to the car wash? She *wanted* her car clean and *thought* that the car wash would clean it.

(2)   Why did John buy a candy bar? He *wanted* something to eat and *thought* that eating a candy bar would help him get through until dinner time.

In short, "we generally explain why people do what they do in terms of desires or goals, and their beliefs both about these goals and about possible means to their goals" (Giere, 1985, p. 86). In such a system, to investigate a person's understanding of belief requires consideration of belief-desire reasoning more generally. I believe that there are important differences in children's versus adults' belief-desire reasoning and hence in their resulting naive psychologies. Nevertheless, I wish to claim that by age three, children's naive psychology is commensurate with adults' in several fashions: (1) in including a conception of belief and (2) in contrasting beliefs with desires while (3) at the same time joining them in a causal reasoning scheme.

Our understanding of children's belief-desire reasoning can be informed by several different research literatures, including those of story comprehension, moral judgment, person perception, and metacognition. For example, Stein and Trabasso have shown that four- and five-year-olds understand the psychological causality involved in simple stories about people who have certain goals, possess certain beliefs, and utilize their knowledge to attain their goals, and having succeeded or failed are appropriately happy or sad or angry (Stein and Levine, in press; Nezworski, Stein, and Trabasso, 1982). The topic is in need of further investigation, however, because empirical studies in these traditions rarely, if ever, directly examine children's reasoning about beliefs. The notable exception is the recent research on children's understanding of false beliefs (beginning with Wimmer and Perner, 1983).

In Wimmer and Perner's work a standard false belief task includes the following features. A character, for example Maxi, watches as a target, chocolate, is hidden in a location, the kitchen. While Maxi is away, unbeknown to him, the chocolate is moved from the kitchen to another location, the living room. Now Maxi wants some chocolate. Will he look in the kitchen or the living room? Children four years of age and older succeed on false belief tasks of this sort by predicting that Maxi will search in the kitchen (see the summary of children's performance on more than 10 different versions of the task as provided in Perner, Leekham, and Wimmer, 1987). This appropriate prediction of the character's action from information about the character's beliefs and desires suggests an impressive understanding of mind in older preschoolers. And it demonstrates a specific understanding of mental states of conviction—beliefs—in that the child must predict Maxi's action on the basis of Maxi's false belief. However, children younger than four years fail these false belief tasks. They do not respond randomly; they consistently err by predicting that the character will search where the chocolate really is rather than where he should believe it to be.

What are we to make of this failure? One possibility is that young children do not understand belief at all and hence do not engage in belief-desire reasoning. On this account, reasoning about false beliefs might be seen as being diagnostic of reasoning about beliefs in general (Dennett, 1978), and the prediction that a character's behavior will correspond to reality rather than to belief reveals young children's inability to understand the mental, subjective aspect of beliefs. An alternate possibility is that false belief reasoning is a particularly difficult form of reasoning about beliefs (perhaps it is especially confusing or complex). In this case, young children might be capable of engaging in belief-desire reasoning but still fail the peculiarly difficult task of reasoning about false beliefs. In this chapter I present evidence that three-year-olds understand beliefs; chapter 9 offers an account of wh y they also fail false belief tasks.

Initial Belief-Desire Prediction Experiment

Karen Bartsch and I (Wellman and Bartsch, 1988) have investigated the early development of belief reasoning. We included beliefs and desires because the two are inextricably intertwined, but our special focus was belief. We began by trying to determine when children understand that beliefs are independent from desires in the sense that the exact same desire will lead to quite different actions depending on the actor's beliefs. That is, When do children understand that beliefs are a necessary addition to information about desire to explain an actor's actions?

Each child was told stories depicting a character's desire and belief and then was asked to predict the action of the character. An example is: "Sam *wants* to find his puppy. His puppy might be hiding in the garage or under the porch. But Sam *thinks* his puppy is under the porch. Where will Sam look for his puppy: in the garage or under the porch?" Sensible prediction of the character's action can result from utilizing the information about his belief coupled with information about his desire.

We call stories such as this *standard belief* tasks (table 3.1). Unfortunately, children might make accurate predictions on standard belief tasks without knowing much about beliefs. For example, suppose the child responded by predicting the last location mentioned. Since the last thing he or she was told was that "Sam thinks the puppy is under the porch," the child simply answers "the porch." To control for this possibility, in part, we devised *not belief* tasks (table 3.1). In not belief tasks, the child was told, for example, "Sam thinks his puppy is *not*

Table 3.1
Critical Features and Example Stories for the Belief Reasoning Tasks

Task	Critical Features	Example
Standard belief	Desire: Character's desire explicitly mentioned. Belief: Character's belief explicitly mentioned. Target: Actual location of object unknown.	Sam wants to find his puppy. It might be hiding in the garage or under the porch. Sam thinks his puppy is under the porch. Where will Sam look for his puppy (garage or porch)?
Not belief	Desire: Character's desire explicitly mentioned. Belief: Character's belief that object is *not* in one locations is explicitly mentioned. Target: Actual location of object unknown.	Sam wants to find his puppy. It might be hiding in the garage or under the porch. Sam thinks his puppy is *not* in the garage. Where will Sam look for his puppy?
Not-own belief	Desire: Character's desire explicitly mentioned. Belief: Subject's belief is first solicited, then character is attributed opposite belief. Target: Actual location of object unknown.	Sam wants to find his puppy. It might be hiding in the garage or under the porch. Where do *you* think Sam's puppy is? (e.g., under the porch) That's a good guess, but *Sam* thinks his puppy is in the garage. Where will Sam look for his puppy?
Changed belief	Desire: Character's desire explicitly mentioned. Belief: Character has initial belief, but then changes to opposite belief. Target: Actual location of object unknown.	Sam wants to find his puppy. It might be hiding in the garage or under the porch. Sam thinks his puppy is under the porch. Where will Sam look for his puppy? *But,* before Sam can look for his puppy, Sam's mom comes out of the house. Sam's mom says she saw his puppy in the garage. So now Sam thinks his puppy is in the garage. Where will Sam look for his puppy?

Table 3.1 (continued)

Task	Critical Features	Example
Inferred belief	Desire: Character's desire explicitly mentioned.	This is Jane. This morning Jane saw her magic markers in the desk, not on the shelf. Now Jane wants magic markers. Where will she look?
	Belief: No belief explicitly mentioned, but character is said to have previously seen target in one location, not the other.	
	Target: Actual location of object not known.	
Inferred belief-control	Desire: Character's desire explicitly mentioned.	Look, there are magic markers in the desk *and* there are magic markers on the shelf. This morning Jane saw the magic markers on the shelf, not in the desk. Now Jane wants magic markers. Where will she look for magic markers? Are there magic markers in the (other location) too?
	Target: Subject sees that target objects are in *both* locations.	
	Belief: No belief explicitly mentioned but character is said to have previously seen target in one location, not other.	
Explicit false-belief	Desire: Character's desire explicitly mentioned.	Jane wants to find her kitten. Jane's kitten is really in the playroom. Jane thinks her kitten is in the kitchen. Where will Jane look for her kitten? Where is the kitten really?
	Target: Object is said to really be in one location.	
	Belief: Character is said to believe object is in other (wrong) location.	

Discrepant belief

Desire: Character's desire explicitly mentioned.

Target: Subject sees that target objects are in *both* locations.

Belief: Character is said to believe target is in one location, not other.

Look, there are bananas in the cupboard and bananas in the refrigerator. Jane wants a banana. Jane thinks there are only bananas in the cupboard; she doesn't think there are bananas in the refrigerator. Where will Jane look for bananas? Are there bananas in the (other location) too?

Relevant belief

Target: Subject sees that target objects are in *both* locations.

Belief: Character is said to believe target is in one location, not other.

Desire: Character's desire explicitly mentioned.

Look, there are books on the shelf and books in the toy box. Amy thinks there are books only on the shelf; she doesn't think there are books in the toy box. Amy wants some books. Where will Amy look for books? Are there books in the (other location) too?

Irrelevant belief

Target: Subject *and* character see that target objects are in *both* locations.

Belief: Character is said to have a belief about one location that is *irrelevant* to her desire.

Desire: Character's desire is explicitly mentioned.

This is Amy. Look (to subject and to Amy), there are books on the shelf and books in the toy box. Amy thinks the toy box is brown; she doesn't think the shelf is brown. Amy wants some books. Where will Amy look for books? Are there books in the (other location) too?

in the garage." The correct prediction is therefore the unmentioned location (the porch).

Suppose, by chance, that the protagonist's belief—"Sam thinks his puppy is under the porch"—consistently coincides with the child's own belief; that is, the child thinks puppies really hide under porches, not in garages. In that case, the child might be correct not by understanding belief but simply by predicting what she herself would do: "The puppy is lost; I'd look under the porch." To begin to control for this possibility, we devised *not-own belief* tasks (table 3.1). In not-own belief tasks the child was told, for example, that Sam wants to find his puppy and that the puppy might be in the garage or under the porch. At this point the child was asked, "Where do you think the puppy is?" After the child stated her belief, she was told that the protagonist had the opposite belief. Thus, when a child said she thought the puppy was under the porch, she was told, "Well, that's a good guess, but Sam thinks the puppy is in the garage." Then the child was asked to predict where Sam would look for the puppy.

Not-own belief tasks share some important features with false-belief tasks, although the two are not identical. Not-own belief tasks resemble false-belief tasks in that there is a conflict between two beliefs, the child's own and another's; the child must ignore her stated belief and predict the other's act on the basis of the other's belief.

Finally, we employed a fourth version of the task, *changed belief* tasks (table 3.1). Changed belief tasks always began with a standard belief task. For example, first the child was told about Sam's desire and Sam's belief and was asked to predict Sam's action (the standard belief task). Then the child was told, "Before Sam looks for his puppy, his mom comes out of the house. Sam's mom tells Sam she saw his puppy in the garage. So now Sam thinks his puppy is in the garage" (the changed belief task). That is, Sam now has the opposite of his earlier belief, and the child was asked again to predict where Sam will look for his puppy.

Correct responses to a changed belief task indicate that the child knows that beliefs can change and that the same desire coupled with two different beliefs leads to two different actions; this reflects the child's understanding of the independent contribution of belief as well as desire to the formulation of an action. Also, because Sam changes his initial belief before he looks for the dog, a correct response shows that the child appreciates that beliefs do not inevitably result in action—the independence of belief from action.

Method

Thirty-two preschool children were tested; 16 three-year-olds (3–5 to 3–11, $M = 3$–9) and 16 four-year-olds (4–1 to 4–9, $M = 4$–5). Children were presented with three instances of each of the four tasks—standard, not, not-own, and changed belief tasks—for a total of 12 stories. Because changed belief tasks always followed standard belief tasks that utilized the same story protagonist and topic, children were essentially presented with three types of stories and three instances of each type or nine stories (three of which included both a standard belief and a changed belief question). The nine stories involved a character wanting to find a puppy, to eat some raisins, to plant seeds, to buy candy, to give a toy, to play on outside play equipment, to make a tent, to build a doll house, to find a hat. The three instances of each general type were presented in a group, with the order of particular stories extensively counterbalanced. During each story, the child was first shown a drawing of the protagonist's face and then a drawing of both possible locations. The child responded either verbally or by pointing to a location.

Results

The top portion of figure 3.1 depicts the design of the study and the relevant competing hypotheses. Correct responding means predicting according to the character's beliefs—for example, the unmentioned alternative in not belief tasks and the subsequent rather than the original belief in changed belief tasks.

   The upper-left-hand graph indicates that if children understand belief, they should be uniformly correct across all versions of the task. The upper middle graph depicts expected results if children simply predict that the character will search at the last-mentioned location. In this case, they would err consistently on not belief tasks. The upper-right-hand graph depicts performance if children simply predict what they themselves would do. In this case children could be fortuitously correct on standard and not belief tasks if their own beliefs just happened to coincide with the belief attributed to the actor. However, if they were correct in this manner on a standard belief task, they should be incorrect on a subsequent changed belief task. And if they simply stated what they themselves would do, then they should be consistently incorrect on not-own belief tasks as well.

   The data are shown at the bottom of figure 3.1. Three- and four-year-olds were consistently correct, averaging 85% and 89% correct, respectively. Children's responding at both ages and in all task ver-

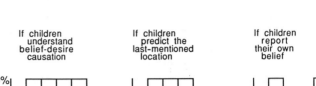

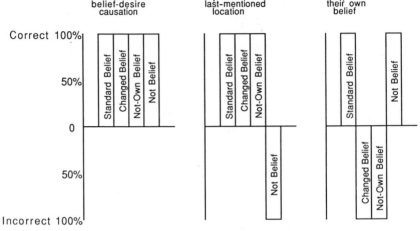

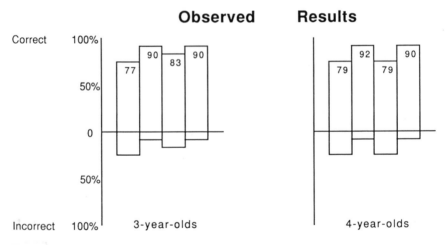

Figure 3.1
Predicted and observed results for the initial belief-desire prediction experiment.
From Wellman and Bartsch (1988).

sions was significantly above a chance level of 50%. Individually children received three instances of each of the four story versions and thus gave a total of 12 responses. Nine correct responses of 12 is significantly above change ($p < .05$, one-tailed); 12 of 16 three-year-olds (75%) and 13 of 16 four-year-olds (81%), performed at or above this level of consistency.

Three-year-olds performed well, but our sample consisted of mostly older three-year-olds ($M = 3$–9). Therefore, we tested eight younger children, ages 2–9 to 3–6 ($M = 3$–2). These children averaged 84% correct. They were correct 67% of the time on standard belief tasks, 92% on not belief tasks, 98% on the not-own belief tasks, and 79% on changed belief tasks. Five of the eight children were correct on 9 or more of their 12 questions; the remaining three children were correct on eight of the 12.

Discussion

Children's high level of performance was compelling. Even three-year-olds had little difficulty in predicting a character's action in accordance with the character's beliefs. Our stories presented characters who had definite desires but desires consistent with both alternative actions. Only the character's belief determined the appropriate option. Correct responses thus are consistent with a conception of beliefs as independent from desires in the sense that beliefs are seen to provide needed information not available in information about desires.

It is important to emphasize the experimental logic of this research. Four different belief-desire tasks were used. Taken singly, correct performance on any one task does not convincingly demonstrate belief-desire reasoning because the individual tasks admit to alternate interpretations. Collectively, however, alternate interpretations are discounted by good performance on one version of the task or another. The uniformly good performance of three- and four-year-olds across all tasks is thus an important aspect of the data. Our next experiment built on this logic. This second experiment included additional belief-desire tasks to minimize further the possibility that response strategies other than an understanding of belief account for younger children's good performance.

Second Belief-Desire Prediction Experiment

A high degree of accuracy by three-year-olds on belief reasoning tasks is seemingly at odds with the established results from the traditional false-belief task. False-belief research (Gopnick and Astington, 1988; Perner et al., 1987; Wimmer and Perner, 1983) suggests that children younger than four or four and a half years are consistently inaccurate at belief reasoning by predicting that an actor with a false belief will search for an object where it really is, not where the actor believes it to be. This is the opposite of what an understanding of belief should yield.

In this second experiment, we attempted to clarify and reconcile these discrepant findings. One possibility was that there is no discrepancy; our three-year-olds might just have been advanced, more like Wimmer and Perner's four-year-olds. If so, success on false-belief tasks and on our belief-desire tasks may actually develop concurrently. To address this, we tested the same children on both sorts of tasks.

Two further possibilities were that false-belief tasks are unnecessarily difficult or that our tasks are spuriously easy. With regard to the former, note that in contrast to our tasks, on Wimmer and Perner's false-belief task the child is never told the protagonist's belief—"Sam thinks his dog is in the garage." Instead the child must infer the protagonist's belief. The child knows that the character saw the object hidden in one location and did not see it moved to another. From this, the child must infer that the character believes the object is still in the first location. Perhaps this inferred-belief requirement make the traditional false-belief task relatively difficult. Indeed, Wimmer (Wimmer, Hogrefe, and Sodian, 1988) has suggested that this is the essence of young children's difficulty. If so, a false-belief task with no inference requirement, where the subject is simply told that the protagonist believes that the object is at the wrong location, should be mastered earlier, as are our tasks.

It is also possible that our belief-desire tasks allowed children to respond correctly without understanding belief. Suppose, for example, that the young child has no conception of belief and hence does not understand belief statements ("Sam believes his dog is in the garage"). Instead the child might simply attempt to determine the real state of affairs and then, knowing the actor's desire, predict the actor will act to fulfill his desire. We call this general possibility use of a reality assessment strategy. One specific version of a reality assessment strategy might be as follows. First, the child might simply translate belief statements into reality statements: "Sam believes his dog is in the garage" becomes "Sam's dog is in the garage." Second, the child would reason: "Sam wants his dog; it's in the garage, so Sam will look in the garage." If children engage in this sort of reality assessment reasoning, then they could be correct, for example, on our standard belief tasks. Similarly, if asked to predict a protagonist's action in our not-own belief tasks the child might have interpreted the statement "that's a good guess but Sam thinks . . ." to be a statement as to what is really true rather than merely a description of Sam's belief. In fact, Perner (1988) has suggested that a version of a reality assessment strategy might also account for early success on not-own belief tasks. Therefore, we included two new conditions in this experiment to control for the use of reality assessment strategies: inferred belief-control tasks and discrepant belief tasks.

Method

Four types of tasks were used. There were *not-own belief* stories similar to those used in the first experiment (table 3.1): "Jane wants to find her kitten. Where do *you* think the kitten is: in the playroom or in the kitchen? Well, that's a good guess, but Jane thinks the kitten is in the [opposite location]. Where will Jane look for the kitten?" In order to provide false belief tasks as comparable as possible to these not-own belief tasks, we constructed simplified versions, called *explicit false-belief* tasks (table 3.1). In these tasks, children did not have to infer the protagonist's false belief but were told it directly: "Jane's kitten is really in the playroom, but Jane thinks the kitten is in the kitchen. Where will Jane look for her kitten?" Explicit false-belief tasks of this sort should prove easy if children's difficulty in the traditional task is that it requires inference of belief.

To test directly whether young children find inference of belief difficult, we included stories requiring an inference of belief from the the protagonist's perceptual access to the relevant situation, *inferred belief* tasks (table 3.1). Here correct prediction of action requires attributing an inferred belief to the protagonist: "This is Jane. This morning Jane saw her magic markers in the desk, not on the shelf. Now she wants her magic markers. Where will she look?"

The fourth type of task was included to defeat the possibility that children make their predictions by reality assessment strategies rather than on the basis of the protagonist's beliefs. Reality assessment strategies seemed most viable on the inferred belief task, so we devised *inferred belief-control* tasks (table 3.1). On these tasks, the stories told of identical objects hidden in each of two locations. The protagonist was said to have seen only one of these objects earlier: "There are magic markers in the desk, *and* there are magic markers on the shelf. This morning Jane saw the magic markers in the desk, but she did not see the magic markers on the shelf. Now Jane wants magic markers. Where will she look for magic markers?" Children were also asked whether the desired object was in the other location ("Are there magic markers in the desk too?") to ensure that they remembered all the information correctly. We reasoned that this sort of task could control for two slightly different variations of reality assessment. First, suppose children simply take the see statement (Jane saw the magic markers on the desk not the shelf) as a statement about reality (the markers really are on the shelf, not the desk). In that case they should fail on the control question (are there markers in the desk too?). Correct answers to the control question would rule against this sort of reality assessment strategy. Second, suppose children assess the story information more deeply but still only to determine where the target really is; then they predict the actor will look there. In this case, if children understand the story information correctly in inferred belief-control stories, they will know that targets are in both locations. After determining that both locations contain the desired items, they should be equally likely to answer that the protagonist would look in either or both locations. This sort of reasoning generates a different prediction as to Jane's action from the one generated by an inference as to the character's belief. If children infer Jane's belief correctly, Jane should look in the desk because she saw markers there, and thus that is where she believes them to be.

Forty preschool children participated: 16 three-year-olds (range 3–0 to 3–11, $M = 3$–7), 13 younger four-year-olds (range 4–0 to 4–6, $M = 4$–3), and 11 older four-year-olds we called the 4½-year-olds (range 4–7 to 5–0, $M = 4$–9). Each child was tested individually in a single session. The experimenter presented two instances of each of the four task types (explicit false-belief, not-own belief, inferred belief, and inferred belief-control). The two stories of each type were always presented consecutively, but the four types were presented in counterbalanced orders across each age group. Each of the eight stories concerned a different protagonist, desired object, and locations, and these topics were counterbalanced over the types of stories.[1]

Each story was accompanied by two drawings: a picture of a child's face ("This is Jane") and a picture of the two locations drawn in such a way that the object might be in the location though it could not be seen.

Results

Figure 3.2 presents the proportion of correct responding by age group. To be correct, children had to predict the location appropriate

Observed   Results

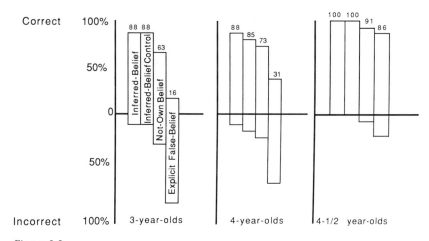

Figure 3.2
Percentage of correct responses given to the different task types used in the second belief-desire prediction experiment. From Wellman and Bartsch (1988).

to the character's beliefs. In addition, on inferred belief-control tasks, children had to assert correctly that there were items in both locations, and on explicit false-belief tasks, they had to assert that the item was really in its correct location. Performances on the inferred belief, inferred belief-control, and not-own tasks (which did not differ from one another) averaged 80%, 82%, and 97% for three-, four- and four and a half-year-olds, respectively. Only performance on the explicit false-belief tasks changed with age; it was below a chance level of 50% for three-year-olds, did not differ from chance for four-year-olds, and was above chance for four and a half-year-olds.

Each child heard six different inferred belief, inferred belief-control, and not-own stories. Responding to five of six correctly is significantly above chance ($p < .05$, one-tailed). Ten of 16 three-year-olds (63%), 9 of 13 four-year-olds (69%), and 10 of 11 four and a half-year-olds (91%) performed at or above this level of consistency.

Finally, we were interested in the direct comparability of not-own belief and explicit false-belief tasks. If being correct on both of the two instances of each story type is considered passing, then 13 children passed the not-own tasks while failing explicit false-belief tasks and only one child showed the reverse pattern. Thus, as clear in figure 3.2, three- and four-year-olds who failed the explicit false-belief stories were typically correct on not-own belief stories.

Discrepant Belief Tasks

An especially troubling possibility is that young children might use reality assessment strategies to reason about tasks such as ours. Therefore, we tested three-year-olds on additional tasks designed to control for this possibility. These discrepant belief tasks (table 3.1) were like the standard belief tasks of the first experiment in that they required children to predict the character's action from a stated desire ("she wants bananas") and a stated belief ("she thinks bananas are in the cupboard"). As in the inferred belief-control tasks, however, there were actually target objects (bananas) in both locations, and the subject knew this. As argued in the description of the inferred belief-control tasks, subjects using reality assessment strategies should either fail the control question or should predict that the character would search in either location or both (because bananas are really in both). An understanding of belief should lead to the single correct prediction coupled with a correct understanding that target items are in the other location as well.

Discrepant belief tasks also parallel not-own belief tasks in several important ways. In a discrepant belief task, like a not-own belief task, the child subject has his own belief—in this case, the correct belief that bananas are in both places. The story character, however, has a different belief—in this case, that there are bananas only in the cupboard. To be correct, the child must predict the character's action on the basis of the character's belief, not on the basis of the child's own belief. In the first experiment, three-year-olds averaged 83% correct on not-own tasks; in the second experiment this average fell to 63%. While these percentages do not differ significantly from each other, we wished to demonstrate more firmly that three-year-olds are largely correct on problems where there is a discrepancy between one's own and the other's beliefs. Testing three-year-olds on discrepant belief tasks served this purpose by providing data on a more controlled version of not-own belief tasks.

Fifteen three-year-olds (3–3 to 4–0, M = 3–8) participated. Each child was given three instances of a discrepant belief task. For example, in one instance, the child was shown drawings of a cupboard and a refrigerator with paper-flap doors. The child was told, "Look; there are bananas in the cupboard [the experimenter opened the cup-board to show the bananas] and there are bananas in the refrigerator [the experimenter opened the refrigerator]." Both doors were shut, and then the child was shown a picture of a story character and told, "This is Jane. Jane wants a banana. Jane thinks there are only bananas in the cupboard; she doesn't think there are bananas in the refrigerator. Where will Jane look for a banana?" After the child answered this question, he or she was asked, "Are there bananas in the refrigerator too?" The three different story instances involved a character looking for bananas, mittens, or magic markers.[2]

Three-year-olds were 82% correct on these discrepant belief tasks—where correct meant predicting the actor's behavior on the basis of the actor's belief. This level of performance was significantly higher than a chance performance of 50% correct. All correct predictions were followed by correct answers on the control question designed to ensure that subjects knew that the target objects were in both locations ("are there bananas in the cupboard too?"). Nine of 15 children (60%) were correct on three of three discrepant belief tasks; five of the remaining children were correct of two of three, and one was incorrect on all three.

Discussion

There were two primary findings in this second study. First, inferred belief tasks, not-own belief tasks, and discrepant belief tasks yielded comparable and high performance in three-year-olds. Thus the inferred belief and discrepant belief tasks take their place with not-own tasks and the standard, not, and changed belief tasks of the first experiment, as part of the package of belief-desire reasoning tasks solved by quite young children. Consistently high performance across all these tasks provides an interlocking variety of controls against alternate interpretations. An important addition to these controls is provided by the inferred belief-control and the discrepant belief tasks. Consistently correct performance on those tasks would not be possible if children were using reality assessment strategies instead of reasoning about beliefs.

The inferred belief tasks (of both varieties) also provide a substantive addition to the tasks used in the first experiment. Correct performance on inferred belief tasks shows that three-year-olds' belief-desire reasoning abilities extend beyond situations in which the actor's beliefs are explicitly stated. In our inferred belief tasks, subjects were not told the protagonists' beliefs ("he thinks . . ."), but such beliefs could be easily inferred from the fact that the actor saw the relevant items.

The second primary result is that in spite of three-year-olds' demonstrable belief-desire reasoning skills, such children still fail false-belief tasks. Note that our explicit false-belief tasks were very simple ones in which subjects were straightforwardly told of the protagonist's belief ("Sam thinks . . ."). In spite of this, three- and many young four-year-olds predicted the actor would look where the target really was, not where it was believed to be.

Consistently incorrect performance on explicit false-belief tasks brings with it an additional important control. It is conceivable, although I think it is unlikely, that in tasks such as ours, young children misconstrue "think" statements as action statements. That is, a statement such as, "Sam thinks his dog is in the garage," could be mistranslated into something like, "Sam will look in the garage," a mental verb simplistically being interpreted as an action verb. If children engaged in such mistranslation, they could be correct on many of our tasks because the subject is told "Sam thinks . . ." However, three-year-olds' consistent failure on the explicit false-belief tasks rules out this possibility. On these tasks, young children heard that "Sam thinks an object is at one location," but they consistently predicted that Sam would look in the other location. These results also speak against related alternatives, such as the possibility that belief terms are just translated into desire terms ("Sam thinks the dog is in the garage" becomes "Sam wants to go to the garage").

Originally Wimmer and Perner (1983) contended that the essential difficulty of false-belief tasks was that they required consideration of contradictory beliefs. More recently, Flavell (Flavell, Green, and Flavell, 1986) and Gopnik and Astington (1988) suggested something similar: young children are unable to conceive of alternative beliefs or representations as applying to the same object or state of affairs. That is, young children will fail on tasks where they must simultaneously consider two different beliefs or representations of one target (in the case of false beliefs, the child's own belief as to the object's location and the protagonist's conflicting belief). However, in an important sense, our not-own belief tasks require consideration of two contradictory beliefs as well: the child believes the object is in one location, the protagonist believes it is in the other location, and the protagonist's action must be predicted on the basis of his or her belief, not the child's. Further, in both the inferred belief-control and discrepant belief tasks, the child's own beliefs are discrepant with, if not actually contradictory to, the character's beliefs. In fact, this seems a critical aspect of an understanding of belief—that different people can have different beliefs (and this in part accounts for why they engage in different actions). Our data suggest that this is a part of the conception of belief well within the grasp of three-year-olds.

Belief-Desire Reasoning without Belief?

I wish to consider more extensively a proposal by Perner (1988) that inspires some provocative analyses of how young children might solve belief-desire reasoning tasks without a genuine conception of belief. A clear example of how three-year-olds might operate without a conception of belief can be derived from Perner's analysis of how they might solve our not-own belief tasks (Perner 1988). In this analysis, Perner acknowledges (as would I) that three-year-olds themselves have beliefs, that is, they have their own knowledge or understanding of various real situations. Indeed, he claims that they often predict others' actions by considering only the real external situation (as coded in their own knowledge of the situation). When asked where Sam will look for an object, they report their own knowledge of where the object is. In our terms, this constitutes use of a reality assessment strategy. However, three-year-olds are at times ignorant; they may not know what is really so. Indeed, on our not-own belief tasks, they do not know where the target is. In such cases, Perner contends, they could simply employ an interesting default strategy. When reality assessment fails, three-year-olds could search their own knowledge for any association between the protagonist and one of the alternatives. Since the story statement, "Sam thinks the object is at location 1" associates Sam with "object at location 1" (and not with "object at location 2"), the child predicts Sam will look at location 1 (not 2). To my mind, there are three essential parts to this analysis: (a) employment of a reality assessment strategy, (b) employment of an associational strategy, and (c) prioritizing one strategy over the other.

The associational strategy deserves some elaboration because it is an intriguing alternative to crediting three-year-olds with a genuine understanding of belief. Perner is vague in his description of how young children might associate characters and alternatives, but one important possibility is that a child forms an uninterpreted link between character and situation, a nonspecific association between the two. Sam is connected with "object at location 1" in the child's mind; Bill could be connected with "object at location 2." Clearly three-year-olds could use belief statements from an adult to construct such nonspecific associational links: "Sam thinks the object is at location 1" could simply link Sam with "object at location 1" for the young child in a general and nonspecific manner. Thus, younger children may not understand that Sam believes (knows, thinks, guesses) that "the object is at location 1" or "at location 2"; rather, belief statements (among others) simply connect Sam with one of the alternatives.

Such an associational strategy alone cannot account for three-year-olds' performance. Most clearly, in false-belief tasks the character is associated with the false alternative, "object at location 1" (when the object is at location 2), but three-year-olds predict that the character will look at location 2. Our explicit false-belief tasks provide the clearest example of this to date. The object is at location 2 but the character is associated only with location 1 (by the "he thinks it is at location 1" statement). In this situation, three-year-olds do not predict on the basis of the character's "association."

For these reasons, I believe, Perner proposed that three-year-olds' strategies are prioritized. They first try a reality assessment strategy; if that cannot be used (if reality is unknown), then they look for an association between the character and the locations (the associational strategy). Perner (1988) says, "Children's task is to predict where [the character] will go in the actual world and so the most obvious search for [the character's] destination would be the knowledge base, which reflects the external situation. However, in the knowledge base there is no record about the [object's] location. . . . the next best strategy is to consult [the character's] belief" (p. 156), that is, to search for an association between the character and an alternative. Such a prioritized list of strategies could yield the observed incorrect answers on false-belief tasks coupled with correct answers on not-own belief tasks; this was the specific pattern of results that Perner considered. However, such a proposal cannot account for the larger pattern of results presented here. It is especially inconsistent with three-year-olds' correct answers on the inferred belief-control and discrepant belief tasks. Suppose that three-year-olds' first priority is to determine where the targets are, as Perner proposes, and predict the character will search there. In inferred belief-control and discrepant belief tasks, there really are items in both locations, and the child knows this. But on these tasks three-year-olds do not predict that the character will look in both locations or in either location without preference. Instead, they correctly predict the character will search in accordance with his belief.

This discussion addresses Perner's original proposal as I understood it and as we discussed it in Wellman and Bartsch (1988). However, it is possible to expand on Perner's proposal a bit by avoiding the notion of a prioritized strategy list and simply positing that young children have two weighted response tendencies that they sum together in predicting actions. One tendency is to consider the real situation; for example, when the target is at location 1, weight location 1 as a likely place for the character to go. The second tendency is to consider associations between the character and the alternatives; for example, when the character is associated with location 2, weight location 2 as a likely place for the character to go. These tendencies are essentially identical to the reality assessment and associational strategies, except that they yield decision weights rather than mandating choice of one location or another. These decision weights would then be summed to predict the character's choice of action. Additionally, let us stipulate that children weight reality as being more important than the character's association; this is reasonable and also is in keeping with the gist of Perner's proposal. These two weighted tendencies encompass no understanding of belief, but (given the assumptions) appropriate predictions would be generated to all the tasks used in the preceding two experiments.

To illustrate, arbitrarily suppose that children weight reality as approximately twice as important as associations in their thinking about action. Concretely, let us say reality is worth 100 decision units whereas associations are worth 50 in the child's scale of things. Now consider discrepant belief tasks (or alternately inferred belief-control tasks). In such tasks, the child knows that there are target items in both places. Roughly this means that location 1 and location 2 will be weighted equally with respect to reality since both contain the target. In my arbitrary example, each alternative location receives 50 weighted decision units (and reality totals 100 arbitrary units). In addition, the child hears that the character "thinks" the target is at location 1. This is understood not as specifying a belief but as simply associating the character with location 1. Thus location 1 but not location 2 receives associational weighting as well. Concretely, location 1 will be weighted 50 units, and location 2 will receive 0 units (and associations total 50 arbitrary units). Summing up, location 1 receives a total weight of 100 (50 + 50), and location 2 receives a total weight of 50 (50 + 0), so that the child predicts the character will search at location 1. This is, of course, the correct answer, but in arriving at it by this hypothetical process, the child utilizes no concept of belief, merely appropriately weighted reality and associational tendencies.

This same decision process could work in our other tasks. In standard-belief or not-own belief tasks, for example, the real placement of the target is unknown; the reality weights are thus equal for each of the two locations (either 50-50 or 0-0). When the "belief" statement associates the character with one alternative, that location is weighted over the other, and it would then be correctly chosen. Or consider false-belief tasks. Importantly, on these tasks, reality is known. Say that the target is at location 1; since the child knows this, location 1 receives a weight of 100. The character, however, is associated with location 2; location 2 thus receives a weight of 50. The false-belief error is generated because reality itself is a weightier consideration for the child than are associations (100 > 50).

I will term this hypothesis the response tendency proposal. The following experiment contrasts this response tendency proposal with the proposal that young children straightforwardly understand belief, the belief proposal.

Third Belief-Desire Prediction Experiment

According to the response tendency proposal, belief statements ("Sam thinks . . .") function only to create a simple association between characters and alternatives. According to the belief proposal, belief statements appropriately provide the child with information about the character's conviction, a specific conviction—for example, that Sam thinks the target is in a specific location. If the response tendency proposal is true, any belief statement, even one specifying an irrelevant belief, creates the needed association. An irrelevant belief will do because the child is not interpreting the belief statement as specifying a belief but simply as connecting character and alternative. If the belief proposal is true, however, and children understand belief, then some beliefs will be relevant to the character's actions and some will not. Only beliefs relevant to the character's desire predict action. For example, if the character thinks the desired item is at the specified location, that belief is relevant to his desire and thus to his action. If, however, the character thinks (irrelevantly) that the location is blue or green, this belief is not relevant to his desire to find the object and thus does not constrain his search actions.

In this experiment, Karen Bartsch and I tested three-year-olds on two tasks: irrelevant belief tasks and relevant belief tasks. In relevant belief tasks, there were target items in both locations, and the subject knew this. The subject was told that the character believed that the items were in only one of the locations. These tasks are thus identical to discrepant belief tasks (table 3.1); we termed them relevant belief tasks in this experiment to contrast them with the irrelevant belief tasks. In irrelevant belief tasks, items were also in both locations, and the subject knew this. The character similarly had a belief about one location, but the character's belief was irrelevant to finding the object.

Method

Thirty-five three-year-olds participated. Seventeen children (11 boys and 6 girls, $M = 3$–6, range 3–1 to 4–0) were given relevant belief tasks; 18 children (10 boys and 8 girls, $M = 3$–7, range 3–1 to 4–0) were given irrelevant belief tasks.

Each child was given three tasks. The three relevant belief tasks were comparable to the discrepant belief tasks used earlier (table 3.1) but modified slightly to parallel more exactly the irrelevant belief tasks of this experiment. On relevant belief tasks, the child was shown two locations, for example, a picture of a shelf and a toy box (with paper flaps that could open and shut). The child watched as the adult opened both locations and then shut them, demonstrating that there were target items in both. A cardboard story character was introduced next, and the character's belief (and desire) was specified: "This is Amy. Amy thinks there are books only on the shelf; she doesn't think there are books in the toy box. Amy wants some books. Where will Amy look for books?" At this point the child predicted the story character's action. The questioner paused noticeably so that the child could specify that the character would search at both locations if inclined to do so. If a single location was specified, the child was asked whether there were target items in the other location too, to ensure that children understood and remembered that both locations contained the desired objects.

Irrelevant belief tasks paralleled relevant belief tasks in format except that both the child and the story character knew there were objects in both locations. First the two locations and also the story character were introduced; then the child and the character were shown that there were target items in both locations: "Look. There are bananas in the refrigerator, and there are bananas in the cupboard." Then the locations were shut and (as in the relevant belief task), a belief was specified for the character, but in this case an irrelevant belief about color: "Amy thinks the cupboard is white; she doesn't think the refrigerator is white." The belief about color was irrelevant because it has no bearing on the character's desire to find bananas. Then the character's desire was specified and the search question asked: "Amy wants some bananas. Where will Amy look for bananas?" A pause ensued to allow children to indicate that the character would search both locations. If a single location was chosen, the child was asked if there were target items in the other location too. Children were correct on these control questions for the irrelevant and relevant belief tasks 96% of the time. Thus, children nearly always remembered that the items were in both places.

Results

According to the response tendency proposal, children's predictions of the character's action should be identical in both relevant and irrelevant belief tasks. In each case, children should judge that the character will search the location specified in the belief statement because that statement, even if irrelevant, creates the decisive association between character and location. According to the belief proposal, however, action choices in the two tasks should be different. According to the belief proposal, in relevant belief tasks the child should predict search only at the belief-specified location because the relevant belief has direct bearing on the character's desire. In the irrelevant belief task, however, the belief statement mentions a belief that should have no bearing on the actor's conception of where the target is. According to the belief proposal, therefore, in irrelevant belief tasks, both locations are reasonable places for the actor to search, and thus children should predict that the actor will choose either or both locations.

To compare these hypotheses, we considered children's correct responses to the relevant belief tasks and their pseudocorrect responses to the irrelevant belief tasks. Correct responses on relevant belief tasks were children's predictions that the actor would search in accord with the belief specified in the relevant belief statement. Pseudocorrect responses on the irrelevant belief task were children's inappropriate predictions that the actor would search at the location specified by the irrelevant belief statement. According to the response tendency proposal, correct responses on relevant belief tasks should equal pseudocorrect responses on irrelevant belief tasks. According to the belief proposal, correct responses on relevant belief tasks should significantly exceed pseudocorrect responses on irrelevant belief tasks. Further, the belief proposal predicts that either children should say the actor will search both locations on irrelevant belief tasks or that pseudocorrect responses should be at chance indicating random or indifferent choice of either location.

The data support the belief proposal. Children did at times predict the story character would search in both locations. In accord with the belief proposal, children were more likely to judge that the character would search both locations on irrelevant belief tasks (18 choices of both) than on relevant belief tasks (6 choices of both). However, choice of both locations was infrequent; therefore, the focal data concern children's correct and pseudocorrect responses. Three-year-olds' correct and pseudocorrect responses were not equal on the two tasks, inconsistent with the response tendency proposal. Instead responses differed appropriately across the two task types. Specifically children's correct responses on relevant belief tasks (67%) significantly exceeded their pseudocorrect responses on irrelevant belief tasks (42%). Because there were three response options (location 1, location 2, or both), correct and pseudocorrect responses can be compared to a chance value of 33%. Correct responses on relevant belief tasks significantly exceeded chance; pseudocorrect responses on irrelevant belief tasks were at chance.

Correct responses on relevant belief tasks in this experiment (67%) were slightly lower than correct responses on the parallel discrepant belief tasks (82%) in the previous experiment. Essentially this difference occurred because of the slight tendency to indicate both locations during the pause provided after the child's initial response. If "both" responses are dropped from the data, children's correct responding to the relevant belief tasks of this experiment averaged 78%, significantly above a chance value of 50% and quite similar to the 82% correct responding to discrepant belief tasks in the prior study. If "both" responses are excluded from the data on irrelevant belief tasks, children's pseudocorrect responding is still at chance, averaging 52%. Figure 3.3 summarizes these data and the relevant predictions.

Discussion

These data are straightforward. Children do not simply mistranslate belief statements as specifying associations between a character and an alternative. They appropriately understand them as belief statements and hence distinguish between certain sorts of relevant and irrelevant beliefs. Performance on the irrelevant belief tasks not only provides an important control; it also adds substantive information about young children's belief-desire reasoning. In the irrelevant belief tasks, children are presented a character who desires targets and sees that targets are in both of two locations. In this respect, the irrelevant belief tasks constitute a variation on the inferred belief tasks of the second experiment but depict a case where the character should believe there are targets in both locations. In that situation, the actor should be judged to be indifferent between the two locations. Accordingly young children predicted that the character would search both locations or either location randomly, as appropriate by belief-desire reasoning.

Children's judgment that the character would choose either location indifferently on the irrelevant belief tasks further confirms the validity of the discrepant belief and inferred belief-control tasks of the

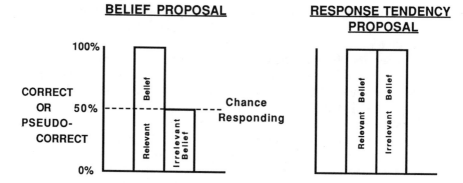

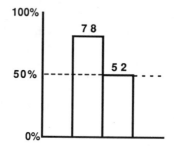

Figure 3.3
Responses to relevant and irrelevant belief tasks in the third belief-desire prediction experiment. Predicted responses for the belief proposal and the response tendency proposal are shown at the top. Observed performance for three-year-olds is shown at the bottom.

prior experiment. In that experiment, we hypothesized that if children use a reality assessment strategy and if they know there are items in both locations, then they should choose either or both locations. Performance above this hypothetical chance baseline was thus interpreted as confirming an understanding of belief. Children's responses to the irrelevant belief tasks in this experiment confirm that hypothetical chance baseline. In a situation where the character should be indifferent as to which of the two locations he chooses, in this last experiment three-year-olds gave "both" responses or randomly chose either location.

Conclusions

I have dwelled at length on the response tendency proposal because it represents a class of proposals to the effect that three-year-olds can succeed on belief-desire reasoning tasks without a conception of belief and because it is an especially powerful and intriguing instance of its class. Indeed, this proposal and our experimental test of it encompass several other possibilities as well. For example, in several recent papers, Perner (1989, in press) has clarified his description of three-year-olds as understanding people only as "associated with" or linked to alternatives rather than understanding beliefs. Perner advances the claim that children in our original experiments (the first two reported here) do not understand belief statements like "Jane thinks her dog is in the garage" to be thinking-that statements. That is, they do not take them as describing beliefs—the thought *that* the dog is in the garage. Instead they understand such statements as a peculiar sort of *thinking-of* statement; that is, they take the statement to mean something like "Jane is thinking *of* the garage" in the sense of "she thinks well of the garage" or "she thinks much of the garage." In short, such thinking-of interpretations "carry the implication of *interest* or even outright preference" for one of the alternatives (Perner, 1989, p. 317). That is, "3-year-olds can cope with attributing to people interesting or desirable possibilities ('thinking of') but not misrepresentation ('thinking that')" (Perner, 1989, p. 318). If so then such thinking-of statements narrow the character's desire appropriately on many of our prior tasks. For example, on our discrepant belief tasks, if there are targets in both locations but the actor prefers one location, then predicting he will search according to his preference correctly solves the reasoning problem but with no recourse to a conception of beliefs.

Such a proposal is also disconfirmed by the results of this last experiment. Similar to the response tendency proposal, the thinking-of proposal should predict equal performance on the relevant and irrelevant belief tasks. In each case three-year-olds should predict the character will search the location specified in the belief statements because that belief statement, even if irrelevant, provides the decisive thinking-of attribution and thus the decisive preference. According to the belief proposal, action choices on the two tasks should be quite different. The thinking-of proposal therefore yields predictions identical to the response tendency proposal, as depicted in figure 3.3. However, as illustrated in that figure three-year-olds' judgments conform to the belief proposal instead.

In total three-year-olds' different performances on relevant versus irrelevant belief tasks and consistently correct performances on not belief, not-own belief, changed belief, standard belief, inferred belief, inferred belief-control, and discrepant belief tasks are inconsistent with a whole range of alternative interpretations. Response strategies or tendencies, such as basing one's choice on the location mentioned last or first or such as translating belief terms ("think") into action meanings ("will look") or desire meanings ("wants to go to"), including preferences ("thinks well of"), cannot produce the pattern of appropriate responses given by three-year-olds. And further possibilities such as predicting on the basis of one's own stated belief, reality assessment strategies, and association between the character and an alternative, a prioritized list of such strategies, or even weighted response tendencies of these sorts cannot produce the observed patterns of response. The straightforward conclusion that young children understand belief within a sensible belief-desire reasoning scheme is compelling.

Three-year-olds construe human action in terms of a concept of belief as do adults. Three-year-olds do not conceive of people as being nonspecifically associated with propositional content, for example, Sam is associated with "object at location 1." Instead they conceive of people as believing or not believing, knowing or not knowing certain alternative states. The data also show that three-year-olds know that such mental states are the causes of overt actions. Against the background of their successes, three-year-olds' failure to solve false-belief tasks remains an interesting finding but not a criterial deficiency. False-belief errors suggest that young children have yet to master certain aspects of belief-desire reasoning rather than that they fail to engage in such mentalistic reasoning at all. In fact I think that false-belief tasks present complications to young children beyond a genuine understanding of belief itself. I will deal with these issues in chapter 9. That discussion permits me to resolve the apparent contradiction between children's understanding of belief but their failure on false-belief tasks.

In saying that three-year-olds genuinely understand beliefs, I do not wish to attribute to them a notion that is as articulated or as developed as an adult's conception. However, I do wish to claim that three-year-olds' conception contains two essential features. First, they conceive of beliefs as intentional entities in Brentano's (1874/ 1973) sense. That is, they know that to have a belief is to have a mental state that is "about" an external state of affairs. This itself involves some understanding of mental states, some understanding of real states or situations, and the recognition that a mental state can be about or correspond to a real state. Both beliefs and desires are intentional in this sense; thus I claim that three-year-olds understand beliefs as being different from desires. I will say more about this difference in chapter 8. For now, to have a desire is to have a positive disposition toward an object or state, to want it. To have a belief, however, is to have a conviction about a state of affairs, to think that it is the case. This distinction between beliefs and desires, that is, between intentional states that are dispositions versus those that are convictions, is a crucial one. I believe that three-year-olds grasp this crucial distinction because on our tasks they predict that a character with a single desire will engage in different acts depending on his or her conviction about the relevant state of affairs. In addition, they judge that a character equally disposed toward several options (wanting magic markers, which reside in both a cupboard and a drawer) will execute a single specific act given a specific conviction (a belief that markers are only in the drawer). That three-year-olds have and utilize such a conception of belief is an impressive and important achievement.

The research reported in chapters 2 and 3 touches on two separable aspects of mental life. The first concerns the freedom of thoughts from things, of mind from reality. This might be called the hypothetical or imaginary character of mind. The freedom to manipulate images mentally and to think of decidedly not real things and events represents cases of this aspect of mind. Because of this freedom, the mental world can be populated with imaginary, counterfactual, fantastical entities that can be posited, manipulated, and reasoned about in ways not applicable to the physical-temporal processes that constrain physical objects and events. The second aspect of mind concerns the correspondence of mind and reality, an aspect involved in such notions as true beliefs or knowledge and in the notion of mental causation of manifest behaviors. This might be termed the causal aspect of mind. The notion of belief studied in this chapter represents the prototypic case of this aspect of mind. Adults understand that the mind encompasses both hypothetical and causal aspects. The data in chapters 2 and 3 suggest that young children also have an appreciation of both of these aspects of mind.

The studies reported in chapter 2 (especially Wellman and Estes, 1986) have been available to colleagues interested in these matters for several years. If one knows those results and knows, from the Wimmer and Perner studies, that children fail to understand false belief until about four years of age, then it is easy to arrive at the following proposal: children aged 2½-three years understand the hypothetical nature of mind but fail to understand the causal nature of mind.

Several writers have recently advanced this general proposal in one form or another. Leslie (1988), for example, concludes that two- and three-year-olds understand the essential mental quality of mental states but not their causal roles. Two- and three-year-olds, according to Leslie, have only a physicalistic understanding of causation, and it is not until age four that their understanding includes an appreciation of mental causation (Leslie, 1988, pp. 37–38). Similarly, Forguson and Gopnik (1988) suggest that three-year-olds understand the imaginary aspect of mind but not its causal aspect (in my terms). They "seem able to differentiate between real things and desires, dreams, imaginings, thoughts, and the like. To make these contrasts, however, 3-year-olds do not have to take cognizance of the fact that they are also mentally representing the real objects and states of affairs" (Forguson and Gopnik, 1988, p. 236). Only older children come to understand mental states that "are full-fledged, serious beliefs. They are representations that are supposed to correspond with the way the world really is" (p. 236). Of course, this is also Perner's (1988) general point in claiming that three-year-olds seems to understand "belief" as merely an association of a character with a state of affairs. All of these positions are advanced in Astington, Harris, and Olson (1988), and indeed those editors summarize across the various chapters in their book to conclude, first, that "children acquire a set of concepts for representing mental activities such as thinking, dreaming, imagining, and pretending . . . sometime between their second and fourth years." Second, "they become skilled in using these concepts for predicting and explaining actions. . . . This achievement, the use of mental concepts to understand and predict what is said and done, begins, at least for children in our culture, when they are about 4 years of age" (Olson, Astington, and Harris, 1988, p. 5). In short, there is an emerging view that three-year-olds understand the hypothetical nature of mind and only later, at about four, do children understand the causal nature of mind.

In contrast, I claim that by three years of age, children understand, in essential form, both the hypothetical and the causal nature of mind. The data of chapters 2 and 3 and the data I will present in chapter 6 make this claim undeniable, to my mind. If children understand something of both the hypothetical and causal aspects of mind, then what exactly is the young child's theory of mind like? I have argued that children's understanding of mind is part and parcel of their commonsense mentalistic psychology. Then what is the young child's mentalistic psychology like? In the next chapter, I provide a more thorough characterization of this commonsense mentalistic belief-desire psychology, which also makes clear the coherence and systematicity inherent in our everyday thinking about the mind.

Chapter 4

Commonsense Belief-Desire Psychology

One way to describe this chapter is to say that it sketches the contents of our commonsense mentalistic psychology. Another is to say that it tackles the issue of theoretical coherence, a topic introduced in chapter 1. To this point I have shown that young children understand the fundamental ontological distinction between mental and physical phenomena and that they understand an important causal relation between mental states and real-world actions. But does young children's understanding of these matters properly constitute a coherent (commonsense) theory?

It is impossible to tackle the question of coherence in the abstract, to specify the type and amount of coherence required to constitute a theory. Some minimal sort of mutual definition and interconnectedness between key theoretical terms is required, as I have loosely demonstrated for preschoolers in Wellman (1988a). But how much and what types of coherence certify someone as possessing theorylike knowledge? Such questions are perplexing when considered generally; they are more tractable if we consider specific articulated theories. Given a proposed theory and its network of terms and relations, it is a difficult but feasible task to assess whether a person grasps that specific coherent body of knowledge. I will adopt this approach to tackling the question of coherence in children's understanding. I will describe a coherent belief-desire psychology and then assess whether young children have such a commonsense psychology. If they do, I will have demonstrated their grasp of the needed theoretical coherence. I will also have provided a rough description of children's early commonsense psychology.

Viewed in this fashion, a theory's coherence merges indiscriminately with that of its ontology and causal-explanatory framework. Theoretical entities and terms, such as beliefs and desires, function together to provide causes, supports, prerequisites, and explanations for one another. A person's appropriate reasoning within such a system manifests both the coherence of their systemic understanding and reveals his or her understanding of the relevant entities and framework, in this case, a belief-desire system for understanding actions and thoughts.

I will outline both adults' and children's belief-desire psychology because I believe that they are similar in several ways, and I cannot make clear my description as to children's theory without basing it on a description of adult belief-desire thinking. Moreover, to describe adult thinking I rely on the fact that each of us, as a naive adult, is familiar with and competent in belief-desire reasoning and can fill in some of the thin spots in my sketch from his or her own everyday understanding.

Because I depict our commonsense psychology, it is in this chapter that my endeavors most closely parallel those of Fritz Heider. My description outlines the theoretical network of everyday constructs such as belief, desire, and intention in a fashion akin to Heider's attempt to flesh out the workings of can, try, difficulty, and luck.

The Theory-Theory

In retrospect, a great deal of recent scholarship seems to converge on the postulation of a commonsense mentalistic psychology, an everyday theory of action and thought. In the past 20 years the merits of a theory-theory, the theory that our everyday understanding constitutes a theory of mind, have become increasingly apparent to both philosophers and psychologists. It is surprising only that it took so long for us to see that the term *theory* is more than just a catchy description, that it might do serious work for us:

> In philosophy, the attractiveness of the theory theory is a result of disenchantment with both Cartesian and behavioristic analyses of the concept of the mental. Once one begins to think of both of these as presenting cripplingly oversimplified pictures of what we are doing in ascribing states of mind to people, one can come to think of them as strangely similar in their limitations. Each takes as central an uncomplicated capacity to make observations: reflection, introspection, on the Cartesian account, the observation of behavior on the behaviorist account. Each then takes the ascription of states of mind to oneself and others from this observational basis to require just induction and the definition of terms. (Morton, 1980, p. 8)

But the everyday process of attributing states of mind now seems much more complex, a process of abduction rather than simple induction. Ascriptions of mental states seem to be "inferences to a best explanation," inferences to a larger meaningful account. In part, mental states cannot be simple empirical generalizations because there is no set of observable activities in self or other that consistently correlates with inferred mental states. There are no actions inevitably connected to having a desire, no consistent introspectable state of conviction essential to having a belief. If no neutral observational or experiential data dictate the inferences of mental states, what does? Observation and experience play their parts but, in addition, some intervening conceptual filter seems to stand between observation or experience and knowledge of mind, a theoretical lens that organizes the latter out of the former. Moreover, the states being inferred—hopes, intentions, wishes, fantasies—must operate together in several ways. We assume a connectedness among such mental terms and descriptions. In the extreme, therefore, mental states—Joe's wishful thinking—seem to be theoretical constructs whose meanings partake of a variety of relationships within a web of constructs. Attribution of a target mental state depends at least as much on the target's presumed coherence with other states as it does on an anchoring in observation or introspection. In total, our use of common mental terms, our everyday assumption of other minds, and the methods we use for assessing our own and others' minds are reminiscent of the construction of theoretical explanations in science (see Churchland, 1984).

Within psychology, similar concerns have pushed social psychologists to postulate that people hold "implicit theories of personality." We view our own and others' behavior as being more stable and coherent than it is, for example. Thus, in our everyday psychology we are engaged in something more constructive than simply assessing the frequency of various behaviors and states and the empirical correlations between them. In everyday understanding, this constructive enterprise includes the attribution to ourselves and others of a variety of psychological constructs. "The observations or inferences we make are principally about intentions, attitudes, emotions, ideas, abilities, purposes, traits, thoughts, perceptions, memories—events that are inside the person and strictly psychological" (Taiguri, 1969, p. 396). We utilize such constructs as a way of bringing theoretical clarity to the chaos of infinitely different observable acts or states. Thus attributions are framed as much by our underlying assumptions about behavior as by our observation of it. Indeed, we seem to assume that unobservable psychological states constitute the bedrock realities of personal description and that manifest behaviors constitute only overt appearances.

Everyday reliance on a theory of mind is also evident in literary enterprises. Fiction, for example, presents a world of created characters and plots. Authors construct and present credible fictional characters by fabricating and describing characters' beliefs, desires, emotional reactions, perceptions, plans, and traits, that is, by instantiating a package of hypothetical features within the framework of naive psychology, by specifying details within the commonly accepted machinery of psychological explanation. This analysis of the writer's enterprise supports the notion that commonsense psychology functions very much like a scientific theory, a guiding conceptual structure for an everyday hypothetico-deductive endeavor. Thus, character construction is a common example of the instantiation of theoretical terms within a larger theoretical framework. David Lewis (1972) makes this clear in his discussion of theoretical identifications. Lewis asks us to imagine that

> we are assembled in the drawing room of the country house; the detective reconstructs the crime. That is, he proposes a *theory* designed to be the best explanation of phenomena we have observed: the death of Mr. Body, the blood on the wallpaper, the silence of the dog in the night, the clock seventeen minutes fast, and so on. He launches into his story:
>
> X, Y and Z conspired to murder Mr. Body. Seventeen years ago, in the gold fields of Uganda, X was Body's partner. . . . Last week, Y and Z conferred in a bar in Reading. . . . Tuesday night at 11:17, Y went to the attic and set a time bomb. . . . Seventeen minutes later, X met Z in the billiard room and gave him the lead pipe. . . . Just when the bomb went off in the attic, X fired three shots into the study through the French windows . . .
>
> And so it goes: a long story.
>
> The story contains the three names, "X", "Y", and "Z". The detective uses these new terms without explanation, as though we knew what they meant. But we do not. We never used them before, at least in the senses that they bear in the present context. All we know about their meanings is what we gradually gather from the story itself. (p. 250)

Yet eventually, we know an extraordinary amount about X, Y, and Z simply because of their descriptions, roles, and relations within the detective's hypothetical account. This can happen because these terms play a role within a coherent larger set of constructs and relations, that is, within a coherent theory. In this way, fictional literature attests to the theorylike functioning of our commonsense psychology.

There is in all this an intriguing convergence of analysis. Everyday understanding of persons constitutes a mentalistic lay-psychological theory. Given this convergence, it is surprising that so little effort has been spent on describing what the theory is, beyond asserting that it must exist. This seems an important part of the task. I find it impossible to evaluate the theory-theory or to research the focal naive theory itself without a more detailed specification of what it must be like. I begin to sketch such a specification here.[1] My sketch has not emerged from a program of empirical research. I believe it is worthy of such research, however, because it provides a coherent and recognizable picture of our everyday mentalism.

To my mind discussions of implicit personality theory among social psychologists tend to mischaracterize our everyday psychology by focusing too exclusively on trait constructs. Trait constructs, I believe, are only one sort of elaboration on a more basic theoretical infrastructure. It seems to me to be closer to the mark to follow philosophers' general parsing of our everyday constructs into those aligned with beliefs and those aligned with desires. For this reason I concentrated on children's understanding of beliefs along with desires in the research in chapter 2. Something like a general belief-desire analysis has seemed plausible to a great many thinkers:

> Whenever someone does something for a reason, therefore, he can be characterized as (a) having some sort of pro attitude toward actions of a certain kind, and (b) believing (knowing, perceiving, noticing, remembering) that his action is of that kind. Under (a) are to be included desires, wantings, urges, promptings, and a great variety of moral views, aesthetic principles, economic prejudices, social conventions, and public and private goals and values in so far as these can be interpreted as attitudes of an agent directed toward actions of a certain kind. (Davidson, 1980, pp. 3–4)

> At least since Hume the philosophy of mind and action has been dominated by the view that the underlying structure of our commonsense conception of mind involves two basic types of states: those that play the role of beliefs, and those that play the role of desires or evaluations. These types of states are to be understood broadly. Belief may be all-or-none, or may come in degrees. Desires include a wide range of "pro-attitudes"—wanting, judging desirable, caring about, and so on—and also may admit of degrees. So, for example, the attempt to understand the structure of rational motivation solely in terms of an agent's "utilities" and "probabilities" endorses this desire-belief framework. (Bratman, 1985, p. 3)

> In our everyday dealings with one another we invoke a variety of commonsense psychological terms including "believe", "remember", "feel", "think", "desire", "prefer", "imagine", "fear", and many others. The use of these terms is governed by a loose knit network of largely tacit principles, platitudes, and paradigms which constitute a sort of folk theory. . . . Commonsense offers explanations: people act as they do because they have certain beliefs or wants or fears or desires. (Stitch, 1983, pp. 1–2)

The importance of these quotations is that their authors argue for the centrality of commonsense, belief-desire reasoning for our everyday understanding of persons. Still, such a gross description needs considerable fleshing out to provide even a crude theory sketch.

Everyday Mentalistic Psychology

In our everyday thinking we commonly explain what people do by appeal to their hopes, plans, beliefs, fears, and aspirations. The phrase *belief-desire reasoning* provides a rough and abbreviated description for the elaborated framework that underlies such everyday psychological explanations. Since this commonsense framework posits mental causes for our actions, belief-desire reasoning rests on a naive mentalism, and hence it is central to our commonsense understanding of the mind. Such reasoning is especially interesting because it encompasses and presupposes important understandings about human action and mental states.

The phrase *belief-desire reasoning* is only a rough description because the terms *belief* and *desire* are to be understood quite broadly. At the same time, the phrase is an abbreviation because beliefs and desires, even broadly construed, denote only two of a variety of psychological causes for actions. The abbreviation seems apt because these two classes are central to the entire larger framework, which rests on a basic triad of constructs: beliefs, desires, action.

The description that follows proceeds in two phases. I start with a greatly oversimplified description of belief-desire reasoning, which captures several core features of the system. Then I present a more embellished description, which, although still simplified, captures more fully the richness and complexity of everyday adult understanding of this topic. There is a presentational advantage in this approach: the simplified caricature paves the way for the more accurate larger view.

The Simple Version

A graphical outline for simplified belief-desire reasoning is presented in figure 4.1. It depicts both core concepts and some connections between them. I will begin my overview of belief-desire reasoning by discussing the concepts and connections shown there.

Actions

Even the simplest presentation of the nature of belief-desire reasoning must include a consideration of the sort of events commonsense psychology attempts to explain. If belief-desire reasoning is the causal explanatory framework for a naive theory of mind, what is the domain of phenomena it is designed to explain? The answer, in part, is the domain of (human) action. Here are some examples:

(1)   Why did Bill go to the barber shop? He wanted his hair cut, and he thought the barber there could do it.

(2)   Why did Jane buy a Macintosh? She wanted a new computer and thought that the Macintosh was the best buy for the money.

These examples might encourage the conclusion, by analogy with definitions of scientific psychology, that the phenomenon to be explained is behavior. This analogy should be resisted. The term *action* is better than *behavior*. *Behavior* is misleading because it suggests that the actions to be explained might best be described in terms of overt responses. Further, *behavior* includes such phenomena as involuntary, autonomic reflexes. In contrast, the domain of explanation for naive psychology is limited to intentional actions. Involuntary reflexes (sneezes, blinks), biological outcomes (fevers, muscle tremors), and physical bodily motions (being buffeted by the wind, run over by a car) are outside the domain of naive psychological explanation (and are probably in the domains of naive biology and naive physics).

The qualifier "intentional" is important in the characterization of actions. The focus of belief-desire reasoning is voluntary action—action the actor has undertaken for a reason, such as going to the barber shop or buying a Macintosh. Unintended accidental actions are also focal: "Joe was trying to clean the gun, and it accidentally went off." But they are focal because their "true" explanation (within commonsense psychology) depends on intention as well. Unintended actions are the unintended outcomes of intended actions: "Joe was *trying* to clean the gun." Commonsense psychology assumes that intentional action, broadly defined, drives the vast proportion (or at least the

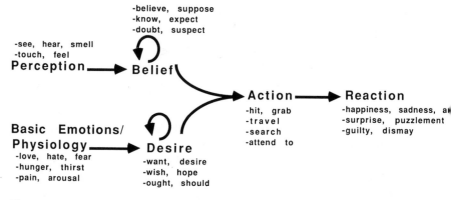

Figure 4.1
Simplified scheme for depicting belief-desire reasoning. A version of this scheme
was first presented in Wellman and Bartsch (1988).

interesting portion) of human behavior, although not every act is itself intended.

Human actions of the sort explained by our everyday psychology
are also intentional in another sense. Even the initial level of description involved is not behavioral (the right hand raising the toothbrush
to the mouth) but intentional (attempting to brush your teeth). The
description of the action to be explained thus presumes the relevance
of some goal-related, belief-desire description. This means that the
basic dependent unit of analysis, the actions-to-be-explained, are entrenched in a mentalistic theory from the inception of the explanatory
process. This is arguably true of most theorizing; even the observation terms of a theoretical domain are theory ridden.

The term *behavior* would thus be too broad; actions, not all behaviors, are at issue. The term *behavior* is also too narrow. This is because
certain mental phenomena (for example, beliefs and desires) are
themselves members of the domain to be explained (as well as members of the theoretical constructs used to do the explaining). Thus, we
can ask, Why did John *think* it was Sunday? Why does Mary *want*
chocolate ice cream? We answer such questions by belief-desire reasoning, including appeal to mental constructs such as other beliefs
and desires, just as we would do for overt actions. Thinking and
wanting are not behaviors, but they are relevant human actions in
the broad sense (they are mental actions) and hence are proper targets for belief-desire explanations.

Since I am advocating calling this system of explaining human actions a folk or naive or lay or commonsense psychology, it is important to clarify in what sense this explanatory system is a psychology.

It is not scientific psychology as often defined as the study of behavior. It is psychology in the everyday sense of the study of people's "mental lives" (James, 1890/1950).

Beliefs and Desires
We typically try to predict and explain what people do in terms of their wishes, knowledge, wants, misconceptions, fears, expectations, and doubts. These constructs can be roughly divided into two complementary groups: beliefs (understood broadly as including the actor's knowledge, convictions, suppositions, ideas, and opinions) and desires (understood broadly as including all the actor's pro and con attitudes, such as lusts, wants, wishes, preferences, goals, and hopes, as well as self-imposed obligations, values, and aspirations). According to commonsense psychology, appeal to both these core concepts is needed to provide an explanation of intentional actions. To do something intentionally is to have a desire *and* to engage in the act because you believe it will help satisfy your desire:

(3)   Why did John go to the store? He *wanted* something to eat and *remembered* he could buy it at the store.

(4)   Why did Joe hit Bill? He *thought* Bill was going to hit him, and he *wished* to defend himself.

(5)   Why did Sue put on her swimming suit? She *knew* it was time for swimming and *hoped* to be the first one in the water.

Both beliefs and desires are needed for the full explanation of intentional actions, but often one or the other of these constructs is clearly more informative in a given situation, and thus its complement may reasonably go unmentioned:

(6)   The kitten was under the chair, but Jill was looking for it under the sofa. Why? She thought it was under the sofa.

(7)   Why is Bill going to the dentist? He's afraid that he has a cavity.

In (6), Jill must want to find her kitten, but that is not mentioned; in (7), Bill must believe that dentists can fix cavities. These examples illustrate an important distinction between the nature of a full explanation and the nature of an acceptable explanation. An acceptable explanation can simply presume common knowledge of certain beliefs or desires. This is acceptable because of a general conversational maximum: be relevant (Grice, 1975). An adequate explanation need not mention all pertinent facts if they can be assumed to be known or inferred.

While beliefs and desires are distinctive in expressing two different sorts of mental states or attitudes, they are similar in being intentional states in Brentano's terms (and as discussed in chapter 3). Their intentional status is also at issue when philosophers refer to such mental states as propositional attitudes. As propositional attitudes, beliefs (or thoughts, or guesses) are about some content, a content that can be captured in a proposition. For example, one might have the belief that "snow is cold," the guess that "Joe's birthday is Wednesday." Similarly, desires (those of interest here) are propositional desires (or fears, or wishes), that is, desires *that* something occur. For example, there might be the desire to "eat ice cream" or the fear that "there will be a snowstorm." In noting this aspect of beliefs and desires, I do not wish to take a stand on the philosophical controversies centering around the label "propositional attitude" with respect to the status of propositions and the nature of attitudes. I only wish to claim that this label appropriately highlights an important aspect of beliefs and desires—that such mental states include two pieces of information: the relevant mental attitude, state, or process (belief, desire) and the proposition or content that is believed or desired.

Both beliefs and desires evidence a distinctive logical property, that of logical opacity. This stems from their status as descriptions of internal mental states, not states of the world. For example, a simply declarative statement such as "the premier of China just died" may be true or false. Whatever its truth value, however, the truth of other statements is logically affected. If it is true that "the premier of China just died," then "the premier of China did not die" is logically false. And if Deng Xiaoping is the premier of China, then "Deng just died" is also logically true. However, these logical extensions do not hold if we are talking about beliefs and desires, because beliefs and desires are logically opaque. If it is true that "John thinks the premier of China just died," it is not necessarily true that "John thinks Deng just died." If "John hopes the premier of China just died," it is not necessarily true that "Deng just died" even if Deng is the premier, and it is not even true that "John hopes that Deng just died." Logical opacity is crucial to our ability to reason about the mental world because it allows us to think and reason about another's mental states even when these are misconceived or plainly wrong (see Leslie, 1987).

In this regard both beliefs and desires represent those curious hybrid units of explanation outlined in chapter 3; they are part internal, part external, part subjective, part objective. That is, they refer both to some possible state of external affairs (that it will snow) and to a mental state (he thinks, he wants). To reiterate, from the point of view of practical explanation of action, this dual character is decidedly useful. Beliefs and desires, in some sense, span the mental-physical divide. Hence, they can be said to provide an appropriately mental cause (a belief-desire reason) for a physical event (a manifest action). That is, they can if one accepts the tenets of commonsense psychology.

Because beliefs and desires partake of two-place characterizations, then following Gricean conversational maxims once again, it is often appropriate to refer to a belief or desire by mentioning either only the relevant attitude or only the relevant proposition. The unmentioned component can reasonably be assumed to be known or inferred. For example:

(8)   Why did Joan go to the ice cream store at 2 A.M.? She had a craving (for ice cream).

(9)   Why did he buy a Black and Decker drill? (He thinks) It's the best.

As specified, both the terms *belief* and *desire* are to be understood generically in this analysis. Consider a subconcept under desire worthy of a separate discussion—that of preferences. By preferences I mean generalized dispositions toward certain things such as "preferring basketball over baseball" or generally "liking to ride horses." Preferences therefore are desire states somewhat akin to wants; compare, for example, "liking to ride horses" and "wanting to ride that horse." Preferences figure prominently in explanations of recurrent activities.

(10)   Why does Bill got to the stable every Monday? He likes riding horses.

(11)   Why doesn't Jill play baseball? She prefers basketball.

Preference explanations of activities often fail to mention relevant beliefs, but such beliefs seem operative in some form anyway. Thus in (10), some belief like "and he thinks he can get free rides" might complement the preference information; in (11), some belief like "and she thinks she can only practice one sport enough to be good at it" might operate. Preference explanations of activities thus partake of the general belief-desire form. Like other desires, preferences can be construed as propositional attitudes. "He likes to ride horses" notes both a mental attitude ("liking"), and a content or object of the attitude (in propositional form, "to ride horses").

Beliefs and desires are causally recursive; beliefs cause other beliefs and desires cause other desires. This is depicted by the circular arrows in figure 4.1 and in examples such as these:

(12) Why did he go to the store? He wanted to buy some string.
      Why? He wanted to wrap a package. Why? He wanted to
      send it to his mother. Why? He wanted to celebrate her
      birthday.

(13) Why did she go to college? She thought it would enhance her
      earning power (and she wants to make lots of money). Why?
      She thinks most high-paying jobs require a college degree.
      Why? She knows that a degree is required to go on to medical
      or law school but not to be a janitor or supermarket cashier,
      and she thinks those sorts of examples are representative of
      lots of jobs.

(14) Why did Sarah hit Bill? Bill hit her first, and she wanted to
      protect herself. Why? She felt bullied and wanted to maintain
      her self-respect.

One aspect of the recursive quality of belief-desire reasoning is reflected in means-end reasoning. Example (12) depicts a means-end
chain: one action can be desired as (or believed to be) a subgoal to
another, which may be only a means to another. Additionally, beliefs
and desires can be nested in other beliefs or desires. Example (14)
illustrates such a nesting; Sarah's protecting herself is a form of defending her honor. This chaining and nesting means that any one
action can be described in several fashions (Sarah's hitting Bill, protecting herself, defending her self-respect). Appeal to one or another
of the various descriptions can provide an informative explanation for
someone's action.

There is another way in which various beliefs or desires influence
one another and thus tend to cohere together in clusters. In particular, beliefs rationally constrain other beliefs. To believe that bats are
mammals is to believe a host of additional things about bats as well.
Example 13 shows this rational influence of beliefs on each other.
Furthermore, being shown that two of one's beliefs are mutually
contradictory initiates processes that aim to reestablish rational coherence or cognitive balance—processes of denial, reasoning, reinterpretation, and revision of one's beliefs.

The coherence of desires with other desires does not have the rational character appropriate to beliefs, but mutual influence between
desires also exists according to our everyday conception. For example, some desires are so fundamental, adults believe, that they organize whole families of related desires. Why does she want this job? She
wants a job. Why does she want a job? For money. Why does she
want money? To buy things. Why does she want to buy things? So

as not to be needy for food, for shelter, and so on. Specific wants (this job) are grounded in fundamental desires for comfort, for life itself, for personal satisfaction.

In summary, intentional actions are caused by beliefs and desires. Beliefs and desires provide the reasons for the actor's actions and also provide the internal mental causes for overt actions (see Davidson, 1963). Everyday appeals to belief-desire reasoning often omit mention of the belief or desire, but both are implicitly presumed. Similarly, explanations in terms of beliefs or desires may omit mention of either the propositional or attitudinal aspect of the mental states.

Perception, Physiological States, and Basic Emotions
Thus far I have considered only the basic triad of beliefs, desires, and actions. Even in its simple form, the relevant causal chain is longer than this. Specifically, as depicted in figure 4.1, perceptions cause beliefs; basic emotions and/or physiological states, such as deprivation and arousal, cause desires (and actions result in outcomes which produce reactions).

(15)   Why did Jill think her kitten was under the sofa (when he was really under the chair)? She saw him go under the sofa (and didn't see him scoot from there over to the chair).

(16)   Why did Joan want an ice cream? She hadn't eaten anything for days. Or, she loves sweets.

Perceptions as well as physiological states and basic emotions provide input to the mind from extramental sources. Perceptions, according to naive psychology, tell us about the external world of real objects, spaces, and events. One's knowledge and credible beliefs are thus forged in part from perceptions (and in part from one's other beliefs).

Physiology and basic emotions also provide inputs to the mind. In this case, however, the input, while external to the mind, is internal to the body. The input from these sources fuels desires, whereas perceptions fuel belief. The distinction between desires (wanting to do something, wishing that something would happen) and basic emotions (hate, anger, fear, anguish) is an important but also an imprecise one. The potential confusion between specific desires and particular emotions is evident in the broad scope of the generic term *feeling*. One can "feel that something would be nice" (a desire) but also "feel hungry" (physiology) and "feel sad" (basic emotion). "Feeling that something would be nice" counts as a desire because of its intentional, propositional attitude nature. Emotions and emotional reactions such as love, pleasure, and sadness ground one's propositional desires but do not constitute desires themselves. Thus, as shown in figure 4.1, emotions influence action through their role in forming desires. The role of emotions is further elucidated in considering the concept of reactions.

Reactions

Actions result in outcomes, and these give rise to various reactions. Like actions, the outcomes of interest here are not well captured in the terms of behaviorism, that is, in terms of external observable events. Outcomes too are entrenched in mentalistic (intentional, belief-desire) descriptions. An analysis of relevant outcomes would include the following three sorts:

1. The outcome of an action can satisfy or fail to satisfy the actor's desires, that is, achieve or fail to achieve his goals. If the actor desires something and his actions achieve it (or desires to avoid something and he successfully avoids it), then satisfaction results. Satisfaction, generically, encompasses such emotional reactions as happiness, pleasure, contentment, and relief. Or if the actor desires something and fails to achieve it (or desires to avoid something and fails to avoid it), then dissatisfaction results. Dissatisfaction, generically, encompasses such reactions as anger, unhappiness, hurt, and disappointment.

2. The outcomes of an action can accord with or fail to accord with the actor's beliefs about that action. The actor can believe something (expect something to occur), but it does not occur (or expect the absence of something and it does occur), resulting in surprise. Surprise, generically considered, encompasses such reactions as puzzlement, curiosity, and the like. Or the actor can believe something (expect something) and it does occur, reflected in neutral acceptance.

3. The outcomes of an action can fall inside or outside the scope of the actor's intentions. Some outcomes of an action fall inside the actor's intentions; that is, the outcomes are directly related to the actor's beliefs and desires. In these cases, the outcomes produce the sorts of reactions already explained in (1) and (2). However, an action can also have unintended, unforeseen outcomes. The production of unintended outcomes can result in puzzlement, guilt, dismay, or perhaps even glee or private gloating, depending on the nature of the unintended result.

Reactions, of course, are emotional states of the actor. Thus, to be complete, figure 4.1 should have an arrow running from reactions back to basic emotions or, better, should depict reactions as a subconstruct under the Basic Emotions/Physiology heading. However, reactions are emotions that stem from the outcomes of belief-desire-produced acts, so it is fitting to place them on the right-hand side of the figure.

Summary
Even this oversimplified introduction to belief-desire reasoning captures some of the richness and generativity of this everyday causal-explanatory framework. It also begins to suggest why such a system seems well characterized as a theory, a mentalistic theory of human action encompassing a theory of mind. This framework seems to be a theory because it dictates a domain of phenomena-to-be-explained—human action and mental states—including which sorts of behavior are relevant (intentional or accidental acts) and which not (reflexes, physically induced movements). The framework dictates the employment of theory-laden descriptive terms for describing the relevant phenomena (the intentional description of actions, something like a propositional-attitude description of beliefs and desires). The framework also establishes the sort of causal explanation to be credited as explanatory in this theoretical domain (belief-desire explanation). Finally, in this system mental states, such as beliefs and desires, are private, internal, and not observable in others. However, such states are theoretically anchored in other relevant constructs. Thus, we infer others' beliefs and desires (and at times our own) from, among other things, perceptual experiences (what he sees), physiological history (how long it's been since he's eaten) and emotional expressions and reactions (when he's happy or surprised).

On the other hand, this oversimplified version is insufficient in several respects. Most important it does not comprehensively capture the full set of notions involved in adults' commonsense psychology. The elaborated version of the theory, presented next, moves closer to such a comprehensive account.

The Elaborated Version

The simplified version of commonsense mentalistic psychology captures several features of our everyday psychology; it captures something of the belief-desire reasoning that we use to predict, explain, justify, and understand human actions. Even the elaborated version I will now present, however, cannot be considered definitive; it aims at the more modest (but still sizable) goals of being plausible and useful. It attempts to capture plausibly something of the richness and the structure of many of our everyday understandings about the mind. And it aims to articulate some of the more advanced understandings that constitute the conceptual targets for children's developing conceptions. To be virtuous in these regards, the description need not be without flaw; it need only be on the right track.

Figure 4.2 provides an embellished graphical depiction of the elaborated theory. Note that the belief-desire-action triad of figure 4.1 is preserved and central in figure 4.2. In fact, given the prior discussion, the core concepts of belief, desire, and action are included in figure 4.2 only by their shorthand labels.

The elaborated theory depicted in figure 4.2 is more complex than the simple version in two ways. First, additional core concepts are included—for example, intention and thinking. Second, the links between the core concepts, which indicate various causal connections, are increased in number as well as labeled in terms of their essential character. In this regard, in addition to the central forward-moving causal chain depicted in figure 4.1—from perception and emotions, to beliefs and desires, to action (depicted by bold arrows in figure 4.2)—there are other branching and even backward-moving causal links.

Thinking

The construct of thinking, in its generic sense, is an everyday description for cognition. As such, thinking in figure 4.2 adds considerably to the original core concept of belief in figure 4.1. Beliefs, as I have discussed them, are a subset of all possible cognitive products and processes. Beliefs (considered as cognitive states or products) are the products of formative thinking processes such as reasoning, learning, and remembering. Believing (as a process) is a process of crediting the reality of some state of affairs. It is thus related to such processes as knowing, fantasizing, imagining, dreaming, and importantly, reasoning. In short, belief is a subset of cognition or thought, broadly conceived, a special theoretical construct designed to capture the causal impact of thinking on the world of actions and events. Notions of thinking in its broader senses thus embellish and situate the core construct of belief in its proper larger mental ecology.

For adults, this larger mental ecology encompasses at least a crude conception of the mind as a central information processor. The mind engages in thinking; it remembers, infers, stores information, interprets perceptual information, and so on. From these cognitive activities, it forms a knowledge base, a set of understandings about self and world (and indeed mind). Beliefs describe certain aspects of this knowledge, namely, one's mental states of conviction about states of affairs.

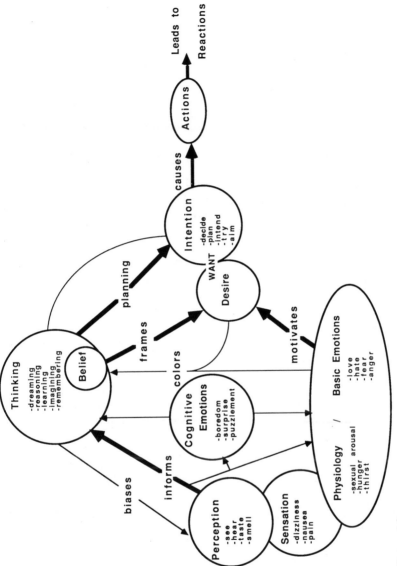

Figure 4.2
An elaborated scheme for depicting belief-desire reasoning.

Intention

Intention is central to an expanded everyday understanding of action. Basically intention seems to emerge out of the core concept of desire. This is hinted at in the dual nature of the term *want*. *Want* is used ambiguously to denote desires—Bill wants candy—and closely related intents—Bill wants to go to the candy store.

(17)   Why does Bill want (plan) to go to the candy store? Because he wants (desires) candy and believes there is some at the store.

Intentions are separable from desires, in naive psychology, though they share the term *want*. Intentions and desires are conceptually distinct because within commonsense psychology one can have a desire (a wish, a hope, a fancy) to do something but in spite of this never actually intend (plan, aim, decide) to do it. Intentions are not a sort of desire; rather intentions function to actualize (some but not all) desires. Thus, desires and intentions are separable core concepts, desires fueling intentions and intentions actualizing desires. Intentions are also distinct from actions. This is evident in that intentions can concern the future; one has an intention to do something later (see Bratman, 1985).

Intention, as is shown in figure 4.2, is the meeting ground where belief and desire join forces in a plan of action. An intended plan of action is designed to achieve certain desires and designed on the basis of certain beliefs. In naive psychology, intentions are the proximal cause of actions. Hence in commonsense psychology actions are essentially intentional; they are to be explained in terms of the actor's intentions:

(18)   Why did Bill shoot Harriet? He wanted to (intended to) kill her. Or, he only intended to frighten her, but he shot her by mistake.

Intentions in turn can be unpacked in terms of their component beliefs and desires:

(19)   Why did Bill intend to frighten Harriet? He was afraid Harriet would hurt him and thought there was no other way to make her leave him alone.

As Anscombe (1957) emphasized, everyday intentions are specific to particular descriptions. Thus, to explain an (intentional) act is in part to describe it in terms of the relevant description (he intended "to frighten her" but not "to shoot her"). Only certain descriptions of the actor's intent are causally related to action because those descriptions capture the relevant propositional aspect of the actor's beliefs and desires. Thus, we (and Bill) can insist that it is his intent to frighten that caused him to act as he did, not an intent to kill.

In summary, intentions are a critical part of a comprehensive commonsense theory of action; belief-desire reasoning "goes forth" through the construct of intention. Intentions are plans to actualize certain desires; intentions harness various beliefs onto actions.

The explicit appearance of the concept of intention in figure 4.2 brings with it several elaborations over the skeletal scheme in figure 4.1. We commonly speak of intentions in two separable senses. Bratman (1984) calls these the two faces of intention. First, in many simple cases, one's intentions are simply one's relevant beliefs and desires. To act intentionally is to act from beliefs and desires. If I scratch my ear right now, I do so because I intend to; that is, I desire to stop an itch and believe that scratching will do the job. My intention in this everyday analysis is inseparable from the belief-desire-action triad. In this sense of intention, intention can be omitted as a core concept (as was done in figure 4.1).

In other cases, however, intentions are separable from their constitutive desires. For example, we often depict one's intentions as first interacting with other intentions before controlling action. Making one's intentions fit together is in fact a notable aspect of deciding on one's actions. Thus, reasoning about complexes of intentions, in self and in others, forms an important part of the explanation of action, and in this sense intention warrants a separate space in figure 4.2. This face of intention is clearest perhaps in the case of future intentions—for example, I intend to go to the store after work. Given this intention, I may also decide to stop by the shoe repair shop ("it's right on the way") and decide to forgo my prior intention to have a beer with Joe after work until a later date. This sort of everyday reasoning about and among intentions can be called planning (Wilensky, 1983; Bratman, 1984, 1987). References to planning and the complex relations among intentions figure prominently in everyday explanations of action.

(20) Why did Harry fly Northwest? That flight was the only one leaving at a good time, and it made a one-hour stop in Chicago so he could get together with his mother at the airport. She lives nearby.

(21) Why didn't you go to Joan's reception? I couldn't fit it into my schedule.

Planning
The bold arrows in figure 4.2 depict the primary forward causal connections from perception and emotion, to belief and desire, through intention, to action. These arrows are thus similar to the links depicted in figure 4.1. In figure 4.1, one arrow links beliefs and desires. In figure 4.2, this single connection is replaced by two bold connections (and some minor ones as well) because the presence of intention as a separate core construct requires the depiction of two sorts of connections melding beliefs and desires into actions. One of these connections, the more obvious and primary one, is labeled planning.

In commonsense psychology, we understand that beliefs about the state of the world are marshaled together with desires to form intentions, or plans for action. This connection is analogous to the single merged arrow in figure 4.1. The label "planning" characterizes the contribution of belief to intention. The construal of belief as embedded in the larger realm of thinking embellishes any basic description of planning. Specifically, simple intents recruit basic beliefs (the intent to go to the candy store is based on the belief that candy is at the store). Complex plans, however, can require complex reasoning processes (deciding to take the bus to the store; or reasoning that shopping for several items at once is more efficient and thus planning to shop for candy and milk together). The basic link between belief and desire (through intention via planning) is thus considerably richer in the full commonsense theoretical understanding of 4.2.

Framing and Coloring
In addition to this primary linking of beliefs and desires (by intentions), two other direct links between belief and desire are depicted in figure 4.2. First, there is a link from belief to desire termed "frames." A person's rational beliefs and thinking help frame and characterize his or her desires. Recall in this vein that desires, unlike emotions, encompass more than just affective valences. Desires are intentional or propositional; they are desires that something occur or be obtained. Example desires include a "wish to be stronger," "a hope that it won't rain," "a desire for French cooking." Since desires are propositional, beliefs are involved in the framing of such desires. A desire for French cooking rests on some beliefs about what French cooking is.

Note also the distinctions that exist between our various desire-attitudes such as wishing, wanting, and hoping. The difference between wishing for something and wanting it, for example, can hinge in part on one's belief in how likely or effortful it would be to achieve the proposed thing. Realization of the improbability of obtaining or experiencing something can thus move that something from one's list of wants and aims to one's list of wishes and dreams. In short, rational belief plays a role in the process of framing and prioritizing desires.

Framing links belief to desire. Reciprocally, "coloring" links desires to belief. Desires and strong emotions are commonly said to color one's thoughts. For example, a vested interest in some state of affairs can make certain propositions about it more believable (because of desire and prejudice) than they would be on rational grounds alone.

Informing and Biasing

A set of reciprocal links also exists between thinking and perception. Primarily (as noted by the bold arrow in figure 4.2), perception provides the raw material for thought. In this way perception informs thought; however, perception is not just a simple supplier to thought but is invested in thought as well. Everyday psychology, like scientific psychology, clearly acknowledges the fact that thoughts constrain perception. This comes out in everyday notions such as having "preconceived ideas" or "biased" and "distorted" observations. It also is clearly operable in the action of various active perceptual processes, such as attention. Thus, there is need for the "biases" link from thinking to perception along with the "informs" link in the opposite direction.

Tracing links such as coloring and biasing makes it clear that in commonsense psychology, there is an acknowledged larger cycle of influence from emotions to desires to thinking to perception, which forms a backward chain parallel to the forward progressions of perception to thinking and emotion to action. Specifically, emotions and desires can color one's thoughts to such an extent that thinking biases one's perception. When that happens, one sees only what one already believes or "only what one wants to see."

In the more typical forward direction of influence, perception not only informs thought but emotion as well. Actual fears, hates, and fancies spring, in part, from perception of fearful, loathsome, or desirable objects (snakes, gore, attractive persons). Emotions are clearly caused in part by such everyday perceptual encounters. However, emotions have a predominantly internal component as well, grounded in physiological states such as arousal and deprivation, and formed by basic feelings such as fear, love, and anger.

Cognitive Emotions

Many cognitive states or attitudes fall under the general heading of belief, such as doubting, believing, and suspecting. Some cognitive attitudes of this sort possess a definite affective or emotional coloration as well as a belief attitude. Examples are approval and boredom. These sorts of attitudes (it's boring that the game was cancelled) can be termed cognitive emotions because the affective component requires much prerequisite cognition (the cognitive evaluation needed to lead to approval) and these states have motivational force or valence to them. For example, curiosity has an emotionlike force to it (satisfied or dissatisfied curiosity creates reactions like satisfied or dissatisfied hunger or lust). A "cognitive emotion," as depicted in figure 4.2, is thus both a concept and a link. Such emotions are an intermediate concept between emotion and thinking that stake out one bidirectional connection between those core concepts.

Further Elaboration

Because the schema in figure 4.2 is constrained to a two-dimensional page, already filled with concepts and links, I have reserved presentation of several additional aspects of the commonsense psychological theory for clearer presentation in figure 4.3. Figure 4.3 is an attempt to clarify the system in figure 4.2 by utilizing a contrived but helpful three-dimensional format.

Traits

The most important additional aspect to be captured is presented as if it were an additional layer laid on top of the core schema. This is depicted by the bold oval termed "traits." In naive psychological explanations, we often refer to traits such as intelligence, cleverness, vanity, integrity, shyness, selfishness, and rebelliousness. These traits are presumed to be more enduring aspects of one's psyche. As such, they organize and ground many of one's specific beliefs, desires, and emotions. Such traits can characterize the thinking-rational aspects of the mind (intelligence), the basic emotional and physiological influences on mental life (fearfulness, agedness), or clusters of more specific desires (lustiness, timidity, introversion). They can also be derived from the cognitive emotions (curiosity). Specific beliefs and desires are often explained as springing from such larger traits (the desire to wear pretty clothes may spring from a vanity or, perhaps, from an insecurity about one's attractiveness). Because of this grounding of specific beliefs and desires in traits, traits figure prominently in causal explanations of actions.

(22)   Why did Bill crash the party? Bill's so thoughtless; he just wanted to and didn't stop to think it would be embarrassing and inappropriate.

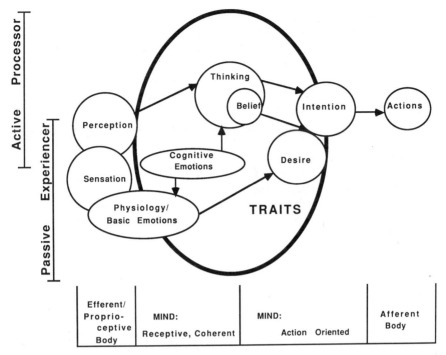

Figure 4.3
A final elaborated scheme for depicting belief-desire reasoning.

(23)   Why didn't Jill come to the party? Jill's so shy. She didn't
       believe anyone really wanted her to come; she was afraid
       she'd have a terrible time.

Efferent/Afferent
The horizontal dimension depicted along the bottom of figure 4.3 presents a different sort of elaboration on figure 4.2. It is an attempt to
depict more explicitly an aspect of the theory that has been only implicit so far. Specifically, the partitioning along the bottom of the figure captures an efferent/afferent distinction integral to the larger
mental system. Mind can be directed outward to perception or to action. In some primary sense, however, mind itself occupies an internal mental world; it constitutes a world-independent core of ideas
and mentation, at least as mind is construed in commonsense psychology. This core has its own internal coherence (beliefs influence
beliefs) somewhat dependent on a receptivity to perceptual input but
independent of actualization in actions. Thus, in the summary at the

bottom of figure 4.3, this core internal mind is termed the receptive-coherent mind, and it encompasses thinking.

At the same time, the introverted mind has extroverted aspects. The extroverted mind faces two directions but especially toward action. Belief, desire, and intention partake essentially of the action-oriented aspect of the mind. Indeed, these three interlocking theoretical constructs are "designed" to capture the mental world in a form conducive to explaining action. It is part of the job description of a belief or of a desire that it connect to action in significant ways. In Searle's (1983) terms, the direction of fit of desires and intentions is for world to fit the mind. At the other end of the continuum, the direction of fit of perception (and of some sorts of thinking) is for mind to fit the world.

Passive/Active

The left-hand vertical edge of figure 4.3 captures another dimension of organization. This is a characterization of everyday psychology that seems considerably more arguable to me than the two prior ones. In everyday Western psychology at least, thinking, reasoning, and intending are often seen as active processes, whereas sensation and even desiring are regarded as the products of passive experience. We are the creatures of our basic desires; emotions and urges "overwhelm" us; fears "immobilize" us; infatuations "sweep us away." It is because we see emotions as confronting us rather than ourselves as manufacturing them that we also concede emotions their compelling influence on thinking, coloring thoughts, distorting judgments. Relatedly, the role of perception in emotion is more to ignite various emotional responses. Perceived things and events frighten, disturb, and elate us. Though we are subject to our emotions, we are, in contrast, active agents in our thinking. We "have" our thoughts, we "form" our plans, we "make" our decisions.

This active-passive contrast is not exact. Disturbing ideas can intrude on our thinking; our memory can fail us. Conversely we can exert some control or influence on our emotions. We can fan the flames of our hatred and dampen our ardor. Perception as a concept in particular seems to span this passive-active division. We both actively attend to and passively experience the perceptual world. In spite of these exceptions, this crude active-passive generalization often surfaces in our everyday thinking; emotions grip us, whereas our thoughts and decisions are forged and crafted by us.

Conclusions

Even this more elaborated sketch of everyday adult belief-desire psychology is extremely simplified. Like any other theory, it is partly a cooperative enterprise, not necessarily adequately grasped by any single individual but managed and developed by a group of adherents and users. Its implicit and cooperative aspects naturally result in unclarities and even controversies. Even a casual glimpse at the philosophical controversies surrounding the nature of intention, representation, and propositional attitudes, or the psychological controversies in characterizing trait constructs, implicit personality theories, practical reasoning and the like, makes it clear that we are far from adequately characterizing people's everyday naive psychology or even agreeing on what such characterizations should characterize.

How plausible or useful, then, is my description of our everyday reasoning about human behavior? I do not contend that my descriptions of commonsense psychology is complete or best. My aim is only to draw a characterization sufficiently apt to partake of two virtues. An apt description should, first, aid in the proper typing of this body of naive knowledge. If our everyday conception of persons and minds approximates the characterization outlined, in general if not in detail, then identifying this knowledge as a naive theory seems increasingly reasonable. I will expand on this point in chapter 5.

Second, my larger goal is a distinctively developmental one. I wish to chart the developmental course of this sort of understanding. Characterizing the developmental target—what adults know—is often helpful in such an endeavor. Knowing the eventual outcome of developmental achievements helps to estimate the trajectory of a course of development. But to achieve this virtue, I do not have to capture the outcome precisely. I need to be only inspirationally close—that is, to achieve a characterization that sets our sights adequately (not fully accurately) so as to suggest some important developmental progressions. I believe that this overview serves these purposes and turn to the task of describing young children's commonsense psychology.

Young Children's Belief-Desire Psychology

I began with a simplistic description of adult belief-desire reasoning, outlined in figure 4.1, and then elaborated it into a more complex version, in figure 4.3. This served a useful presentational purpose. I now wish to propose that the simplified theory in figure 4.1 also provides an approximate description of children's first belief-desire psychology.

I believe that in the course of development, there is conceptual change within our belief-desire psychology; adults and young children possess distinctly different belief-desire psychologies. Therefore, figure 4.1 is not an apt description of adult everyday psychology in several key respects, but it can provide an approximate description of three-year-olds' theory. In subsequent chapters I say more about these developmental and conceptual differences, but it is useful to provide a quick overview here, using the differences between figures 4.1 and 4.3 to begin to outline the sorts of theory revisions made in the course of normal development.

1. I believe that the child's understanding of mind itself is different from the adult's. I described this difference in chapter 1 by distinguishing between a conception of mind as a repository of beliefs and ideas versus mind as an information processor. Children have an entity notion of mind, adults more a process one. The comparison between figures 4.1 and 4.2 conveys this difference by two primary changes. First, in figure 4.2 belief is just one small part of thinking understood broadly. That is, an elaborated understanding of such processes as remembering, thinking, and inferring frames and colors adults' more specific understanding of belief.

Additionally, the role of thinking itself is changed and expanded in figure 4.2 over figure 4.1. This can be seen as a shift from a more passive to a constructive or active mind. In figure 4.1, the mind passively receives its beliefs from perception (if you see something under the table, you know it's there). In figure 4.2, mind more actively interprets and construes such perceptual information to construct ideas, beliefs, impressions. Moreover, thinking frames desires, biases perception, and produces such active cognitive emotions as curiosity. If the mind is viewed as constructive in these ways, then the possibilities of error and individuation become more characteristic. A constructive mind can produce illusions, yield false beliefs, and ignore or misinterpret perception. Since the mind's products are not so tightly dependent on the nature of the world, my thoughts can more obviously be different from yours.

2. A second conceptual and developmental change, I hypothesize, concerns the construal of intention. In figure 4.1, and for young children, actions are intentional, but that means simply that they are purposeful; they are caused by beliefs and desires. A person's intentions therefore are simply the direct beliefs and desires that cause his or her acts. In figure 4.2, in contrast, intention has a refined and independent existence. People are seen as having crystallized intentions that are more than simple purposes or intents; they are instead plans

of action. To reiterate, in adult commonsense psychology, these two senses of intention coexist. To intend to go to the store in some cases means simply to mean to do it on purpose, that is, to do it because of motivating desires and relevant beliefs. However, an intention to go to the store can also be a description, for adults, of a developed and committed plan. Such a concrete plan is different from action itself but is also different from the initiating desires and beliefs from which it was developed. This second sense of intention, apparent in future-intentions and in formal plans such as itineraries, rests on a construct within adult commonsense psychology unavailable to young children.

3. There is as well, in comparing figures 4.1 and 4.3, a fundamental difference with regard to the presence of the construct of traits. Temporally and situationally stable traits provide an additional level of psychological analysis of action for adults. This is a prevalent adult solution, I believe, to an obvious problem. Individual beliefs and desires in fact tell us little about behavior. If John believes the store has cookies and wants cookies, he may or may not go to the store; it all depends. It all depends on the nature of his larger aggregated beliefs and desires. He may go if he believes the store has cookies, and believes that no other store has cookies, and believes that the walk will do him good, and believes that he is a thin fellow and so is unconcerned about his weight, and he likes to walk. Indeed, such a person may go to the store simply as an exercise and not get cookies.

To reason about someone's actions, we must get a handle on these larger packages of belief-desire factors. Traits like virtue, concern, and rationality seem to provide leverage on this problem. Adult employment of belief-desire psychology proceeds against a backdrop of deeper descriptions of people's characters—whether John is hot-blooded, impulsive, and romantic with a tragic worldview, or pragmatic and reflective albeit an overoptimistic Pollyanna.

Children's first belief-desire psychology, I hypothesize, has not yet come to grips with this problem—that is, the need to ground belief-desire thinking on a more stable, less evanescent infrastructure. Therefore young children have not embraced the adult solution—that is, stable character traits or perhaps something even more sophisticated (see Morton, 1980). Note, however, that the child's naive psychology does, by my account, include the notion of preferences, under the generic rubric of desire. Recall that preferences ("he likes riding horses") are the special desire explanations for recurring activities ("riding horses" rather than "riding Old Paint into town"). As such, an understanding of preferences includes an acknowledgment of temporally consistent patterns of behavior and a rudimentary explanation of such consistency by more stable dispositions.

These differences between early child and adult belief-desire psychology are important. I will return to them and document them in later chapters. To begin, however, I wish to focus on the similarities between the two theories, child and adult. As the overlap between figure 4.1 and 4.2 suggests, I think there are important similarities. That is, I claim the theories are different but commensurate rather than radically discrepant. Because of this, in a rough fashion, we can use the scheme depicted by figure 4.1 as an approximate sketch of three-year-olds' belief-desire psychology and as a simplified version of adults'. I believe that children's understanding of constructs that appear in both figures, like the construct of belief, is different, in part, from that of adults. Recalling what I have said in general about how theoretical concepts depend on one another for their larger meanings and what I have said specifically about how an understanding of thinking, for example, frames an understanding of belief, then given the differences in the concept of thinking from adult to child, the child's concept of belief and hence his belief-desire reasoning could not be exactly the same as ours. But it could still be substantially similar and familiar.

What would it mean for three-year-olds to hold such a recognizable and familiar theory? Even the simplified knowledge and reasoning outlined with respect to figure 4.1 is substantially more comprehensive than anything demonstrated in the belief-desire studies reported in chapter 3. An obvious task is to see whether and in what way young children's understanding encompasses the comprehensive sorts of belief-desire reasoning implicated by even the simplified scheme of figure 4.1. Four main sorts of belief-desire reasoning seem clearly implicated by that scheme. First, children should be able to predict actions given relevant information as to an actor's beliefs and desires. Second, not only should children be able to predict actions from beliefs and desires, but they should also be able to explain actors' observed actions by spontaneous appeal to their beliefs and desires. Third, children should also be able to predict someone's emotional reactions from information about beliefs, desires, and outcomes. Finally, just as children can infer actions from information about the actor's beliefs and desires, they should be able to infer beliefs from information about the actor's perceptions and desires from information about the actor's physiological states.

Providing data and discussion on these four points seems the simplest way of documenting and elaborating young children's initial belief-desire psychology. Some relevant data are provided by the studies in chapter 3, but more empirical work is needed. I provide more data and hence a more detailed characterization of children's first belief-desire psychology in chapter 6. First, however, I wish to clarify more precisely, in chapter 5, the status of everyday theories. Since I claim that everyday belief-desire reasoning is a theory, I wish to be clear about what sort of theory I think it is and why.

Chapter 5
Everyday Theories

If we look at the progress of recent work on human conceptual understanding, we can see a research tradition emerging. Investigators in several disciplines increasingly talk of commonsense theories, folk theories, children's theories, intuitive theories, and so on. And some serious claims have been advanced: that conceptual change and thus important aspects of cognitive development can be construed as a type of theory change, that this sort of theory change is akin to theory change in science, that cultural worldviews are instantiated in naive theories, that intuitive theories account for people's resistance to instruction, and that everyday theories supplant similarity-based conceptions (in current scientific thinking and in the individual's own learning or development). This is only a potential research tradition, to my mind, because in spite of much pregnant discussion, the tradition could remain stillborn. Several troubling questions exist. In what sense does everyday knowledge constitute a theory? What are the similarities and differences between everyday theories and scientific theories? What are the specific implications and the utility of construing everyday knowledge as theories? In this chapter I address these questions and stake out a more detailed version of the general position that human knowledge is framed by everyday theories.

Much of the current discussion about commonsense theories is imprecise. In fact, different authors seem to mean different things by referring to commonsense theories, and the common set of dicta espoused by all those appealing to this construct may prove remarkably small.[1] The early days of easy appeal to naive theories are behind us; it is time to refine our analyses. Refinement requires being specific about several issues; thus I will restrict the use of some terms and draw some uncommon distinctions. This is necessary, I believe, in order to craft an interesting and viable position.

One issue requires preliminary consideration: the nature of the proposed relation between commonsense and scientific theories. There exist strong and weak versions of the claim that all human knowledge is steeped in theory. The strong version is that everyday knowledge is organized in structures that are identical in character and function to scientific theories. The weak version is that human knowledge is theorylike in some sense. Sometimes the weak version may claim essentially one sort of similarity between scientific theories and theorylike human knowledge, for example, that human conceptual knowledge is coherent (Murphy and Medin, 1985).

It is unlikely that the strong version of the position is the case. Too many differences seem to exist between naive and scientific knowledge. Ordinary knowledge is not so consistent as scientific theory, nor are the concepts in ordinary language as precisely defined as in chemistry or electronics, for example. It is equally unlikely that a weak version devoid of specifics will prove useful. To say simply that knowledge is theorylike in some sense constrains the central notion too little. To include all coherent knowledge as theorylike fails to specify the relation that naive theories have to other coherent sorts of knowledge such as scripts, schemas, and mental models. To be useful, a weak version of the position must provide a specific characterization as to what commonsense theories are like, what similarities and dissimilarities they share with other theories. In this chapter I advocate a particular characterization of the weak position, that "theory" is a superordinate concept encompassing two different subordinates—everyday theory and scientific theory. I first discuss scientific theories not because scientific theories and commonsense theories are identical (they are not) but because there is a body of developed discussion available about scientific theories to help us better characterize naive theories.

There is certainly no consensus about the nature of scientific theories in philosophy of science or in science itself. Indeed, there has been considerable controversy about the nature and virtues of scientific theories; however, some striking insights have emerged, albeit amid further controversies. These insights into the nature of science show it to be both more complex and more deceptive in nature than depicted in the past. In particular, scientific theories, at least at one level of analysis, can be seen to be less formal, less logical, and more akin to other coherent belief systems, such as religion or philosophy, than once supposed. While this understanding of scientific theories introduces some disconcerting problems into our estimation of the validity and progressiveness of science, it makes scientific theories a more useful source of information about naive human understanding. In short, this perspective suggests there may be sizable overlap between scientific theories and everyday thought.

Two distinctions are of primary importance for my discussion. One is a distinction between framework and specific theories. The second concerns two different perspectives on theories. The first perspective considers theories as entities because they are bodies of knowledge that can be described and characterized as coherent, existing systems. The second perspective considers theories as processes, focusing on theorizing as an activity.

Framework Theories versus Specific Theories

In recent philosophy of science, and in scientific practice, the term *theory* is used to refer to at least two different sorts of things. On the one hand, there are specific theories, which refer to scientific formulations about a delimited set of phenomena. To use psychological examples, theories at this level would include the McClelland-Rummelhart model of the acquisition of past tense, Piaget's theory of object permanence, the Rescorla-Wagner theory of classical conditioning, and Freud's theory of the oedipal complex. On the other hand, the term *theory* is also used to refer to more global theoretical traditions or camps. Examples in psychology include behaviorism, psychodynamic theory, connectionism, and Piagetian theory. Such global or framework theories, as I will call them, are articulated and instantiated in a variety of specific theories; specific theories exist within a larger theoretical tradition or framework.[2]

Philosophers of science have called framework theories paradigms (Kuhn, 1962), research programs (Lakatos, 1970), or research traditions (Laudan, 1977). There are several important differences in these various writers' characterizations of framework theories, but for my purposes I will focus on some provocative commonalities.

In general, framework theories are said to inspire, engender, frame, and constrain specific theories that constitute, articulate, or instantiate the more global theoretical positions. This relationship allows a division of labor. By generally grounding a theoretical tradition, framework theories permit specific theories to address details. Detailed theories can therefore simply presume certain background conditions, categories, and facts without explicitly defending or testing them. These assumptions are underwritten by framework theories. "By sanctioning certain assumptions in advances, the research tradition frees the scientist . . . to pursue specific problems of interest" (Laudan, 1977, p. 92).

More specifically, framework theories define the ontology and the basic causal devices for their specific theories and even constrain some aspects of accepted methodology:

A research tradition provides a set of guidelines for the development of specific theories. Part of those guidelines constitute an ontology which specifies, in a general way, the types of fundamental entities which exist in the domain or domains within which the research tradition is embedded. The function of specific theories within the research tradition is to explain all the empirical problems in the domain by "reducing" them to the ontology of the research tradition. . . . Moreover, the research tradition outlines the different modes by which these entities can interact. Thus, Cartesian particles can only interact by contact, not by action-at-a-distance. Entities, within a Marxist research tradition, can only interact by virtue of the economic forces influencing them. (Laudan, 1977, p. 79)

By virtue of their ontological dictates, framework theories define domains. Behaviorism is about behavior, cognitive science about cognition, quantum mechanics about a subatomic domain of matter. Specific theories advance more detailed explanations of phenomena within these globally defined domains and consonant with the larger explanatory framework.

Because of their basic definitional role, framework theories are well buffered from traditional empirical test. Thus, in Kuhn's view, the course of normal science is the articulation and testing of specific theories within a paradigm; paradigms themselves are not subjected to empirical tests. Paradigms are changed in periods of revolution that can be better characterized, according to Kuhn (1962), as periods of sociological and ideological change than as the logical, empirical development of new theories from old. According to Lakatos (1970), research programs have an inner "hard core" of shared commitments that is protected from empirical modification because it specifies the basic aspects of the program. Only repudiation of the research program itself, which requires replacement with a viable alternative program, touches this inner core.

Intriguingly, framework theories are seen as being especially relevant to issues of change and progress in science. Specific theories change only within the confines of their theoretical tradition. Such specific changes are often data driven and can be regarded as progressive, but framework theories guide specific theory changes. Furthermore, framework theories themselves emerge and change, but the change processes that come into play in these cases seem somewhat discrepant from those dictating specific theory changes. They are less directly dependent on empirical data, more dependent on nonempirical concerns such as consistency, scope, and theoretical problem-solving efficacy, and, hence, more contentious. Concern with framework theories has required philosophers of science to deal with special and intriguing aspects of theory change and development. This was Kuhn's inspiration, though there is much disagreement about the details of the change processes he proposed for framework theories and his resulting estimation of scientific progress and realism.

I believe that a particularly useful level of analysis for finding similarities between scientific and commonsense theories is that of framework theories. A level of analysis more replete with dissimilarities is the comparison of commonsense and scientific specific theories. Moreover, commonsense framework theories capture a particularly important but neglected sort of everyday knowledge. In this regard, our everyday theory of mind, our mentalistic commonsense psychology, is, I propose, a framework theory. Finally, to clarify my earlier analysis, two of the features I considered central to commonsense and scientific theories—their specification of basic ontological commitments and their provision of general causal explanatory frameworks—are characteristic of framework theories.

The theory of mind outlined in chapter 4 serves to define an ontology and a domain—indeed, the theory defines "mind" as we ordinarily understand it. The theory also dictates a causal-explanatory framework—belief-desire reasoning—that engenders but does not precisely specify more detailed causal explanations. Within such a framework theory, one can develop specific theories. A primary way in which we do this in everyday thinking is the development of specific idiographic theories, detailed theories about the mind and actions of specific individuals. Consider the specific theory that a writer might develop in instantiating a character in a novel, for example, Fitzgerald's presentation of Gatsby. Or more prosaically and empirically, consider the specific theories we might develop about people we know—about Ronald Reagan, for example, why he acts and thinks as he does. In this specific theory, we would need to posit some concrete details about Reagan—his traits, his individuating network of specific beliefs and specific desires. We would use data and inference to develop our theoretical analysis, observations, and evidence as to Reagan's specific mental workings. Then, in the case of some act or decision on Reagan's part, we could put forth a specific prediction or a specific explanation from our idiographic theory.

Suppose we need to explain Reagan's decision to invade Grenada. In this explanation, we would instantiate a specific explanation for the specific theory by detailing such matters as what information Reagan did and did not have available at what times, what his relevant desires and goals were in this instance, what beliefs were brought into play to develop his specific plan of action, and what background traits and habits of mind were relevant. This specific theory and our application of it to derive this specific explanation would be empirically revisable. Enough new data about Reagan could revise the theory or even refute it; we could go from thinking of Reagan as thoughtful and perceptive to thinking of him as careless and impulsive, for example. New data of less comprehensive scope could cause us to revise our derived explanation even if we maintained our original specific theory; actually Reagan was ignorant of certain information and so was acting blindly, not maliciously. To formulate and revise such a specific theory, we operate within the confines of the framework of belief-desire reasoning outlined in chapter 4 but do not test that framework. Even if we refute our specific theory about Reagan's thinking, we do not refute the global theory. Indeed, we would probably go on to hold a new specific Reagan theory but a Reagan theory undoubtedly within the same global framework. Framework theories provide the confines for such creative theory revision.

Our framework theory of mind frames not only specific idiographic theories but also specific topic theories. For example, the framework theory houses and constrains everyday understanding of specific mental capacities or faculties such as intelligence or memory. An everyday understanding of memory, often called metamemory (Flavell, 1971), embodies specific beliefs about memory processes, tasks, capacities, strategies. Such a specific theory articulates and elaborates a single topic within the framework theory—memory. The larger framework theory constrains and supports this specification, for example, by defining memory as an internal mental faculty related to thinking and reasoning, informed by perception, providing information to planning and action.

My investigations have been aimed at depicting the development in children of a framework theory of mind, not the more specific theories that such a framework would also engender. I am especially interested in this level of analysis for several reasons. First, if commonsense framework theories do constrain and guide naive specific theories, then the explication of framework theories is needed to understand commonsense theories in general. Also, if I am correct, it is in such framework theories that our basic ontological commitments and worldviews reside. They are thus particularly important for understanding cognition and cognitive change. Finally, it is at the level of framework theories and relevant global issues that it is easiest for me to see bridging similarities between everyday knowledge and scientific theories and therefore easiest to see the utility of construing everyday knowledge as theories. This is an important point. To say that both scientific and lay theories are distinguishable instances of a more general class is to posit essential commonalities, along with important distinctions. Helpful commonalities become obvious, I feel, if we consider certain commonsense theories to be comparable to scientific framework theories.

Process versus Entity Considerations

Several important differences between scientific and everyday theories exist as well, and these become especially clear when considering how theories arise and how they function for their holders, that is, in considering process rather than entity issues. So far, my descriptions of commonsense theories and of scientific theories have focused on entity characterizations. I have talked of framework scientific or commonsense theories as entities that constitute certain ontologies and causal-explanatory infrastructures and that frame or "house" specific theories. Specific theories are entities of more precise scope and character that depend on and instantiate framework theories for limited, specified phenomena. However, often, within philosophy of science and in scientific practice, theories are characterized by their process features. In some of these characterizations, scientific theories are construed as necessarily the products of a special sort of testing and formulation called theorizing. For example, Morton (1980), who originated the theory-theory label to refer to the view that naive knowledge of the mind is a theory, argues that the theory-theory is wrong. Naive knowledge of mind, according to Morton, is not a theory but something less impressive, what he terms a "scheme." Morton claims that naive knowledge is not a theory, in part, because it does not function and evolve as theories do. Specifically, it does not foster, nor is it a product of, the sorts of empirical testing and rigorous theorizing that are the hallmarks of scientific theories. Our commonsense psychological schematism thus differs profoundly from scientific theories in terms of process:

> Science is the best way of running a theory; we build into it whatever we find to be good theory-managing technique. So any body of beliefs that is not part of science will be either a poor imitation of a scientific theory or something that is not a theory at all, for example a scheme. (p. 7)

> Theory is risky. It depends on a delicate balance of conjecture and fact, imagination and prudence. . . . Free imaginative hypotheses are allowable in science just because they take place

within a network of tests, observations, and opportunities for critical reflection that ensure public criticism of hypotheses and give refuting considerations a chance to appear. Science would not work otherwise. . . . Where could common-sense psychology fit in? It does not seem to be mostly empirical generalizations; beliefs, desires, memories, and regrets are too far from observation. And it certainly does not embody scientific balances and controls. (p. 29)

Part of Morton's contention is that the lack of proper scientific theorizing indicates that commonsense psychology falls short of being a theory; however, I feel that it is possible and necessary to separate theories from scientific theorizing. Certainly within philosophy of science it has been important to separate framework theories from too narrow a view of scientific theorizing. The formation and revision of framework theories does not necessarily require certain forms of scientific theorizing once regarded as definitive of theorizing itself. In the analysis of scientific framework theories distinctions of this sort help support the contention that theories as entities and scientific method as a process are separable. Hence, it certainly seems possible to consider that there are theories—for example commonsense theories—that are not the products of rigorous explicit theorizing.

This characterization of commonsense theories as not being the product of rigorous theorizing is particularly necessary and apt with respect to children's theories. Young children have theories—or at least one theory, a commonsense (framework) theory of mind—but those theories are not the product of scientific theorizing. Children do not craft their theories on the basis of explicit, rigorous activities akin to scientific formulation and test. Indeed, they do not "test" their commonsense theories at all in the sense of explicitly considering them revisable, as explicitly induced from or confirmed by data. Most of our commonsense theories are acquired by processes of everyday knowledge acquisition in childhood. These processes are not well understood, but they surely are not the processes of formulation and testing employed in scientific theorizing. Scientific reasoning in this sense is either not available to young children or at least not employed on commonsense framework theories.

Developmental psychologists have studied the development of "scientific reasoning" for many years (Inhelder and Piaget, 1958; Siegler and Liebert, 1975; Kuhn and Brannock, 1977). Inhelder and Piaget, for example, directly likened formal operations to scientific reasoning and thus studied the acquisition of certain scientific abilities: considering all possible combinations of variables, formulating controlled experiments by holding all variables constant save one, reasoning inductively to a generalization from data and deductively from hypotheses to test. According to Inhelder and Piaget's analysis, such abilities are absent in children and acquired only in early adolescence. Current research presents a more complex picture. Young children engage in hypothesis-testing endeavors with some similarities to the hypothesis testing of experimental scientists. Young children engage in systematic observation (Piaget, 1953), consider alternative possibilities in certain situations (Somerville and Wellman, 1987), and actively acquire information to rule out certain possibilities and confirm others (Bryant, 1973; Shultz, 1982; Fabricius, Sophian, and Wellman, 1987). Still, these endeavors seem to fall short of explicit scientific reasoning, perhaps most obviously in that these early strategies lack self-conscious attempts to think about a theory (rather than merely hold one and use it). That is, the systematicity of scientific method depends on efforts to make explicit, and also to suspend, one's belief in a theory so as to formulate objectively one's hypotheses and to evaluate objectively the evidence acquired and needed. This differentiation of theory and evidence, and attempts to think more explicitly about both, seems to be an acquisition of pre-adolescence (Kuhn and Phelps, 1982).

According to one sort of analysis, therefore, thinking is not noticeably scientific until late in development. From this perspective we certainly could not attribute theorizing to young children, and thus no theories that require such theorizing. Even if we stipulate that the hypothesis-testing endeavors of younger children constitute theorizing in some minimal sense, it is implausible to think that early framework theories arise from such efforts. When such "theorizing" is evident, I claim, children can at best be seen as testing and revising specific theories or, more likely, specific explanations within a framework theory; they are not subjecting their framework theories to explicit consideration and test. Recall my earlier example of an adult's idiographic theory of Ronald Reagan. The parallel for a child might be a theory of Aunt Jean, her thoughts and actions. Such a theory, a detailed mentalistic account of Aunt Jean, would be formulated from data and could be revised in the light of new data. For example, what Jean does and says provides the data for abduction (within the framework theory) of a specific theory, the Aunt Jean theory. Children could, at times, consider some alternative hypotheses as to Aunt Jean's states of mind (whether she is sad or tired, serious or joking) and then actively test such hypotheses. But children do not test and revise the framework theory; they simply hold it.

In short, everyday theories do not result from theorizing itself but are theories nonetheless, and this seems to be particularly easy to accept if we focus on everyday framework theories. Everyday cognition is typically less formal, less explicit, less self-aware, and less rigorously empirical than scientific formulation and testing of specific theories. Yet it can give rise to bodies of knowledge that are theories, everyday theories, and that function in other aspects of everyday thought just as theories function in scientific thought. Here is one example of such everyday theoretical work guided by everyday framework theories.

In science, one formulates specific theories within the confines of a framework scientific theory. In this manner framework theories influence the workings of specific ones, especially their formulation and revision. In everyday thinking, I argue, one similarly formulates specific explanations within the guidelines of everyday framework theories. Within science, empirical data make contact with specific theories, which are revised accordingly; framework scientific theories are much less subject to empirical test. Within everyday cognition, observations and new data cause one to formulate, refute, and revise specific explanations; but commonsense framework theories, the global ontologies and causal presumptions that guide and constrain the formulation of specific explanations, are not up for empirical revision in the same way.

In scientific practice, specific theories can be and are contrasted with data. However, what counts as data in the first place is theory ridden at the level of framework theories. Framework theories define, in part, what counts as admissible evidence. This is similarly true for commonsense theories. For example, belief-desire psychology specifies what actions are and that they are belief-desire dependent. Given that constraint, one can observe another's actions and use such data to infer, confirm, and refute hypotheses about that person's specific beliefs and desires. But parsing human behavior into actions, beliefs, and desires in the first place is theory laden; it is dictated by the ontology of our framework commonsense psychology. This multilevel arrangement—of observations, then specific theories, then framework theories—means that two apparently contradictory things can both be true: that theories are genuinely accountable to data (and hence revisable by new data) but that data themselves are theory laden. As this often works, specific theories are accountable to data, but data are dependent, in a broad fashion, on global theory. I believe these multilevel dependencies between data and theory hold for commonsense as well as scientific theories.

Within philosophy of science, the existence, functions, and characteristics of framework scientific theories have been seen as problematic for our high estimation of science. That data and observation are theory ridden, for example, or that certain theoretical notions are immune to empirical test, calls into question the realism and progressiveness of scientific theories (Scheffler, 1967; van Fraassen, 1980). However, this characterization has clear parallels in commonsense thought and thus, for my purposes, makes the postulation of everyday theories, especially everyday framework theories, apt and informative.

Specific Conceptual Structures

This description of the differences and similarities between framework commonsense theories and framework scientific theories raises the question of the existence, nature, and scope of specific commonsense theories. If there are framework commonsense theories comparable to framework theories in science, are there specific naive theories analogous to specific scientific ones? The answer is: *yes, but.* In fact, the answer is: *yes, but, but.*

It seems obvious that some sorts of narrower bodies of more specific everyday knowledge do exist, housed under and influenced by our framework theories. Under lay mentalistic psychology, for example, there exists specific conceptual knowledge about memory, intelligence, mental imagery and illusion, and so on. And the larger global framework also encompasses specific naive idiographic efforts, such as the Reagan theory discussed before. Calling some of these specific bodies of knowledge *theories* has attractions; I have done this in the preceding discussion and will resort to this terminology again in chapter 11. This is the *yes* to the question of the existence of specific commonsense theories. But (the first *but*) these conceptual structures are noticeably dissimilar to specific scientific theories, at least to our best specific scientific theories. Consider Einstein's special theory of relativity. Specific scientific theories of this sort are more verifiable, more empirically tested, more formal and precise, and more consistent than any sort of everyday thinking. This is because specific scientific theories are the products of rigorous scientific practices and they show it; specific naive theories are not. Process-entity differences between science and everyday thinking thus loom especially large at this specific level of comparison. Still, it is useful to talk of everyday specific theories because they function in relation to their framework theories as specific scientific theories function in relation to their framework theories. It is the relation of specific theories to framework theories that holds across everyday cognition and science even when scientific and everyday thought are so different. Specific everyday theories are a certain type of more detailed and more restricted theoretical endeavor guided by their everyday framework theories, just as specific scientific theories specifically instantiate their scientific theoretical frameworks.

But (the second *but*), even though laypersons have some specified theories, such theories do not constitute the only sort of concrete, instantiated conceptual structures housed under global theories. This is true in science and commonsense. Scientific global theories frame isolated hypotheses and theory fragments as well as theories. Even more strikingly, our everyday knowledge of the world, framed by naive framework theories, is a compendium of a variety of conceptual structures—scripts, schemas, mental models, associative nets, raw empirical generalizations, practical lore, and rules of thumb, as well as something on the order of specific naive theories. Because of this variety of everyday cognition, we should be wary of premature, uncritical adoption of the "theory" label to designate specific conceptual structures. Not all organized human knowledge about identifiable cognitive contents is theory. We muddy the waters by indiscriminate use of the phrase and failure to articulate the real differences between such structures, the difference between a script and a specific theory, for example.

What are the differences between everyday theories and other specific conceptual structures, such as scripts? The view that everyday knowledge is framed by commonsense framework theories helps distinguish between naive theories and other coherent packages of everyday knowledge. With respect to scripts, Susan Carey's analysis appeals to me, if we refine her use of theory to mean framework theory. Carey says:

> Explanation is at the core of theories. It is explanatory mechanisms that distinguish theories from other types of conceptual structures, such as restaurant scripts. To see this, consider such questions as "Why do we pay for our food at a restaurant?" or "Why do we order before the food comes?" The answers to these questions are not to be found within the restaurant script itself; the answer to the first lies in the domain of economics, where questions of the exchange of goods and services are explained, and the answer to the second lies in the domain of physics, since it involves the directionality of time. (Carey, 1985a, p. 201)

In fact, even scripts provide some explanatory grist for our thinking. We pay for our food before receiving it at fast food restaurants but after eating it at sit-down establishments. Why? In part, the answer appeals to the force of routine, which is so well captured by scripts: "because that's how they do it." Carey herself admits that "all conceptual structures provide some fodder for explanation" (p. 201).

A more profound point is the reverse of her statement: theories are at the core of explanations. That is, many explanations show the imprint of more basic modes of explanation, which inhere in framework theories. These basic modes of explanation take their character from the broader causal-explanatory framework of global theories and take their scope from the ontologies of such theories. Explanatory force and sensibility are grounded in our naive framework theories.

What are scripts, then? Scripts are more specific conceptual structures designed in part to capture temporal regularities in frequently encountered streams of events. Scripts cross-cut theories in this fashion; they are more specific but do not precisely instantiate our framework theories. Still, as Carey's example illustrates, some aspects of scripts are made sensible only by reference to and dependency on our framework theories. Imagine asking a series of "why" questions about phenomena captured by our specific structures. For example, in the restaurant script: (1) why do we pay for our food? (because it is an exchange: we pay; the owner cooks), (2) why doesn't the owner pay? (because he has to make a living), (3) why does he have to make a living, and how does he do it? Prolonged question-answer exchanges of this sort tend to gravitate toward framework theories. That is, questions and answers begin to circle around within certain domains of explanation, domains founded on and framed by naive framework theories. The above questions and answers revolve around naive economics, to reiterate Carey's basic point. Explanations at this level develop a sort of circularity, or rather, a kind of self-supporting coherence, dependent on the coherence of terms and principles of the framework theory.

A similar sort of relationship seems to exist between our framework theories and schemas. Consider story schemas. Story schemas such as those in story grammars (Mandler and Johnson, 1977; Stein and Glenn, 1979; Rumelhart, 1975) capture in part the regularities of sequenced story events. Underlying such schemas, however, is a deeper level of causal analysis on which story schemas depend (Nezworski, Stein, and Trabasso, 1981; Omanson, 1982; Trabasso and Sperry, 1985). As the analysis of story texts by Trabasso and van den Broek makes clear (Trabasso and van den Broek, 1985), the causal glue of story grammars, depicting the extended actions and reactions of psychological protagonists, depends on commonsense psychological causation; that is, the basic story grammar depends for its causal "force" on everyday belief-desire psychological theory.

Finally, I wish to consider the relationship between framework theories and more specific problem-solving representations such as mental models (Johnson-Laird, 1983), reasoning diagrams (Larkin and Simon, 1987), or practical inference schemas (Cheng and Holyoak, 1985). This is an important issue; it is part of the larger topic of how framework theories function to guide everyday reasoning. Theories are entity-descriptions of people's conceptual knowledge; such knowledge must be instantiated in more detailed working models to solve specific problems. An important point here is that framework theories do not dictate everyday reasoning about specific problems within their domains; they do influence such reasoning but do not completely specify it. In this regard recall that framework theories do not even dictate the specifics of specific theories in their domain. They constrain and inform such theories, but the formulation of specific theories requires the articulation of specific theoretical proposals as well, proposals that instantiate the framework notions with respect to a more detailed set of phenomena and findings. Framework theories play a similar role in our attempts to solve specific reasoning problems. Framework theories, I claim, constrain specific problems representations, which therefore reflect the imprint of the theories framing them. But more is needed to create and utilize specific problem representations than a framework. The reasoner must articulate or devise more detailed and procedurally precise reasoning devices or models based on the particular situation and problem specified.

To illustrate, consider an extension of the Ronald Reagan example. Suppose I am the leader of a foreign country sitting down with Reagan to negotiate some agreement or treaty. One important step in my thinking is that I frame the situation as a problem in assessing and influencing Reagan's beliefs and desires; that is, I construe the problem to solve as a problem generally within belief-desire psychology. But more is required than that. Thus, I might additionally represent the situation to myself as akin to a poker game: my problem is to keep "my cards" secret, to try to infer Reagan's "cards," to bet and bluff appropriately, to concede certain hands but attempt to come out ahead in the total game. Or alternatively, I might adopt a different sort of specific problem representation within my general framework. I might construe the situation more like a courtship ritual—say my problem is to win Reagan's hand, to demonstrate my true affection for him and my ability to provide for him in the future. In any event, I claim, I often scrutinize the actual problem situation ("What are Reagan's cards exactly?" "Is that a bluff or a serious bet?") to flesh out a more specific representation. And then I reason within or manipulate this specific representation in various procedural ways; that is, I use it to simulate the course of events and infer my optimal conclusions and actions.

There are two points to make with respect to this example. First, framework theories do not simply provide such specific problem representations; I might use a poker game representation, a courtship representation, or some other specific representation altogether. But second, framework theories are not irrelevant; they frame my efforts to find or devise a specific representation; to reiterate, both of the specific representations proposed involve belief-desire construals of the relation between Reagan and me. In either sort of representation I must attempt to understand and manipulate Reagan's beliefs and desires (not his anatomy or digestion for example). Therefore, in order to solve many reasoning problems, the reasoner must recruit or construct specific problem representations by appeal to a relevant framework theory as well as to the target problem's specifics.

I do not wish to say much more about the nature or workings of specific problem representations now. Following others (Johnson-Laird, 1983; Holland, Holyoak, Nisbett and Thagard, 1987) I will loosely call such specific problem representations mental models, although I am aware of the limitation and unclarities in that usage (Rips, in press). I do not think these difficulties cloud my more general points that specific problem solutions often recruit something on the order of mental models and yield mental simulations of events by such models, that such models are not simply dictated by our framework theories, but that our framework theories still frame and constrain such specific problem representations in important respects. The analogy to computer simulation research is helpful here. Framework theories (connectionism) do not dictate specific simulation models (the Rummelhart-Norman model of past tense), but they frame such endeavors to a substantial degree.

Advantages

The analyses I have set out make credible the notion of commonsense theories, especially commonsense framework theories. If the notion is credible, then we are licensed to push the theory analysis further.

Why should we do so? Why should an "everyday theory" perspective be considered as a potential research tradition, worthy of development and effort? We might so consider it to the extent that it offers the resources of an emerging research tradition: if it cuts through some basic conundrums of existing struggling research traditions, if it provides a positive research heuristic, an exploitable central vision of its domain, and if it inspires and propagates credible specific theories that can be validated and developed more critically. As a research tradition or theory itself, a theory perspective is not directly refuted or warranted by specific empirical tests, yet to attract scientific investment, it must have the three prospects just listed. In my estimation, considering everyday knowledge as inhering in everyday framework theories offers these needed attractions as a program for understanding and investigating everyday cognition. Therefore, it is worth detailing the attractions more clearly.[3]

The Problem of Domain-Specific, Content-Dependent Cognition

Part of my enthusiasm for construing global aspects of children's cognitive development in terms of commonsense global theories is that such a construal holds promise of appropriately managing a central problem confronting the study of cognitive development: the problem of domain-specific, content-dependent cognition. This problem is a legacy of our prior research traditions.

Most directly this problem is a legacy of Piagetian theory. Piagetian theory rests on the notion that cognition is organized by underlying cognitive structures. For Piaget such structures have several necessary, interlocking aspects. Most critically, cognitive structures are, according to the theory as it is typically understood, content independent and domain general. Content independence means that a more or less unitary sort of thinking applies similarly to a vast array of dissimilar tasks or cognitive contents. For example, concrete-operational thinking applies in largely similar fashion to number, time, area, weight, length, morality, and so forth, and this results in some crucial similarities in the child's thought across these different contents. That is why the acquisition of the various conservations is said to occur at roughly the same stage. Since this sort of concrete operational thinking and its pertinent structures apply across many (though not all) domains regardless of their specific contents (such as, number versus space), such structures are also domain general. Sensorimotor, preoperational, and formal operational cognition similarly structure thinking in many domains, or so the theory goes.

The content-independent, domain-general nature of Piagetian cognitive structures is evident in, and indeed defines, both the vertical and horizontal dimensions of Piaget's stage theory (Flavell, 1971a). Consider first the vertical aspect—how later stages relate to earlier ones. Concrete operational structures (the eight concrete operational groupings) succeed preoperational structures (qualitative identities and functions) and precede formal operational structures (the INRC group). Since these different structures organize thinking quite differently, cognition undergoes qualitatively different forms with development. Because of this, according to the theory,, children evidence the major sequence of stages of cognitive development. Since the structures organizing these stages are decidedly different, these stages define a series of developmentally different thinkers, who have different resulting worldviews. These sorts of stages and structures also have a concomitant horizontal aspect. Since thinking about a great many contents is organized by the same structure (and reorganized similarly by stage changes), these stages and structures are quite broad, putatively influencing much of the child's cognition at any one time. Thus, cognitive development has its telling synchronies, according to the theory.

The last 25 years have revealed serious problems with the notion of content-dependent, domain-general cognition. Children's thinking, and adults' as well, seems content dependent. This problem is evident in the discrepancies between our current understanding of adult thinking and Piaget's depiction of formal operations. Because of their formal, abstract nature, formal operational structures are especially general and content independent. And of course such structures are the targeted endpoint of preceding developments in Piaget's theory. As a result, the character of formal operational thinking is especially significant. But adult cognition does not seem to have the formal, logical character depicted by Piaget (Cheng and Holyoak, 1985; Evans, 1982). Instead, adult thought seems quite dependent on concrete materials, contents, examples, and props. It seems to be a not particularly unified collection of routines and systems rather than a general, formal edifice. Adults reason in nonformal ways subject to a variety of biases, limitations, and errors that vary according to their familiarity and expertise with various domains of thought (Nisbett and Ross, 1980).

Moreover, cognitions pertinent to different domains of thought seem to have different rather than similar developmental paths. An understanding of number, for example, does not seem to involve the same sorts of knowledge and processes as an understanding of space. Consequently these two sorts of cognitions seem to have different developments (compare, for example, Gelman and Gallistel, 1978, with Stiles-Davis, Kritchevsky, and Bellugi, 1988). Even the conservations that Piaget studied do not enter into the child's cognitive repertoire with the generality or synchrony required of content-independent, domain-general cognitive machinery (Brainerd, 1978; Flavell, 1971a; Toussaint, 1974). All in all, content-independent, domain-general formulations of cognition and cognitive development now seem more wrong than right (Gelman and Baillargeon, 1983; Carey, 1985b).

The downfall of this unified account of cognition raises a new set of problems, however; a content-independent, domain-general perspective had several not insignificant attractions as a framework for cognitive research. Perhaps most prominently such a perspective held hope for making the study of cognition manageable. That perspective posited a small number of basic structures that characterize cognition in important general ways. Focusing on those structures thus provided important leverage for a large range of issues and topics if the theory was true. If the theory is not true, if cognition is instead domain specific and content dependent, then the picture may be one of innumerable cognitive skills or entities whose organization may be ad hoc. If so, what and how big are the proper units of analysis, and how are we to achieve a manageable bigger picture? The recent history of research in cognitive development renders these questions anything but academic. Not only do researchers now consider and investigate thinking separately with respect to specific domains, such as number, moral issues, space, and biology, but analyses and research have gone beyond this toward still smaller "contents" or "domains." Models and explanations for a wide variety of small domains of cognition are pursued. Examples include the child's understanding of the number zero (Wellman and Miller, 1986), of balance scales (Siegler, 1976), of a single memory strategy such as organization (Tenney, 1975), and of dinosaurs (Chi and Koeske, 1983).

Fischer's skill theory (1980) exemplifies this sort of reasonable but confusing perspective on cognition. Fischer distinguishes task domains from skill domains. A task domain centers on a single task and "only minor variations in the same task, in contrast to the broad grouping of behaviors across tasks in skill domains" (p. 484). At times, Fischer's examples of skill domains are broad, including, for example, cognition, learning, problem solving, language, and social skills (p. 521). At other times, skill domains are more specific, encompassing basket-making skills, reading skills, skills for drawing maps (p. 513) conservation of substance, conservation of volume (p. 515), and specific social role skills (p. 513). In the end, Fischer admits skill theory "does not deal adequately with skill domains" (p. 524).

Task domains are more specific and limited still. An example that Fisher offers (p. 505) is a child playing with two doll replicas, a doctor and a patient. The task is used to assess children's understanding of social roles and especially reciprocal role relations, such as doctor-patient. Fischer states, however, that even minor changes in the task, such as varying the roles from doctor-patient to mother-child (p. 506), mean that a new task domain is involved. Skill theory cannot predict the developmental relation between performance on the two tasks (doctor-patient social roles versus mother-child social roles) because they come from two different domains.

If this is the level of our first-order description of cognition, then the job of assembling an understanding of cognitive development in general will be very difficult, perhaps intractable. In the extreme almost any topic can be a "content," and almost any difference between items or materials can carve out a "domain." Our understanding of children's cognition becomes more accurate at such fine-grained levels of analysis but also more fragmented.

Thus, the bare assertion that cognition is content dependent, domain specific, albeit probably correct, raises serious problems of its own. There are three interrelated problems. First is the extreme specificity of the skills and contents that such a generalization allows, indeed encourages, as the basic infrastructure of knowledge. Second, such a description of cognition offers no principled analysis of what a domain is, though the term *domain* is often used. Domains seem arbitrary, innumerable, and ad hoc. Third, and most central, there is no provision of a positive heuristic for characterizing what domain-specific bodies of knowledge might be like, how they might be generally viewed and analyzed. The assertion that cognition is content dependent and domain specific is at odds with one research tradition (the Piagetian one), but it provides no clear sense of a viable alternative tradition.

An Alternative Research Program

Construing children's knowledge as the acquisition of commonsense theories has the makings of an alternative research program that charts an appropriate course through some of these conundrums. That is, it does so if we focus on children's framework theories.

1. On analogy to framework scientific theories, commonsense theories provide a useful and viable characterization of the general nature of domain-dependent, content-specific cognition. Specifically,

framework scientific theories are content dependent and domain specific in coherent, easy-to-see ways. A framework scientific theory, such as behaviorism in psychology, posits certain theoretical constructs and structures. The constructs—operants, reflexes, conditioned stimuli and responses, various conditioning schedules—provide a coherent, structured account of phenomena in its domain. But compare such a theory to a framework theory in biology—for example, evolutionary biology—or in economics—for example, Keynesian macroeconomics. Each account (behaviorism versus macroeconomics) provides an organized, coherent system of constructs and explanations, but the systems are quite different. The workings of theoretical behaviorism have no parallel in macroeconomics. Classical conditioning's structures, terms, and accounts are nothing at all like the Keynesian theoretical apparatus. The theories are obviously domain specific, not general. The reason is that the theories are content dependent. The central theoretical apparatus of behaviorism is based on certain content-dependent terms—behavior, stimuli, responses. This basic ontology defines the units for the theory. The content of the theories of behaviorism versus macroeconomics is quite different, mandating quite different sorts of analytic treatment because overt individual behavior and aggregated market forces are quite different sorts of things.

My point is that framework scientific theories easily flesh out the notion of content-dependent, domain-specific knowledge in familiar but inspiring ways. Such a characterization provides a positive heuristic as to what content-dependent, domain-specific cognitive structures are like, and by analogy it becomes easy to imagine how an individual's cognition might well be entrenched in content-dependent, domain-specific cognitive structures, namely, naive framework theories.

2. Similarly, construing commonsense knowledge as theories, and focusing on global theories that frame more specific explanations, also seems to provide a foothold on the slippery problem of defining a domain. This is crucial: if indeed cognition is domain dependent, how are we to identify the domains of everyday cognition?

A commonsense framework theory is like the broad belief-desire framework described in chapter 4. That theory, like every other framework theory, defines its own domain—in this case the domain of thoughts and actions. That domain, as described in chapter 4 (and not the domain of behavior), defines the relevant content and scope of the commonsense theory of cognition. More specific theories can articulate and develop within this global territory, but the framework theory defines the domain. It does so because it specifies the relevant ontology—mind, ideas, beliefs, desires, intentional actions, rather than behavior, stimuli, operants, reflexes. Ontological commitments inhere in framework theories, and hence framework theories define domains. In this way, the domains of commonsense cognition are definable; we can define them by mapping the nature and scope of commonsense framework theories.

Although this analysis points the way to a method for outlining the basic domains of cognition—their terms, boundaries, and scope—it does not specify what those domains are. It cannot. The specification of such domains requires the specification and characterization of people's actual framework theories. The data presented in this book with respect to children's naive psychology show, as a case study, that it is possible to characterize a framework theory in such a fashion that the relevant domain of naive thought is revealed. But the task of characterization must be undertaken in each domain because theories are domain specific and content dependent. One must know the nature of naive psychology to know that the domain is mind, not behavior. In addition, since domains are theory dependent (dependent on the ontological specifications and commitments of the encompassing framework theory), if and when framework theories radically change with development, then the domains of commonsense cognition themselves change. Thus, the domains of interest for children versus adults might differ.

Having said that the task of discovering domains is in part an empirical one, dependent on the charting of extant naive framework theories, and that framework theories are possibly different at different ages of development, then clearly there is no current chart of such naive domains. Still, on analogy to science there are several sources of inspiration for some informed initial guesses—philosophy of science and science itself. Specifically, current mature scientific disciplines themselves carve phenomena into different domains—physics, chemistry, biology, psychology, economics. Many of these divisions evolved from and extend commonsense thinking. We could do worse than to use these disciplines as initial signposts to begin analyses of everyday content-dependent knowledge.

3. Defining the domains of human thought in this framework theory-dependent fashion may have an additional attraction: the number of relevant domains should be few. Since framework theories are global and encompassing, it might well be that persons hold only a small number of such theories. In part this is an issue of level of analysis, but there does seem to be an informative, broad level of analysis to be used here. On my analysis people do not explicitly theorize about framework theories. Thus they do not simultaneously

hold competing framework theories (naive behaviorism versus naive mentalistic psychology). They only simultaneously hold complementary theories (naive mechanics and naive psychology). If so, then a small number of such theories may well frame and constrain a host of more specific understandings that people construct. For example, for adults the total number of framework theories might be fewer than 10 or so. There might, for example, be a naive mentalistic psychology, a naive physics (probably a naive mechanics of an impetus sort), a naive mathematics, and perhaps a few naive social sciences like a naive political science and a naive economics. People's more specific naive understandings would fall under one or another of these framework theories. A lay specific theory of the weather might fall under naive metaphysics for one person and naive physics for another, depending on from which domain (which lay framework theory) the relevant causal phenomena and explanations are recruited.

Children especially might well have a small number of framework theories. And a different, larger set of adult framework theories could emerge from these. Carey (1985a), for example, has speculated that young children might have only a (framework) naive mechanics and a (framework) naive psychology. There has been recent disagreement with her position that a third commonsense theory, naive biology, emerges out of an earlier naive psychology only at about age six to eight years. But even if young children have three framework theories rather than two, then such global theories are still an important level of analysis, and everyday mentalistic psychology seems a likely member of the original formative set.

Points 1, 2, and 3 suggest that domains, ontology, and theories are wrapped up together. Or at least they can be cogently pursued together given the notion of framework commonsense theories. Consideration of commonsense framework theories thus provides an avenue for addressing the difficult questions of how to define and assess the domains of commonsense cognition and how to do so in a way that constrains or at least organizes an explosively large possible set of domains. These are the central virtues of the theory research program. There are some additional attractions as well.

4. For many people an attraction of Piaget's theory was his focus on qualitative, nonbiological changes in development. Piaget was well aware of quantitative developmental changes (that the adult or older child might just know more or think faster than the younger child), but he felt that qualitative changes also marked cognitive development—ways in which an adult or older child thinks profoundly differently from a younger one. The preoperational child who fails to

conserve quantity has, according to Piaget, a very different under-standing of amount than the older child who easily solves such con-servation problems. The younger child's world is therefore different from our own in failing to construe objects and substances in terms of fixed amounts, invariant under many transformations and truly changed only by addition or subtraction of new quantities. Similarly, the animistic, realistic, preschooler of Piagetian theory has a very dif-ferent worldview than the older child. Piaget insisted that such qual-itative changes in thinking resulted from endogenous changes in the child's system of cognitive structures, that is, in reorganizations, re-equilibrations, of the child's thought. These changes were not pri-marily the result of exogenous changes, such as adult socialization or maturational biological changes in the brain, but rather the result of ways in which prior conceptual systems engender new discoveries, which in turn engender further conceptual change.

The qualitative changes that Piaget pinpointed (such as those from preoperational to operational thought) and the endogenous explana-tions he crafted (his description of how the concrete-operational groupings structurally emerge from preoperational predecessors) now seem doubtful. Still, the general picture of qualitative conceptual change has its attractions. Such qualitative reorganizations or change in worldview seem to punctuate the history of ideas, for example. And many people feel that pervasive conceptual reorganizations are obvious in their own intellectual development—for example, in their experience of going from being an outsider to an insider with respect to some new culture or tradition, the experience of going from being a novice in some field to becoming reasonably expert, or the experi-ence of watching a child or student suddenly grasp a key idea, for example, Helen Keller's uncovering the essence of speech. In such progressions one often has the feeling of seeing a worldview substan-tially shift, change, or realign. Cognitive development may well en-compass such important shifts.

Again, viewing human knowledge as being framed by naive global theories provides a place for such shifts, on analogy from scientific theory change to naive theory change. Framework scientific theories change; such changes involve formative changes in scientists' world-view, shifts in the very definition of domains of inquiry and para-digms of explanation. In the history of science such changes are amenable to endogenous analyses that trace the formulation of new ideas to creative advances upon older notions and do not seem tied to biological change. Einstein's physics is different from, but was en-gendered out of, Newtonian physics. We do not explain this advance by attributing a more biologically developed brain to Einstein than to

Newton but by citing the development of certain insights and ideas. Such analyses form a natural rather than mysterious part of the story of cognitive development if we view cognitive development as encompassing theory changes, specifically framework theory changes.

This discussion is obviously related to the question of restructuring of knowledge: Is knowledge radically restructured in the course of cognitive development? This question and an answer to it has been articulated by Carey (1985a). It is not necessary for me to paraphrase or to endorse her specific arguments here. Regardless of the specifics of her position, she makes clear that we must consider the possibility of analogous content-dependent, domain-specific conceptual changes in cognitive development. Theory changes in science become a demonstration of the plausibility of such changes in the individual's developing cognition.

5. Learning something new is often a difficult endeavor. This is the problem of resistance to instruction. Teaching physics or statistics to college students does not always take (chapter 9 in Holland, Holyoak, Nisbett, and Thagard, 1987; White, 1983; di Sessa, 1982); certain childhood acquisitions—for example, the Piagetian conservations—are difficult to train (Beilen, 1971; Brainerd, 1974). Resistance to instruction often results in a reaction of practical disbelief: Why don't pupils just learn these things? The content is not that difficult. The Piagetian reaction was a domain-general interpretation: changes in thinking of these sorts require changes in deep domain-general logical structures.

From a theory perspective, both reactions are misguided. If people's understandings are entrenched in naive framework theories and if learning requires changes in these theories, then failures of instruction are to be expected. Theory changes and framework theory changes require basic shifts in ontology and explanatory frameworks; such shifts are not accomplished in a few hours of instruction unless already well launched outside the specific training situation. But such shifts do not necessarily reflect domain-general shifts. Domain-specific restructurings, that is, theory shifts, provide a possible alternative explanation.

Students come to instruction with a set of ideas, indeed often a coherent, well-supported system of beliefs, that is at odds with new teachings. This has become especially obvious in science education. If the history of science is any guide at all, then changing such preconceptions requires long periods of accommodation and transition, at times conceptual revolutions. Thus educational change can be viewed as analogous to theory change in the history of science. Such a perspective makes sensible the prevalence of resistance to instruction and provides some insights on how to overcome it. For these reasons, science educators have become increasingly interested in construing students' preinstructed knowledge as commonsense theories (McCloskey, 1983; Champagne, Klopfer, and Gunstone, 1980; Clement, 1983; Vosniadou and Brewer, 1987). For example, some researchers believe that preinstructed knowledge of physics constitutes definite theories because it resembles an earlier theory in the history of science (McCloskey, 1983). Others think that naive physical thinking consists more of a fragmented collection of ideas without the systematicity or coherence of scientific theories (di Sessa, 1985). Both may be right. Specific physical knowledge may or may not be well conceived as a specific scientific theory, but specific knowledge structures are entrenched in naive framework theories nonetheless. Understanding and causal explanation are framed by such global theories, and hence scientific instruction may require confrontation with and accommodation by one's framework theories. To the extent that it does, resistance to instruction will exist.

6. Thinking of conceptual knowledge in theory terms is helpful for framing another set of issues in developmental psychology. Loosely put, this concerns the relation of knowledge and action. It seems sensible that what a person knows influences how he or she acts; indeed this is a tenet of commonsense psychology and contemporary cognitive science as well. However, psychologists have at times been remarkably optimistic in their expectations for and research into this relationship. They often act as if they held an implicit theory that conceptual knowledge should be tightly tied to action or performance. My own experience of this is clearest with respect to the literature on metacognition, generally, and metamemory specifically.

In the 1970s developmental researchers became quite interested in studying metamemory, the child's knowledge of his or her own memory (see Flavell and Wellman, 1977). The construct of metamemory rests on the distinction between engaging in an activity (remembering) and knowing about that activity (metamemory). One of the initial appeals of the construct was that metamemory should be informative for our understanding of memory behavior, on the assumption that a rememberer's memory activities are caused in part by his or her ideas about memory—his or her construal of certain tasks and beliefs about what sorts of strategies and memory activities are appropriate and helpful. But disenchantment quickly set in (see Cavanaugh and Perlmutter, 1982). Empirically, specific metamemories as assessed in certain situations had little impact on their parallel memory activities. A typical study of this sort assessed metamemory and also children's parallel memory activities to see whether they were tightly related.

For example, children's belief as to whether organizing items together aided remembering was assessed, and then whether children organized to-be-remembered items together when faced with memory tasks was observed (Salatas and Flavell, 1976; Wimmer and Tornquist, 1980). Often there was little relation. Children who knew about organization were not especially likely to use it (Salatas and Flavell, 1976).

Studies such as these seem based on expectation of a tight link between discrete cognitions and overt activities. Construing everyday knowledge as entrenched in and framed by theories sets a different sort of expectation.

On analogy to science, it seems clear that theoretical knowledge does not directly dictate actions; at best it indirectly informs them. A scientific theory—for example, our best theoretical understanding of physics—dictates very little concrete activity, even in such obviously related endeavors as designing space rockets or bridges. Indeed, another whole discipline—engineering—is needed to build bridges and develop rockets. Our best physics informs, constrains, and inspires engineering practices, but engineering draws on other knowledge and lore as well. Similarly, consider the relation between astronomy and celestial navigation or that between economics and the activities of the Federal Reserve Board. Theory does not dictate practice.

> The theories of the physical sciences differ from those of the diagnostic and applied sciences much as maps differ from itineraries. . . . A map of South Lancashire does not specifically tell us how to get to Liverpool. To a man making a map, all routes are as good as each other. The users of the maps will not all be going the same way, so a satisfactory map is route-neutral: it represents the region mapped in a way which is indifferent as between starting-points, destinations, and the like. An itinerary, however, is specifically concerned with particular routes, starting-point and destinations, and the form it takes is correspondingly unlike that of a map. (Toulmin, 1967, p. 109)

These sorts of slippage between theories and practice are all the more noticeable when we consider framework theories. Framework theories do not even dictate the precise development of specific theories; at best they provide rough guidelines for such creative endeavors.

If naive knowledge inheres in theories, the relation of cognition to action parallels that between theory and practice. Metamemory frames understanding of memory activities and can even be used to derive some practical implications. But this is a far cry from the expectation of tight metamemory-memory links. In commonsense as well as science, the application of theory to practice is often not clear, competing strategies could all be supported by the same theory, and the derivation of a theory's more specific implications for action in any one situation is not determinate or inevitable.

This analysis does little to solve the issue of the relation of knowledge and action, but it helps by pointing away from simplistic expectations. No difficult questions are answered, but some progress is made in getting the questions right. Surely the sort of framework theory I have outlined has profound implications for how persons interact with other minds and use their own (see chapter 10). But those implications do not straightforwardly entail the causation of specified actions by specific concepts. Many concrete activities will be produced, therefore, more under the aegis of specific applications, such as specific mental models, practices, and rules of thumb than under theoretical entailments per se. Such applications are framed, but not dictated, by naive theories, especially naive framework theories.

Viable Research Program

An attractive research tradition solves some problems confronting prior traditions, provides a positive research heuristic, and engenders credible specific theories. Therefore, if a theory perspective is to be a viable research program, it must prove able to inspire and frame more specific theories, more detailed descriptions of phenomena within its domain that are verifiable and informative. More specifically, my version of a theory perspective should produce research that details some actual naive framework theory. Most of this book is an attempt to provide such a product, an attempt to sketch a single naive framework theory and its development: a theory of mind. Such an attempt, if productive, underwrites and advances the larger research tradition in the most concrete possible fashion. After concluding this chapter, therefore, I will return to the more specific task of articulating and researching developing theories of mind.

Conclusions

Consider the following collection of at times contradictory propositions about theories:

    1. "Not any collection of beliefs forms a theory. The unity of a theory, the way its terms rest semantically on one another and its assertions can be spread over a group of people, is something

that most sets of assertions cannot have. Number all the commonly held beliefs, and take the theory consisting of the prime numbered ones. There are no experts, no tests or techniques, no ways of generating it. It couldn't evolve as a unit or be criticized as one" (Morton, 1980, p. 6).

2. "Consider large-scale theories. . . . Typically such a theory consists of a set of sentences—usually general sentences or laws. These laws express the relations that hold between the various properties/values/classes/entities. Such properties and entities are expressed or denoted by the set of theoretical terms peculiar to the theory. . . . Theoretical terms do not, in general, get their meanings from single, explicit definitions. . . . They are implicitly defined by the network of principles that embed them" (Churchland, 1984, p. 50).

3. Theories are the products of theorizing; the paradigm case for a theory therefore is scientific theory, run and operated by scientists.

4. There are experts who formulate, articulate, and revise theories. But this simply allows a useful division of labor; no one has to understand the whole theory, and the theory may be invoked and utilized by many who understand only little of it (Putman, 1975).

5. Theories are held together by a captured ontology, a sense of what they refer to. "A research tradition, we have said, is a set of assumptions: assumptions about the basic kinds of entities in the world" (Laudan, 1977, p. 97).

6. Theories encompass causes and explanations for a targeted set of phenomena. "Explanation is at the core of theories. It is explanatory mechanisms that distinguish theories from other types of conceptual structures" (Carey, 1985a, p. 201).

7. "Science is the best way of running a theory; we build into it whatever we find to be good theory-managing technique. So any body of beliefs that is not part of science will be either a poor imitation of a scientific theory or something that is not a theory at all" (Morton, 1980, p. 9).

8. "A scientific theory TC is an axiomatized system where T are the theoretical postulates or basic laws of theory . . . and C are correspondence rules specifying the admissible applications of T to observable phenomena" (Suppe, 1974, p. 27).

9. Theories postulate covering laws; they explain individual phenomena by deducing them from such general laws. A theoretical explanation "has the form of an argument, an argument whose premises (the *explanans*) contain the explanatory information,

and whose conclusion (the *explanandum*) describes the fact to be explained. Most important, the premises include a *nomological statement*—a law of nature, a general statement expressing the patterns to which nature adheres" (Churchland, 1984, p. 57).
10. Theories, at least our best theories in the mature sciences, genuinely refer—their theoretical entities designate real events/ entities in the world, albeit nonobservable ones—are "approximately" true, and later theories are measurably closer to the truth than prior theories in the same discipline (see Boyd, 1981).
11. A theory is a proposal—a proposal about underlying realities hypothesized to undergird everyday appearances, a proposal about principled regularities hypothesized to organize chaotic-seeming events and instances.

By now, many of these enumerated positions should be clear. Propositions 1 and 2, for example, specify two different aspects of coherence as I have discussed it: that a theory is a peculiarly unified set of beliefs and that by virtue of this unity theoretical terms are defined by their position in a web of terms and constructs. Propositions 5 and 6 refer to ontology and to causal-explanatory framework, respectively. Propositions 3, 7, 8, 9, and 10 align theories, to varying degrees, with science and scientists. In contrast, propositions 4 and 11 make theories more universal in character and availability. From this contrasting perspective, science provides good case studies of theories and theoretical methods, but nonscientific theories also exist, run and operated by cultures of knowing and language communities other than groups of cooperating scientists.

Some of these proposals require brief elaboration. Proposal 8, for example, is one way of phrasing the "received view" about scientific theories in an earlier positivistic age. But this view of scientific theories now seems inadequate. The implied claims as to axiomatization, theory-observation distinctions, and correspondence rules embedded in this formulation are now generally agreed to be problematic (see Suppe, 1974). Proposal 9 is a softer version of a nomological-deductive view of scientific theories.

Proposal 10 involves claims about the inevitable realism and progressivism of theories. As noted in point 11, theories in science and everyday life often purport to be about real entities, about the underlying realities driving experienced phenomena. The task of both science and everyday understanding is to attempt to strip away the phenomenal veil, to portray a deeper, more substantial reality. Indeed, as Horton (1979) claims, both science and religion "attempt to explain and influence the workings of one's everyday world by discovering constant principles that underlie the apparent chaos and flux of sensory experience" (p. 355). The special thrust of proposal 10, however, and certain claims in philosophy of science, is that developed scientific theories not only aspire to such realism but can be said to attain it or at least to be progressing toward attaining realism in important, measurable fashions. This is a hotly contested issue in philosophy of science, even for our best theories (van Fraassen, 1980; Churchland and Hooker, 1985).

This list of various notions about theories helps place my present position among a range of possibilities. One could develop a position that attempts to deny theory status to any commonsense knowledge (by invoking criteria such as 3, 7, 8, or 10). It would, on the other hand, be possible to develop a position that attributes theory status to much of human knowledge (by invoking only propositions 6 or 11, for example). My position is to talk especially of framework theories, which essentially involve 2, 5, and 6—coherence, basic ontological prescriptions, and causal-explanatory dictates—and which by virtue of these essential features evidence 1, 4, and 11 but do not require scientific formulation or management and hence do not require 3, 7, 8, or 10. To be clear with regard to proposal 10, I do not claim any special sort of realism or progressivism for commonsense theories. Some theories cash out as realistic; others do not, regardless of their aims.

Morton's (1980) position—that the theory-theory is wrong, that our naive understanding of mind is not a theory—can also be more fully understood by placing it with respect to these several claims. In part, Morton's reservation is a process one—that theories depend in an essential manner on scientific theorizing. Morton's concerns, however, are deeper than I have yet portrayed them. "The two great points of contrast between schemes and theories are in how they change and how they refer to their subject matter" (p. 22). With respect to these issues Morton advocates a realistic, progressivistic stance. Theories "zero in on . . . truths"; they refer to real entities and they progress, by the coordination of theoretical hypotheses with observed facts, toward more and more veridical explanations captured in general laws. But this is not true of commonsense psychology. In that case, "particular explanations and attributions . . . don't seem to depend on our possession of completely general truths, or on our being able to refer to causes that are operating beyond the case at hand. This is an intuition that is hard to capture if we conceive of commonsense psychology as a theory. Then what realism demands is that there be determinate properties that the terms of the theory refer to, and that the assertions of the theory be true. . . . But . . . the situation for commonsense psychology . . . is different" (p. 25). "There is a real possibility" that "our commonsense intuitive conception of the mental [may be devoid of] general beliefs that are both literally true and describe the real causes of the events we use them to explain" (pp. 24–25). In short, commonsense psychology may rest on no covering laws (point 8 or 9, depending on one's meaning) and be neither realistic nor progressive (point 10).

In contrast, my position is that realism and progressivism are not critical for theories, whether or not they are characteristic of our best theories. Morton's concerns may make commonsense psychology a static, failed theory worthy of rejection (see also Churchland, 1981; Stitch, 1983), but it can make commonsense psychology not a theory at all only if one requires realism and progressivism as essential in theories. If that is the requirement, however, then only a few (and perhaps no) scientific theories are theories either.

One issue of special import with regard to commonsense belief-desire psychology (and with respect to scientific cognitive psychology) concerns a general nomological-deductive view of science and theories as articulated in proposal 9. It is possible to argue that commonsense psychology lacks general covering laws or even that such laws are impossible within that explanatory framework (Davidson, 1974; MacNamara, Govitrikar, and Doan, 1988). To some this means that such a psychology fails to be a theory or at least fails to be a science. However, the general nomological-deductive perspective on explanation has been increasingly challenged (see Cartwright, 1983; Salmon, 1984), and it is possible to argue cogently that neither theories nor science require general laws of this sort (MacNamara, et al., 1988). I take no position on this controversy other than that psychological explanation of the belief-desire sort is sufficiently definite and defendable to qualify as a theory of the framework theory type (see also Fodor, 1987).

Articulating and evaluating what theories are is a crucial and difficult task for forging a theory perspective on conceptual knowledge. It is crucial because the whole viewpoint depends on our sense of what theories are and how they work. It is difficult because, as some of these conflicting proposals indicate, the notion of theory itself is imprecise and underdeveloped. There is disagreement even as to what scientific theories are, and they form the root of the analogy. This difficulty is indicative of the depth and importance of the issues, not necessarily indicative of problems with the construct. Indeed, if commonsense theories are fundamental to cognition, then their analysis requires addressing some of the deepest issues in our understanding of human knowledge. I do not claim to have resolved these deep issues but to have staked out a reasonably clear position that inspires and warrants the research in this book and that may help advance the theory perspective in general.

Chapter 6

Young Children's Belief-Desire Psychology

My aim in this chapter is to document young children's earliest belief-desire psychology, both its existence and scope. I propose that the scheme in figure 4.1 and its elaborated description in chapter 4 outlines this childhood commonsense psychology. Figure 4.1 and its description are at best a rough outline—cryptic, abbreviated, and inadequate in several ways. The research that follows is not designed to validate that scheme as a precise description of children's belief-desire reasoning. Instead I wish to ask, Suppose that children's belief-desire psychology has something like the features and organization outlined in figure 4.1, then what sorts of reasoning about action should result, and do young children evidence those sorts?

The scheme outlined in figure 4.1 implies several related competences. First, someone whose theory is characterized by something like that scheme should be able to predict actions given relevant information as to an actor's beliefs and desires. Data with respect to younger children's predictions of these sorts were presented in chapter 3. Second, someone with a belief-desire psychology of the sort depicted in the figure should be able not only to make forward inferences, predicting actions from beliefs and desires, but also appropriate backward inferences, explaining actors' observed actions by appeal to their beliefs and desires. When asked, for example, "Why is Jane looking for her kitty under the piano?" their explanation should mention some relevant desire (she wants her kitty) or a relevant belief (she thought it was there) or both. An investigation into children's explanations of this sort will be presented in this chapter. Third, not only does the scheme in figure 4.1 imply abilities to make forward and backward inferences about actions, beliefs, and desires but also abilities to infer characters' emotional reactions to the outcomes of their actions. Two studies of children's understanding of two quite different reactions, happiness and surprise, will be reported here. Finally, if the scheme in figure 4.1 is any guide, then young children ought to be able to infer a character's beliefs from information as to that character's perception and infer desires from information as to physiological states. Children's performance on the inferred belief conditions in the studies in chapter 3 provides some of this information, and I will discuss those findings and some other data as well, in this chapter.

A Study of Children's Explanation of Actions

In the studies reviewed in chapter 3 Karen Bartsch and I investigated young children's ability to predict an actor's actions when given information about that actor's beliefs and desires. In the research presented here (Bartsch and Wellman, 1989), we examined young children's ability and inclination to reason backward from actions to beliefs and desires. Backward reasoning involves explaining a character's action by appealing to beliefs and desires. This sort of explanatory appeal to beliefs and desires is evident in the following examples:

(1) Why did Bill go to the barber shop? He wanted a "new look" and thought a haircut would achieve it.

(2) Why did Sue buy a yellow sweater? She likes sweaters, wanted to get a new one, and thought that the yellow one looked best.

(3) Why did John go to the candy machine? He was hungry and wanted a candy bar, and he thought he'd seen the kind he liked in the candy machine.

As outlined in figure 4.1, these examples illustrate how everyday explanations of human action are organized by the constructs of desire ("wanted") and belief ("thought") and, further, recruit a network of related constructs, including physiological states ("hungry"), and perceptions ("seen," "looked"). Beliefs and desires can be described as mental states; other constructs such as physiological states cannot, although they are used in the same system of reasoning.

We were interested in such explanations for several reasons. If children understand human action in terms of something like the reasoning scheme in figure 4.1, then they should be able to reason from it in more than one way—for example, to generate explanations as well as predictions. Moreover, explanations could be especially revealing. Examination of children's explanations for action could provide information as to whether children spontaneously utilize belief-desire reasoning when asked open-ended "why" questions, in addition to being able to derive correct inferences when supplied with explicit premise information about an actor's beliefs and desires, and reveal whether children's larger reasoning scheme includes constructs beyond beliefs and desires, psychological constructs of the sort included in figure 4.1 or even figures 4.2 and 4.3 (such as traits).

Examining children's explanations of actions could help confirm that young children's reasoning includes an understanding of belief as well as desire. Belief-desire reasoning depends on a crucial distinction between beliefs as mental states of conviction and desires as mental states of disposition. An important part of my claim is that children as young as 3 years understand and use a construct of belief. Conceivably, however, very young children might construe action only with respect to desires. Consider the standard belief tasks of chapter 3 again. In such tasks, a desire encompassing both locations was described (wanting a dog that might be in either the garage or the porch). The belief was more specific (thinking the dog is in the garage). Since three-year-olds were largely correct (77%) in predicting that the character would look in the single belief-specified location, we concluded that they understood that beliefs are distinct from desires in that beliefs provided essential information not provided by desires alone.

It is possible, however, that young children solved such tasks by understanding only desires and preferences, not beliefs. That is, in the standard belief task, perhaps the belief information ("Sam thinks the puppy is under the porch") was misinterpreted as indicating a disposition rather than a conviction (as something like, "Sam wants to look under the porch"). Even on discrepant belief tasks, children may have attributed to the character a preference for the location he is said to have the belief about. For example, perhaps when children heard, "Fred thinks there are only magic markers in the desk, and not on the shelf," they interpreted that statement to mean something like "Fred likes the desk and not the shelf," and so predicted accordingly and correctly. Although children's differential performances on relevant versus irrelevant belief tasks (see chapter 3) argue against such a possibility, still it would be comforting to have convergent evidence from another sort of task.

Examining children's explanations provides such a task. If three-year-olds construe action only with respect to desires, then their explanations of action should reflect this limitation. Such children would not be expected to explain a character's action by invoking the beliefs or knowledge of the character, they would invoke only desires. Whereas in the prediction tasks of chapter 3, children might misinterpret the provided belief information as desire-information, in explanation tasks they are free to recruit whatever antecedents they choose. In this case, if young children construe actions simply in terms of desires and preferences, then it seems unlikely they would ever use belief terms to explain action. Or if they used such terms, they would misuse them. We were interested, therefore, in whether young children would spontaneously invoke beliefs as explanations for actions and in the degree to which their belief explanations would be convincing and appropriate.

Method

Children were presented with simple descriptions of a character engaging in a specific action and then were asked to explain the character's action. Three different kinds of actions were described in order to provoke a variety of explanations. Neutral descriptions specified a single simple action—for example, "Jane is looking for her kitten under the piano. Why do you think Jane is doing that?" The two other sorts of descriptions depicted characters acting contrary to their apparent desires. In anomalous belief descriptions, the contradiction was generated by providing further information about the action situation—for example, "Jane is looking for her kitten. The kitten is hiding under a chair, but Jane is looking for her kitten under the piano. Why do you think Jane is doing that?" In anomalous desire descriptions, the contradiction depended on further information relevant to the character's desires—for example, "Jane hates frogs, but Jane is looking for a frog under the piano. Why do you think Jane is doing that?"

Children's appeals to both beliefs and desires as explanations were of interest, as was their use of other psychological constructs. When subjects mentioned perceptions, physiological states, emotions, preferences, or general traits, these were treated as appeals to the larger reasoning scheme but not to beliefs and desires specifically. Figure 4.1 indicates why and how perceptions, physiological states, and emotions differ from beliefs and desires. Our reason for keeping preferences and traits separate from desires and beliefs was methodological more than substantive; we wished to be cautious in attributing understanding of beliefs and desires to young children. Preferences ("she likes apples") are forms of desires ("she wants to eat an apple"). But in young children's utterances, most statements about preferences use the term *likes,* and statements using *likes* could not clearly be distinguished from statements of basic emotions (she loves apples). To be conservative we resolved this ambiguity in this study by treating preferences as being more similar to basic emotions than to desires. Traits, of course, can be derived from desires ("she's greedy") or from qualities of mind ("she's smart"), including beliefs ("he's wrong-headed"). Again, to be conservative we did not count such trait explanations as belief or desire explanations more narrowly. Trait explanations do not refer to beliefs and desires narrowly because they do not designate both a mental attitude and a relevant proposition (contrast "she's greedy" to "she wants to eat an apple").

There were 60 participants: 23 three-year-olds (M = 3–6, range 2–11 to 4–0), 22 four-year-olds (M = 4–4, range 4–3 to 4–11) and 15 adults (M = 31 years, range 21–59 years, 6 men and 9 women). Each person was presented nine short action descriptions—three each of the neutral, anomalous desire, and anomalous belief varieties. In addition to the examples given, other neutral actions were: "Joe is putting candy in his mouth" and "Mary is buying an ice cream at the grocery store." The other anomalous desire actions were: "Beth hates apples, but she's taking a bite of this apple," and "Jeff hates snakes, but he's trying to catch a snake." The other anomalous belief actions were: "This is a rock that looks like a peanut, but Sam is putting it in his mouth," and "The drugstore does not sell balloons, but Andrew is going to the drugstore to buy balloons." All nine explanation items were presented in a single session, in one of two random orders. Each story was accompanied by a drawing of the story character performing the action but in such a way that the target item was not depicted.

Each action description was followed immediately by the explanation question: "Why do you think [Jane] is doing that?" When a subject's initial response did not refer specifically to a desire or belief of the character, the adult prompted the subject by asking either a desire prompt, "What does [Jane] want?" or a belief prompt, "What does [Jane] think?" If prompts were needed, desire prompts were given on the anomalous desire stories and on one of the neutral stories; belief prompts were given on the anomalous belief stories and on two of the neutral stories.

Coding

Children and adults gave a variety of explanations. Each person's response to a single action was coded twice—first, to characterize an unprompted explanation (what was said before any belief or desire prompt) and second, to characterize a complete explanation (the subject's comprehensive explanation, taking into account what was said both before and after the belief or desire prompt). Examining prompted as well as unprompted explanations was important because everyday explanations are typically incomplete. An appropriate explanation need not mention both the belief and desire.

Prompting can reveal whether subjects nevertheless appreciate the nonmentioned explanatory construct.

Each response was first coded as being one of three general types: (1) an explanation referring to psychological causes, including the protagonist's desires, beliefs, or other psychological constructs of the sort discussed in chapter 4 (perceptions, physiological states, preferences), (2) an explanation referring to nonpsychological causes like external states of affairs, physical causes, or explanations that may have been but were not clearly psychological ("because the kitten is lost"), or (3) a failure to generate an explanation at all ("I don't know"). If a response included any reference to psychological states, it was coded as a psychological response even if it appeared in conjunction with a nonpsychological explanation ("The kitten is under there, and Jane knows it's there").

Explanations falling into the first general category, psychological explanations, were further categorized into beliefs and desires narrowly construed and other psychological constructs, including physiological states ("She's hungry"), perceptions ("He saw balloons there once" or "To see if the frog's under there"), emotions ("He's sad), mind changing ("She changed her mind about apples"), oughts ("She has to try a bite each time"), pretense ("He's just pretending to eat it"), preferences ("She likes apples"), and traits ("He's mean"). If an explanation involved a belief or desire, it was coded as a belief-desire explanation, even if another psychological state (a preference) was also mentioned ("She likes apples and wants to eat one").

Within the category of belief and desire explanations, a desire response was one in which the desire was mentioned either explicitly or implicitly. Explicit desire explanations in principle could include use of several relevant desire verbs such as *want, desire,* and *hope* ("She hoped to find her kitten"). In fact, however, all the desire explanations involved *want,* except for one use of *hope* by an adult. Implicit desire responses (sensible references to desires but without mention of a desire verb) were coded as such only if provided after a desire prompt (in response to the prompt "What does Jane want?" the answer "to find her kitten").

A belief response was one that referred to the protagonist's belief, either explicitly or implicitly. Explicit responses, in principle, could include any belief verb, such as *think, know,* and *guess* ("She thought it was under the piano"). In the data, 87% of belief responses used the word *think.* All the remaining belief responses involved the word *know,* with the exception of one use of *expect* and one use of *believe* from adults. Implicit responses were coded as such only after a belief prompt (in response to the prompt "What does Jane think?" the answer "that the kitten is under the piano").

Explanations appealing to beliefs or desires varied in sensibility and relevance. For example, "because she thinks it's a record player" was offered as a belief explanation for why Jane was searching under the piano for her kitten, but it was not a relevant or sensible explanation. Belief and desire explanations, therefore, were also coded as to whether they were relevant or irrelevant.

Reliability between two independent coders, as assessed on a subset of one-quarter of the data, was .85. Disagreements were resolved by using the more conservative rating.

Results

Children's unprompted explanations and their complete explanations provided complementary evidence regarding their understanding of actions. Figure 6.1 presents an overview of both sorts of data. As would be expected, because they included responses to the belief or desire prompts, complete explanations were more likely than unprompted explanations to refer to psychological causes generally and to beliefs and desires specifically. Note the similarity between adults and children in the levels and patterns of their explanations. A substantial majority of the unprompted explanations of three-year-olds, four-year-olds and adults referred to the sorts of psychological states shown in figure 4.1. And a large proportion of these specifically recruited beliefs and desires. For three-year-olds, 60% of their psychological explanations specifically mentioned beliefs and desires; for four-year-olds the figure was 69%, and for adults 67%. The same sort of similarity between children and adults is evident with respect to complete explanations. I will briefly summarize the results for the unprompted explanations, complete explanations, and explanations specifically invoking beliefs.

Unprompted Explanations
Although subjects usually attempted to give an unprompted explanation for the actions of story protagonists (79% of the time), they did not always do so. Failures to attempt an explanation were classified in a separate category, as explained. Unprompted explanations were generated 70% of the time by three-year-olds, 75% of the time by four-year-olds, and 96% of the time by adults. All subjects generated unprompted explanations to some stories, and even three-year-olds did so 70% of the time. Therefore, the results in figure 6.1 and in the

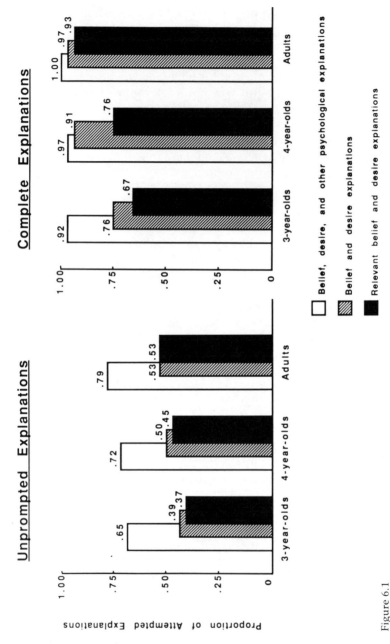

Figure 6.1
Types of unprompted and complete explanations given by children and adults in the study of explanations of action. Data reported are proportions of attempted explanations. From Bartsch and Wellman (1989).

following analyses consider the various types of explanations as proportions of the attempted explanations.

As is clear in figure 6.1, unprompted explanations of both children and adults referred mostly to psychological causes, and most of these involved specific mention of beliefs and desires.[1] Because these explanations were made before a prompt was given, they involved explicit mention of a desire term (essentially *want*) or belief terms (essentially *think* or *know*).

For each unprompted belief or desire explanation given, we assessed whether the explanation was relevant or irrelevant to the story facts. Very few belief or desire responses were irrelevant—only 2%, 5%, and 0% of all the attempted explanations for three-year-olds, four-year-olds, and adults, respectively.

With regard to constructs other than belief or desire within the larger framework of psychological reasoning, 17% of all unprompted explanations were attributions to preferences ("She likes kittens"); references to traits, perceptions, physiology, and so forth comprised less than 10% of the attempted explanations. Age differences were apparent only for traits. Only 1 of 45 children (a three-year-old) ever mentioned traits, whereas 8 of 15 adults did so, χ^2 (1) = 19.22, $p < .01$.

Complete Explanations
In coding complete explanations, we took into account what was said both before and after any prompt. Very few subjects of any age failed to give some sort of explanation in this case; some sensible explanation was generated 93% of the time by three-year-olds, 97% of the time by four-year-olds, and 99% of the time by adults. Therefore, again, the data in figure 6.1 and the following analyses considered explanation types as a proportion of attempted explanations.

Figure 6.1 depicts the mean proportions of the three nested explanation types (psychological state, belief-desire, and relevant belief-desire) for complete explanations. Children and adults generated almost solely psychological state explanations (95%), and there were no differences among age groups. For explanations specifically referring to beliefs or desires, there were age differences, but even three-year-olds provided such explanations three-fourths of the time; the proportions were 76%, 91%, and 97%, for three-year-olds, four-year-olds, and adults, respectively. Again, most of subjects' complete belief-desire explanations were relevant. Conceivably, prompting might have provoked irrelevant or nonsensical belief-desire explanations, at least from young children, but irrelevant explanations comprised only 9%, 15%, and 4% of all attempted explanations for three-year-olds, four-year-olds, and adults, respectively.

Belief Explanations
These analyses suggest that although children differed somewhat from adults in their explanations, they relied chiefly on a belief-desire reasoning scheme, and they did so almost exclusively when complete explanations are considered. How often did these explanations specifically invoke beliefs rather than desires? This question is especially relevant to the claim that young children's participation in belief-desire psychology involves more than an understanding of desires alone. Two aspects of these data are of special interest: children's spontaneous use of belief terms in their explanations, best seen in analyses of their unprompted explanations, and the appropriateness of children's belief explanations, best considered in detailed analyses of subjects' complete explanations.

Unprompted Belief Explanations.   On average, unprompted explanations appealed more to desire (32%) than to beliefs (20%). For example, desire explanations comprised 28% of attempted explanations for three-year-olds, whereas belief explanations comprised 10%. This comparison assesses the prevalence of belief versus desire explanations, but it does not reveal the extent to which individual subjects used belief at all. Twelve of 23 three-year olds (52%), 14 of 22 four-year-olds (64%), and 14 of 15 adults (93%) gave unprompted belief explanations at least once. Because these explanations occurred before any prompts, they required explicit use of a relevant belief term—either *know* or *think*—to be categorized as a belief explanation.

Complete Belief Explanations.   Even subjects who did not spontaneously mention belief in unprompted explanations often gave specific references to beliefs following our mild prompt. Seventeen of 23 three-year-olds (74%) gave at least one belief explanation in their complete explanations, compared to 20 of 22 four-year-olds (91%) and all 15 adults. Most belief explanations appeared on the anomalous belief items, and this was true for each age group. Anomalous belief items provoked belief explanations 72% of the time, with the next largest proportion overall appearing on the neutral items (38%). Because belief attributions occurred most frequently on the anomalous belief items and because these items allowed us to assess the appropriateness of belief explanations quite precisely, I will focus primarily on subjects' complete explanations of those three items.

For anomalous belief items, 53%, 83%, and 86% of all complete explanations for three-year-olds, four-year-olds, and adults, respectively, involved belief explanations. A large proportion of subjects in all age groups responded to the three anomalous belief items with belief explanations at least once. Subjects who gave a belief explanation of these items included 74% of the three-year-olds (17 of 23), 91% of the four-year-olds, and 100% of the adults. All of these subjects provided at least one relevant belief explanation, except for one subject among the four-year-olds.

In addition to being judged as relevant or not, each explanation for the anomalous belief item was evaluated as to whether it resolved the anomaly. For the anomalous belief items, an answer that resolved the anomaly was one that attributed either a false belief or ignorance to the protagonist. For example, for the item about Jane searching for her kitten under the piano when the kitten was really under the chair, explanations such as "She thinks the kitten's under the piano" or "She doesn't know the kitten's under the chair" resolved the anomaly. Such answers could be given spontaneously; for example, one three-year-old said, "cause she thinks the cat is under the piano," when asked why Jane was doing that. Anomaly-resolving answers could also be given in response to the prompt. For example, another child, in response to the question of what Jane thought, said "that the kitty is under there." These sorts of sensible responses indicated an understanding of belief as different from desire. Such responses cannot stem from a dispositional misuse of belief terms because the child cites a belief that is a sensible explanation for why the character is looking where his or her desire will not be satisfied. This is an important way in which conviction differs from disposition; mistaken convictions, or ignorance, lead one to do things that thwart rather than satisfy one's desires. On anomalous belief items, 47%, 70%, and 87% of the explanations for three-year-olds, four-year-olds, and adults, respectively, resolved the anomaly by appealing to either ignorance or false belief. Further, 70% of three-year-olds, 86% of four-year-olds, and 100% of adults gave at least one such anomaly-resolving belief explanation.

These results concerning anomaly-resolving explanations focus on appropriate use of either ignorance or false-belief explanations. What of false belief specifically? Sixty-five percent of three-year-olds, 82% of the four-year-olds, and 100% of the adults gave at least one false-belief explanation. False-belief explanations attributed a positive belief (thinks, thought, knew) rather than ignorance (didn't know) to the character ("she thinks the cat's under the piano"). Fifteen (of 23) three-year-olds generated 25 false-belief explanations.

We attempted to follow a subject's mention of a false belief ("She thinks it's under the piano") with a control question ("Where is the kitten really?") to determine whether false-belief explanations included an understanding of the true situation (whether the subject knew where the kitten was). In this way, we could be certain that apparent reference to a false belief did not simply reflect a misunderstanding of the story. All such control questions were answered correctly. Moreover, for all subjects who ever attributed false belief, there was at least one instance of their doing so in conjunction with correctly answering the control question, demonstrating that they knew the true facts of the story and had not simply misinterpreted the information.

Discussion

Generally there was notable similarity in responses across all the ages tested; three-year-olds and adults provided comparable explanations for the actions presented to them. There were also some substantial changes with age in subjects' responding.

A central finding was that three-year-olds did not differ from adults in terms of their use of a psychological belief-desire framework, broadly defined. That is, to the extent that they gave any explanations of the action at all, three-year-olds explained actions by referring to beliefs, desires, preferences, perceptions, and so forth as frequently as did adults, in both their unprompted and their complete explanations. This is evidence that quite young children share with adults at least the rudiments of a common belief-desire psychology, something akin to that outlined in figure 4.1. It might seem that we were quite lenient in counting appeals to belief, preferences, emotions, and so on as all falling under a psychological belief-desire framework, but we made this designation a priori based on the analysis in chapter 4, and, in addition, subjects were quite free to refer to behavioristic causes (a history of conditioning), physical causes (the wind blew him there), physical situations (the kitten is gone), or biological causes (reflexes or muscle tremors). Adults did not recruit such explanations with any frequency; neither did children. That is our point: quite young children share with adults a familiar psychological construal of human action.

With regard to children's invocation of beliefs or desires specifically (not including preferences, perceptions, and so forth), three-year-olds did not differ from adults in their unprompted explanations. And belief-desire explanations were by far the commonest explanation for action across all the ages studied here, in both unprompted and complete explanations. Adults did give proportionately more belief-desire explanations in their complete answers than did children; nevertheless, belief or desire explanations comprised 76% of even the three-year-olds' attempted complete explanations, and 67% were relevant to the action being explained. Thus, three-year-olds relied primarily on beliefs or desires in their attempted explanations and did so in a generally sensible fashion, as did adults. Belief-desire explanation appears to be well within the capabilities of even these young children; indeed it is their predominant mode of explanation for simple actions.

Did three-year-olds' explanations of action refer only to desires and never to beliefs? This is what one would expect if indeed three-year-olds understand desires or dispositions but fail to appreciate the role of beliefs. More than half of the three-year-olds spontaneously mentioned belief terms in their unprompted explanations. It is difficult to see why a child who construes action solely with respect to desire would spontaneously recruit belief terms in explanations when straightforward desire terms (such as *want*) were available. Clearly, such desire terms were available to these three-year-olds; all but two used the term *want* explicitly and sensibly at some time or other in relevant desire explanations.

More important, children not only used belief terms spontaneously but used such terms appropriately to refer to characters' convictions as distinct from their desires. This is best seen in children's provision of anomaly-resolving belief explanations to the anomalous belief items. While the proportion of belief attributions increased with age, fully 70% of the three-year-olds gave at least one belief explanation that was judged to be relevant and that also resolved the anomaly for the anomalous belief items by citing the character's ignorance or mistaken beliefs.

For adults, it is so natural and automatic to explain an action by attributing it to the actor's belief that such reasoning can seem inevitable or even trivial. This raises the suspicion that three-year-olds could not do otherwise. In fact, one colleague who saw our results suggested that belief explanations are simply "logically entailed" by, or are mere repetitions of, the information directly given in the story. This argument rests on the assumption that an action statement like "Jane is looking for her kitten under the piano" actually includes or logically implies the assertion that "Jane thinks her kitten is under the piano." But the latter statement does not follow from the former simply on the basis of formal logic or indeed in any content-free manner. The only way that statement can be derived from the first is if the child assumes that beliefs and actions are linked in a causal framework. That is, only a content-rich scheme such as that shown in figure 4.1 would support the appropriate derivation. This is our primary contention. Children are making an inference but one that is based on an understanding of beliefs (and desires), not just on some content-independent logic.

Similarly, to argue that three-year-olds are doing nothing more than merely repeating in other words what they were told in the story is misleading. It suggests, for example, that children have no other choice but to appeal to beliefs. Yet they do have other sensible options. They might, for example, say that Jane looks for her kitten under the piano because she found her kitten there yesterday and the day before that (a behaviorist answer). Or they might simply answer that Jane wants her kitten, never appealing to her beliefs. Even when prompted with, for example, "What does Jane think?" a correct answer that resolves the anomaly on anomalous belief items (that "her kitten is under the piano") is not mere repetition of the story information. If children were merely repeating what they heard, then they should be equally likely to select another phrase available in the initial story, such as "the kitten is really under the chair" or "she is looking for her kitten." Although the term *think* is mentioned in the prompt question, a response such as "that the kitten is under the piano" reveals an understanding of belief in that it reflects neither the reality of the kitten's location as mentioned in the story nor the place where the actor's desire would actually be satisfied. Moreover, the range of other responses that a child could give to such a question is extensive. For example, children could have responded to a "think" prompt with answers such as "she thinks she wants her kitten," using the term *think* in an empty fashion, only to state the character's desire. Indeed, children occasionally produced this sort of response; however, such answers were coded as desire responses, not belief ones. The "think" prompt, therefore, is clearly an open-ended question that can be answered in a variety of ways by a young child. Only an understanding of beliefs, as distinct from overt actions and reality, would result in the consistently appropriate and specific responses that we observed.

In addition to commonalities across age groups, we found several differences between the ages studied, especially between the children and the adults. Although both children and adults attempted an explanation for nearly every story eventually, children attempted fewer explanations before any prompt was given. With respect to belief explanations particularly, age differences were apparent. While most three-year-olds explained action by belief at some point, the prevalence of such explanations increased with age. On anomalous belief items, those action descriptions most designed to provoke belief explanations, 53% of three-year-olds' explanations referred to belief, whereas the comparable figure for adults was 86%.

In the light of the great commonalities across age, these age differences seem to reflect mainly gains in fluency and explicitness within an enduring basic reasoning system rather than evidencing a fundamental change from one reasoning system to another. Adults were less often at a loss for an explanation and more often referred to beliefs without any prompting. Even so, adults' and three-year-olds' explanations seemed of a common sort, stemming from the same larger system of psychological reasoning. Belief-desire reasoning is a core feature of that larger system, and even three-year-olds reasoned by belief as well as desire at times. This commonality in psychological explanation is evident in the quantitative aspects of the data and is also strikingly apparent if one simply hears young children's explanations. To illustrate, table 6.1 presents a random assortment of three-year-olds' relevant belief and desire explanations for actions from the current study. These explanations seem to be straightforward attempts to engage in belief-desire reasoning as we all know and use it.

Table 6.1
Randomly Selected Relevant Belief and Desire Explanations from Three-Year-Olds

"He wants candy."
"Because he wants a balloon." (What does Andrew think?) "He thinks he wants a balloon."
"Because she wants it."
(. . . putting a rock that looks like a peanut in his mouth . . . why . . . ?) "Because it looks like a peanut." (What does Sam think?) "It really is a peanut."
"Because he wants to eat it."
"Because he thinks there are balloons there, because he wants a balloon to hold."
"She wants to."
(. . . looking for kitten under chair . . . why . . . ?) "Because she thought there was one under there."
(. . . looking for frog under piano . . . why . . . ?) "Because she thought one was under there."
"Because she wants to put the frog in a cage."
(. . . going to store for ice cream . . . why . . . ?) "Because she's hungry." (What does Mary think?) "They sell ice cream at the drugstore."

One exception to the basic commonality between adults and young children's explanations concerns the use of trait explanations. Adults at times referred to explanatory character traits; children essentially never did. I will discuss this development more fully in chapter 11.

Our findings demonstrate that three-year-old children not only engage in belief-desire reasoning but that they may have some appreciation of the existence and implications of false beliefs. This depiction of substantial numbers of three-year-olds as at times understanding false belief is, at first glance, at odds with other research. Specifically, three-year-olds consistently fail even extremely simple versions of false belief prediction tasks, such as the explicit false belief task used in chapter 3. The data from the current experiment suggest that three-year-olds may not be as confused about false beliefs as prior findings suggest. In chapter 9 I will discuss three-year-olds' understanding of false belief in detail. In that discussion, and as first outlined in chapter 3, I will maintain that three-year-olds have a significant difficulty with false belief while at the same time evidencing a genuine understanding of belief. I save that discussion for chapter 9; my point here is simply that three-year-olds' explanations clearly evidence their appeal to both beliefs and desires. Hence their explanations of actions show the presence of a naive belief-desire psychology of the sort outlined in figure 4.1, just as did their predictions of action in studies in chapter 3.

First Study of Children's Understanding of Emotional Reactions

What do young children know, if anything, about the sorts of emotional reactions that result from belief-desire-caused actions? The sort of belief-desire psychology encompassed by figure 4.1 includes two primary and different sorts of emotional reactions: generically happiness reactions versus surprise reactions. Roughly, if you want something and get it, you are happy; whereas if you want it and fail to get it, you are unhappy. Similarly, if you believe something will happen and it does not, you are surprised; if you believe something will happen and it does, then you are not surprised. Children's understanding of these two sorts of reactions would show their understanding of several aspects of belief-desire reasoning. First and foremost, it would demonstrate their ability to predict appropriate emotional reactions as dictated by the theory. Beyond that, however, appropriate understanding of these sorts of reactions further confirms an understanding of the two basic constructs of belief-desire reasoning: belief and desires.

Belief-desire reasoning distinguishes among three independent factors: beliefs, desires, and external reality. One can believe something to be true or believe that something will occur, but that something can instead be false or fail to occur. Similarly, one can want something to happen (or hope or fear it will happen) but that something does not happen. Finally, beliefs and desires are not only independent from reality; they are also distinct from each other. To believe that something will happen is vastly different from desiring that it will happen, as in the belief that death is inevitable. These different sorts of independencies among beliefs, desires, and reality are indexed, according to the analysis in chapter 4, by actors' different reactions to the outcomes of their acts. Happiness-unhappiness reactions reflect the independence of desires from reality. Surprise-nonsurprise reactions reflect the independence of belief from reality. And the differential reactions of happiness versus surprise serve to distinguish beliefs from desires. If young children engage in belief-desire reasoning, they should be able to judge desire-outcome and belief-outcome scenarios appropriately with respect to these reactions. In a first study Karen Bartsch and I tested whether four-year-olds could do this (Wellman and Bartsch, 1988).

Method

Sixteen four-year-olds (4–2 to 5–0, $M = 4$–8) participated (11 boys and 5 girls). Each was presented two sorts of simple stories. In want stories, a protagonist either wanted or did not want something; in think stories, a protagonist thought or did not think he or she would get something. In each story, the protagonist either got or did not get that thing. As a result, there were eight types of stories: +want+get, +want−get, −want+get, −want−get, as well as +think+get, +think−get, −think+get, and −think−get. An example +want+get story was: "Here's Mary. Mary drinks juice at snack time. Today she wants to have orange juice because she didn't get orange juice for breakfast. Look; Mary gets orange juice for snack." For each story, the child was asked to rate the happiness and also the surprise of the protagonist.

Want stories presented six simple desires: wants orange juice, wants to go to the park, wants a puppy, wants it to rain, wants blue gum, wants Dad to read a dinosaur book. Think stories presented beliefs in the form of simple expectations about the future, for example, thinking (believing) that some unidentified juice is orange juice or thinking that an unidentified pet is a puppy. There were six beliefs, each corresponding in content to the six desires listed.

To complement the example want story, an example think story ($-$think$+$get) is as follows, along with an outline of the procedures for story presentation. The child was shown a drawing of a story character's face. "This is Lisa. Lisa thinks it won't rain today. She likes it when it rains, and she likes it when it doesn't rain, but she thinks it won't rain today." At this point, to be sure that the child understood the essential story information, he or she was asked, "So, what does Lisa think?" On rare occasions, children answered this question incorrectly, in which case the story was repeated. Then the child was told, "That's right; Lisa thinks it won't rain today." The drawing of the character's face was turned over and a picture of the outcome was presented: "Look; it rains."

Each child heard the eight story types—twice. They heard the stories once in a session where they rated whether the protagonists felt happy on a three-part scale (happy, just OK, sad), and once in a different session where they rated whether the protagonists felt surprised on a two-part scale (surprised or neutral). Children rated each story and on every other story were asked to explain their rating, for example, "Why does Lisa feel like that?" Each session began with a warm-up task designed to familiarize children with the scale being used.

Each of the eight story types came in several versions, with different protagonists and different target objects, and these features were extensively counterbalanced, as was whether children rated the stories for happiness or for surprise in their first or second session.

Results

According to the analysis of belief-desire reasoning outlined in chapter 4 and in figure 4.1, happiness is especially linked with desire, and surprise is especially linked with belief. The predicted ideal responses are thus those presented at the left of figure 6.2. Do children conform to these ideals, evidencing the ideal happiness pattern more for want stories (where it is especially appropriate) than for think stories and evidencing the ideal surprise pattern more for think stories than for want stories? Yes, as the observed findings shown in figure 6.2 indicate. The ideal happiness pattern was much more apparent for want stories than for think stories, and the ideal surprise pattern was more apparent for think than for want stories. Such data suggest that children understand belief-desire specificity.

To elaborated briefly, we termed the $+$want$+$get and $-$want$-$get stories the concordant want stories (because of the concordance between desires and outcomes) and the $+$want$-$get and $-$want$+$get

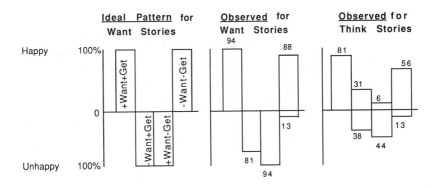

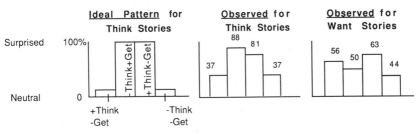

Figure 6.2
Ideal and observed responses for happiness and surprise ratings in the first study of children's understanding of emotional reactions. For happiness ratings a three-place scale was used (happy, neutral, unhappy). Data depicted are the percentages of happy or unhappy choices. Neutral choices are not directly depicted but constitute the remainder. For this reason the percentages depicted are typically less than 100; total percentages can reach as high as 101 because of rounding errors. For surprise ratings only two choices were given (surprise, neutral); the data depicted are the percentage of surprise choices; neutral choices constitute the remainder. From Wellman and Bartsch (1988).

stories the discordant stories. The predictions require that there be significant differences on happiness ratings for concordant versus discordant want stories and significant differences on surprise for concordant versus discordant think stories. As figure 6.2 shows, that is what occurs. Children say the character will be happy on concordant want stories and unhappy on discordant ones; children say the character will be surprised on discordant think stories and essentially not surprised on concordant ones. In addition, if subjects understand belief-desire reasoning, then they should evidence greater discrepancy in their happiness scores for concordant versus discordant want stories than they evidence for concordant versus discordant think stories. As the top line of figure 6.2 shows, this was so (the ideal happiness pattern was more apparent for want than for think stories: t (15) = 4.31, $p <$ .001 one-tailed). Similarly there should be, and was, a greater discrepancy in surprise ratings for concordant versus discordant think stories than for want stories (the ideal surprise pattern was more apparent for think than for want stories: t (15) = 1.68, $p =$ .058, one-tailed).

For each child, six stories in a session had unique protagonists and topics (Joe wants blue gum; Lisa thinks it will rain). Two protagonist-topic pairs were repeated in each session in two different stories (Lisa thinks it will rain and it does, and Lisa thinks it won't rain and it does). This arrangement allowed us to compare children's ratings of the same protagonist experiencing the exact same outcome but when having quite different desires (or beliefs). Eight children received same-protagonist, same-outcome, different-desire pairs; seven of the eight children appropriately rated these different-desire pairs as different in happiness (with one tie). Eight children received same-protagonist, same-outcome, different-belief pairs; six of the eight appropriately rated these different-belief pairs as different in surprise (with one tie and one reversal).

Discussion

This experiment demonstrated a reasonable degree of facility by four-year-olds with a specific sort of belief-desire reasoning: predicting belief-outcome versus desire-outcome reactions. The data show that four-year-olds have some understanding of both desire-dependent emotional reactions, such as happiness, and belief-dependent emotional reactions, such as surprise. In comparison to the studies in chapter 3 these data show that four-year-olds can utilize belief-desire reasoning not only to predict appropriate actions from beliefs and desires but also to predict emotional reactions. In this study children could not correctly predict the protagonists' reactions simply by linking certain emotions with certain objective outcomes (for example, by always predicting happiness to result from generally positive events, such as getting a puppy). Correct responses required a consideration of the actor's individuating subjective beliefs and desires. Correct performance (judging that getting a puppy leads to happiness if it is wanted but unhappiness if it is not) also showed that young children clearly recognized that internal states such as beliefs and desires are independent of outcomes, that is, from reality. Beliefs are different from reality in that the same event or outcome will produce quite different emotional reactions depending on one's belief. The same reasoning applies to desires. Moreover, children's differential rating of beliefs and desires, with respect to happiness and surprise, further showed that children differentiated these two different sorts of internal psychological states.

These findings showed that while four-year-olds have a significant understanding of surprise reactions—reactions stemming from the characters' beliefs—they are better still at understanding happiness reactions—reactions stemming from the characters' desires. As figure 6.2 shows, childrens' responses more closely approximated the ideal pattern for happiness ratings than for surprise ratings. This raises the question: What of three-year-olds? Two other studies (Yuil, 1984; Stein and Levine, 1986) demonstrate that three-year-olds understand something of relevant emotional reactions with respect to desire. Stein and Levine used tasks similar to our want stories. They presented three- and six-year-olds with four story types. The stories presented all combinations of a protagonist's wanting and not wanting an object crossed with obtaining or not obtaining it. After hearing such stories (Jimmy wants a toy car and gets one), children were asked to say how the protagonist would feel (happy, sad, or angry). Stein and Levine's data straightforwardly show that even three-year-olds (range 3–1 to 4–7, $M = 3$–9) predict the reactions appropriate to the various desire-outcome eventualities. They understand that wanting and obtaining leads to happiness; not wanting and avoiding (not obtaining) leads to happiness; wanting and not obtaining or not wanting and obtaining lead to sadness and anger. Those data thus show that three-year-olds understand some essential relations between desire and emotional reaction. Do they also understand some essential relations between belief and emotional reactions such as surprise? Mita Banerjee and I have begun to address this question (Wellman and Banerjee, 1989).

Second Study of Children's Understanding of Emotional Reactions

Our first attempt to study three-year-olds' understanding of emotional reactions was a relatively straightforward extension to younger children of the methods described for the first study. We presented three-year-olds appropriate stories and asked them to rate the protagonists' emotional reactions. Confirming the Stein and Levine and also the Yuil findings, three-year-olds easily understood the relation between desires and happiness. However, they showed no understanding of surprise reactions as differentiated from happiness reactions. Across story types three-year-olds did judge that the character would sometimes be surprised and sometimes not, but they seemed to judge as if to be surprised meant the same as to be happy (and to be not surprised meant the same as to be unhappy). This was especially clear on stories of the following sort: "Joey *wants* hot oatmeal for breakfast because he likes oatmeal. Joey *thinks* he will get hot oatmeal, because he saw an oatmeal box in the kitchen. Joey gets cold spaghetti." On stories such as these the character should be judged differently with respect to happiness and surprise, that is, as not happy (because he did not get what he wanted) but surprised (because his expectations were false). Three-year-olds in our data uniformly judged the character's surprise and happiness as the same; that is, Joey was not happy and not surprised.

This preliminary attempt thus failed to show any understanding of surprise as a belief-dependent emotional reaction in three-year-olds. Recently Perner and Hadwin (1989) have used a method like the one described in our first study (Wellman and Bartsch, 1988)—presenting children with story characters who have specific desires or beliefs coupled with story outcomes that match or mismatch those psychological states and then asking subjects to rate the character's happiness and surprise. In their data, they found obvious understanding of happiness reactions in three- and four-year-olds but no understanding of surprise until age five. Their data therefore call into question whether even four-year-olds, and certainly whether three-year-olds, understand anything with respect to emotional reactions, such as surprise, which are dependent on a person's beliefs rather than desires.

Note, however, that our initial studies and Perner and Hadwin's studies attempted to assess young children's understanding of belief-dependent emotional reactions by the rating of a character's surprise. Children's difficulty on such tasks could stem from a more specific misunderstanding of surprise rather than a general failure to understand that some emotional reactions depend on beliefs. Specifically, young children may think that surprise is intimately joined with happiness. For example, when parents talk to young children about "surprises," they typically do so in ways that join surprise and happiness. Children are told, for example, that they will get a surprise for their birthday or for Christmas, and such surprises are inevitably pleasant. For children to hear "I have a surprise for you" from visiting grandparents means they will receive something nice or fun, albeit something (perhaps) unexpected. Young children may almost never hear of a surprise that is horrible, painful, or distinctly unpleasant. If children understood surprise in this limited fashion, as something inevitably pleasant, then they would perform poorly on our tasks and on similar ones such as those used by Perner and Hadwin. They might do so in two different fashions.

First, a child asked to rate a character's surprise in our studies might, in essence, ask himself if the character is happy. If the character is happy, the child would then judge that the character is surprised ("pleased") and if not happy then not surprised ("not pleased"). Many three-year-olds in our preliminary attempt did just this. Second, in all our stories, and in Perner and Hadwin's as well, when a character is described as getting something unexpected (Jill's dad reads a book about kittens when she was expecting he would read about dinosaurs), the outcome is typically pleasant in some absolute sense (after all her dad does read her a nice story). In such situations—those of characters experiencing generally pleasant outcomes—a child who misunderstands surprise as inevitably joined to pleasantness might well judge that all the story characters are "surprised." That is, all the characters should be mildly pleased even if not truly happy (they get something pleasant even if not exactly what they wanted). In our first study, a substantial number of four-year-olds evidenced this pattern of response, and this seems to be true of Perner and Hadwin's subjects too (see their pp. 32–33). Moreover, other researchers have asked young children to rate various emotional expressions (to pair emotion words, such as *surprise*, with various photographs of facial expressions). These studies have shown that preschoolers match the term *surprise* to happy expressions, and thus for them "surprise" seems to mean something nice or pleasant (Bullock and Russell, 1984; Russell and Bullock, 1986).

In the study described next, Mita Banerjee and I used a different method. We presented children with characters who had a specific emotion (Bill visited his grandma, and when he got to her house he saw that it was painted purple. He was very surprised.) and then asked children to explain the character's emotion ("Why was Bill so surprised?"). In essence, we reasoned that if children understood that surprise was belief dependent (albeit perhaps also denoting a pleasant experience), they would, at times, refer to Bill's beliefs in order to explain his surprise. For example, they might say that "he didn't think the house would be purple."

Method

The participants were 23 three-year-olds (3–2 to 3–11, M = 3–7) and 20 four-year-olds (4–2 to 5–0, M = 4.8). We tested each child on four different emotional reactions: two that depend on the relation between a person's desires and outcomes (happy and sad) and two that depend on the relation between a person's beliefs or knowledge and outcomes. One of these belief-dependent emotions was surprise. In an attempt to extend our consideration of belief-dependent emotional reactions beyond surprise, the second was curious. To be curious is to be lacking in knowledge or in a definite verified belief about an outcome.

There were two stories of each type. The happy stories described a character getting juice for snack or receiving a visit from grandma (and thus being very happy). The sad stories concerned a character who sees rain out the window or who goes to a library that has no picture books (and being very sad). The surprise stories concerned characters who saw giraffes on an ordinary farm or who visited grandma and found that her house was purple (and being very surprised). The curious stories were about characters who found a big wrapped box in a closet or saw another child bring a closed bag for show and tell (and being very curious). After each story the subject was asked to explain the character's emotion: "Why is the character so happy [sad, surprised, or curious]?" As a follow-up to this first open-ended question, the child was also asked two more specific questions: "What is the character wanting?" and "What is the character thinking?" Children heard the eight stories in two different orders; they always received the open-ended question first and then both the wanting and thinking questions in counterbalanced order.

Results

We were interested in children's responses to both the open-ended and the more specific questions. For responses to open-ended questions, appeal to the character's belief on the surprise and curious stories versus appeal to the character's desires on the happy and sad stories would indicate some understanding that certain emotional reactions are belief dependent in addition to the understanding that certain emotional reactions are desire dependent. However, consider the surprise stories for a moment. Following our earlier discussion, children might understand surprise as meaning happy or nice in addition to meaning something unexpected. If so, then it would be appropriate for them to answer the initial open-ended question ("Why is the character so surprised") with a desire explanation ("He likes purple"). The child could still evidence an understanding of the belief-dependent nature of surprise (that a surprising outcome is unexpected), however, by answering the specific thinking question appropriately. That is, a child who understands in any sense that surprise is belief dependent should say something like, "He didn't think it would be purple" or "He thought it would be white," when asked specifically about the character's thoughts. A child who had no understanding of the belief-dependent nature of surprise would instead fail to answer this thinking question appropriately. Thus, responses to either the open-ended or specific questions could reveal children's understanding of the belief dependence of certain emotions such as surprise, in addition to the desire dependence of emotions such as happiness.

Responses to Open-ended Questions
Responses to the open-ended question were coded as either appeals to desires or appeals to beliefs. Appeals to desires included mention of the character's wants, preferences, or values (she wants orange juice; it's her favorite). Appeals to beliefs included mention of the character's thoughts, knowledge, ignorance, or desire to know (she thought it would be white; he doesn't know what is there; he wants to know what's inside). Both appeals to desires and appeals to beliefs used some sort of explicit mention of mental terms (wants, likes, thinks, knows). Other responses besides appeals to beliefs or desires also were produced, including the simple mention of the objective situation (it's purple; it's raining), uninterpretable answers, and "don't knows."

Sixty-six % of all four-year-olds' open-ended explanations of the happy and sad stories appropriately appealed to desires; similarly 57% of four-year-olds' open-ended explanation of the surprise and curious stories appropriately appealed to beliefs. Nineteen of 20 four-year-olds mentioned an appropriate desire as the explanation for the character's emotion on at least one of the four happy or sad stories; 17 of 20 four-year-olds mentioned an appropriate belief or knowledge state as the explanation for the character's emotion on at least one of the four surprise and curious stories. Three-year-olds showed comparable understanding of desire-dependent emotions: 55% of the three-year-olds' open-ended explanations for the happy and sad stories appropriately appealed to desire, and 18 of 23 mentioned an appropriate desire as the explanation of the character's emotional reaction on at least one of the four happy or sad stories. Three-year-olds' understanding of belief-dependent emotions was noticeably poorer; still, many evidenced some understanding in their open-ended explanations. Only 22% of three-year-olds open-ended explanations of the surprise and curious stories appealed to beliefs; but 12 of 23 three-year-olds mentioned an appropriate belief as the explanation of the character's emotional reaction on at least one of the four surprise and curious stories.

Responses to the Specific Questions
Children's responses to the specific thinking and wanting questions clarify their open-ended explanations and might also reveal understanding of the belief-dependent nature of emotions such as surprise, even if young children misinterpret such emotions as tightly linked to desire. Specifically, if children understand that a surprise reaction depends on a mismatch between belief and outcome (in addition to denoting a pleasant outcome), then when asked what a surprised character is thinking, they should appropriately appeal to the character's discrepant expectation (he didn't think it would be purple).

Children's responses to the specific thinking and wanting questions were coded as appeals to appropriate beliefs or appeals to appropriate desires. For the surprise stories appeals to appropriate beliefs included the character's thoughts or ignorance (he thought that "it would be white"; that "there were no giraffes"). For curious stories appeals to appropriate beliefs included the character's thoughts or ignorance ("he doesn't know what's in the box") and to desiring to see or know the hidden contents ("he wants to know," "he wants to find out what's in there"). For happy and sad stories, appeals to appropriate desires included mention of the character's wants, preferences, and values just as for the open-ended questions.

Ninety-six percent of four-year-olds' responds to the wanting question for happy and sad stories were appropriate desire responses; all 20 four-year-olds provided an appropriate response for at least one of the four happy and sad stories. Similarly, 74% of four-year-olds' responses to the thinking questions for surprise and curious stories were appropriate belief responses; 19 of 20 four-year-olds provided an appropriate response for at least one of the four surprise and curious stories.

Three-year-olds' level of performance was comparable to that of four-year-olds for desire-dependent emotions; their understanding of belief-dependent emotions was, in comparison, worse but nonetheless substantial. Ninety-six percent of three-year-olds' responses to the wanting question for happy and sad stories were appropriate desire responses; all three-year-olds provided an appropriate response to at least one of the four happy and sad stories. Fifty percent of three-year-olds' responses to the thinking question for surprise and curious stories were appropriate belief responses; moreover, 19 of 23 three-year-olds provided an appropriate belief response to at least one of the four surprise and curious stories.

A further comparison helps clarify these data. Imagine a hypothetical child who fails to understand the dependence of emotional reactions such as surprise on a character's prior beliefs. Instead, this hypothetical child understands surprise only in desire terms. That is, he or she understands surprise only as an emotional reaction like happy, resulting simply from the match or mismatch of a character's desires with outcomes. If such a child was told that a character was surprised (as we did in our stories), it would mean something like if an adult were told simply that the character was happy. Such a child should be extremely unlikely to provide appropriate belief responses to the thinking questions on surprise and curious stories since for such a child the description of the character as surprised conveys no information as to the character's belief state. Of course, a child like this might provide an occasional belief response by chance but not often. Indeed such a child would be as likely to provide belief responses to the thinking question asked of happy and sad stories as to the thinking question asked for curious and surprise stories because in neither case has she any clue as to the character's thoughts. On the other hand, if children do understand surprise and curious to be belief-dependent emotional reactions, then to be told, for example, that a character is surprised is to be told something about the character's belief (that the character was not thinking that the specified event would happen). In short, the imaginary child who fails to understand surprise or curious as belief dependent should give equally few belief responses to the thinking questions for curious and surprise stories and for happy and sad stories. In contrast, the child who understands something of the belief dependence of curious and surprise should give more belief responses to the thinking question for those stories than for happy or sad.

In this regard, 74% of four-year-olds' responses to the thinking question for curious and surprise stories were appropriate belief responses, whereas only 13% of their responses to the thinking question for happy and sad stories provided belief responses of any sort. Similarly, 50% of three-year-olds' responses to the thinking question for surprise and curious stories were appropriate belief responses, whereas in comparison only 17% of their responses to the thinking questions for happy and sad stories provided any belief response at all. In short, young children in this study treated emotional descriptions such as surprise and curious as providing information pertinent to the character's belief states, whereas emotional descriptions such as happy and sad did not. This is appropriate if children understand the belief dependence of certain emotions (surprise) and the desire dependence of others (happy).

Discussion

These findings demonstrate once again that young children understand that emotions such as happy and sad are dependent on the character's prior desires. Beyond this now familiar result (Wellman and Bartsch, 1988; Yuil, 1984; Stein and Levine, 1986; Perner and Hadwin, 1989), the data also indicate that children understand emotions such as surprise and curious to be dependent on the character's belief states, although this understanding is also masked by young children's tendency to think that such emotions are intimately dependent on desires as well. For example, children seem to think that a surprise is something unknown in advance or unexpected but definitely pleasant. Nonetheless, four-year-olds and three-year-olds do understand that such emotional reactions depend on beliefs and in this way can be distinguished from others, such as happy and sad, that do not. Three-year-olds are not as firm in their understanding of such belief-dependent emotions as they are in their understanding of desire-dependent emotions such as happy and sad, but nonetheless they show significant understanding.

There is much more to be learned about children's understanding of emotional reactions such as surprise and curious. Still, the findings shed light on the general issue I wish to address in this chapter; they extend and strengthen the claim that three-year-olds possess a belief-desire psychology something like that in figure 4.1, incorporating an understanding of beliefs as well as desires. They extend and strengthen this claim in two ways. First, they show that even three-year-olds understand the nature of emotional reactions as stemming in part from the character's mental states such as beliefs and desires. More specifically they understand that there are two sorts of such emotional reactions: those stemming from the character's belief states and those stemming from the character's desire states. Second, our method in this study was to ask children to explain a character's emotional reactions. Thus the findings also show that three-year-olds can move backward along the causal chain depicted in figure 4.1, explaining the nature of certain events by appealing to their appropriate antecedents. This study is similar in that regard to the explanations study reviewed at the beginning of this chapter on children's explanation of actions.

Children's Understanding That Perceptions Inform Beliefs

The studies in chapter 3 show that three-year-olds can predict actions given information as to the beliefs and desires of the actor; that is, they can move forward along the causal chain depicted in figure 4.1. The studies in this chapter have shown that three-year-olds also can explain actions and emotional reactions by appeal to beliefs and desires and, further, that they understand the differential natures of such reactions as happiness versus surprise and their special links to desires and beliefs, respectively. The main remaining aspect of figure 4.1 to consider, therefore, concerns young children's understanding of the origins of beliefs and desires. I will concentrate on young children's understanding that beliefs can originate in perception.

Recall the inferred belief tasks reported in chapter 3 and for comparison some of the other belief tasks described in that chapter (see table 3.1). In the other sorts of belief tasks used in chapter 3, the child was explicitly told the character's belief (Sam thinks his dog is in location 1) and asked to predict his action. In inferred belief tasks, however, the child was told the character's perceptual experience (Sam saw his dog in location 1) but nothing about the character's belief. A belief-desire reasoner could still infer the character's belief from the information about perception (since Sam saw the dog in location 1, he believes it's there) and then, just as in the other belief tasks, predict the character's action. In fact, three-year-olds were highly successful on inferred belief tasks (88% correct). They were equally successful at predicting action on inferred belief tasks as they were on tasks where beliefs were explicitly mentioned.

Even more convincingly, three-year-olds were correct on inferred belief-control tasks (88% correct). On these control tasks, the stories told of identical objects hidden in both of the two locations, so the child knew target objects were in both places. But the character was said to have seen targets in only one of the locations. Three-year-olds seemed to understand that the character's perception would lead to a belief discrepant from reality (he thinks the object is in only one location) and predicted the actor's actions accordingly. At the same time, three-year-olds also asserted (correctly) that there were targets in the other location too. Thus they could not have been answering on the basis of a reality assessment strategy (translating "Sam saw targets only in location 1" to "there really are objects only in location 1") because they knew full well that there were objects in both locations.

I conclude from these data that young children know (at least) one very simple aspect of the link between perception and belief depicted in figure 4.1, something like the understanding that seeing leads to believing and not seeing leads to ignorance (Taylor, 1988). Our inferred-belief tasks were so simple that correct responses to them do not warrant crediting young children with much knowledge about, or much facility regarding, the derivation of beliefs from perceptions. For example, there would be much more to know about the influence of perception on beliefs—such as that perception can be wrong or incomplete and thus lead to false beliefs, that visual perception can lead to one belief (perhaps that a surface is rough) but touch or another sensory modality to another belief (that the surface is smooth). And there would be much more to know about the origins of beliefs—for example, not only do beliefs arise from perceptions but they also arise from other beliefs by inference, and even from other mental processes such as distorted memories, or dreams. Still, understanding that beliefs (Sam thinks it's in location 1) can arise from seeing (he saw it in location 1) seems to be a genuine awareness of the fact that (if not exactly how) perception leads to belief as depicted in figure 4.1. Our data suggest that appreciation of this very rudimentary fact, entailed by the sort of belief-desire psychology outlined in figure 4.1, is within the grasp of quite young children.

As it turns out, however, this is a controversial claim, in part because Wimmer (Wimmer, Hogrefe, and Sodian, 1988; Wimmer, Hogrefe, and Perner, 1988) has made the exact opposite claim: that three-year-olds and even many four-year-olds fail to understand this simple perception-belief link. And he provides solid evidence for his view. Wimmer arrived at his position by considering the Wimmer and Perner (1983) false-belief data. According to those data (and those of Perner et al., 1987) children failed to predict a character's action from his or her false beliefs until around age four. Wimmer attempted to determine why children fail these tasks. Recall that in the Wimmer and Perner false-belief tasks children are told, for example, "Maxi put his chocolate in a drawer. When he is away playing, his mother removes it and puts it in a cupboard. Now Maxi wants some chocolate. Where will he look?" In this sort of task, the character's beliefs are not explicitly stated but must be inferred from the fact that Maxi saw the chocolate placed in the drawer and did not see it moved (and hence must believe it is still in the drawer). Thus, Wimmer hypothesized that children's difficulty might be in inferring the character's false belief from his perceptual experiences. Beyond this, Wimmer proposed that children may have a general deficit at inferring beliefs (false beliefs or straightforward beliefs) from the character's seeing.

To test this more general notion, Wimmer, Hogrefe, and Perner (1988) conducted several studies of the following sort. Pairs of children were shown a closed box, which when shaken clearly had something inside. Then the lid of the box was opened so that only one child could see into it. The subject child was asked about the target child, "Does he know what is in the box, or does he not know that?" both when the target child had and had not seen into the box. (Subjects were also asked about their own knowledge, but, as Wimmer cogently argues, this question can be answered simply by the subject's having knowledge rather than understanding about knowledge.) To be correct, the child must answer that the other knows (has acquired the relevant belief) when he has seen into the box but does not know when he has not seen. Almost no three-year-olds ever gave this correct pattern of response. In fact, only about 50% of the four-year-olds gave correct responses. Hence, Wimmer concludes, in general young children do not understand that visual access leads to belief, and specifically this could account for their failure on traditional false-belief tasks.

Our data from the inferred belief tasks of chapter 3 contradict Wimmer's position and data in two ways. First, with respect to false belief, if difficulties with inferring belief are what account for young children's failure on traditional false belief tasks, then three-year-olds should succeed on our explicit false-belief tasks. They did not. So the false-belief error remains even when inference of belief is not at issue. Second, with respect to the general proposal, if three-year-olds are unable to infer knowledge from perceptual access, then they should fail our inferred belief tasks. Yet they passed such tasks with ease. Again, the inferred belief-control task is particularly convincing here because children know there are items in both locations but predict Sam's action solely on the basis of Sam's perceptual access.

At this point we have two contradictory sets of results: our results suggesting young children understand a simple perception-belief link and Wimmer et al.'s suggesting they do not. It is possible that in our tasks children were not inferring the actor's belief but still were predicting actions correctly. We do not know for sure that children in inferred belief tasks inferred the character's belief because we did not ask them what the characters knows or believes and so did not demonstrate directly that children make that inference. We simply asked them to predict the action, whereas Wimmer et al. asked children to state what the character knew.

However, Pillow (1989) has found that three-year-olds correctly understand the existence of a link between perception and belief even when queried directly about beliefs (rather than actions). In the first of Pillow's studies, three-year-olds were questioned about a puppet's viewing of a hidden object. A colored toy dinosaur was hidden in a container. The puppet viewer or the child looked inside the container; then the child was asked, "Does the puppet know what color the dinosaur is in here?" and "Do you know what color the dinosaur is in here?" Three-year-olds attributed knowledge and perceptual experience to the person (either themselves or the puppet) who had viewed the hidden object but not to the person who did not view it. In a second study, three-year-olds were asked to indicate which of two puppets, one who had viewed a hidden object and one who had not, would be able to tell them the object's color. Three-year-olds chose the correct puppet significantly more often than chance; they were better than 70% correct in the first study and 75% correct in the second.

What procedural differences account for the differences between ours and Pillow's versus Wimmer's results? Some recent research by Pratt and Bryant (1988) may have identified the critical factor. Pratt and Bryant argue that Wimmer et al.'s (1988) question format was too complex. Wimmer et al. asked children a double question: "Does he know what is in the box, or does he not know that?" Pratt and Bryant found that even in a seemingly straightforward task about simple possession, children became confused with a double question—for example, "Does he have the red counters, or does he not have them?" So in two studies, Pratt and Bryant simplified the questioning procedures. In the first study children had to judge which of two assistants knew the contents of a box: one who lifted the box but did not look into it or one who simply looked inside. The question was, "Who knows what is in the box: John or Fiona?" Young children (range 3–8 to 4–7) answered this question correctly on 84% of their trials, and all children were correct on four or five of their five trials.

The second study paralleled Wimmer et al.'s task (1988, experiment 1) almost exactly, except for the complexity of the question. Two children either saw or did not see into a box, and the subject was asked about the target child, "Does she know what is in the box?" Seventy-five percent of the three-year-olds (3–4 to 3–11) were correct with this procedure, whereas only 13% were correct with the double question in the Wimmer et al. research.

Taken together, these results establish that three-year-olds have an initial grasp of the fact that beliefs can arise from perception. This seems all the more likely since in the Shatz et al. (1983) data on the use of mental terms in young children's speech, the focal child uttered several statements of the following sort well before the fourth birthday (reported in Wellman, 1985b):

1. Child: This is wheat bread. . . . Do you know this is wheat bread because it's made from wheat?
    Father: Yep, I know that.
    Child: I didn't know that.
    Father: Then how come you told me?
    Child: Because I tasted it.
    Father: You didn't know until you tasted it?
    Child: No. I thought it wasn't wheat bread.

2. Father: What's under there?
    Child: A mouse.
    Father: A mouse?
    Child: Yeah. Do you want to see if it's really a mouse?

3. Child: Let's go outside.
    Father: It's wet outside.
    Child: I'll look out and see if it's raining. I don't see any rain.

Examples 1 and 3 show a three-year-old clearly talking about sources of information for his own knowledge. Example 2 shows sensitivity to visual sources of information for another's knowledge.

Although I am claiming that Wimmer was wrong, his proposal was a cogent one resting on an important distinction. Wimmer did not claim that young children understand nothing about seeing; he claimed that they failed to understand that seeing produces beliefs. The critical distinction is thus along the lines of the distinction between "seeing" and "seeing that" (Dretske, 1969). I can see a car and not see that it is a car; I can comprehend that you see an object but still not appreciate that you know it is a car or ball or what have you. Children could know quite a bit about seeing and not know anything about seeing-that, that is, not know anything about the internal mental products of seeing, such as beliefs, knowledge, and ideas. It is clear from the work on young children's understanding of visual perspective taking (e.g., Flavell, 1978) that young two- and three-year-old children do know a lot about seeing. For example, such young children know that if your eyes are closed you won't see X, that you may see X when I don't, and so forth. These results stem from numerous tasks where young children have been asked to judge what they or someone else sees. Still, they may not have understood that beliefs arise out of seeing. Indeed, when describing level 1 knowl-

edge about seeing, that level that he feels characterizes the understanding of two- and three-year-olds, Flavell (1978) initially said:
"Looking at and seeing may be tacitly interpreted by the Level 1 child
as just another overt act or behavior, much like touching it or picking
it up. . . . The Level 2 child, on the other hand, seemingly would
have to represent O's (the observer's) view of the object as something
akin to a visual experience or impression—more like an internal image than an external action" (p. 48). In short Wimmer could have
been right, but the evidence now seems to show that he was not, at
least with respect to three-year-olds. It may be that still younger children do not understand that perception generates belief.

Conclusions

I believe that it is undeniable that by age three children are engaged
in the same everyday-psychological enterprise as are adults—construing people as having minds and understanding action by the internal mental states of the actor. More specifically, it seems clear that
by three years of age, children understand the basic ontological distinction between mental states and entities versus physical states and
objects. Moreover, they possess most, if not all, of the pieces of the
belief-desire reasoning scheme in figure 4.1. Specifically, they (1) can
appropriately predict actions given information as to the actor's beliefs and desires. (2) They explain actors' actions by stating they are
caused by internal beliefs and desires. In doing (1) and (2) they see
beliefs as an importantly separate construct from desires. They also
(3) can appropriately infer the presence or absence of belief given information as to the character's seeing or not seeing a relevant situation and can use that inferred belief appropriately to predict action.
And they (4) understand the nature of the proper emotional reactions
given the concordance or discordance of the actor's desires and outcomes and also beliefs and outcomes. While the data needed to characterize fully three-year-olds' competence at all the sorts of reasoning
encompassed by figure 4.1 are not currently available, there certainly
is sufficient evidence to claim that three-year-olds operate with a conception of mind very much like the familiar adult one, embedded
within a larger belief-desire reasoning scheme recognizably like the
one depicted in figure 4.1. Therefore, three-year-olds' knowledge
evidences the requisite sort of coherence, rests on the mandated ontological distinctions, and is centrally tied to a powerful causal-
explanatory framework. In short, their knowledge constitutes a
theory. Specifically, it constitutes a familiar mentalistic framework
psychology encompassing, indeed resting on, a theory of mind.

Early achievement of a mentalistic everyday belief-desire psychology and its concomitant theory of mind is not to be overestimated; very young children still have trouble sorting out the respective roles of beliefs and desires. Indeed they have much to learn about the mind that forms and holds beliefs, and they have important realizations yet to achieve about the nature of beliefs and representations. These are issues I will discuss in chapter 9. The three-year-old's belief-desire psychology, although recognizable, is not the same as the adult's. Nonetheless, this accomplishment is not to be underestimated. That three-year-olds have and utilize a theory of mind is an impressive and important achievement. It means that their view of human action and thought is not unlike our own.

Chapter 7

Further Clarifications of the Theory and the Data

This chapter brings together a loose assortment of issues that have fallen between the cracks in my presentation to this point. Primarily I wish to tackle two suspicions: that most three-year-olds do not know and understand as much about the mind as those three-year-olds who have participated in our studies and that three-year-olds do not really have a theory of mind; they have something more straightforward and less abstract. I begin, however, with a point of clarification concerning methods.

Knowledge of Others' Minds

The research reported in chapters 2, 3, and 6 examined children's knowledge of both their own and others' mental states and their understanding of how behavior of self and other is mentally caused. Most of the research, however, has emphasized children's understanding of others' minds—another child, a story protagonist, an adult. This has been for methodological rather than substantive reasons. Substantively my view is that the child is acquiring a generic theory, one applicable to self and other. Of course, application to self or to other may raise special problems in one area or another—we may be quick to see others' mistaken beliefs but slow to see our own, for example—and require some differing procedures. Nonetheless, I claim that the basic theoretical architecture applies: both my actions and yours are construed in terms of beliefs and desires, and both my mental contents and yours are construed in terms of the basic distinction between internal mental states and entities versus external events and manifest behaviors.

Why, then, has most of the research focused on others' minds? Because children's judgments and explanations of other minds often avoid a problem inherent in judgments of their own mental states. The problem is this: I am interested in whether young children conceive of beliefs and desires but I assume that children have beliefs and desires or something similar. The possession of beliefs and desires in the first instance is not the same as, but can be easily confused with, the possession of the appropriate concepts.

Suppose, as in chapter 6, I am interested in whether children know about the relation between seeing and knowing. To test this I show a child a closed box and an open box and in each case ask, "Do you know what is in the box?" The child answers correctly in both cases. Does this show that she grasps something of the connection between seeing and knowing? No; the child can answer simply by having or not having the relevant knowledge. When the box is closed, she does not know and says no; when it is open she has seen inside and does know and says yes. Although the child answers questions about "knowledge," and does so correctly for occasions of both seeing and not seeing, correct answers do not indicate knowledge of the seeing-knowing relation. Instead, the child's own seeing simply generates knowing, and then reporting her own knowing constitutes correct responding. But, what if I show the child what is in the box and do not show another character? Then I ask the child of the other, "Does he know?" Here the child would be incorrect by reporting her own knowledge. If she simply reports her own knowledge, in this case she has seen and so knows and therefore, when asked "does the character know?" she would answer incorrectly. In this way it is possible to distinguish an understanding of beliefs from having beliefs. The child's possession of knowledge can be contrasted with the other's possession of knowledge (child knows and other does not), and we can see if the child differentiates her answers for self and other appropriately.

This methodological tactic was incorporated into the original false-belief tasks (Wimmer and Perner, 1983). In false-belief tasks the child-subject knows where the target is, but the protagonist does not. Understanding false belief thus reveals a true understanding of belief (rather than a simple possession of beliefs) because the subject must attribute to the other a belief different from his or her own. Similarly, this tactic was incorporated into our studies, even, for example, when we were interested in the child's understanding of his own mental state as in the mental imagery studies of chapter 2. In those studies we tried to frame our questions so that they required the child to judge and conceive of his own mental states and entities rather than just report them. For example, we asked children not only if they had an image but if they could see that image. But we also contrasted judgments of their experience with judgments of another's. Thus, it was especially compelling that children said they could "see" their images but that another person could not. When children differentiate their own and another's experience of the same mental state in this fashion, it indicates that the child has a conceptual understanding of the nature of the phenomenon beyond simply having an experience of the phenomenon.

I claim that by age three, the child's theory of mind encompasses the minds of self and other. Indeed, that is part of what the theory is: a general and generative set of concepts applicable to individual minds, not simply an experience of one's own individual mind.

Johnson's Proposal

Recently Carl Johnson (1988) has proposed that young children's (three-, four-, and five-year-olds) understanding of mind is not a theory. According to Johnson, what young children evidence and recruit *is* the experience (plus reporting) of mind, not a constructed understanding of mind. This is a complex and serious proposal. As I understand it, the proposal encompasses four essential elements, which outline a position worthy of extended consideration:

1. Young children have minds and thus, of course, have mental experiences—dreams, perceptions, beliefs, intentions. In other words, young children have conscious, phenomenal experiences—experiences such as that of dreaming, seeing, wanting to do something.
2. Conscious experience is not a uniform undifferentiated whole; it is structured. Dreaming is a different sort of experience from believing, for example. Indeed, conscious experience is richly structured. Our conscious experience is organized (just by the nature of our minds themselves, not by virtue of an understanding of mind) into a variety of different types that constitute an organized set of categories.
3. When young children are asked questions about mental phenomena—about mental images, beliefs, or surprise—they answer by simply reporting from the organized structure of their conscious experience, without benefit of any constructs or achieved conceptions such as a concept of "belief." Their answers report on their own firsthand experiences; they do not evidence or stem from a theory of mind, that is, stem from third-person conceptions about mental states and processes. In this sense, preschoolers' knowledge of the mind is "intuitive" (Johnson, 1988, p. 47) whereas the knowledge of mind of school-aged children is "constructed" (p. 56). Since preschoolers' conscious experience is richly structured, however, their answers

are impressively coherent and sensitive to many important distinctions.

These three tenets taken together could possibly account for a young child's knowledge of her own mind. But children can also talk about the nature of others' minds, or minds in general, and indeed predict others' behavior on the basis of others' mental states quite different from their own. Thus, Johnson also proposes:

> 4. Young children accomplish predictions of others' minds directly, by "simulation" (p. 58), without benefit of inference from a theory of mind. In essence, children project themselves into the other's position and then read off their own state of mind (or action tendency) when asked questions about another. Thus, young children do evidence knowledge of others' minds, but this is not objective knowledge of mind based on mental constructs but subjective experience, projected. Children's knowledge is therefore "limited by their ability to imagine or simulate states of people in the world" (p. 58).

To be clear, the main difference between my position and Johnson's is not that only one (his) acknowledges the importance of subjective experiences as providing information about the mind. I too contend that such experiences importantly aid and inform the child in achieving a theory of mind (see Wellman 1985a, and chapter 8). Similarly, the difference is not that only one (mine) emphasizes the coherent impressive knowledge of mental life available to very young children. Johnson too claims that past accounts failed to credit and characterize young children's impressive achievements. The difference is that Johnson claims the young child's impressive knowledge is read off from firsthand experience—firsthand experience of subjective states (dreams, thoughts, desires). My claim, in contrast, is that even young children do more than this: they not only have experiences, they have knowledge about such experiences, indeed they have a rudimentary theory about such phenomena. This theory goes beyond an implicit acknowledgment that thoughts and objects, for example, are different in a firsthand fashion and includes a conception of thoughts and objects as different in specifiable fashions (the ontological aspect of a theory of mind), and it goes beyond an ability to provide correct answers about people's actions by simulation and encompasses an ability to generate such predictions inferentially from conceptual knowledge or constructs such as beliefs and desires (the causal-explanatory aspect of a theory of mind). In short, by age three children not only have minds (rich, structured, knowledgeable minds) but also a beginning theory of mind.

There is a corollary to this difference in position as well. In keeping with his firsthand account, Johnson suggests that the young child's sole source of evidence for his or her knowledge of mind is firsthand experience. Johnson puts this forth as an "antidote" (p. 47) to the opposite notion, which he sees as endemic to a theory position. "What is perhaps most misleading about the theory metaphor is that it suggests that children are approaching the problem of other minds from a third person perspective, inferring the existence of abstract theoretical entities to explain the behavior of others. While states like desiring, thinking, and willing may seem like abstractions from the outside, they appear to be the very substance of experience from the inside" (p. 57). My position is that the child's understanding of mind is founded, in part, on third-person inferential endeavors. However, I wish to avoid a strict dichotomy—that the child's knowledge is based on either firsthand experience or third-person inferences. It is both. Since it is both, however, I do maintain that third-person inferences as to the causal explanation of others' behavior, and indeed objective construal of one's own behavior and mind, motivate and inform the child's theory-building enterprise. The meanings of such terms/constructs as *belief*, *desire* and *dream* may be anchored in certain firsthand experiences, but by age three children have not only the experiences but the theoretical constructs, and they can utilize the constructs within a theory; that is, they employ rudimentary belief-desire psychology (as elucidated in chapter 4).

Beyond simply asserting these differences in position, is there any evidence to decide between them? I think there is. First, as our demonstrations of children's abilities to infer others' minds and actions have become more complete—for example, have come to include their success at not-own belief tasks, discrepant belief tasks, anomalous belief explanation tasks—then it becomes increasingly difficult to maintain that such correct performance stems exclusively from abilities to simply put oneself in the other's position and read off one's firsthand experiences or tendencies. The child who answers, "You can't see my image, but you could see *your* image in your head" (see table 2.4) seems to do more than simply adopt another's position and report from it in a firsthand manner. Such answers seem to comment on the distinction between my mental states and yours in an articulate conceptually acute fashion. Similarly, answers like, "Your mind is for moving things and looking at things when there is not a movie or a TV around" (see table 2.4) may in part involve reporting on firsthand experience but beyond this also explicitly construe and conceptualize a mental state objectively. Still, such data are not completely telling; some sort of articulated firsthand experience account could be devised to handle such performances.

Further evidence exists, however. The essence of Johnson's account is that young children's knowledge (before the school years) rests solely and ineluctably on the relevant firsthand experience. Knowledge of dreaming, before age six or so, is dependent on, or even stronger directly read off of, the experience of having dreams. Knowledge of believing is read off of having beliefs. Crucial counterevidence would exist, therefore, if we found a child without the relevant firsthand experience (had never had a dream, for example) but who still had the relevant knowledge. Such knowledge would constitute a clear case of inferred knowledge, whose meaning is constructed rather than read off and whose meaning is available because of the construct's entrenchment in a theoretical web of constructs and belief. In this regard, note that the experience of vision qualifies as an appropriate firsthand conscious experience. Indeed Johnson includes seeing (pp. 53–54) as a relevant conscious mental experience and in an earlier presentation of his position (Johnson, 1986) spoke at length about young children's visual experiences.

All this sets the stage for the following argument. Blind children by age three or four attribute seeing to others and not themselves. Indeed, their knowledge of seeing is rather good. Such knowledge could not result from the firsthand experience of seeing. It constitutes instead, I claim, attribution to others of a theoretical category of experience (seeing). Admittedly knowledge of seeing could be grounded indirectly in experiences of touching and hearing, but such knowledge could not be read off of or simulated from one's own firsthand experience of seeing. Thus the knowledge is, in important part, constructed and inferred, and it is posited in others, in a third-person fashion, because of its theoretical-explanatory role and utility. If blind children commonly engage in this sort of theoretical endeavor, it seems senseless to deny a similar sort of constructive-theoretical knowledge to ordinary three-year-olds.

That is the nature of the argument. The data to support the argument would come from data on young blind children's understanding of vision and attribution of vision to others. Landau and Gleitman (1985) provide data of exactly this sort. Most telling are their data examining in detail the meaning of sighted verbs such as *look* and *see* for a blind preschooler, Kelli. Importantly, Landau and Gleitman's data focus on a distinction between Kelli's understanding and use of *look* and *see* as applied to herself versus as applied to others. When

applying *look* and *see* to herself, Kelli used the terms to mea\
ing or apprehending by touch. But when applying the ter\
sighted mother or a sighted experimenter, Kelli used the \
refer to exploration by sight and apprehension by vision. This\
est in a series of experiments where Kelli (at age three and a half),
when asked to "let me see/look at the front of your shirt," for example, drew attention to the target by orienting or pointing to it at a
distance, that is, out of the viewer's reach; at the same age appropriately differentiated between showing versus giving someone something and letting someone see versus letting them touch something;
and at age four and a half understood that other people cannot see
through opaque barriers that she can hear through.

Landau and Gleitman demonstrate persuasively that as young as
age three and a half, Kelli understood about vision in others, to the
extent of knowing that a sighted person can look through windows
although she herself cannot reach through them, can see objects out
of reach, and cannot see objects behind opaque barriers even though
she herself can hear them. This happens not by simulating her own
firsthand experience of seeing but by constructing an understanding
of vision inferentially and using it as a theoretical term to understand
others' actions, that is, by positing a mental state in others quite different from her own firsthand experience.[1]

My point is not that such theoretical endeavors are exotic and rare,
the province of special knowledge-creation efforts initiated to overcome glaring deficiencies in special children. The knowledge of sight
of young blind children does seem exotic and special. But its early
achievement shows the presence (and power) of ordinary everyday
childhood theory building. If I am correct, then the knowledge of
sighted three-year-olds about the mind is no less impressive and theory laden but is a common and everyday achievement. Belief-desire
psychology is an everyday acquisition of three-year-olds no matter
how impressive. And it is an impressive piece of theory building, no
matter how ordinary.

Harris's Position

Recently Paul Harris (1989) offered an informative elaboration of
Johnson's general position. He provides a more detailed analysis of
how children "simulate" others' mental states, in Johnson's terms,
and thus how they easily answer questions about other's beliefs and
desires. The process, Harris argues, requires only a common but distinctive use of everyday imagination:

In order for you to understand my beliefs and assumptions, you need not share them. You may readily know what I believe and why without believing it yourself. Conversely, I may appreciate what you intend or perceive at this moment, but scarcely need to intend or perceive the same thing.

What does my understanding amount to in such cases? One way to state it is as follows: if I appreciate what you feel or perceive at the moment then I can *imagine* what you feel or perceive. I do not actually experience a mental state like yours. Imaginative understanding does not involve a contagious transmission of mental states from observed to observer. Rather, when you feel embarrassed or proud, I observe this and imagine what emotion I would feel were I in your shoes. As a result, I generate an "as if" or pretend emotion. Unless I have contributed to or in some way shared your success or discomfiture, I do not feel any genuine pride or embarrassment myself. Similarly, if I am a spectator at tennis, I can appreciate, by an act of imaginative projection, what you perceive as you receive a service. I can imagine myself in your position with the ball coming towards me, and if my imagery is vivid enough, I may even generate, again in an "as if" mode, some of the sensations that you experience: the effort of trying to reach the ball, the recoil of the racquet, and so forth. I can imagine all of these sensations without actually having them. (Harris, 1989, pp. 52–53)

I find this a compelling analysis of how easily and frequently even young children can reason about other minds and hence predict their actions by such imaginative processes. My objection comes only when Harris opposes imaginings of this sort with theoretical knowledge and asserts that children understand others' mental states by imagination rather than a theory of mind: "Young children have beliefs and desires, and they can report them. Their understanding of psychology is based upon their experience, rather than on deduction from a set of theoretical postulates" (Harris, 1989, p. 77). In more detail, he says:

I have argued that children come to understand the links between beliefs, desires, and emotions. To what extent are they operating with what has come to be called a "theory of mind" (Astington, Harris and Olson, 1988)? A theory usually involves the postulation of unobservable entities whose interrelations can be shown to explain and predict observable events. For example, a theory of planetary motion might involve the postulation of gravity, and centripetal force, that permit the explanation and prediction of observable events such as the orbit of a planet. Similarly, it has been argued that the postulation of unobservables such as beliefs and desires can be used to explain and predict what people say, do and feel. Therefore, if children have recourse to such unobservables they should be credited with a theory of mind (Wellman, 1988). . . . However, there are ways in which the child's theory of mind is quite unlike a theory of planetary motion. Gravity is an unobservable, theoretical postulate. I do not think that we can say the same of beliefs and desires. . . . Children have desires and beliefs, and they can report them. So far as they are concerned, there is nothing hidden or unobservable about their own mental states, whatever the opacity of other people's. Therefore, children do not invoke unobservable entities. They invoke mental states that they experience every waking day. Second, children do not postulate such states when they explain someone's behavior. They simply imagine wanting or believing a particular state of affairs. This is not to deny, of course, that the imagination plays a role in the generation of such theoretical entities as gravity, but it does not play a role by projecting from our own personal experience. There is no sense in which we explain planetary motion by imagining ourselves to be a planet subjected to a given set of gravitational forces. In short, the psychological process by which a theory of mind is constructed bears little relation to the psychological process by which scientific theories about the non-psychological world are constructed. (Harris, 1989, pp. 75–76)

This argument is incorrect, I think, in part because it begins with an inadequate depiction of how theories operate, even with respect to scientific theories, and in part because it fails to distinguish some importantly different levels of analysis, specifically the difference between framework theories and specific conceptual representations, such as mental models.

It is misleading to oppose theorizing and imaginative projections. When Einstein devised and utilized such thought experiments as imagining how a clock would report time inside a vehicle traveling at the speed of light, he was engaged in theory construction and application by processes of imaginings. The use of imaginative projections is complementary with, indeed typically encompassed by, rather than antithetical to our theories. For similar reasons, I object to Johnson's opposition of simulations versus theories. I believe that the two often operate together. Framework theories constrain specific mental models; specific mental models are devices for instantiating larger conceptual understandings and then arriving at additional predictions by "working" the mental model. That is, we often run simulations of various events by our mental models as a way of applying larger conceptions to certain parts of problems. Such simulations do theoretical work for us and are not theory free. Certainly researchers in artificial intelligence do not consider the utilization of simulations to be theory free; they consider them to be theories, to instantiate larger theoretical approaches, and to represent theoretical exercises.

Part of Harris's objection seems to be based on the suspicion that children's knowledge of beliefs and desires cannot be theoretical because children do not postulate beliefs and desires from the armchair, out of nothing, "theoretically" as it were. Instead, this objection goes, children experience their own beliefs, desires, emotions, perceptions. These are not theoretical constructs or unobservables for children, it is claimed, but firsthand experiences extended to make sense of others. This suspicion seems misplaced. It rests in part on a false impression as to the character of scientific theories and as to the nature of theoretical constructs or unobservables. I agree that children's observational-experiential data base in this realm is large and immediate. Even infants accrue an extensive history of firsthand experience of their own cognition, motivations, and internal states; they amass innumerable experiences of interaction with and observation of others who, of course, display and express emotions, cognitions, and desires. However, the wealth of this experience does not mean that children's understanding is not theorylike and requires no theoretical concept or abstractions. On the contrary, because there is so much experience and information available to children in so many punctuate and commingled episodes and events, they must develop a coherent conceptual framework to organize and make sense of these experiences. They must distill some sort of general constructs, such as beliefs and desires, out of the stream of specific personal experiences that indiscriminately interleaves specific beliefs, specific desires, sensations, emotions, and so forth. What organizes these experiences for children in such a fashion that they are able to simulate another's desires instead of, for example, simply imagining a stream of consciousness, a flow of intermingled sensations, in the other? Children achieve orderly imaginings because they have recourse to a commonsense framework theory. This is one important function of scientific theories: to derive and impose conceptual order on a wealth of chaotic observations. This is also an essential function of belief-desire psychology, and this is the sort of theoretical understanding that I propose children have achieved, substantially, by age three. Belief-desire psychology is a theory in this sense, an everyday theory forged from innumerable data, rather than constructed in the absence of data. Theoretical constructs such as beliefs and desires generalize over such experiential data.

The presence of children's framework belief-desire psychology can be seen in the very workings of their imaginings. Such imaginings and simulations are the everyday working out of mental models that children (and adults) construct to solve problems in understanding others' behavior. As such, these models are constrained and informed by the child's framework theory. Why, for example—to understand everyday behavior, or to answer our experimental questions, or to understand story protagonists' actions—do children imagine a character's beliefs and desires instead of his or her heartbeat or respiration or any of a number of states and sensations that the subject can experience and thus can imagine in others? Children concentrate on imagining some things (beliefs and desires) and not others, I claim, because of their role in acceptable explanations as framed by their framework theory (belief-desire psychology). In total, I am indebted to Harris for his insightful analysis of how, and how often, children use imagining to solve the problem of understanding others' minds; however, I claim that such imaginings show the imprint of, not the absence of, a framework theory of mind.

Atypical Data?

I have likened my task to that of the cultural anthropologist—that is, I am seeking to characterize a different worldview on the basis of evidence from informants. For the anthropologist, the attempt is to characterize the worldview of another culture using native informants. For the child psychologist, the attempt is to characterize the worldview of earlier life-ages using child informants. The methods can be different, involving in my case use of carefully designed experiments, but there are notable similarities. One is that the anthropologist typically uses not just any man on the street but "good" informants. I use, initially at least, "good" child informants.

The research reported here has been conducted primarily with middle-class, verbally articulate children of average and above-average intelligence. Ninety percent of the data reported in our studies thus far come from children enrolled in one of three middle-class preschools in Ann Arbor, Michigan. When trying to get an initial understanding of children's worldview, I do not begin with inarticulate or unintelligent children; that would make the process exceedingly difficult. Of course, my claim is that the picture painted by good informants is typical of most children, in essence, if not in complete detail.

I assume that articulate, advantaged children may be somewhat better at revealing their conceptions but that the nature of the conceptions themselves, in the case of such a basic topic as this one, are shared by children at large (at least in Western culture). I believe this assumption is true, but the suspicion arises that the picture painted here applies only to a small group of advantaged children.

There are several ways to refute this concern. In some of our studies we have carefully included children from quite diverse populations. In Johnson and Wellman (1982), for example, subjects were children from Ann Arbor but also from average school systems in Pittsburgh. When we compare responses from children in our primary subject population to these other groups, no differences are evident; the same substantive conclusions remain. Our findings have also been replicated by others. For example, the main findings of Wellman and Estes (1986) have been replicated (and extended) with preschoolers in England (Harris, Marriot, and Whittall, 1988). Conversely, aspects of our data also replicate those of others. For example, children's performances on the explicit false-belief task of chapter 3 replicate performances in more than 10 other false-belief prediction conditions conducted primarily with children in England and Austria (see Perner et al., 1987). More striking, children's correct false-belief predictions beginning at about age four, as evident in our studies and in Wimmer and Perner's, are also evident in Down's syndrome children with mental ages as young as four and a half (Baron-Cohen, Leslie, and Frith, 1985).

A further sort of replication was reported in chapter 2. There I showed that our data on children's understanding of mental entities replicate those collected by Laurendeau and Pinard (1962). There are many reasons that that particular replication might have failed. We might have tested an overprivileged sample of children who have arrived at their sophisticated ideas atypically early in development. The difference might also reflect important cohort differences; our children were tested in the late 1980s, Laurendeau and Pinard's in the late 1950s. Perhaps with increased early childhood education or increased exposure to television and computers, young children today are more knowledgeable about these matters than children in prior years. However, the two sets of data were largely the same (table 2.5). This comparison showed that the findings reported in chapter 2 would be essentially typical of a "completely representative sample of children" from Montreal in the late 1950s (see Laurendeau and Pinard, 1962, chapter 6) as well as typical of a haphazard sample of middle-class and advantaged children from Ann Arbor in the late 1980s.

Concern with the Singular Reliance on Language

I wish to uncover the young child's acquisition of a theory of mind and its subsequent development. I do not wish merely to chart children's learning the meaning of mental terms. Concerns arise, therefore, because the methods I have used are all language dependent. Such methods can prove ambiguous. Specifically, if children do poorly on a task, it can be unclear whether this is due to linguistic-communicative or conceptual deficiencies. Nonetheless, understanding and use of mental terms is an integral part of my methods and the methods of other investigators in this field. There are two essential reasons for this reliance on language. First, in many cases there is no better alternative. Fortunately, and second, lack of better alternatives is due, in part, to the fact that language-dependent measures prove extremely revealing. Language development does not map conceptual development in any strict sense, but language-dependent tasks can be used to do so. Indeed, almost all techniques cognitive psychologists use to assess a person's knowledge involve verbal instruction of the subject or require his or her verbal response in some form. It is true that studies of visual attention in infants (and some other methods with adults and children) provide exceptions to this generalization, but limited exceptions. Besides, the methods I have used are fruitful with children as young as two years. However, use of such language-dependent measures brings with it the obligation to protect the research from their limitations. I have tried to discharge this obligation in two ways: by use of improved methods for questioning young children that diminish the language burden on the child and use of controls and analyses to confirm that when children's responses are conceptually inadequate, they are nonetheless linguistically adequate.

In general, methods for questioning children about their knowledge can be language dependent in two fashions: requiring comprehension of presentations and questions by the child and requiring verbal responses from the child. Earlier research at times was questionable in both respects. For example, Piaget (1929; Kohlberg, 1969; Laurendeau and Pinard, 1962; Broughton, 1978) asked children open-ended questions such as, "What are dreams made of?" Such questions are poorly constructed and likely to be miscomprehended by young children. The questions are ambiguous, and the expressive burden on the child is large. Our tasks use precisely formulated non-ambiguous questions. In addition, they require from the child at first a simple judgment—for example, "yes" or "no."

A related issue concerns the sorts of items or situations about which children are questioned. Children's answers to a single sort of item or situation are rarely revealing in themselves. A pattern of responses across items or conditions is needed—for example, contrasts between mental entities and close impostors or contrasts between standard belief, not-own belief, discrepant belief, and changed belief tasks. Our results show that given such comparisons, children's conceptions are clear not only in their initial judgments but in their subsequent explanations as well. In essence, the methods used in this book depend on carefully chosen task-type × question-type designs. These designs yield response matrices where different sorts of conceptual understandings result in different patterns of responses (see figures 2.4, 3.1, and 6.2).

In our earliest studies (Wellman and Johnson, 1979; Johnson and Wellman, 1980; Shatz et al., 1983) the focus was on conventional mental terms. Children were asked judgment questions, such as "Did X *know* Y"? In our later research, mental terms are less focal. In some cases, children heard tasks where mental terms (*remember, think, dream*) were used but the judgments themselves asked whether, for example, a character "could *touch*" an entity. In our studies on belief-desire reasoning, we used only the two most common and early understood mental terms, *want* and *think*. And in our last mental imagery study, we diminished the use of conventional mental terminology. In that imagery study, images were labeled "pictures in your head." This terminology does not use any commonly used mental terms (*think, remember, guess, know*).

Finally, it has been possible, even when using methods that are language dependent, to rule out some sources of linguistic incompetence as accounting for the results. For example, much talk about the mental world relies on complex sentences requiring predicate complements: John believed *that Mary was lost*; I know *how to fix the car*; I wish *it would rain*. However, in Shatz et al. (1983) we were able to show that children could control such linguistic expressions before they began to use mental terms for mental reference and that when they began to talk about the mental world, children could do so with simple sentences not involving predicate complementation. These data allowed us to be more confident that children's earlier lack of mental reference was not simply due to certain sorts of linguistic immaturities.

The experimental research reviewed in this book includes similar controls. Consider the studies in chapter 2 again. If children answer appropriately for real items (especially the close-impostor items) we know that, at the least, they can comprehend questions of the required complexity and form. If they provide linguistically complex explanations for close-impostor items, then we know that they are capable of a baseline level of necessary expression. Of course, it has not been necessary to emphasize the presence of these sorts of controls up to this point because of young children's correct performance. This serves as the best control possible. If the child is shown to understand appropriately some term or some task situation, then this must depend on appropriate conceptions. In fact, even inappropriate use or comprehension can often reveal appropriate conceptions. The child may use a set of terms incorrectly but in such a way as to honor an important conceptual distinction. This is exactly what we found in Johnson and Wellman (1980). In that study children's use of the terms *remember, know,* and *guess* was not like adults'; it developed substantially over the ages four to nine years. Nonetheless, it was clear that even four-year-olds used such terms to refer to mental states in contrast to the observable behaviors of themselves and others. In sum, I believe that the research reported in this book can be taken as providing a reasonably sensitive measure of young children's developing theories of mind.

Chapter 8
Before Three

In the preceding chapters I have described what I take to be the naive psychology of young children, at about their third birthday. Because this is a patently mentalistic psychology, it encompasses and rests on a theory of mind. In this chapter I look back from three and examine the origins of three-year-olds' impressive achievements. I will look a bit at infants but will focus mostly on children in the third year of life (from two to three), whom I will call two-year-olds. I offer primarily proposals, not data. I will report some confirmatory data for one of my proposals; nonetheless this chapter is much less anchored in empirical evidence than chapters 2, 3, and 6. We still need detailed research on children younger than three but it is possible to advance some cogent hypotheses about these early developments.

I intend to consider such questions as where initial belief-desire psychology comes from and why and how children first develop a theory of mind. Two different though complementary sorts of answers can be considered to such questions. These should be distinguished at the start because they are often confused. One sort of answer focuses on mechanisms. That is, it would attempt to specify or even model those types of experiences and processes of acquisition that cause children to acquire initially and to amend developmentally their theories of mind. A second sort of answer concentrates on origins. This would attempt to specify not the detailed mechanisms of acquisition but the earliest glimmerings of this sort of conception and the earlier precursors from whence notions of mind spring. In this chapter I will be concerned more with origins than with initial mechanisms.

I want to utilize once again the crude breakdown of an understanding of mind into two aspects noted at the end of chapter 3: the hypothetical or imaginary aspect of mind and the causal aspect of mind. These are, in the first case, an appreciation that mind is quite different from matter, of the ontological distinction between mental entities and states versus physical objects and events, and in the second case, an appreciation of how beliefs are "about" the world and of how acts stem from beliefs and desires. To have a theory of mind is to appreciate both of these aspects in a suitable, coherent manner. I attempt to identify probable precursors of three-year-olds' theory of mind by examining earlier partial understandings of these two aspects: the imaginary and the causal. By separating them for this analysis, I do not mean to suggest that they are at first separate in the child's understanding and must be merged in some final step of acquisition of a theory of mind; that may or may not be true. Still, it is possible to begin to identify the earlier sources of these two basic understandings within a theory of mind. I will discuss very young children's understanding of the causal aspect first, followed by their understanding of the imaginary aspect of mind.

From Simple Desires to Ordinary Beliefs: The Causal Aspect of Mind

Having characterized three-year-olds' causal understanding of mind as similar to adults' in explaining actions in terms of beliefs and desires, I now wish to examine the causal understanding of two-year-olds. Let me note again the importance of the construct of belief in our everyday psychology. Desires motivate behaviors, but beliefs frame them. Persons' actions can thwart their own desires (Jane wants her kitty, which is under the chair, but she's looking for it under the piano) because beliefs are also at work (Jane *thinks* it's under the piano). In essence, I will now propose that three years is about the earliest age at which children understand belief and thus can participate in belief-desire reasoning. More specifically, while three-year-olds evidence a beginning grasp of an understanding of belief, two-year-olds do not. However, two-year-olds are not ignorant of human action; they too evidence a coherent naive understanding of action but one distinctly different from that of adults and one that I have begun to call a simple desire psychology (Wellman and Woolley, in press).

I will talk here in a shorthand manner about two-year-olds and contrast them to the three-year-olds. This is purely a convenience. More exactly, I believe that understanding of belief and several other aspects of mind first appear in very old two-year-olds, in the months right before the third birthday. This marks acquisition of a belief-desire psychology and hence of the sort of theory of mind described in chapter 6. Even this is inexact, however. I do not believe that the conceptual developments I am charting are tied to chronological age at all in any precise way and am simply using age as a convenient marker for talking about a sequence of early developments. My collaborators and I do find that among samples of middle-class children of the sort studied here (and typical of the children used in other related studies) that very late in the third year many children first evidence an early understanding of belief. What is of importance, however, is that the understandings I talk of in this chapter precede understanding of beliefs, not that they characterize all or only two-year-olds.

The Proposal

I consider briefly three broad classes of psychological theory: behaviorism, internal state theory, and cognitive theory. For my purposes, I depict behaviorism as an attempt to explain action solely on the basis of functional relations between observable states, specifically dependencies between observable states of the world (stimuli) and observable behaviors of the organism (responses). In behavioristic theories of this sort, no attributions about the "insides" of the organism are made; the organism simply constitutes an input-output device achieving certain input-output functional relations.

An internal state psychology, in contrast, postulates internal states of the organism. An example is classic drive theory. In drive theory organisms are attributed certain internal states, drives (such as hunger), whose waxing and waning propel and direct behavior. Note that drives, albeit internal states, are not cognitive states; that is, they are not mental representational states. In the everyday terms of figure 4.1, drives are something on the order of physiological states and basic emotions and can be coupled with more specific desires and preferences.

In a broad sense, cognitive theories are internal state theories. But they constitute a specific refinement of internal state theory, postulating certain very distinctive internal representational states that function to provide an internal mental world for the organism. From a cognitive perspective, understanding behavior requires one to understand the contents and status of these mental representational states. In the everyday terms of figure 4.1, a person's beliefs and knowledge also cause action.

Given such a crude taxonomy, one could ask two sorts of questions. First, what kind of organism is the two- or the three-year-old? That is not my question. I assume that understanding such young children requires a cognitive account of some sort. My question instead is, What characterizes young children's naive psychologies? How do children conceive of people for the purposes of explaining their actions, for example? Do they conceive of them in behavioristic, internal state, or cognitive terms? The data reported in chapters 2, 3, and 6 make clear that children as young as three years are not behaviorists; they understand human action by positing unobservable internal states. In addition, they are not merely internal state psychologists but more narrowly are cognitivists. Specifically, theirs is a mentalistic naive psychology, incorporating a rudimentary conception of belief. In contrast, most two-year-olds are more like internal state psychologists. Theirs is a simple desire psychology focusing not on basic drives but on simple object-specific desires.

This claim inspires two questions. First, since philosophers often treat beliefs and desires as similar, can they be distinguished in the way I wish to—one as cognitive and representational, the other not? Second, what might simple desire reasoning—predicting actions on the basis of a person's desires alone with no conception of belief—look like?

I term two-year-olds' understanding a "simple" desire psychology; by that I mean it rests on a simplified understanding of desire—an understanding of desire unlike the adult one although recognizable. In adult understanding as philosophers treat it, a person's desires are typically construed as similar to beliefs. Thus, both desires and beliefs are called propositional attitudes. Beliefs are beliefs about a proposition: Joe believes that that is an apple. In this construal, beliefs are understood as representational. "Joe believes that that is an apple" means something like that Joe has a cognitive representation of the world and in that representation the designated object is an apple. A person's desires can be construed similarly, that is, as desires about propositions, about possible represented states of affairs. "Joe wants an apple," then, is understood as something like, "Joe wants that there be an apple and that he obtain it." This makes sense because in adult belief-desire psychology, desires are intimately tied to beliefs. If Joe wants an apple, then Joe must believe an apple exists. Since a person's desires are also representational in this sense, it is feasible to talk of desires for not-real, nonexistent imaginary things. We say things like "Joe wants a unicorn" or "Joe wants to be the best ski jumper ever."

It is possible, however, to imagine an alternative conception of desire, unlike our typical understanding of belief, in which desires are not representational. In this alternative simplified conception, "Joe wants an apple" embodies no notion of Joe's representing an apple, simply wanting one. In this simple conception, desires are not attitudes about a proposition but attitudes about an actual object or state of affairs. Figure 8.1 is an attempt to capture this simple conception of desire and to contrast it with a conception of belief. That figure graphically portrays someone (the person on the right) thinking of

Desire (wants an apple)

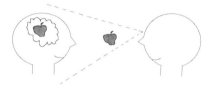

Belief (thinks that that is an apple)

Figure 8.1
Graphical depiction of simple desires (top) and ordinary beliefs (bottom).

another's (the person on the left) internal state. At the top the person on the right is thinking of the other person's desire. At the bottom the person on the right is thinking of the other's belief. The internal states of the target person (on the left) are shown in something like the way the first person construes them. In the case of simple desires, the conceiver can simply think of the target person as having an internal longing for an external object. In the case of belief, however, it seems the conceiver must think of the target person as representing the apple somehow. This graphical depiction is meant only to be suggestive, but the key idea seems important: that any valid conception of belief evidences appreciation of the fact that persons live not simply in a world of objects and events but also in a world of representations of objects and events. A simple understanding of desires is conceivable, however, that does not require any understanding of representations.

In initially distinguishing internal state psychologies from cognitive psychologies, I aligned simple desires with drives as internal states and contrasted them with cognitive representations such as beliefs. It is important, however, to distinguish simple desires from drives as well as from beliefs. Both drives and simple desires—for example, being hungry and wanting an apple—describe internal states energizing the organism toward certain outcomes—relieving hunger or obtaining an apple. But drives describe the organism's internal physiological state (he's hungry; she's thirsty); simple desires describe a specific object (or event or state of affairs) that is sought. Conversely drives are silent about objects; desires are silent about physiological state. For example, being hungry can be satisfied by an apple, an orange, or a sandwich. The object is not specified by stating the drive. But "wanting an apple" is not satisfied by a sandwich; the object is essential.

The necessary specification of an object makes desires, even simple desires, similar to beliefs in an important respect. Simple desires, in this proposal, and beliefs, more ordinarily, are intentional constructs in the sense that they are about some "object." This is an important similarity, often noted (Brentano, 1874/1983; Dennett, 1979). However, according to my proposal, all intentional states need not be representational. To reiterate, we can imagine a simple desire description that refers simply to a pro-attitude toward an actual object. The relevant outcome with respect to such a simple desire concerns simply obtaining the object. In sum, the "object" of a simple desire is an object, event, or state of affairs in the world. The "object" of a belief, however, no matter how simple, is a proposition about objects, events, or states of affairs. Beliefs encompass attitudes of "entertaining" a proposition, and the relevant outcome concerns truth or correspondence. In this sense, beliefs are necessarily propositional and truth relevant; simple desires are not. Simple desires are intentional but not representational. A simple desire psychology, therefore, resting essentially on a conception of internal states directed toward obtainment of objects in the world, is quite different from a belief-desire psychology that rests centrally, if not wholly, on a conception of internal cognitive states representing truths about the world. I am not claiming that a conception of simple desires captures everyday adult understanding of desires. Our everyday adult conception is more complex, more inextricably intertwined with the business of belief. But a simple desire notion of this sort is possible.

What sort of reasoning about actions might be encompassed by a simple desire psychology? In brief, a simple desire psychology attributes to the actor certain internal desires, recruits various sources of knowledge about the external world, and generates inferences about how actions in the world stem from and fulfill (or not) the actor's desires. More specifically, simple desires such as wanting a drink of water or desiring a certain toy are seen as causing the organism to do certain things. For example, simple desires cause actors to engage in goal-directed actions (seek water, avoid fire), to persist in goal-directed actions (if the route to water is blocked, seek an alternative), and to have certain emotional reactions (getting what you desire yields happiness). Such a desire psychology can therefore provide some simple but cogent accounts and predictions of various acts. Thus, if a desire psychologist knows that "Betty wants an apple," he can predict that Betty will look for the apple. He can predict that "Betty will look for the apple" under the general maxim that people act to fulfill their desires. And if he knows "Betty wants the apple" and that "the apple is in the cupboard," he can predict that Betty will look in the cupboard. It is critical to understand this example. In this example, the simple desire psychologist knows that the apple is in the cupboard and utilizes this knowledge in predicting where Betty, the character, will look. Critically, the desire psychologist does not attribute such a knowledge state to Betty but sees Betty as having a desire and sees the world as having desired objects. The desire psychologist recruits his knowledge of the world together with his knowledge of Betty's desires to predict Betty's desire-caused action-in-the-world; he predicts Betty will act so as to fulfill her desire. He does not attribute knowledge of the world (a belief-representational state) to Betty. A desire psychologist can also predict that if Betty finds the desired apple, she will be happy, under the general maxim that getting what you want makes you happy. If Betty does not find the apple, she will be unhappy or angry.

As an internal state psychology, simple desire psychology rests on an important distinction between internal states and external reality. Desires are independent of actual, realized outcomes; one can desire things that do not happen. I do not mean that a simple desire psychologist attributes to others desires for nonexistent objects or impossible events. I mean instead that simple desire psychology honors the distinction between wanting and getting. I want *that* (very real existent) apple, but I may or may not get it.

My proposal is that most two-year-olds have a simple desire psychology and engage in only desire reasoning about actions, although by three years, or just a little before, children have and utilize a concept of belief. Jacqui Woolley and I have conducted two studies to provide initial support for this proposal (Wellman and Woolley, in press).

A Study of Two-Year-Olds' Understanding of Simple Desire Psychology

If two-year-olds possess a simple desire psychology, this represents an intriguing, indeed critical, acquisition. Desire psychology is an internal state psychology of some utility and complexity, albeit not a cognitive, representational psychology. It is important, therefore, to document more clearly whether such young children can engage in simple desire reasoning.

Method

Sixteen older two-year-olds (*M* = 2–10 months; range 2–7 to 3–1) participated. As shown in the left-hand portion of figure 8.2 these children made judgments about the actions (top of the figure) and emotional reactions (bottom of the figure) of story characters in each of three types of situations. In the finds-wanted situation a doll character wants something that may be in one of two locations; the character searches in a first location and gets the object. The finds-nothing situation was identical to finds-wanted except that upon searching in the first location, nothing was there. The finds-substitute situation was identical to finds-wanted except that upon searching in the first location, the character found an attractive object but not the one said to be wanted.

In making action judgments children had to predict the character's subsequent action—that is whether he or she would go on to search in the second location or would stop searching at the first. An understanding of the implications of characters' desires should lead to a prediction of continued search in the finds-nothing and finds-substitute situations but not in the case of finds-wanted. In making emotion judgments children had to state the character's emotional reaction—happiness or sadness. An understanding of the role of desires in mediating emotional reactions should yield a prediction of happiness in the finds-wanted situation but sadness in the finds-nothing and in the finds-substitute situations.

For example, children were shown a cardboard cutout of Sam, drawn from the back (so as to depict no facial expression), and were told that Sam wants to find his rabbit. They were told that the rabbit might be hiding in either of two depicted locations and then shown Sam walking to one of the locations, opening it, and either finding the desired object (a cutout of the rabbit) or something else (a dog) or nothing. In action stories, ones in which the child had to judge the character's search actions, children were also told that Sam wanted the rabbit to take it to school, and a third location (the school) was depicted. After Sam had looked in the first location, children were asked what the character would do next: "Will he look in the [other hiding location] or will he go to school?"

Emotion stories, ones in which children had to judge the characters' emotional reaction, were identical to action stories except that no final destination was mentioned. Children were simply told, for example, of Sam who wanted a rabbit, shown Sam looking in one of the two hiding locations, and shown him finding the rabbit there or not. Then, to elicit emotion judgments, the children were asked how Sam felt: "Does he feel happy or does he feel sad?"

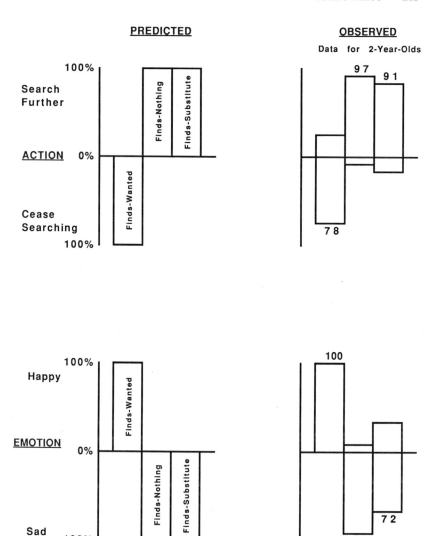

Figure 8.2
Predicted (left) and observed (right) responses for the action and emotion judgments from the study of two-year-olds' understanding of simple desires. From Wellman and Woolley (in press).

There were six stories—two instances of each of the three types. Each story was told twice, once for action questions and once for emotion questions. The six stories were about six children (three boys and three girls) who wanted to find a dog, a horse, a bike, a box of crayons, a rabbit, and a pair of mittens.

Results
Figure 8.2 provides a graphical depiction of the results alongside the predicted patterns of results if children understand the role of simple desires. Children appropriately predict continued searching for finds-nothing and finds-substitute story characters but not for finds-wanted. They appropriately predict happiness for finds-gets but sadness for finds-nothing and finds-substitute stories.

Each child judged six stories with respect to action and six with respect to emotion. Being correct on five or six of the six judgments represents above-chance performance ($p < .05$, one-tailed). Thirteen of 16 children (81%) were correct on five or six of the six action judgments, and 13 of 16 children were similarly correct on the emotion judgments. Two different characters were presented to each child as getting the exact same object—for example, Sam wants a rabbit and gets a dog (finds-substitute story) and Johnny wants a dog and gets a dog (finds-wanted). Understanding of desire requires judging these actors differently even though they got the same thing. That is, Johnny should be happy with a dog because it was desired, whereas Sam should be unhappy with a dog because he desired a rabbit. Ten of 16 children were correct on both of their pairs of this precise contrast for action judgments and 2 were correct once. Ten of 16 children were correct on both of their pairs of this precise contrast for emotion judgments and 3 were correct once.

Discussion
These data document that older two-year-olds reason about actions and reactions by desire. Two-year-olds correctly predicted actions from information as to a character's simple desires, including the appropriate continuance and cessation of search, and they correctly predicted emotional reactions, even to the extent of predicting that two characters finding the same attractive object would be happy or sad depending on their relevant desires. Children's correct responses evidence not only the generation of correct inferences but also an appreciation of the basic distinction between desires and external outcomes. Children could not be correct on our tasks simply by predicting happiness or ceased searching upon finding an objectively attractive object. To be correct, finding an object (a dog) must be

predicted to have quite different action and emotion implications depending on if the object was desired. Actions and reactions stem from desires, which inhere in persons, not in objects, and our data suggest that two-year-olds know this at least for simple desires of the sort used here.

If very young children are simple-desire, rather than belief-desire, psychologists, then they should both succeed at desire reasoning tasks and fail at comparable belief-desire reasoning tasks. The ease with which young children solved desire judgment tasks in our first study suggests that they were able to utilize desire reasoning. In a second study we attempted to demonstrate that children of this age also fail comparable belief reasoning tasks.

A Study of Young Children's Understanding of Beliefs versus Desires

We hoped to show that two-year-olds understand simple desires but fail to understand beliefs. To do this, we needed belief tasks that were quite simple so that two-year-olds might pass them, and we needed to construct simple desire reasoning tasks of a comparable sort. We began with the simplest yet valid belief reasoning tasks we could find and then devised analogous desire reasoning tasks. In the research reviewed in chapter 3 Karen Bartsch and I employed a series of tasks evidencing an early understanding of belief in young three-year-olds. In this study Jacqui Woolley and I sampled two of those tasks—not-own and discrepant belief tasks—that seemed representative of the larger set.

The desire reasoning tasks that we devised in this fashion provided some important extensions of the desire reasoning tasks used in the first study. For example, returning to the methodological concern raised in chapter 7, we certainly grant that even two-year-olds have desires, that they are motivated by internal dispositions on the order of desires, preferences, and so on with respect to objects in the world. We also grant that young children can act so as to fulfill their own desires and that they have emotional reactions dependent on the satisfaction or failure of their own desires. Therefore, suppose that in the first study, children simply have desires and that they have the same desire as that stated for the protagonist—the child subject desires a rabbit, and in the story Sam wants a rabbit. When asked whether Sam will search beyond the first location, the child simply reports his own action tendency: he would search if the rabbit was still missing and would stop when it was found. When asked to rate Sam's emotion, the child simply reports his own—happy when the rabbit is found and unhappy if it is not. To control for this possibility in our second study, we utilized a not-own desire task, where the child's preference and that of the story character differed. We hoped to show that young children predict the character's action and emotion on the basis of the character's desire and not their own.

Method
We used not-own belief tasks (see table 3.1) as an example of belief reasoning tasks and constructed not-own desire tasks to be comparable. In not-own desire tasks, the child was told about a character with two options (swimming in the pool or playing with the dog by the doghouse). Then the subject was asked his or her own preference (what would you want to do?). After citing their own desire, they were told the character has the opposite desire and asked to predict the character's action (go to the pool or go to the doghouse). If two-year-olds correctly predict the character's action based on the character's desire, they must have some understanding of desire as a cause of action over and above simply having desires. If successful performance on not-own desire tasks contrasts with failure on not-own belief tasks, this would provide an example of desire reasoning prior to belief-desire reasoning.

In a similar fashion we constructed no-preference desire tasks to parallel discrepant belief tasks (see table 3.1). In no-preference desire tasks, as in discrepant belief tasks, children saw that target objects are really in both locations (markers are in the desk and in the toy box). Then they were told Bill's desire (to find markers). In this situation, reasoning simply that Bill will act to fulfill his desires should lead to a prediction of no preference for either location, and hence children should predict that Bill will look in either or both locations. Correct performance on no-preference desire tasks therefore would demonstrate that children understand an aspect of desire reasoning not tested before: indifference between equally desirable choices. Correct performance on no-preference desire tasks but not on discrepant belief tasks would document the presence of desire reasoning before belief reasoning.

Twenty young children participated ($M = 3$–0, range 2–9 to 3–3, 10 boys and 10 girls). Each child got 12 tasks—three of each of the four types: not-own belief, not-own desire, discrepant belief and no-preference desire. Each task concerned a different protagonist. Discrepant belief and the no-preference desire tasks contained the same object and locations and differed only in the inclusion of belief information in the former.

Results

Consider first children's performance on not-own belief versus not-own desire tasks. Children averaged 73% correct responding on not-own belief stories but 93% correct responding on not-own desire stories. More important many children understood desire but not belief. Being correct on three of the three instances of each task represents a substantial degree of understanding, unlikely by chance alone. Only 9 of 20 children (45%) were correct on all three not-own belief stories, whereas 17 of 20 (85%) were correct on all three not-own desire stories. Nine children passed the three desire tasks but failed the parallel belief tasks, whereas only one child showed the reverse pattern.

These young children were also poor at the discrepant belief tasks. Only 5 of 20 (25%) were correct on all three discrepant belief tasks; for comparison 17 of 20 were correct on all not-own desire tasks.

Consider next children's performance on discrepant belief versus no-preference desire tasks. This comparison is complicated because on no-preference desire tasks, correct performance means choosing both locations equally. Nonetheless, if young children understand a role for desire in causing behavior but not a role for beliefs, then two predictions should follow. First, young children should make similar predictions on discrepant belief tasks as on no-preference desire tasks because if they fail to appreciate the actor's belief, then discrepant belief tasks become equivalent to no-preference desire tasks. Second, children should judge that the actor will search in either or both locations on no-preference desire tasks because search in either location will satisfy the actor's desire.

Our test of the first prediction—that performance should be similar on both no-preference desire and discrepant belief tasks—used correct responses on discrepant belief tasks as a baseline. On these tasks, the actor was portrayed as having a specific belief, so there was a single correct response. Since no-preference desire tasks paralleled discrepant belief tasks exactly with regard to the objects, locations, and desires specified (the sole difference being the extra belief information provided in discrepant belief tasks), we calculated parallel pseudocorrect scores on no-preference desire tasks. That is, we arbitrarily gave children credit for a pseudocorrect response on a no-preference task if they chose the location that was correct on the parallel discrepant belief task. Children averaged 60% correct on discrepant belief tasks and 46% pseudocorrect on no-preference desire tasks (F (1, 16) = 2.60, ns). Thus, as predicted, very young children responded similarly to both tasks.

The second prediction was that on no-preference desire tasks, children should say that the actor will search either or both locations. Accordingly, children's pseudocorrect responses on no-preference desire tasks (46%) were not different from a value of 50%. Fifty percent represents equal distribution of responses across the two locations and is what would be expected if children were choosing either location based on an understanding of the character's indifference between the two locations. However, such performance might also reflect only chance performance in a two-choice task rather than an understanding of indifference. Fortunately, other aspects of the data confirm that children were appropriately judging that the character would be indifferent.

In the no-preference desire condition, for example, children explicitly mentioned that the character would search both locations on 23% of their responses, confirming at least a partial understanding that indeed both locations would fulfill the character's desire. (For comparison, no "both" responses were given to not-own desire tasks and only 7% were given to the parallel discrepant belief tasks.) More important children's responses on no-preference desire tasks can be compared to their responses on not-own desire tasks. Pseudocorrect responding was 46% on no-preference desire tasks; correct responding was 93% on not-own desire tasks. The same children thus chose single correct locations on not-own desire tasks and chose either location on no-preference tasks. This differential responding across critically different desire tasks demonstrates an appropriate understanding of desire. Children do not respond randomly to desire reasoning tasks; instead they correctly predict a choice where one is appropriate (not-own desire) and correctly predict indifference where it is appropriate (no-preference).

Discussion
These young children were largely correct on tasks requiring reasoning about human action on the basis of actors' simple desires. At the same time they performed significantly more poorly on tasks requiring understanding of actors' beliefs. Indeed, individually, many two-year-olds passed desire tasks but failed comparable belief-desire tasks.

What do these data mean? Young children's failure at the belief tasks coupled with success on the desire tasks demonstrates that simple desire reasoning precedes belief-desire reasoning, if our belief reasoning tasks were simple yet valid—that is, if children understand the task formats, language, and situations while still failing these tasks and only slightly older children do pass these tasks.

With respect to the first requirement—showing that children understand our task formats—the pattern of results obtained is important. Many two-year-olds systematically failed the belief reasoning tasks, but they passed comparable desire reasoning tasks. The same children's correct performance on comparable desire reasoning tasks argues against the possibility that the general vocabulary or response formats of the tasks we employed were too difficult for children of this age. Such young children were convincingly competent at our specific task formats even when they failed to incorporate an understanding and utilization of belief into their psychological reasoning. Moreover, the data in table 8.1 demonstrate that only slightly older children pass these belief reasoning tasks with ease. Across these studies and those reported in chapter 3, we have now collected data from children ranging in age from 2 years, 5 months to 5–0 on both not-own belief tasks and discrepant belief tasks. Table 8.1 presents this aggregated data. The youngest children (2–5 to 3–0) are at chance on belief reasoning. At only a slightly older age, however, children are markedly above chance on belief reasoning.

An alternative explanation for our results might argue that perhaps two-year-olds understand belief but are not familiar with the term *think*. In our methods we used the term *think* to convey a character's belief to the subjects ("Suzi thinks there are bananas in the refrigerator"). Unfamiliarity with or miscomprehension of the term may have masked young children's understanding of the concepts. However, children of this age are clearly conversant with the term *think*; indeed they spontaneously produce *think* and *know* in their everyday utterances beginning about the second birthday (Limber, 1973; Bretherton and Beeghley, 1982). Perhaps children are familiar with the term but nonetheless our statements to them were too difficult for them to understand. Our statements did require use of predicate complement constructions involving two verbs: "Sam *thinks* that his dog *is* in the garage." Again, however, children are familiar with and use such constructions themselves beginning shortly after the second birthday (Limber, 1973). They even use such constructions with the term *think*, although not for mental reference (Shatz et al., 1983). Furthermore, our desire statements ("Sam wants to find his rabbit") employed parallel predicate complement constructions. Two-year-olds clearly understood complex statements of this sort in our tasks.

Of course, if I am right about two-year-olds' everyday psychology, there is an important sense in which they do not correctly understand mental terms like *think*: although they spontaneously use mental verbs such as *think*, *know*, and *forget* earlier in the third year of life,

Table 8.1
Comparison of Young Children's Understanding of Belief and Desire

Not-Own Belief Tasks[a]			Discrepant Belief Tasks[a]			Experiment 2 Not-Own Desire Tasks			Experiment 1 Emotion Prediction Desire Tasks			Experiment 1 Action Prediction Desire Tasks		
Age	N	Percent Correct[b]	Age	N	Percent Correct[b]	Age	N	Percent Correct[b]	Age	N	Percent Correct[b]	Age	N	Percent Correct[b]
2-5 to 3-0[c]	17	66%	2-5 to 3-0	11	57%	2-9 to 3-0	11	96%*	2-7 to 3-0	16	89%*	2-7 to 3-0	16	88%*
3-1 to 3-5	15	90%*	3-1 to 3-5	13	67%	3-1 to 3-3	9	90%*						
3-6 to 4-0	16	80%*	3-6 to 4-0	11	80%*									
4-1 to 5+	16	80%*												

a. Data aggregated from Experiment 2 of this research and Experiments 2 and 3 of Wellman and Bartsch (1988).

b. The mean of children's scores where each child's score is the percent correct across three different trials.

c. For not-own belief tasks (but not the others in this table) we have collected enough data from two-year-olds to provide a somewhat finer age breakdown. Nine children aged 2–5 to 2–9 have been tested on not own belief tasks, their mean correct is 53% (not significantly different from a chance value of 50%). Eight children aged 2–10 to 3–0 have been tested; their mean correct is 80% (significantly different from chance at $p < .05$). This suggests that old two-year-olds, right before their third birthday, are the first age group that demonstrates any understanding of belief.

*Significantly greater than chance (50%) at $p < .05$.

only right before age three do children use the term *think* to talk about a person's beliefs. That is, children fail to understand a construct of belief until late in the third year and thus, although aware of the term and even using it, do fail to understand appropriately the term *think*.

These findings shed light on early desire reasoning and on early belief-desire reasoning as well. With respect to desire reasoning, summing across both studies, two-year-olds correctly predicted characters' actions given information as to the characters' desires, including predicting cessation of search when desires were fulfilled, predicting continuance of search when desires were unfulfilled (even when the character found an attractive object but not the desired object), predicting that the character would engage in a specific activity opposite to the child's own desired activity, and predicting that characters would be essentially indifferent to which of two locations they would search if both locations contained the desired objects. These young children also correctly predicted characters' emotional reactions, including predicting happiness when outcomes fulfilled desires and predicting unhappiness when outcomes failed to fulfill desires. Taken singly, correct performance on any one of these reasoning tasks is not definitive. Collectively, however, consistently correct performance on all of these tasks is quite convincing with respect to young children's prediction of actions and emotions resulting from a character's desire.

Two-year-olds' highly correct responding in these cases (averaging essentially 90% correct on the desire reasoning tasks used here) is all the more remarkable since such young children so often perform poorly on laboratory tasks of this sort requiring sustained attention to verbal materials and deliberate choice among several response options. One important aspect of our tasks is that all require understanding of simple desires, that is, straightforward longings for external objects. I believe that young children's understanding of desires is limited to such simple desires, but our data do not prove that. The data do provide evidence of a reasonable facility and expertise with interpreting people's actions as the result of internal desirelike dispositions, and hence with desire reasoning. This is an impressive acquisition of an understanding of human action in very young children. Our data also suggest that understanding of belief-desire psychological causation, in contrast to simple desire causation, is beyond the grasp of children until just about the third birthday.

More about the Proposed Transition from Simple Desires to Ordinary Beliefs

My proposal concerning the transition from a simple desire to a belief-desire psychology encompasses three separable aspects: (1) that an understanding of desires precedes beliefs, (2) that a nonrepresentational understanding of mental states (specifically, simple desires) precedes an understanding of mental representations (ordinary beliefs), and (3) that this transition takes place at about age three, with two-year-olds understanding simple desires and three-year-olds understanding beliefs as well. This proposal is novel in several respects, especially with regard to (3), but it has similarities to some other recent proposals, especially with regard to (2), and receives some support from other research, especially with regard to (1).

From Desires to Beliefs
Our data on two-year-olds' understanding of desire are in accord with several other recent findings suggesting that in the year from age two to three young children evidence a sizable developing understanding of human action as stemming from the internal goals and motives of the actor. In their spontaneous speech, children begin to talk about internal psychological states such as wants, internal physiological states such as hunger, and emotions such as happiness, sadness, and anger at right about their second birthday (Bretherton and Beeghley, 1982). More impressive than just the appearance of such words in the child's language is the nature of children's conception that underpins their comprehension and production of such words. Bretherton and Beeghley (1982) claimed that two-year-olds used words such as *want* or *mad* in appropriate causal fashions. More rigorously, Hood and Bloom (1979) analyzed the naturally occurring causal utterances of eight children studied longitudinally from approximately two to three years. They found that children's causal explanations were almost wholly references to psychological causation. They provided detailed analyses of children's causal utterances and found them to be correctly ordered and commendably sensible. Thus they conclude: "Children did talk about intentions and motivations in their causal utterances which could be support for Piaget's characterization of the child's first causal relations as expressing . . . psychological causality" (pp. 29–30).

More recently, Huttonlocher and Smiley (Huttonlocher, Smiley, and Charney, 1983; Huttonlocher and Smiley, 1987; Smiley and Huttonlocher, in press) have been intensively investigating young children's understanding and use of action verbs. Such verbs can refer to overt aspects of a person's behavior (*bouncing, breaking*) or can include reference to psychological aspects of a person's action, such as their goals and desires (*getting, pulling, avoiding*). To say that someone is getting something (going to get their toy) is to describe their intent or desire as much as their behavior. Huttonlocher and Smiley believe children first understand others' actions only in terms of observable features: "When children first apply verbs to the actions of others, they apply only a subset of verbs, . . . namely those that encode perceptually simple acts. We argued that these actions can be categorized on the basis of directly observable features" (Smiley and Huttonlocher, in press, p. 3). More important for my proposal, these authors conclude that by early in the third year, children construe others' actions as the result of internal states and thus appropriately apply verbs of psychological agency: "As children approach 2 ½ years, they begin to describe other people as subjects of experience, using words like *get, give,* and *want* in relation to others. At this time, we believe the child's word use provides evidence of having acquired the critical elements of the adult notion of person" (Huttonlocher and Smiley, 1987, p. 2). By two years, therefore, children's understanding of action verbs encompasses something like an understanding of simple desire.

In comparison to two-year-olds, however, older children acquire more than simply a refined and perfected desire psychology. They develop a belief-desire psychology, a sense of psychological causation that rests on and requires consideration of the actor's mental convictions about the world as well as his or her goals. This places an important caveat on any claims that two-year-olds understand "psychological causation" or "the adult notion of person." The psychological causation understood by two-year-olds, while indeed impressive for such young children, is quite different from that of adults.

Our findings in these two studies show that very young children fail to understand belief-desire reasoning and that such children utilize a simpler naive psychology. When such young children fail belief reasoning tasks, they nonetheless pass comparable desire reasoning tasks. Thus, the current data are consistent with a developmental sequence from understanding desire to understanding belief as well. This sequence receives suggestive support from several other sources. In spontaneous language use, very young two-year-olds use such desire words as *want* and related emotion words such as *happy* before they use mental terms such as *think, know,* and *surprise* (Bretherton and Beeghley, 1982). Moreover, young children of two and three years have been found to use deontic modal expressions before epistemic ones. Modal auxiliaries, such as *may* and *must* in English, can refer to notions of ability, intention, and permission—deontic modality—or to notions of probability, conviction, and logical necessity—epistemic modality. Deontic modality as studied with young children seems to me to be aligned with notions of agency, desire, and intent—that is, notions that seem meaningful within desire psychology alone. Epistemic modality as studied with young children seems aligned with notions of belief and conviction—that is, aspects of belief encompassed by belief-desire psychology. Both in English and in other languages such as Greek, two- and three-year-olds consistently evidence use of modal expressions for deontic meanings before they use the same expressions for epistemic meanings (Stephany, 1986).

Recall the study of children's explanation of action (Bartsch and Wellman, 1989) reported in chapter 6. Children were simply told of a character's action ("Jane is looking for her kitten under the piano") and then asked, "Why do you think she is doing that?" On such tasks most three-year-olds gave both belief and desire explanations; however, some young children explained action only by recourse to desire and never by appeal to belief, even when prompted by being asked, for example, "What does Jane *think*?" Of 23 three-year-olds, six consistently provided desire explanations but never mentioned belief even when prompted, and only one child evidenced the reverse pattern. This pattern of results provides support for the progression proposed here: early understanding of desire before understanding of belief. Moreover, the two studies of children's understanding of emotional reactions also described in chapter 6 clearly showed young three- and four-year-old children to be much more knowledgeable about desire-dependent emotions, such as happiness, than they were about belief-dependent emotions, such as surprise. These sorts of difficulties are the legacy, I believe, of children's earlier desire psychology, that is, the legacy of an earlier explanatory scheme that concerns itself solely with the satisfaction of desires.

Nonrepresentational Understanding of Mental States: What and When?
My proposal (here and in Wellman and Woolley, in press) is specifically that children's early understanding of desire is nonrepresentational and, more generally, that such a nonrepresentational understanding of mental states precedes an understanding of representational mental states such as beliefs and imaginings. I further propose that the transition from a nonrepresentational to representational understanding of mental states begins at about the third birthday. Several other writers have made related proposals (Perner

1988, Flavell, 1988). The similarities and differences between these proposals deserve some discussion.

Perner (1988) proposed that children have two quite different understandings about belief and belief descriptions. If young children hear, "Mary thinks the van is at the park," they might appropriately understand Mary as representing a particular state of affairs in her head (along the lines, perhaps, of how I have portrayed belief in figure 8.1). Alternatively, they might simply understand the description "van at the park" to be a description of the world and simply associate Mary with that description. Perner proposes that children until about four years of age do something like the second alternative: "associating" persons (Mary) and situational descriptions (van at park). Such an association between persons and situations constitutes a nonrepresentational understanding of belief. Only at about four years, he proposes, do children begin to understand persons as having representations.

Perner's proposal that a nonrepresentational understanding of mental states (specifically belief) precedes a representational understanding is similar in that respect to mine about simple desires; however, it is also different in several regards. A potential difference is Perner's assertion that young children simply see others as associated with these various situational descriptions. As I originally understood this proposal (Perner, 1988), the idea was that young children construe persons as simply linked to, in an unlabeled or nonspecific sense, certain situational descriptions not others. That is, statements such as that "Mary wants an X," "thinks an X," or "sees an X" all "associate" Mary with an X. If a child understands such statements as simply associating character and situation, then these very different statements equally create a positive association. And statements like "doesn't think," "doesn't want," and "hates" create more or less equal negative associations. In contrast, to construe a person as having a simple desire, as I describe it, is not merely to associate that person with an external object or description but to understand distinctly that the person wants it—a specific labeled internal state rather than an unlabeled association. The person need not be construed as representing what he wants, but his relation to that object is definite; he *wants* it. My position, therefore, is that even two-year-olds do something more specific than simply associate characters and described objects or situations.

More recently, Perner (1989; in press) has elaborated his proposal. Given this elaboration, I now believe that my emphasis on Perner's use of the term *associate* led me to misunderstand his proposal. The associational position as I describe it is a credible and serious proposal, and thus I spent time in chapter 3 refuting it. But it is not actually Perner's (current) position. The crux of Perner's position now is not that young children construe persons as associated in some unlabeled fashion with descriptions of situations; they do come to specific construals of the relation between person and description but construals that are nonrepresentational. Thus Perner says three-year-olds understand a statement like "Mary thinks the van is at the park" in a thinking-of rather than in a thinking-that manner. They understand such belief statements to mean something like "Mary thinks much of the park" or "Mary thinks well of the park" and hence prefers the park. Perner's main point, therefore, much like my own in figure 8.1, is that young children's construal of the relationship between persons and descriptions is nonrepresentational: to "prefer the park" can be seen along the lines of figure 8.1 as an internal state toward an object, unlike to "think that the van is at the park," which requires an understanding of representation. Young children, Perner proposes, may indeed understand persons as specifically wanting an X, or seeing an X, or pretending that X but not truly representing that X. In short, a nonrepresentational understanding of mental states precedes a representational one. On this I think we agree.

Some important differences remain, however. First, Perner believes that the transition to a representational understanding of belief does not take place until age four with the onset of an understanding of false belief. In contrast I think it takes place at about three. Further discussion of our disagreement requires a more precise definition of "representation" and "representational understanding of mind." I offer such a definition of representation in chapter 9, and at that point, I contend that three-year-olds have a representational rather than nonrepresentational understanding of belief and belief statements. I save further discussion of this aspect of Perner's proposal, therefore, until chapter 9.

Second, Perner believes that young children arrive at a nonrepresentational understanding of belief terms and belief statements, such as "Sam thinks his dog is in the garage." I do not think so. I think the developmental progression is from a nonrepresentational understanding of desire to a later representational understanding of belief; Perner seems to think that the progression is from a nonrepresentational to a representational understanding of belief itself. Two sets of data incline me toward my proposal. The first concerns three-year-olds. I do not think that three-year-olds typically misunderstand belief statements such as "Sam thinks his dog is in the garage" to be nonrepresentational descriptions of the character, such as Perner's "Sam thinks well of the garage." In chapter 3, I argued against this depiction of three-year-olds' (mis)understanding of belief in our study comparing relevant and irrelevant belief tasks. Second, I can find no evidence that two-year-olds make such an error either. I believe that the second study described in this chapter and our natural language research as well (Shatz et al., 1983) show that two-year-olds have no sensible understanding of belief terms at all; they do not have an appropriate understanding of belief, but they do not evidence a definite thinking-of misinterpretation of belief either.

Flavell (1988) has also recently suggested that young children move from a nonrepresentational understanding of mind to a representational one. As Flavell puts it, they can construe people as connected to external objects; only older children construe people as representing such objects and events: "Children have learned that they and other people can be epistemically related or 'cognitively' connected to things in the external world in a variety of ways" (Flavell, 1988, p. 244). Children, according to Flavell, understand others as connected to an external object by, for example, seeing it, tasting it, wanting it, and pretending with it. And they understand that such "connections entail inner, subjective experiences" (p. 245). I take this to mean something like my depiction of simple desires in figure 8.1; the child understands the other as having an internal experience (wanting, looking at) directed toward an external object (an apple), albeit not representing the apple in any sense. In this regard, therefore, Flavell also proposes that there is an important developmental transition from a nonrepresentational understanding of certain mental states to a representational understanding.

Still, again there are some differences. Flavell, somewhat like Perner, proposes that three-year-olds have a nonrepresentational understanding of mind and only four-year-olds achieve a representational one. I propose that this transition is made, roughly, at the third birthday rather than at the fourth. Additionally, Flavell argues that young children's understanding that people can be connected to objects include such "connections" as that the person can "think of or about it, remember it, dream of or about it, image or imagine it" (p. 245). This is confusing to me; these seem exactly like ways in which a person represents something rather than nonrepresentational connections to an object. I can conceive of a simple desire (wanting an apple) as a nonrepresentational connection to an apple. But I cannot conceive of what nonrepresentational imaginings, for example, could be like. How can imagining conceivably be parallel to the depiction for simple desires rather than beliefs in figure 8.1? I cannot come up with a sensible picture. Again the disagreement here between Flavell and me hinges on a closer examination of what we mean by "representations," a task I take up in chapter 9. I will return again to a comparison of my position and Flavell's in that chapter.

In spite of postponing some discussion of these various positions, I think it is worth emphasizing that Flavell, Perner, and I similarly propose that there is an early development in the child's theory of mind constituting a transition from a nonrepresentational to a representational understanding of certain mental states. We disagree about the specifics of such a proposal and about the timing of such a developmental transition, but the essential agreement is nonetheless important. Something like the present proposal seems a likely hypothesis to several workers in the field.

Change from Desires to Beliefs
A simple desire psychology could provide a necessary precursor to the child's later discovery of a belief-desire psychology. I believe that belief-desire psychology represents a theory change sponsored by and derived from simple desire psychology. A revision of desire psychology is necessitated by the predictive and explanatory failures of that reasoning scheme, failures that engender a construct of belief.

Early desire psychology provides the young child with significant explanatory resources, allowing the child to predict and understand a variety of actions and emotional reactions as stemming from the actor's internal desire states. A simple desire psychology fails in some respects, however. In particular there are certain phenomena that belief-desire psychology can account for that desire psychology cannot. These achievements depend on a conception of belief as an internal mental state in interaction with, but independent of, desire. Including a concept of belief in one's explanatory apparatus can provide, for example, an explanation for why two persons with the same desire (or the same person with the same desire at different times) might nonetheless engage in two different acts—because they have different beliefs. A conception of belief can also be used to predict a reaction of surprise (not just happiness); getting what you want (or do not want) may or may not be accompanied by surprise depending on whether the event is believed likely or unlikely. Moreover, adding a concept of belief can provide an explanation for why an actor might do something that seems contradictory to his or her own desires—for example, why he or she might look for desired food in the refrigerator when it is really in the cupboard—"because she *believed* it was in the refrigerator." Thus, to reiterate, two characters with the same desire can engage in different actions. They do so because they have different beliefs. Same desires leading to different actions is a common occurrence. It is easily accounted for in belief-desire psychology but is a theoretical anomaly for simple desire psychology. Similarly, actors often do things that thwart their desires. Recall Jane searching for her kitty. That she should look for it under the piano when it is under the chair is an anomaly for simple desire psychology because Jane is not acting so as to fulfill her desire. However, the same behavior is easily accounted for by Jane's false belief. Thinking about actors in internal-state terms at all, that is, with respect to their internal desires, makes it possible for the child to confront such theoretical anomalies. A behaviorist, for example, would not find these examples perplexing; he or she could easily account for them by histories of conditioning. It is simple desire psychology that generates these anomalies. Such anomalies, once generated, require the addition of a very different sort of internal construct to one's theoretical arsenal, specifically a conception of cognitive states of representation and conviction, not merely states of desire and disposition.

The proposal I am advancing concerns itself with the origins of belief-desire psychology—its origination out of an earlier desire psychology. It does not address the question of mechanisms, the sorts of learning and experiences that drive and constrain belief-desire conceptions. Still, the descriptive proposal as to origins is important:

> Any theory of learning must have at least two components: a specification of the initial state and a specification of the mechanisms in terms of which that initial state is modified. "Initial state" here is specified relative to the particular change under consideration. Both components are necessary for stating the constraints on induction that guarantee that learning is possible. Psychologists who decry the lack of mechanisms of conceptual change focus on only half of the problem. Equally important is the specification of the initial state. (Carey, 1985a, p. 200)

Simple desire psychology begins to characterize, if not precisely or completely the "initial state," at least a very early state in the understanding of human action. Moreover, it begins to pinpoint an important early transition—that from a simple desire to a belief-desire psychology. I am not claiming that understanding of desire ceases at this point of transition; it does not. I am claiming instead that an initial understanding of simple desires also results in an understanding of belief and that acquisition of this construct seriously transforms the young child's naive psychology. Indeed, the psychology thus acquired, belief-desire psychology, encompasses the first coherent understanding of mental representational states rather than simple internal dispositions.

Two further elaborations of this position are needed. I claim that a

theory of mind begins at about three years. I make this assertion because belief-desire psychology begins at just about three, and it is
belief-desire psychology that manifests the first real theory of mind.
However, it is not my position that before three years children know
absolutely nothing of the mind. Philosophers often loosely define the
domain of the mind as encompassing a variety of "mental states,"
and such mental states include those of pains, drives, arousal, and
simple desires, as well as beliefs. Thus, since two-year-olds evidence
understanding of simple desires, for example, they clearly are attaining some understanding of mental phenomena. Nonetheless, there is
something essential about the concept of belief in our everyday concept of mind because the concept of mind itself seems to require a
notion of internal representations. Consider, for example, such
phrases as "it's only in his mind" and "my mind is blank slate." A
conception of a simple desire falls short of this ordinary understanding of the mind. Another way of saying this is that it is only from the
vantage point of a belief-desire psychology that the notion "mind"
makes sense. Once it makes sense, then we can talk further about
hunger, and pain, and simple desires as related mental states—but
only then. Some of these states are states of "mind" only by virtue of
their participation in a larger theory such as that in figure 4.1. Therefore, it is only at about three years, when understandings of mental
phenomena cohere into a larger belief-desire psychology, that I feel
that children can be said to acquire a theory of mind. This is somewhat arbitrary, I realize; the developmental story is one of continuous
advances. Still this way of marking the start of a theory of mind
seems sensible.

Equally, it should be clear that my position denies that a belief-
desire construal of action is innate, given to us by evolution rather
than constructed developmentally. Fodor (1987), for one, has claimed
that belief-desire psychology is innately given (p. 132) and, taking a
page from my book, argues that the fact that children as young as
three years evidence belief-desire theorizing is evidence for nativism.
If I am right, however, belief-desire psychology is not available at
birth. Belief-desire explanation is beyond the grasp of infants and toddlers. Neither does it emerge as the result of endogenous maturational processes. A belief-desire psychology is not innately given
because the construct of belief must be constructed out of a notion of
desire. Or better, it is constructed out of theoretical failures of a simple desire psychology.

There is a narrow path here that I believe is the correct one, hov-
ering above the abyss of simple nativism on the one hand and the
abyss of know-nothingism on the other. It is not that infants and tod-

dlers know nothing but they do not know belief-desire psychology either. One sort of intentional explanation is in hand by two years, and it may even be that some sort of intentional explanation proves within the grasp of infants, but not, I contend, those belief-desire explanations so dear to us as adults.

Agency

By two years children are simple desire psychologists. By three years belief-desire psychology develops out of desire psychology. Desire psychology is an internal state theory but not a cognitive, representational theory. Desire psychology does provide an early answer to questions of causation; that is, it posits internal causal states that produce external actions and reactions. The causal aspect of mind obvious in belief-desire psychology is built from this earlier causal analysis. Notice how different this is from Leslie's proposal (1988) that toddlers understand only physical causality and that notions of mental causality emerge out of physical notions of causality. In contrast I propose that even toddlers understand a sort of psychological causality distinct from physical causality—desire causality. Mental causality of the belief-desire sort emerges out of this earlier desire causality.

Desire psychology is an interesting achievement. It posits that others, like self, act on the basis of their own wants, which may well be different from one's own. Where does desire psychology come from? Here it is possible to speculate that it comes from an earlier understanding still, an understanding that others are independent initiators of action. This is what Poulin-Dubois and Shultz (1988) have termed an understanding of agency. There are two aspects to a notion of agency as I wish to use the term. To understand someone as an agent is to understand that the person is independent of oneself and that the person's acts are self-caused. In brief, agents are autonomous causers. An agent in this sense is quite different from a physical object such as a ball. A ball begins to move, for example, only if acted on by an external force; an agent initiates action on its own. An agent in this sense is also different from an organism with simple desires. An entity such as a battery-driven car may qualify as an agent, but its actions do not result from desirelike dispositions. It is possible that infants may have a recognition of agents—entities capable of self-initiated movement or behavior—before an understanding of desire-driven actors and that the latter develops out of the former.

There is ample suggestive evidence of a early understanding of agency, in the above sense, in infancy. Poulin-Dubois and Shultz

(1988) and Stern (1985) present interesting cases for an understanding of agency in infancy. As a brief example, Golinkoff (Golinkoff, 1975; Golinkoff and Kerr, 1978) has shown that by twenty-four months, at least, toddlers consider inanimate objects that act like autonomous agents to be anomalous. That is, such very young children do not attend unduly to an animate agent such as a person moving on its own or to an inanimate object such as a chair moving because an external force is applied to it, but do attend considerably to a chair appearing to move on its own. Poulin-Dubois and Shultz (1988) claim to have shown a similar recognition in thirteen-month-olds.

Relatedly Golinkoff (1983, 1986) has shown that in communication to their parents, one-year-old toddlers treat their parents as independent agents who can be mobilized to actualize the child's goals. There is controversy as to whether such young children's communicative attempts and repairs demonstrate an even greater knowledge of their listeners than evident in this characterization (see Golinkoff, 1986; Shatz, 1983). Still, at a minimum it seems clear that in the year from one to two, toddlers evidence an understanding of others as agents. Perhaps they do so before their first birthday. Leslie (1984) has shown that seven-month-olds distinguish certain animate from inanimate causal sequences (Leslie, 1984). Regrettably, we are still largely ignorant of the infant's understanding of causality. But enough is known to suggest that the two-year-olds' developing understanding of desire-driven actions is based on and could emerge from a long earlier concern with human causality and a prior conception of persons as agents.

In summary, I propose that the causal aspect of mind, achieved at around age three with an initial understanding of belief, rests on an earlier understanding of simple desires, which in turn rests on a long history of concern on the part of infants and toddlers with human agency. Understood in this fashion, three-year-olds' understanding of mental causation is an impressive achievement but a less mysterious one and not necessarily solely innately given.

Sources of Information for the Imaginary Aspects of Mind

What of precursors to the three-year-old's understanding of the imaginary aspect of mind—their appreciation of the internal, not-real, subjective status of mental entities? Simple desire psychology provides a conceptual infrastructure for this aspect of mind too. Simple desires are internal states that are specific to individuals (my desires are not necessarily yours) and discrepant from external reality in the sense of discrepant from realized outcomes. The independence between desires and outcomes (what you want versus what you get) nicely foreshadows the independence between ideas or beliefs and facts (what you think versus what is so). Both the hypothetical and causal aspects of an understanding of belief, specifically, and mind more generally, could emerge out of an earlier simple desire psychology.

There is more to understanding the mental nature of mental entities than this, however. Our adult impression of the internal mental world of ideas, dreams, images is rich and vivid. According to the data in chapter 2, so too is the three-year-old's. It is here that a revised version of something like Johnson's proposal (1988) has its proper role: everyday experience of mind provides one- and two-year-olds with ample information to pull together a rich conception of imaginary mental entities and states by age three.

There is very little research to appeal to on this topic. Still, we can, like Gibson, begin to analyze more seriously the sorts of information available to the infant and toddler that afford a theory of mind. I use the term *afford* advisedly. Among the most compelling aspects of Gibson's theory of perception are his analyses of the information available to organisms in their environment. Similarly, I think that there is a striking amount and quality of information available to quite young children in their everyday experiences that can inform them about the subjective and hypothetical qualities of the mind. We are in need of careful analyses, in a Gibsonian sort of way, that describe the affordances for a theory of mind. Of course, in Gibson's theory, perceptual affordances are said to specify directly the nature of the event for the organism. I do not think that a theory of mind is directly specified for the infant or child in everyday experience; constructive inferential cognition is needed to forge such a theory. I have discussed this at length in examining Carl Johnson's and Paul Harris's positions. In everyday usage, however, before Gibson's specific theoretical adoption, the term *afford* has just the meaning I need: "to have the capacity for providing especially to one who seeks" (Webster's New Collegiate Dictionary, 1979, p. 20). We can analyze affordances for a theory of mind in this everyday sense, describing the experiential information that must richly inform the theory even if it does not specify it. In this section I will begin to describe a few aspects of the young child's everyday experience that have the "capacity" for providing the information necessary for a theory of mind, especially to a constructive organism "who seeks" to make sense of this aspect of personal and social life, that is, to the average one- and two-year-old child. The paragraphs that follow do not achieve the sort of inspired analyses so useful in Gibson, but they demonstrate the possibility of such analyses and make plausible the acquisition of the theory by age three.

Careful thought can reveal the presence of many sources of relevant information. Let us stipulate that toddlers are cognitive organisms of the sort that have dreams, memories, and convictional attitudes such as beliefs and dispositional states such as desires. If so then:

> One primitive source of information is the phenomenological "feels" of different cognitive experiences, that is, the difference between experiencing a dream and forgetting a phone number. Having a dream is very distinct from forgetting a phone number; they differ in vividness, imaginal quality, and mental state (awake versus asleep). It seems highly probable that certain mental experiences are easily distinguished from one another on this basis by even young children. This is not to say that the child knows what dreams are and knows what forgetting is and so knows the two to be different. However, in the course of inevitably experiencing dreams and forgetting the child also experiences certain differences between these states. Such experiential differences can lead to further knowledge of distinctions between mental states or processes. (Wellman, 1985a, p. 199)

To paraphrase, since various mental processes are distinct, this yields potential information to the child about their critical differences, information that could afford certain conceptual distinctions and understandings on the part of the child. Not only do various mental processes have different experiential features among themselves, but they also contrast decidedly with nonmental events and occurrences. If we grant that young toddlers are sufficiently cognitively endowed to have thoughts, then thoughts just are different from objects and acts in the child's experience. Consider the basic distinction between desires and world. Even very young children want and hope for things (a special present, a certain food for dinner). In some cases such desires are actualized and in others not. Such experiences of the satisfaction and thwarting of one's desires afford the basic conceptual distinction between desires and outcomes. The case is similar for beliefs. Young children believe or expect various things (perhaps that boys have short hair) that are sometimes true and sometimes false. This affords the conceptual distinction between beliefs and facts. And children themselves have differential emotional reactions to such occurrences. The experiential difference in reactions such as unhappiness versus surprise, to return to an earlier example, could inform children about the difference between desires and beliefs, respectively.

In short, if very young children simply operate in roughly cognitive, symbolic, mental fashions at all, then their day-to-day experiences must provide them with a great deal of information as to the existence and nature of mind. Whether and when children take advantage of such affordances to build or amend their theory of mind is not known, but it seems improbable to me in the extreme that three-year-old's rich knowledge of the mind does not stem in part from the toddler's rich ubiquitous experience of having a mind.

Johnson (1988) has provided a provocative preliminary analysis of very young children's mental experiences, their "conscious life," in Johnson's terms. While I have tried to refute Johnson's claim that such experiences exhaust the three-year-old's understanding, I am in sympathy to a revised claim that such experiences afford an understanding of mind. I am indebted to Johnson because he begins to outline a serious analysis of the nature, structure, richness, and clarity of such everyday experiences and how such types of experiences could inform parallel categories of mind.

Children's experiences of these sorts of information do not begin at age one or two. Some experiences eventually affording a theory of mind are available in infancy. For example, one aspect of mental states apparent to adults is their subjective character. Mental life has an "internal," in-the-mind or in-the-head, feeling to it. For this reason, mental states and awareness are often wrapped up with conceptions of the self. In one sense, one's sense of self is often mental: I am the person with these ideas and memories, living "behind" my eyes, which are windows onto the external world (for me) and windows to the soul (for others). In another sense, one's sense of mind is individual: memories are mental experiences of a private, firsthand, in *my* mind's eye, character. What sort of information might help children to acquire such notions? Gibson (1979) provides some fascinating analyses of how everyday perceptual experiences may afford such understandings. According to Gibson, information is available to even infants who distinguish the self from the external world and who place the experience of self as located in the body, not outside, and indeed even in the head:

> Our field of view has boundaries, which, although vague and indistinct, are nevertheless boundaries. These consist of the head and the nose. That the nose forms a constant part at least of the adult field of view, is easily checked by closing one eye. Thus the self is a constant feature of the visual field because it visibly oc-

cludes part of the visual world. Such occlusions have regularities that are similar to the occlusions produced by a conventional moving object in that they consist of "an accretion of optical structure at the leading edge with deletion of structure at the trailing edge."

Moreover, as Gibson points out, the other features of the body, the trunk and the limbs, also occlude part of the visual world; but they differ from the head and nose with respect to their distance from the point of observation. The nose and orbit sweep across the surface behind them at the greatest rate whenever one moves one's head. Thus Gibson suggests that the experience of the self as being in the head, or at least as most centrally located within the head rather than the body, has its basis in optical information rather than any unanalyzable intuition.

In addition, an analysis of the optical information available to the infant suggests that there is at least one route—whether or not the neonate takes up that route is another question—by which the neonate can escape the adualism that is assumed by virtually every other developmental theorist regarding the period immediately after birth. The nose, head, limbs, and extremities occupy relatively fixed positions with respect to the point of observation. All other objects in the infant's environment, on the other hand, will be seen to undergo reduction in the retinal size as the infant is transported from place to place or as objects and people spontaneously move away. (Harris, 1983, pp. 744–745)

Of course, we have no evidence that infants actually discriminate or take in these various sorts of optical information. And in my view such information, even if discriminated, does not directly specify a private, mentalistic self. But this analysis does show the availability of a rich sort of information that even infants might use, that is, information that would afford (in the everyday sense of that term) construction of a sense of an internal subject of experience.

In a similar vein, Stern (1985) provides a potential analysis of how infants may construct a sense of self agency—themselves as the causes of their own actions:

Self events generally have contingent relations very different from events with another. When you suck your finger, your finger gets sucked—and not just generally sucked, but with a sensory synchrony between the tongue and palate sensations and the complementary sensations of the sucked finger. When your eyes close, the world goes dark. When your head turns and eyes move, the visual sights change. And so on. For virtually all self-initiated actions upon the self, there is a felt consequence. A constant schedule of reinforcement results. Conversely, acts of the self upon the other generally provide less certain consequences and result in a quite variable schedule of reinforcement. The infant's ability to sense contingent relations alone will be of no help in self/other differentiation. What will help, however, will be the infant's ability to tell one schedule of reinforcement from another, since only self-generated acts are constantly reinforced. (Stern, 1985, p. 80)

These analyses of probable affordances to a three-year-old's theory of mind paint a constructivist picture. In part that is my intent. I believe the child acquires a constructed entity—a theory—and does so by attending to various sources of information and amending earlier understandings. But I do not mean to suggest that the child's constructivist activities go on in isolation, that toddlers or infants undertake solely an independent theory-building enterprise, isolated from social sources of information. A theory of mind is also a social entity, a structure of beliefs held, operated, and transmitted by adults in the child's world. At the very least, the child is told certain things about the mind. Indeed, language to the child provides sources of socially transmitted information about the mind. At least three different sorts of information are afforded by language: explicit teachings about mental phenomena ("dreams aren't real"), a host of mental metaphors ("use your head," "she's brainy," "that's the rough idea"), and, most generally, everyday talk using everyday mental terms (*think, know, idea, dream*). Language acquisition must be an enormous source of information. There are mental verbs to be learned, such as *remember, believe, know, expect,* and *guess*; there are related semantic distinctions, such as factive and nonfactive predicates (see Hopman and Maratsos, 1978); there are nouns such as *brain, mind, idea,* and *memory*. We know that children hear such terms and their mental usages well before their third birthday. Indeed, children start to produce psychological terms at or right after their second birthday including terms of desire (*want*), emotional reaction (*happy*), physiological states (*hungry*), perception (*see*), and belief (*think*) (Limber, 1973; Bretherton and Beeghley, 1982; Shatz et al., 1983). However, our best estimate of when children first actually refer to states of belief and mentation (*think, know, remember*) with their use of such words is right before their third birthday.

At the very least, insights transmitted by others by language provide an important source of information for the child's theory building. Of course, it is possible that children are taught their society's theory of mind rather directly, that language, words, and parental teachings in essence convey a set of conventional beliefs to them. We know so little about the early acquisition of the theory that such a possibility remains open, but it is not a possibility that I favor.

It is extremely unlikely that children merely remember and assemble certain facts they have heard. That is, it is unlikely that their knowledge in this domain is the accumulation of direct teachings about the mind. It is unlikely, for example, because it is unlikely that children are ever "taught" a simple desire psychology as opposed to a belief-desire one. At a minimum, then, children assimilate any "teachings" to their own level of understanding. Indeed, in our study of the brain and mind (Johnson and Wellman, 1982), we showed that when fifth graders were exposed to direct teachings about the mind, they retained little of it and persisted with their own theoretical notions instead. Several studies of children's exposure to information concerning complex concepts have shown that preschool- and school-aged children's learning from such exposures is more determined by what they already know than by what they are shown (Kuhn, 1972; Siegler, 1978; Turiel, 1969). Of course, it may be that very early in conceptual development, in infancy, information from others is much more influential and more directly assimilated, though this seems unlikely. To be sure, understanding of the exact mental terms used in their own language must depend on the child's hearing and acquiring these terms, since mental terms differ from language to language. Some sort of socialization of the child's theory must be taking place, but what sort, and when? This remains a question for further research. The question, however, is not whether concepts of mind are individually created or instead learned; rather it is, How do children arrive at a theory of mind given the variety of rich sources of information available to them?

Pretense

I have concentrated in this chapter on characterizing an early state in the child's acquisition of an understanding of mind—simple desire psychology—and describing some of the sources of information that make acquisition of a theory of mind seem possible and not miraculous. Leslie (1987, 1988) has concentrated on a different task: attempting to specify the cognitive architecture—the underlying information processing mechanisms—that makes possible a theory of mind. Leslie argues that processing information about the mind itself requires a different sort of cognitive wherewithal from processing information about objects. "My approach to understanding these processing mechanisms makes certain assumptions about the nature of human cognition. These assumptions center on the hypothesis that human cognition involves *symbolic computations. . . .* What sort of internal symbol manipulating machinery is responsible for the development of the human capacity to form a theory of mind?" (Leslie, 1988, p. 21).

Why won't straightforward symbol-manipulating machinery do? The essential problem can be seen by comparing a system that has beliefs to a system that has beliefs about beliefs, and especially a system that entertains beliefs about false beliefs. To have beliefs is to be a system that forms representations of the world. Presumably, in the design of such a system, it is highly desirable for that system to strive to form accurate representations of the world, to put a premium on having correct beliefs, a premium on "the veridicality of cognitive processes." It is desirable to have correct beliefs because if a system's beliefs are wrong, for example, then it will search for food in wrong places and make other serious mistakes. But what of a system designed to have beliefs about beliefs? Since beliefs themselves are symbolic entities independent from reality, then to portray beliefs, the system must suspend its drive to represent reality itself correctly. This is clearest in the case of false belief; the system must ignore what is really so and conceive of a belief that is patently wrong. Let's say that it does so; then how can the system work so that a representation of a false belief is not confused with a representation of reality itself? This is important because if the two sorts of representations are mixed indiscriminately—representations that are patently not true and representations that are—then the organism's understanding of the world will become garbled and come tumbling down.

Leslie's assertion is that having beliefs about beliefs therefore places a special information-processing burden on the organism. That burden can be met by only a certain type of information-processing device, one capable not only of representations (reality-pointed representations) but also capable of metarepresentations (reality-suspended representations). Leslie presents a computational sketch of the nature of such an information-processing device.

The developmental implication of Leslie's analysis is that the child must have achieved this sort of processing capability in order to support a theory of mind. Then when does the child achieve such a capability? Here Leslie is able to show that pretend play—pretending a banana is a telephone—evidences the same sort of computational system. Children engage in pretense at about one and a half years and thus from about that time on are capable of achieving a theory of mind.

About pretending, one can ask the sorts of questions asked about beliefs about false beliefs: "Pretense poses deeper puzzles. How is it possible for a child to think about a banana as if it were a telephone, a lump of plastic as if it were alive, or an empty dish as if it contained soap? If a representational system is developing, how can its semantic relations tolerate distortion in these more or less arbitrary ways? Indeed, how is it possible that young children can disregard reality in any way and to any degree at all? Why does pretending not undermine their representational system and bring it crashing down?" (Leslie 1987, p. 412). Again, Leslie sketches the nature of such a representational system, and it is identical to that needed for a theory of mind. The appearance of pretense in the child's play at age one and a half therefore shows that such a representational system is in place. It may be in place even earlier, but pretense evidences its early existence. Of course, such a capability does not equal a theory of mind; it computationally allows a theory of mind.

Conclusions

Well before three years, the child has the computational symbol processing wherewithal potentially to deal with beliefs about the mind— for example, beliefs about beliefs. This is evident in the pretend play of one and a half-year-olds. Before three, the child has an earlier theory of human causality to build from, evident in the two-year-old's simple desire psychology. Before three, the child has a plethora of experiences affording a conception of the imaginary and subjective aspects of mind. All of these accomplishments set the stage for acquisition of belief-desire psychology around the third birthday. And these accomplishments have their own predecessors in such infant achievements as an understanding of agency and the firsthand experience of perception and action.

Chapter 9

From Three to Six: From Copies and Imaginings to Interpretations

In this chapter I tell my story of how the first theory of mind, that of three-year-olds, becomes consolidated and importantly transformed in the years from three to six. Much of what I will say here is not only my story but a story increasingly in the air. That is, researchers interested in children's first theory of mind are coming to some basic agreements. For example, generally it is now agreed that in the years three to six, children elaborate a first theory of mind, that they develop an understanding of mental states as representations, that they become able to see action as caused by mental representational states like belief, and that they come to see mental states such as belief to be informed by experiences with the world.

These agreements occur, in part, because the phrase "from three to six" covers a multitude of sins. For example, I believe that three-year-olds have a basic sense of mental representations; it is part of their rudimentary conception of belief and hence part of their beginning theory of mind. Perner (1988), Flavell (1988) and Gopnik (Forguson and Gopnik, 1988), however, believe that this is not achieved until four or four and a half years. In spite of our differences, we all agree that this is a fundamental achievement attained between three and six. This level of agreement is no trivial matter. The new consensual view tells a story of children's attainments that is quite different from the prior traditional view; it represents substantial agreement about the nature and timing of important milestones. I will return to this consensual level of description at several points throughout this chapter; it is an important task to articulate this accumulating common wisdom. However, I will begin by clarifying differences, differences masked by adoption of the less detailed "three to six" level of analysis. I begin with the differences because they force us to be clear at the outset about what we mean; for example, about what constitutes a mental representation and when young children understand what about false beliefs. To the extent that we achieve increased clarity about such matters, our larger descriptions can aspire to agreement based on mutual insight as to details rather than agreement based on silence as to details.

Much of the confusion and disagreement revolves around the notion of representation and the phrase "representational theory of mind." Many writers now assert that it is at about four or four and a half years that children achieve a representational understanding of mind. Before that, although children might understand about the existence and some of the properties of mental events and entities, they do not understand them to be representations. My view is different. I think that with the advent of an early but cogent understanding of belief, at about age three, children understand the basic notion of a mental representation. The transition from desire to belief-desire psychology thus marks the onset of an understanding of representational states of mind. Three-year-olds do not, however, understand the ineluctably interpretive quality of representations in general or the interpretive quality of mental representations such as beliefs, specifically. What children begin to achieve at about four or five, therefore, is an interpretational or constructive understanding of representations rather than an initial understanding of representation. This is not the whole story, however. Thus, after dealing with children's understanding of representation, I describe several other important acquisitions and advances in the young child's theory of mind. Within this discussion I include my view with regard to children's understanding of false belief.

Representation

> The difference between the 3-year-olds and the 4-year-olds might be summarized as follows: The 4-year-olds have developed a *representational model of mind*. . . . Four-year-old children, then, are beginning to recognize representations as representations, and they are beginning to adopt a metacognitive policy about them: namely, that some of these representations are one's own personal viewpoint; . . . that representations provide information about the way reality stands; that different people have a different informational relation to reality than oneself. (Forguson and Gopnik, 1988 p. 236)

> However, young children tend not to understand that forming cognitive connections to things entails mentally representing those things in various ways. They tend to be largely ignorant of the fact that it is possible to represent a single thing with its single nature in several different ways—ways that would be mu-

tually contradictory if they described the object itself rather than mental representations of it. Thus, they do not clearly understand that even though something may be only one way out there in the world, it can be more than one way up here in our heads, in our mental representations of it. (Flavell, 1988, p. 246)

These two quotations are typical of suggestions that a representational understanding of mind does not begin until four or four and a half years of age. Both suggest that only four-year-olds begin to understand anything about mere, faulty, relativized representations and that only with the advent of such an understanding do children have an understanding of mental representations and hence a representational understanding of mind. To my mind, such claims confuse having an understanding of mental representations at all with having a particular interpretational or constructive understanding of mental representations. Given the legacy of cognitive psychology and our naive adult notions of the essentially interpretive nature of such mental entities as beliefs and opinions, it is easy to view a constructivist conception of representation as the only possible one. But this confounds separable understandings. I turn first, therefore, to the task of achieving some clarity as to what representations are or how they might be construed.

I attempt to separate two different levels of sensible understanding of representation by considering photographs as representations. I do not mean to suggest that photographs provide the essential instance of a representation or that adults or children think of mental representations as generally like photographs, or indeed to suggest that there are any deep parallels at all between photographs and typical mental representations like beliefs or ideas. I simply employ photographs as an analytic device, to establish a reasonably straightforward distinction that can be carried over to a consideration of mental representations. I am aware that the nature of photographs themselves is controversial, but the device is adequate for my purposes. In addition, to provide a contrast, I will compare photographs to fictional drawings as representations.

Imagine a simple situation: a box and a photograph of that box, which I will term the thing-entity and the representational-entity, respectively. What can we say of the photograph in distinction to the box?

1. The photograph itself is an entity separate from and distinctly different from the box itself.
2. Still, the photograph "displays" the box, or can be taken to refer to or stand for the box.

These points together provide the sense behind such statements as "the photograph represents the box" or "photographs are representational entities." Together they mean that a photograph has a dual status as a flat piece of paper (a type of thing-entity in its own right) and as a representational entity, that is, a picture of another entity. One reason the photograph represents or displays the box is that there exist some important correspondences between it and the box; perhaps the photograph shows the box as red and the box is red; perhaps the photograph shows the box as rectangular and the box is rectangular. In total it seems reasonable to say that I understand the photograph as a representation if I understand that it is a separate representational-entity that depicts or stands for some other entity altogether, based on the establishment of certain relationships between representation and referent (between representational- and thing-entities). Of course, the specific kind of relationships between a photograph and its referent (graphical correspondences) does not define representational relations generally. Other relationships (that between word and referent, between a concept and its extensions), even completely arbitrary stipulations, can also be used to create representations. The point is that some such referential relations are necessary.

Now consider a fictional drawing. Suppose that I draw a picture of an imaginary, nonexistent box. I could, of course, make a drawing of some specific real box, but I want to concentrate on the case where I do not. Importantly such a drawing of a box is also a representational entity. Artwork that depicts recognizable objects is called representational art; it contrasts with abstract art. Representational art represents even when it does not depict any specific real physical item. A drawing of a unicorn represents a unicorn even though there are no unicorns; a drawing of a box stands for a box even in the case where there is no real box, no physically extant thing-entity that I draw. A contrast between photographs and fictional drawings highlights an important distinction between two varieties of representations: reality-oriented and fictional representations. A drawing of a box when there is no such real box (no real model for the artwork) is representational, but it is not reality oriented in the sense I mean. In contrast, photographs, as we ordinarily understand them, are reality-oriented representations. A photograph of a box displays a specific real box, the box that was the target of the photo.

This distinction between fictional and reality-oriented representations, as evident in a comparison between drawings and photographs, seems to hold with regard to mental states too. Beliefs and percepts are reality-oriented mental representations; imaginings, dreams, and daydreams are also representational mental states, but they are often fictional. That is, part of the definition of a belief is that it is a description of a person's attempt to capture reality faithfully; it is reality oriented. In contrast, although imaginings also depict things, they are fictional.

Let me return to photographs. I want to distinguish two different sorts of understandings of photographs as reality-oriented representations; these revolve around two different understandings of misrepresentation. To reset the stage, I will talk of a box and of a photograph meant to be of that box (that is, a reality-oriented photograph) but ask: how could the photograph fail to represent the box faithfully?

3. Hit-or-miss representation: Let's suppose that the photographer takes a blank picture, because he aimed the camera off target. Such a photograph is not a representation of the box (in the usual sense). The photograph misrepresents because it has missed; it has failed to display the target, the box. Or suppose I want a photo of a specific box, and the photographer takes a photo of a different box. Again the photograph misrepresents because it has missed; it fails to display the right box. The photographer may also have taken a partial photo—for example, a photograph of one box whereas there were two boxes present. Such a photograph also does not represent the real situation faithfully even if it was intended to. By mistake, it misrepresents, in the sense of having missed part of the target.

4. Interpretive misrepresentation: In addition to this basic level of missed representation, there is another sort of discussion we could have about misrepresentation. The photograph might actually depict my box, but because of the use of filters, it displays the box as blue whereas really it is green. Because of the printing process, the photograph displays the box's surface as grainy whereas it is really quite smooth. That is, the photograph can hit the proper target but misrepresent it in the sense of providing a misconstrual of it. Indeed, so this discussion goes, every photograph is a construal, an interpretation. Even if I feel the photo has captured my box perfectly, this has required composition in the photographer's eye, creative use of filters and light, and embodies only one of a great many possible developing and printing possibilities. In short, every photograph is a creative, interpretive statement and not an automatic copy of reality. This opens up the possibility of misconstrual or interpretive misrepresentation.

Even an understanding along the lines of (1), (2), and (3)—without (4)—evidences an understanding of representation. However, it is only one sort of understanding of representation—the sort that is inherent in what might be called a copy view of photographs. I borrow this phrase from Chandler (Chandler and Boyes, 1982). What I wish to say about a copy understanding of representation was inspired by his analysis of a possible copy theory of knowledge.

Suppose for the sake of argument that photographs truly were completely faithful copies of reality. If so, they would still be representations and could still misrepresent in a hit-or-miss sense (say, by failing to hit the target). Of course, in the light of (4) above it seems unlikely that such a copy understanding of photographic representations is correct. Still, it is a possible conception. Based on this discussion, it seems clear that we can separate two sensible understandings of reality-oriented representations; a copy understanding and an interpretive understanding. Moreover it is possible to imagine three successive levels of understanding. First, there might be a failure to understand representations at all. For example, someone who sees photographs as only thing-entities (a flat piece of paper with interesting colors and designs on it) fails to understand the representational nature of photographs at all. Second, there is an initial understanding of representation, available even if we take representations (such as a photograph) to be true copies of reality. Someone who understands (1), (2), and (3)—but not (4)—has a representational understanding of photographs, albeit a copy rather than an interpretive understanding of photographs. Third, there is an understanding of the interpretive aspect of representations. Someone who understands (1)–(4) has both a representational understanding of photographs and an interpretive understanding of photographic representations.

It is revealing, and helpful in keeping terminology straight, to recall that in artistic circles there has been a debate as to whether photographs are to be considered an art form or instead simply copies of reality. All parties to this debate have considered photographs as representations. The issue has been whether photographs, as representations, are more on the order of copies or constructions, mere recordings or interpretations, representations or expressions (Goodman, 1976; Arnheim, 1974; Gombrich, 1965; Tagg, 1988).

It is probably clear how I intend to apply these distinctions to children's understanding of mental representational phenomena. In brief, my contention is that three-year-olds understand ideas, beliefs, mental images, dreams, and such to be representational. They understand some of these to be fictional representations and some to be reality-oriented representations, but in each case representational. Hence it is incorrect to say they do not have a representational understanding of mind. However, their representational understanding of reality-oriented representations is a copy understanding. Not until four and five years of age do children understand mental representations in any sense as interpretive entities. There are several important distinctions to keep track of here. There is the distinction between representational and nonrepresentational entities. Then within the class of representational entities, there is the distinction between fictional and reality-oriented representations. Finally, with respect to reality-oriented representations specifically, there are two levels of understanding: a copy understanding and an interpretational understanding. Discussing photographs and drawings helps to clarify these distinctions.

First Representational Understanding of Mind

Two sorts of data already presented support the claim that three-year-olds understand the existence and representational nature of mental entities (representational-entities) such as images, thoughts, and beliefs. These data include demonstrations of children's understanding of both fictional and reality-oriented representations.

Consider the studies of young children's understanding of mental entities reviewed in chapter 2. In those studies we did not rigorously segregate fictional from reality-oriented representations, therefore, consider first the general question of whether children understand mental entities as representational or nonrepresentational things. Recall that even three-year-olds readily agree that they can form mental "pictures" of real entities. Along the lines of (1) above, they say that mental entities such as images and thoughts are different in ontological status from the real entities they represent (the thing-entities). In addition, along the lines of (2) above, they say that nonetheless such mental entities are "of" or "about" their thing-entities; for example, mental images are "imaginations" about or "dreams" of the real cup, or are like "television" or "movies." As a way of capturing this representational quality of images, children often explicitly referred to their images as "pictures" of the real entity. Of course, in our mental imagery studies, that is how the adult termed mental images in talking to the children. So a more compelling finding is that in similar studies of children's understanding of thoughts, dreams, and memories (Wellman and Estes, 1986, and the close impostor study of chapter 2), where adults never mentioned the term *picture*, young children still spontaneously referred to their mental entities as "pictures" in their head or mind. Spontaneous comments of this sort were also reported by Piaget (1929) and Laurendeau and Pinard (1962). This sort of spontaneous comment, while noticeable, is not particularly frequent from young children. However, recall that in the second mental imagery study (in chapter 2) we began to compare directly children's understanding of mental images and photographs. Children's patterns of responding revealed a representational understanding of mental images. That is, they responded to mental entities and real photographs similarly with regard to their representational status, albeit differently with respect to their material versus mental status.

Beyond an understanding of mental representation generally, those data also encompass a demonstration of an understanding of fictional as well as reality-oriented representations. With regard to fictional representations, in the third study of Wellman and Estes (1986) even three-year-old children said, for example, that they had never seen "a dog that flies" and that in fact "a dog that flies" does not exist. Nevertheless they asserted that they could think about and dream about "a dog that flies." Also in those studies children often said of mental representations such as dreams that they were just imagination or made up. In short, it seems that three-year-old children understand that some mental representations are fictional: imaginings as I generically term them.

These data also show that children understand that some mental representations are reality oriented. For example, in the mental image studies, children were asked to make mental images of specific real objects. They found this an easy instruction to understand, claimed that they had done so (had made a picture of *that* X in their mind), and treated such mental pictures as mental snapshots or photographs in various ways. Further, in Chapters 3 and 6 I offered evidence supporting three-year-olds' understanding of beliefs as reality-oriented representations. To understand belief as a mental state, but a mental state of conviction about the external world—that is, as simultaneously internal and mental but providing information about the real state of affairs that can be used to act in the world—is to understand beliefs as reality-oriented representations. It is to understand beliefs somewhat along the lines of figure 8.1, that is, to understand that beliefs depict, mentally, an external thing world. Our data show that this is how three-year-olds understand belief; they understand statements such as "he thinks the markers are in the drawer" to convey information about the actor's mental conviction as to real-world entities.

In short, the data provided and reviewed in prior chapters demonstrate that three-year-olds understand many mental entities to be representational. Therefore, I conclude that they have a representational understanding of mind and an understanding that includes a distinction between two different sorts of mental representations: fictional and reality-oriented ones. The next question to consider is whether children at this age understand reality-oriented mental representations in copy or in interpretational terms.

Two sorts of data are relevant to the claim that, at first, young children misunderstand reality-oriented mental representations to be like copies of reality rather than interpretive construals of reality. There are positive demonstrations that young children treat such representations as direct copies, and there are negative demonstrations that they fail to understand such representations as interpretive. As is obvious in my initial remarks about photographic representations, both sorts of evidence revolve around children's understanding of misrepresentation. To start, therefore, it is important to show that three-year-olds have some understanding of misrepresentation at all. They do, I claim, but they have a hit-or-miss type of understanding, not an interpretive-type understanding of misrepresentation.

In figure 9.1 I have provided a depiction to help capture the crucial aspects of young children's earliest understanding of representation and misrepresentation, that is hit-or-miss representation. I am interested in the conceptions of the person on the right. That person sees things in the world, including the target person on the left. My depiction of the person on the left is meant to capture a construal by the person on the right of that target person's ideas. Thus, on the top line, the person conceives of the target person as having a reality-oriented representation in his head of a specific apple, a true belief. On the second line there is no apple, so I mean to depict that the character is imagining an apple, a fictional representation. The top line of the figure reiterates the crude depiction of belief I advanced in figure 8.1, and the second line offers a parallel visual depiction of imaginings. The next lines elaborate on the young child's understanding of reality-oriented representations by depicting the sorts of misrepresentation understood by someone who has a copy view of reality-oriented representations. Those next lines assert that young children also understand that persons can fail to have any representation of the real object (ignorance) and can have mistaken beliefs of at least one variety—incomplete knowledge. In short, I claim that even for three-year-olds the mental world is populated by beliefs, mistakes, and imaginings. And beliefs can come in two forms: hits (true beliefs) and misses (ignorance and incomplete knowledge). Ignorance and incomplete knowledge are the sorts of misrepresentations encompassed by a copy theory of representation because both can be viewed as something like a copy mechanism missing its target. In ignorance, the copier has missed its target completely; in incomplete knowledge, the copier has missed part of the complete target.

What sorts of data support this depiction of three-year-olds' understanding of misrepresentation? First, what about ignorance? Recall that in our explanation studies in chapter 6, three-year-olds at times explained anomalous actions by saying, "He didn't know where it was." And in a series of studies, Hogrefe, Wimmer, and Perner (1986) have shown that even when three-year-olds fail to understand the nature of a character's false belief, they tend to understand that he is ignorant.

What about incomplete representation? Relevant data confirming three-year-olds understanding of incomplete knowledge come from their performance on our discrepant belief tasks as reviewed in chapter 3. Three-year-olds understood that in a situation where targets were in both of two locations, an actor might believe that targets were in only one location and act accordingly. Moreover, the sort of understandings of ignorance and true belief required by a copy sense of representation seem obviously tied to some related understandings that perception engenders mental representations. In figure 9.1 if the target person looks at X, he hits X and represents it; if he does not hit X, he is left with either ignorance or imaginings. In this sort of copy view, there seems to exist a direct link between perception and representation. Hence, it is relevant and important that in chapter 6 it became clear the three-year-olds understand that perception yields belief in certain simple fashions. Indeed the understandings outlined there now seem like part and parcel of the depiction in figure 9.1. That is, three-year-olds seem to know that if a person has seen something, then he knows it (true belief), and if he has not seen it, then he does not know it (ignorance). Also three-year-olds know that the person may have seen only one of several objects and thus have incomplete knowledge; that is, in our inferred belief-control task where there were targets in two locations but the actor had seen them only in one, three-year-olds understood that incomplete knowledge would constrain the actor's action. While these studies all concern seeing, presumably young children might know something of the relation between other forms of perception (such as hearing) and knowing too.

True Belief

Imaginings

Misrepresentations of a Hit-or-Miss Variety

1. **Ignorance:**

2. **Incomplete Knowledge:**

Figure 9.1
Graphical depiction of children's earliest understanding of representations and misrepresentations.

In short, I claim that three-year-olds have an initial understanding of mental representation. Their understanding encompasses both fictional representations (that is, imaginings) and reality-oriented representations (that is, beliefs). However, their understanding of reality-oriented representations encompasses only a hit-or-miss type of understanding of misrepresentation. That is, three-year-olds' understanding of misrepresentation is confined to an understanding of ignorance and incomplete knowledge, as heuristically portrayed in figure 9.1. Hence, I term three-year-olds' understanding an understanding of imaginings and copies.

With respect to reality-oriented representations, there seems to be, therefore, positive, albeit incomplete, evidence that three-year-olds have a copy understanding of representation. There is also negative evidence that three- and even many four-year-olds fail to understand the interpretive nature of representations. I will review that evidence in the next section because those data depict the transition from three-year-olds' copy understanding of representation to four- and five-year-olds' beginning interpretational or constructive understanding of representation.

An Interpretive Understanding of Representation

Three-year-olds have an understanding of mental representation—including a copy-type understanding of reality-oriented representation—and hence a representational understanding of mind. What develops in the years three to six, therefore, is an interpretive understanding of representation. The general phenomenon, first alluded to in chapter 1, is the transformation of the three-year-old's early understanding of mind into a later active, processing understanding. One specific manifestation of this general developmental trend, in fact, perhaps a first manifestation of it, is the child's increasingly interpretive understanding of mental representations. Here my story begins to resemble Flavell's and Gopnik's in certain ways. I think that we would all agree that children achieve an increasing sense of mental representations as interpreted construals of reality in the years three to six.

One source of evidence that might demonstrate young children's increasingly interpretive view of representation concerns children's understanding of what Forguson and Gopnik (1988) have termed representational diversity. If all representations are interpretive products, then you and I are likely to have different ideas in many respects. Your interpretations will not be identical to mine; your construals—based on your own prior ideas, likes, predilections, and so on—will be different from mine. In short our representations will be diverse.

By adopting their descriptive label for this topic, I am not claiming, as Forguson and Gopnik appear to, that three-year-olds have no sense of representational diversity. Three-year-olds have a limited initial understanding of representational diversity because even a copy notion of representation allows room for individual differences. For example, I may see something and hence know it, but you do not and hence are ignorant. I may have a dream (a representational experience), and you do not. In short, as encompassed by figure 9.1, even three-year-olds understand representational diversity, but they understand only the diversity allowed by imaginings and by a hit-or-miss conception of misrepresentation. Thus, as reviewed in Chapter 6 three-year-olds do understand that I may be knowledgeable but you may be ignorant, that I may have complete knowledge where yours is incomplete. As demonstrated in Chapter 2, they understand that mental entities are private; I have dreams, thoughts, and mental images that you do not share. Indeed, the preferred method in these studies is to have children differentiate between their own and another's mental states. Three-year-olds do so. What happens in the years three to six, therefore, is not the initial understanding of differences between individuals in their representations but an increasingly pervasive allowance for such differences and additionally an interpretational understanding of such differences. For example, you and I both see the object and represent it, but we represent it in slightly different ways.[1]

If children are changing from copy to interpretive notions, then they should achieve some substantially new insights with regard to representational diversity in the years three to six. That is, from an enlarged interpretive perspective, someone with only a copy notion of reality-oriented representation should make some telling mistakes. What sort of mistakes? In general, if mental representations actually are the interpretive products of processes of construal, then someone with a copy theory of representation ought to make two sorts of errors in judging representational diversity: in some cases, a copy theorist ought to judge that a person has an appropriate representation when in fact he does not (for example, if the person has some exposure to the object or event but not enough to arrive at the proper interpretation), and in some cases, a copy theorist ought to judge that a person has no representation when he does (for example, the person could not achieve a perceptual copy but could arrive at a representation in an active constructive fashion). From an interpretive, constructive view, perceptual access to an event might be sufficient to provide a "copy"—it might hit, not miss—but be uninterpretable. Conversely, it can be possible to construct a valid interpretation in the absence of the sort of perceptual access needed to produce a copy. There is evidence that three-year-old children make both of these errors but that in the years three to six, such errors substantially decline.

Chandler and Helm (1984) uncovered evidence that young children make the first sort of error. In their task children first saw a picture of an object (an elephant); then the picture was screened so that only a very restricted view was left. For example, a small hole showed only the tip of the elephant's trunk. Children were asked if a naive observer who saw only the contents of the hole would know there was an elephant there. Preschoolers said yes. In essence they appeared to believe that a person who encountered the picture at all would represent it or know it comprehensively.

Taylor (1988) clarified these findings. She found that three- and four-year-olds believe that exposure to a small, uninformative view of an object is sufficient for a person to represent it. Hence such young children claim that a viewer will know he is looking at a giraffe even if exposed to a screened display showing only an unidentifiable spot on the giraffe's back. She concludes that young children think that seeing equals knowing; such a belief constitutes the first sort of error mentioned. Given a copy theory of reality-oriented representation, visually viewing the object at all constitutes a hit and could provide a copy of it. Taylor shows that by five years, children begin to respond more correctly to such tasks, discriminating between informative and uninformative views. Acknowledging that perception may hit the target but still be uninformative is an interpretive notion.

The second sort of error might be manifest as follows. Present children with a situation where an observer does not see an object's identity but could infer it. Given a copy theory, where reality-oriented representation is dependent on a perceptual hit, young children should judge that the person does not know the object's identity. Older children with an interpretive theory of representation could judge that the person inferentially constructs a representation anyway. Allowing for inferential representations—derived knowledge beyond that given by perception—is a constructive, interpretational notion.

Sodian and Wimmer (1987) have shown this. Four-year-olds claim that a person without perceptual experience of an event but with sufficient information to infer its nature does not know what occurs. For example, a child and another character are shown a bag full of red markers. Then, out of sight, one marker from the bag is transferred to a box. When asked if they know what color the marker in the box is, four-year-olds answer it is red. When asked if the other knows, four-year-olds say no, because he has not seen it. Thus four-year-olds can make the inference involved, but they judge knowledge as arising only from hit-or-miss perceptual experiences. Five- and six-year-olds attribute knowledge to the other person because they understand that that person can infer the answer.

These examples represent two aspects of a basic change in children's understanding of representational states such as knowing and believing in the years three to six. The essential change is that children come to understand a variety of informational relations to an event rather than a simple copy relation. Thus, they begin to understand such notions as interpretation, construal, and inference (although they do not use these terms). These are the sorts of active, constructive processes of representation central to an interpretive understanding of representation but outside the pale of a copy understanding of representation.

A Direct Copy Theory: Reconciliation of Three-Year-Olds' Failures on False Belief and Appearance-Reality Tasks

The notion of a copy theory of reality-oriented representations is general enough to encompass several more specific versions. In this section I outline a more specific proposal that I think captures three-year-olds' understanding in more detail. This proposal provides an account of three-year-olds' failures on false belief and reality-appearance tasks.

A Direct Copy Theory

A copy theory of representation, as I see it, might encompass answers to two separable questions. First is the acquisition question: How are reality-oriented representations acquired? The simple answer is that they are copied. Second is the definitional question: What are reality-oriented representations (however acquired)? The simple answer here is, direct copies of reality. In my view the three-year-old's copy theory includes some implicit notions about both questions, but the definitional answer is paramount. That is, three-year-olds' understanding is based on a sense of what direct copies are (faithful depictions of reality) more than on an understanding of how copying, as an acquisitional process, works.

Consider the following characterization of a copy theory of knowledge:

In ways reminiscent of certain early psychological theories of perception (Furth, 1969) [preschool] children seem to proceed as though they believe objects to transmit, in a direct-line-of-sight fashion, faint copies of themselves, which actively assault and impress themselves upon anyone who happens in the path of such "objective" knowledge. Within such a view, projectile firings from things themselves bombard and actively victimize individuals who function as passive recorders and simply bear the scars of information which has been embossed upon them. (Chandler and Boyes, 1982, p. 391)

This passage vividly portrays one way in which a copy theory of knowledge might work, thereby making credible, even in adult mechanistic terms, the general proposal that mental representations could be conceived of as direct copies of reality. However, there is a possible interpretation of this passage that I want to avoid. One might conclude from it that children have not only a direct copy notion of what representations are like but also a detailed conception of how representations are copied onto minds from things (perhaps by projectile impression-radiations). I think they do not. Three-year-olds understand that (reality-oriented) mental representations faithfully copy reality but have much less definite, fleshed-out notions of how that happens. To summarize, it is the direct quality of copies that is the essence of three-year-olds' copy notions, not a conception of the copying mechanism.

Given such a direct copy understanding of what reality-oriented representations are, how would a copy theorist answer the question, "What does someone else think?"—for example, "What does Joe think is in the box?" I believe they would answer like this. Since reality-oriented representations (such as beliefs and photographs) are direct copies, they are representations that faithfully capture reality. The content of such a representation therefore is a copy of reality. "What does Joe think is in the box?" is a request for the content of Joe's belief. The question becomes in essence, What is the content of a faithful copy of reality? And the answer is clearly, "reality." Therefore if the copy theorist knows what is really in the box, say a ball, the answer as to Joe's belief is, "Joe thinks a ball is in the box." In short, beliefs are direct copies, and so the content of a person's belief is reality. I think this sort of copy theory answer accounts in large part for three-year-olds' errors on false-belief tasks. Recall the story about Maxi who saw the chocolate in the kitchen and did not see it moved to the dining room. If a direct copy theorist is asked, "Where does Maxi think the chocolate is?" he reasons. "This is a question about the content of Maxi's beliefs; beliefs are reality-oriented representations and hence they are faithful copies of reality; therefore, Maxi thinks the chocolate is in the dining room."

I think that three-year-olds have a direct copy theory of this sort, but this is not the only conceivable possibility. To illustrate, I briefly describe a different sort of copy theory, what I will call a time-tagged copy theory. I do not believe that three-year-olds have this sort of copy theory, but as I understand it Chandler now thinks that they do (Chandler, 1989; personal communication). In this possibility a copy theorist focuses more on the process of copying and especially the timing of that process. Specifically, in this alternative theory, the reasoner knows that a copy representation is copied from reality at a specific time. A copy (a photograph or belief) therefore is the product of a time-dependent copying process and once made does not change. If the copy depicts a ball in the box, it continues to depict the ball in the box until replaced by a new copy. The time-tagged copy theorist knows that reality can change with time (the ball is taken from the box), but the copy does not change (unless a new copy is made). In this sort of time-tagged copy theory, a copy representation could misrepresent in three ways: the two depicted in figure 9.1 (ignorance and incomplete knowledge) and in an additional way not depicted in that figure. Specifically, a time-tagged copy could misrepresent the contents of the box by representing a past reality rather than the present one. A time-tagged copy theorist therefore should be correct on false-belief tasks. When asked about Maxi's belief, a time-tagged copy theorist would reason, "Maxi's belief is a copy of what Maxi saw. Maxi saw (hence copied) the chocolate in the kitchen; he did not see and (did not copy) that the chocolate is now in the dining room. Maxi's belief depicts that past reality. Hence Maxi thinks the chocolate is in the living room."

I believe that three-year-olds are direct copy theorists, not time-tagged copy theorists. A time-tagged copy theory is a distinct possibility, however. Why do I prefer the direct copy theory? My reasons are essentially empirical. I think three-year-olds understand beliefs to be representations but they fail false-belief tasks. Indeed, by my proposal, the primary reason they fail false-belief tasks is that they are direct copy theorists of this specific sort. Chandler prefers something like a time-tagged copy theory because he feels that three- and even two-year-olds can understand false belief. I therefore discuss next three-year-olds' understanding of false belief.

3-Year-Olds' Misunderstanding of False Belief

There is a debate among interested researchers as to whether children younger than four years understand false belief. The majority view (Wimmer and Perner, 1983; Forguson and Gopnik, 1988; Flavell, 1988; Perner, 1988) is that three-year-olds fail false-belief tasks and that this failure indicates they fail to understand belief or at least fail to have a valid, representational understanding of belief. Others think that three-year-olds understand false belief at times (Bartsch and Wellman, 1989; Chandler, 1988) and that further demonstrations of three-year-olds' understanding will appear in the future. My own position is complex. In general I believe three-year-olds validly understand belief, regardless of whether they pass or fail false-belief tasks. That is, even perfectly valid demonstrations that three-year-olds fail false-belief tasks do not mean that they fail to understand belief generally or that they fail to have any understanding of mental representations. Within this general position, I have been inconsistent as to whether I think three-year-olds understand false belief. In Bartsch and Wellman (1989) we argued that they do, but my current revised position is that they do not; or more precisely, young three-year-olds do not understand false belief, although older three-year-olds are beginning to. I will briefly review the evidence suggesting three-year-olds fail to understand false belief. This is the evidence that leads me to believe that they have a direct copy theory of (reality-oriented) representations. Then I will describe some evidence suggesting that older three-year-olds at times evidence an initial understanding.

Beginning with Wimmer and Perner (1983) more than 20 demonstrations now exist that three-year-olds generally fail false-belief tasks (Perner et al., 1987; Gopnik and Astington, 1988; Moses and Flavell, 1989). They do so even when great care has been taken to make the tasks easy, comprehensible, and straightforward (see Perner et al., 1987). Consider three-year-olds' failure on our explicit false belief tasks (see table 3.1). In spite of passing our not-own and discrepant belief tasks, three-year-olds failed what seemed to us to be the simplest possible false-belief story: ("Jane wants her kitty. Her kitty is under the chair. Jane thinks her kitty is under the sofa. Where will Jane look?").

Given these data, why did I ever assert that three-year-olds understand false belief? I did so because in Bartsch and Wellman (1989) we found that three-year-olds could succeed at explaining someone's behavior as due to a false belief. Recall in the study of children's explanations (study 1 in Bartsch and Wellman, 1989) that when asked about anomalous belief actions (Jane's cat is under the chair; Jane is looking for her cat under the piano; why is she doing that?) many three-year-olds could at times appeal to the character's false belief ("Jane thinks it's under the piano"). Given those data, we hypothesized that three-year-olds' difficulty might be predicting action from false beliefs rather than understanding false belief per se and thus that three-year-olds might be able to explain actions stemming from false beliefs although unable to predict actions on the basis of false beliefs. In a follow-up study (study 2 of Bartsch and Wellman, 1989), we compared three-year-olds' ability to explain actions by false beliefs versus their ability to predict actions from false beliefs. For example, three-year-olds were shown two boxes, one a Band-Aid box with a picture of a Band-Aid on it, and the other a comparable plain white box. Then the child was asked which box had Band-Aids, and the boxes were opened. All children said the Band-Aid box had Band-Aids, but when the Band-Aid box was opened, it was empty and the plain box had the Band-Aids. In an explanation task based on this situation, children were then shown a puppet who "wants a Band-Aid." The puppet was walked to the Band-Aid box and began to open that box. The child was asked, "Why is she doing that?" Sixty-six percent of three-year-olds' explanations correctly appealed to the character's false belief, such as "she thinks Band-Aids are in there." On a prediction task the child was similarly shown a puppet who "wants Band-Aids" but who was placed equidistant between the two boxes. Then the child was asked, "Where will she look for Band-Aids?" In contrast to the explanations data, on these prediction tasks, the same three-year-olds were correct only 31% of the time.

We concluded therefore that three-year-olds could explain actions by false beliefs; their only problem was predicting actions by false belief. And this pattern of results made theoretical sense to us given that two-year-olds are desire psychologists and assuming that three-year-olds have incompletely abandoned that earlier way of thinking. We argued that

> for 3-year-olds at any rate, the false belief prediction tasks present a conflict between reasoning about what would satisfy the actor's desire (Sam wants the candy and it is in the drawer, therefore Sam will look in the drawer) and reasoning in terms of the actor's beliefs (Sam believes the candy is in the cupboard therefore he will look in the cupboard). Faced with this conflict, 3-year-olds predict according to what would satisfy the actor's desire. They do so not because they have no conception of belief; rather, in conflict, three-year-olds weight desire satisfaction over belief. Why this mode of reasoning wins out, we believe, con-

cerns the young child's strong allegiance to the maxim that in general people act so as to satisfy their desires. Young children are disinclined to suppose that an actor will act in a manner to thwart his or her own desires. (Bartsch and Wellman, 1989, p. 963)

I continue to think that this argument has some force. Given their allegiance to the maxim that people act to fulfill their desires, false-belief prediction tasks cause three-year-olds difficulty. In such tasks the child must predict the actor will act so as to thwart his desires (predict the puppet will go where there are no Band-Aids). But I no longer believe that this is the only or even primary difficulty three-year-olds face with false belief. Instead, I believe three-year-olds have a deeper difficulty with such tasks because they have a direct copy notion of belief. And I no longer believe that three-year-olds (specifically, younger three-year-olds) will consistently pass even false-belief explanation tasks.

My reasons are twofold. First (I am indebted to discussions with Debbie Zaitchik and Lou Moses here), if three-year-olds' only trouble was with predicting action from false beliefs, then they should succeed on tasks that remove this requirement. But they do not (Moses and Flavell, 1989; Perner et al., 1987). As one example, consider experiment 2 in Perner et al. (1987). Children were shown a Smarties box (a distinctive candy box well known to British children) and asked what it contained. All said Smarties. They then were shown they were wrong and that the box actually contained a pencil. Next they were asked about a friend waiting in the hall: "What will she think is in here?" Notice that in this task no desire is attributed to the friend ("She wants a pencil"), and if anything the child is likely to think the friend will want Smarties, not a pencil. Second, the child is not asked to predict action; he is simply asked to say what his friend will think. Three-year-olds ($M = 3$–5, range 3–1 to 3–9) failed this task; they were correct only 45% of the time. Thus three-year-olds continue to fail false-belief tasks even when there is no conflict between desire reasoning and belief reasoning. I think they fail because they have a direct copy understanding of belief. When asked about the content of their friend's belief, they know that belief is a reality-oriented representation, and hence a direct copy of reality; therefore their friend thinks there is a pencil in the box. In this way they make the classic false-belief error, failing to say their friend will mistakenly think there are pencils in the box.

There is a second reason that I now think the Bartsch and Wellman explanations data fail to show that three-year-olds in general understand false belief. Just as it was important to qualify my general discussion of two-year-olds' desire psychology, I must qualify any general discussion of three-year-olds' direct copy theory. In short, when I talk about three-year-olds in this chapter, that is simply a convenience. To be more precise, I believe that most three-year-olds fail to understand false belief but that an initial understanding of false belief appears in older three-year-olds right before the fourth birthday. Even this is inexact. I do not claim that these conceptual developments are tied to age in any exact way; I simply use these ages as a convenient marker for talking about a sequence of early developments.

In the Bartsch and Wellman data, for example, 18 of 24 three-year-olds failed our false-belief prediction tasks. Of these, 11 passed false-belief explanation tasks, and 7 failed both sorts of tasks. The average age of the 11 children passing explanation tasks was 3–10; the average age of those who failed was 3–7. Therefore, these data show an early understanding of false belief but in older three-year-olds. Recall from table 8.1 that even very young three-year-olds and some old two-year-olds pass our other belief reasoning tasks (not-own belief and discrepant belief tasks). Such young threes apparently consistently fail false-belief reasoning tasks, even the false-belief explanation tasks in Bartsch and Wellman (1989).

The data in Bartsch and Wellman (1989) also suggest that some old three-year-olds begin to be able to predict false beliefs, as well as use false beliefs to explain actions. Six of our 24 three-year-olds (25%) consistently passed false-belief prediction tasks (passing three of four such tasks). Other research (Perner et al., 1987), when looked at in this fashion, shows an understanding of false belief in some older three-year-olds. Beyond this, however, our data in Bartsch and Wellman suggest that the earliest appearance of an understanding of false belief might come in situations where older three-year-olds must explain anomalous behavior, for example, explain why Jane is looking for her kitten under the piano when it is under the chair. Such actions present a theoretical anomaly for a direct copy notion of representations. Here Jane is acting as if she believes her kitten is under the piano, but if her belief is a direct copy of reality, then she should believe her kitten is under the chair (because that is where it is). Such situations may be the first breeding ground for an understanding of false belief specifically and for the eventual overthrow of a direct copy theory of representation more generally. To summarize, most three-year-olds fail to understand false belief, and this supports a characterization of them as having a direct copy understanding of reality-oriented representations, but late in the fourth year of life older three-year-olds begin to understand false belief and begin to move away from an unadulterated direct copy theory of representation.

Given these data, why does Chandler propose that three- and even two-year-olds understand false belief? In essence he thinks that demonstrations that show such young children as failing to understand false belief depend too much on children's language skills. They constitute false negatives; less verbal methods may reveal unexpected competencies (Chandler, 1988). This is always a possibility. Beyond mere possibility, however, Chandler offers recent data he feels show a very early understanding of false belief (Chandler, Fritz, and Hala, 1989). His data concern young children's deceptive acts.

Chandler, Fritz, and Hala (1989) investigated two and a half-, three, and four-year-olds' ability to engage in deceptive actions in quite simple circumstances. They assert that deception requires a genuine understanding of false belief. Indeed, they claim that if one is deceived, one has a false belief, and to deceive is to create such a false belief. I believe things are more complex than this. I believe this study does show that young children can be deceptive, in one sense, but that deception in this sense does not require an understanding of false beliefs. Children can be genuinely deceptive without attempting to create deceptive beliefs.

In the Chandler et al. task a young child plays a hide and seek game, using a puppet to hide a treasure for an adult to seek. With the aid of a friendly adult, the child must walk the puppet to one of several table-top containers so that it can hide the treasure. A second adult, the seeker, is out of the room while this is done, and the child is told to "help hide the treasure so that [the seeker] won't be able to find it." One important feature of the task is that the puppet, as he walks, always leaves bright but washable purple footprints on the table-top surface.

What might count as deception in this situation? Chandler et al. argue that the following four strategies are all plausibly deceptive:

1. Destroying evidence: Wiping out the puppet's washable footprints.
2. Lying: Telling the seeker the puppet is in an incorrect container.
3. Producing false tracks: Laying down a false track to an incorrect container.
4. Combining strategies 1 and 3: Wiping out the correct trail while at the same time laying a false one.

Chandler et al. found that 70% of the 10 two and a half-year-olds (M = 2–9), 85% of the 20 three-year-olds, and 85% of the 20 four-year-olds engaged in one or more of these strategies in their first two attempts to play the game.

It may be that data from tasks such as these will eventually demonstrate an understanding of false belief in young three-year-olds and even old two-year-olds. If so I will have to revise (once again) my position as to young children's failure to understand false belief and my description of young children's direct copy theory. But I do not think that Chandler's data require this interpretation as yet. I do think that the data demonstrate deceptive behavior in young children, a striking and informative demonstration. I discuss this further in chapter 10. But deceptive behavior can come in several varieties, some of which do not require intentionally creating a false belief in another. For example, by my analysis in chapter 8, even a simple desire psychologist can understand that two persons may want the same object but only one can have it. A simple desire psychologist could engage in certain behaviors to get the object himself (satisfy his own desire) at the second person's, the competitor's, expense. That is, even a desire psychologist might attempt to eliminate competition (thwart the other person's desire). A desire psychologist might engage, for example, in certain actions to make the competitor go away or go someplace else. His intention is not to create a false belief; it is more simply to rid himself of a competitor. His actions essentially say "go away," not "believe this mistaken information so that you will go away." Destroying evidence, producing false tracks, and even some of the "lying" in Chandler's study might simply be efforts to make the competitor go where the target is not. That is, I think the young child is avoiding competition for a desirable object directly by sending the competitor someplace else, rather than indirectly by creating a false belief. An important control in the Chandler et al. study, therefore, would be to ask young children where the competitor thinks the target is. Young children may know that they are sending the competitor to some wrong location, without making an attribution as to his belief, that is, without believing the competitor will think that the target is in that other location. To summarize, the behavior of children in Chandler's task seems to me to be deceptive, but it does not evidence engendering a deceptive belief. And, hence, this does not constitute evidence that young children manifest a time-tagged copy theory rather than a direct one.

Finally, I want to consider a piece of research I believe also supports the view that young children have a direct copy view of reality-oriented representations. For this reason they fail false-belief tasks, and they fail analogous false photograph tasks as well (Zaitchik, in press). Zaitchik shows the child an arranged scene, say a toy duck, a bed, and a bathtub, with the duck on the bed. Then she takes an instant photograph of the scene. While it is developing, she changes the scene so that the duck is put in the bathtub. The child is asked what the photograph will show. Three-year-olds consistently say that the photograph will depict the duck in the tub (as it is now) rather than the duck on the bed (where it was when the picture was taken). They do so in spite of the fact that they correctly remember that the duck was on the bed earlier. By my analysis, three-year-olds construe the photograph as a direct copy of reality and hence believe the content of the photograph faithfully depicts the real situation. Four-year-olds, however, begin to predict that the photo will show the earlier, now incorrect view. (See also O'Connor, Beilin, and Kose, 1981, for related research on preschoolers' beliefs in photographic fidelity.)

In general, I think that the child's early theory of mind progresses from an early direct copy theory of reality-oriented representations to an interpretive or active processing understanding of such representations. Such a characterization of three-year-olds' theory, appropriately qualified, can account for why they pass many belief reasoning tasks yet often still fail to understand false beliefs (and false photographs).

Three-Year-Olds' Misunderstanding of Appearance-Reality

There is another manifestation of this general change from a copy to an interpretive view of representation. Given that we construe the developmental progression here as one of achieving an interpretive understanding of (reality-oriented) representations rather than an initial understanding of mental representations at all, then Flavell's (1988) recent description closely parallels my own. Flavell argues that his studies of children's understanding of the appearance-reality distinction provide another instance of children's increasingly interpretive understanding of mental representations. I agree. Flavell's appearance-reality tasks require children to understand that there are visual illusions (a sponge that looks just like a rock, for example) and to distinguish simultaneously between what the object looks like and what it really is. To distinguish between what the object "looks like" and what it "really is," is in my words to distinguish between a visual representation or percept (a representational-entity) that is different from the thing (the thing-entity). In addition, the child must acknowledge that a misrepresentation has occurred; the representational-entity does not correspond to the thing-entity. And, importantly, the sort of misrepresentation acknowledged is beyond the hit-or-miss type. The misrepresentational problem in these sorts of illusion tasks is not that I mistakenly looked at (and hence representationally copied) the wrong object (a real rock rather than the sponge rock); it is that from the item's appearance I construe it to be a rock, but it is not. This awareness of perceptual misconstruals is beyond the scope of a copy understanding of representation. For someone with a copy notion, to see a plainly visible object is to represent it. I hit the target; I get a direct copy of reality. From this viewpoint, reality-oriented representations are identical in content to reality (or at least that part of reality that they hit). Such a copy notion still leaves room for imaginings—made-up representational entities—but with respect to reality-oriented representations such as percepts, appearance just is reality and vice-versa. This is exactly how three-year-olds seem to respond to Flavell's tasks. They answer appearance questions and reality questions about the item identically, as Flavell has amply documented (Flavell et al., 1986). It is as if they think "I am representing a sponge"; period. There is for them a representation and a reality, but the representation copies the reality. Therefore, three-year-olds say (correctly), "It is a sponge," *and* (incorrectly), "It looks like a sponge."

An increasing understanding of representations as interpretations or construals allows for an increasing role for misconstruals, for the possibility that something looks like X but really is Y. This constitutes understanding of the appearance-reality distinction as Flavell has studied it. Flavell convincingly has demonstrated that in the years four to six, children become increasingly aware of this distinction (Flavell et al., 1986). Hence they evidence an increasing awareness of the interpretive nature of perceptually driven representations.

In my initial description of reality-oriented representations I concentrated on beliefs; now I focus briefly on percepts. It is easy to see how someone might arrive at a copy theory of visual percepts— perceptual representations. Even in our everyday adult talk, we often speak as though percepts were direct uptakes of the external world. Perception mirrors the world; it copies it. Three-year-olds, I claim, take this copy notion of perceptual representation quite literally, just as they do for beliefs.

Embedded in this discussion is an important distinction between imaginings and representational misconstruals. The concept of misconstrual is an important advance beyond that of imagining, although both can yield representations of not real things. Imaginings are within the scope of three-year-olds' understanding, but misconstruals are not. As I portray it in figure 9.1, even three-year-olds understand the imaginary quality of mind—your mind can just make up imaginary "things." These things are representational entities, but they are like fictional drawings, not photographs. Thus, I can draw a three-headed dog even if there are none, and they could never be photographed. For the three-year-old, however, imaginings are strictly segregated from reality-derived representations like beliefs or percepts. Therefore, what three-year-olds do not yet understand is that there exists a basic similarity between these two things, that is, between imaginings versus percepts and beliefs. They do not understand that even percepts, for example, can be like imaginings because all mental representations are constructive endeavors. They do not understand that the reality-oriented representations that seem so direct are actually the product of interpretive, slippery, cognitive process, yielding even in the case of beliefs and percepts an interpretive construal of reality. Three-year-olds conceive instead that in the case of beliefs and percepts, the copy is direct, hence faithful. In the years from three to six this changes.

It is impressive to stress how much things change. By five or six years of age, children begin to understand that this interpretive aspect of representation infects even percepts. This is a major advance because, after all, seeing does so often seem to be just a direct uptake of reality. When children begin to understand the interpretive nature even of visual percepts—which they evidence in Flavell's appearance-reality studies—they provide clear evidence of a new and sophisticated understanding of representation and a new interpretive understanding of mind. To begin to understand, no matter how imperfectly, that even seeing bears the imprint of processes of construal and is therefore akin in that fashion to imaginings is to demonstrate convincingly the acquisition of a new interpretive understanding of mind. Beyond the copy theory evident in three-year-olds, by five or six years children have achieved, at least in an initial fashion, an interpretive theory of mind, so that imagining and believing are now cousins rather than strangers.

The Active Constructive Mind

Children's achievement of an interpretive understanding of representation is part and parcel of a larger achievement: an understanding of mind itself as active and constructive. Children come to view the mind as something on the order of an active construer and processor of information rather than a passive registry of reality. This reconception of mind in active constructive terms begins to be evident at about four or five years.

How can we neatly capture the nature of this new theory of mind and contrast it to the prior theory? I do so by contrasting what I believe is the basic metaphoric ground of the two theories. To preview, the earliest theory of mind—that of three-year-olds—can be seen as having a containerlike nature; the later theory of mind—that of somewhat older children and adults—can be seen as having a homunculuslike nature. These two characterizations provide something like root metaphors for their respective theories. Both metaphors are apparent in adult speech about the mind, but, by my analysis, only the first one characterizes the three-year-old's theory.

A container is a repository; it holds things. In the case of typical containers like bowls and boxes, the contents are physical entities. By analogy, a mind contains things—ideas, thoughts. It metaphorically "houses" these mental entities. This sort of metaphor is evident in sayings like "in your head," "holds a belief," "it's just in his mind." Containers can be big or little, secure or porous, and these aspects of containers can form the basis for mental metaphors such as "he has a large memory," "a lot of smarts," "he has a memory like a sieve" versus "a mind like a steel trap." In the case of common containers such as bowls and bags, the container's contents are acquired passively in that the container does not actively recruit its contents; they are just dumped there. A container-copy metaphor of mind encompasses a similar sort of reception. The mind too receives its contents rather passively; they are directly copied into it. This sort of container notion is therefore congenial with most of the sorts of understanding evident in three-year-olds' initial belief-desire, copy-representational understanding of mind.

A homunculus is a person inside the head; it is a personification of the mind. Adults often do personify the mind: "his mind tricked him," "he quickly grasped that idea," "now he sees the light," "my mind is tired today," "the mind's eye," "that idea escaped him," "that's a seductive thought." A homunculus is an attractive metaphor for an interpretive, construing mind. It emphasizes the mind's active and individualistic aspects—"a lively mind," "a mind of his own." And it does so in an immediately understandable way, by importing our knowledge of people as individual active agents. By analogy, the mind can be viewed (in a crude but useful way) as a person in the head: a person who can be fooled, leading to misinterpretations; a person who can direct and order, leading to actions; an inner person who works with ideas, crafting them, constructing them, sorting them out, just as outer persons work with objects. In using the term *homunculus* I do not mean to suggest that in everyday life people think that there literally is a little person in the head or that the brain physically mimics the human body in some miniaturized or concretized way. People know that the mind is nonphysical; they do not actually think of minds as physically-spatially personified in any sense; they see mental activity only as psychologically personified. A homunculus even in this abstracted form is a horror to cognitive psychologists because it conjures up an infinite regress, but it is a powerful metaphor for everyday understanding of the active mind. I claim that this homuncular way of thinking about the mind is first acquired in the years from three to six, as children move from a passive repository view of mind to an active interpretive view.

This proposal has some attractive developmental features. If I am right in chapters 3 and 6, then even three-year-olds have a rich, organized set of beliefs about people as active agents, that is, as persons. When at a somewhat older age they begin to see the mind itself as active and constructive, it is a natural and useful device to personify the mind. A homuncular understanding of mind can build directly on an earlier understanding of people themselves.

There is another way of describing this change: for three-year-olds the domain to be explained is human action (in the broad sense of both behavior and thought). Mind and mental states—beliefs, desires—enter in as primitive theoretical constructs used to explain action and thoughts. Children at this age have a theory of mind because they refer to and utilize a rich set of mental concepts in order to achieve such explanations. At this point, however, children do not theorize about the mind itself much. They talk about mental phenomena; they organize their mental concepts coherently and in theoretically appropriate ways, but they do not attempt to explain mind itself further. Mind just is; it is just there, holding beliefs, receiving and containing its copies of reality. When mind itself becomes an increasingly active player in the scheme, however, it increasingly demands explanation in its own right. The child therefore begins to theorize about a conception of the mind, not just with a conception of mind. This represents a new level with respect to acquisition of a theory of mind. One of the child's first moves here, and a move adults perpetuate, is to explain the mind itself as "something like" a person inside us, to offer explanations for the mind's "behavior" of the same sort as those we would offer about people. A homuncular theory of mind therefore is the naive, everyday theory that does the same job as the psychologist's more technical information-processing theory of mind. Acquisition of a homuncular theory of mind thus constitutes a notable theory change in children's theories of mind. The full playing out of this theory change will take many years, but it is a change begun in the years three to six.

This proposed characterization of children's understanding of mind itself as progressing from a containerlike to a homunculuslike version is sensible but speculative. It is sensible in that it helpfully organizes into an overall picture several different aspects of children's theories.

It is also sensible in that theories, even scientific theories, often are organized analogically around some root metaphor (see Gentner, 1982). It is speculative, however, in that no research with children has directly tackled this proposed progression and verified it. This awaits further investigation; however, it is not without some suggestive support.

Consider the claim that young preschoolers have yet to achieve an understanding of the mind as an interpretive, executive, mediating entity, as something on the order of a personified central information processor. Carl Johnson and I provided some preliminary data for this claim in a study of children's conception of mind and brain (Johnson and Wellman, 1982). In this research preschool children judged that the mind and brain were implicated in thinking, dreaming, and remembering—that is, in paradigmatic mental acts and states. They denied, however, that mentation was involved in walking or kicking or seeing or hearing. Only elementary school children claimed that the mind and brain were needed for those activities as well, explaining, "It tells your legs where to go" or "You have to think about what you're seeing." Similarly, if asked whether the mind helps your eyes or your ears and conversely whether the eyes or ears help your mind, younger children judged that the mind and the sense organs were essentially autonomous, in the sense of passively connected to one another but not actively influencing one another. Only somewhat older children judged them to be interdependent, in the sense of the mind's actively interpreting sensation and directing the sense organs. In short, explicit consideration of the mind as a central information processor was notably absent in young preschoolers but became more and more apparent as children grew older. Additionally, school-aged children often described this increasingly active character of the mind by personifications, for example, "The mind tells your legs where to go." In contrast, in our studies in chapter 2, children often spoke of mental entities as "in their mind" or "in their head" but rarely personified the mind itself. Only a distinct minority of children, a handful of four-year-olds and five-year-olds, ever personified the mind with statements about their "mind-hands" or "dream hands" (see table 2.3).[2]

From Novice to Proficient Practitioner

In chapter 1, I outlined two sorts of changes in children's theories of mind. One concerned theory changes—when the essential character of children's theory is changed. The discussion in this chapter so far has been an attempt to specify more clearly the nature of an important theory change begun in the years three to six. The other change was in proficiency—when persons become more expert in whatever theory is under consideration. The years from three to six also see proficiency changes.

In any one instance it can be difficult to say whether a change is one of increasing proficiency or of theory transformation. Theory changes are only visible given a broad view of the conceptual terrain. And changes in proficiency undoubtedly contribute to theory changes; for example, only a proficient practitioner of a theory is likely to see theory anomalies for what they are and attempt to deal with them. Still, in addition to the beginnings of a theory change from copy to constructivist theory, the years three to six see some notable changes in the child's proficiency at an initial belief-desire psychology.

For example, while our study of children's explanation of behavior in chapter 6 revealed a basic belief-desire competence in three-year-olds, it also revealed sizable increases in proficiency in the years from three to five. In that study, four-year-olds provided more belief-desire explanations of action than did three-year-olds (see the data on complete belief-desire explanations in figure 6.1). More four-year-olds than three-year-olds gave unprompted belief explanations, and four-year-olds provided more belief explanations than three-year-olds in their complete explanations. In short, while apparently engaged in the same belief-desire explanation of action, four-year-olds were noticeably more fluent at the process than were three-year-olds.

Similarly, although three-year-olds understand that perception leads to knowledge, several studies have shown that in the years from three to six, children achieve large increases in the proficiency and pervasiveness of this understanding. For example, children come to know not only that you and I will know different things if we have had differences in visual access (Pillow, 1989; Pratt and Bryant, 1988) but also that we will know different things if you have been told a "secret" but I have not (Marvin, Greenberg, and Mossler, 1976); or if I watched a videotape with the sound on but for you the sound was off (Mossler, Marvin, and Greenberg, 1976); or indeed that you and I have different knowledge and beliefs if we have different olfactory and tactile experiences as well (Yaniv and Shatz, 1988). Three-year-olds do know that perception leads to belief in the sorts of ways I have now tried to capture in figure 9.1. However, the same studies that demonstrate such knowledge also show that children get better at judging consistently in a variety of task situations that differences in experiences yield differences in knowledge. That is my point here.

Similarly, three-year-olds have a beginning understanding of representation, specifically an understanding of imaginings and a direct copy sense of reality-oriented representations. Still, children get noticeably better at dealing with the distinction between referent and representation in the years three to six. Thus three-year-olds often do provide answers about referents (a dog) when queried about representations (a thought about a dog). This error diminishes in the years three to six.

Relatedly, if three-year-olds have a beginning grasp of belief-desire psychology, then they should have a basic competence at understanding and creating simple stories. Stories hinge on naive psychology, on describing the actions of a protagonist who has certain beliefs and desires, generates certain actions, strives for certain outcomes, and reacts to success and failure. Stein, Trabasso, and colleagues have been pursuing an intensive program of research examining the story understanding abilities of preschool children. They find that even three-year-olds understand simple stories (Stein and Levine, in press). But there are certainly increases in the preschool years in children's abilities to understand increasingly long and complex stories (Stein and Trabasso, 1982; Trabasso, Stein, and Johnson, 1981). Preschoolers become increasingly able to manage belief-desire reasoning in the midst of increasingly complex informational presentations.

One of the most notable changes in proficiency apparent in the preschool years concerns the child's developing ability to deal with false beliefs. An early grasp of false belief is signaled by even some three-year-olds who can generate false-belief explanations for anomalous action and who may even pass very simple false belief prediction tasks. By four and a half years children are consistently proficient at such false belief prediction. Note that the proficiency evidenced by four and a half-year-olds is reasonably comprehensive. Not only do they pass quite simple explicit false-belief tasks of the sort used in chapter 3, they also correctly solve a range of reasonably complicated false-belief tasks. In my view, it is the child's increasing ability to follow stories that accounts for this change. Our belief-reasoning tasks used in chapter 3 constitute about the simplest story line possible (see table 3.1). However, examine an example false-belief story, used by Wimmer and Perner, presented in table 9.1. Here the story line is considerably more demanding. The story encompasses quite a bit of information, and there is a need to infer the character's false belief (from an early nonupdated perceptual experience), as well as the need to predict action from the inferred false belief. By four and a half years children correctly predict the character's action given such

Table 9.1
Traditional False Belief Story

[Boy-doll present, representing Maxi waiting for his mother.]
"Mother returns from her shopping trip. She bought chocolate for a cake. Maxi may help her put away the things. He asks her: 'Where should I put the chocolate?' 'In the blue cupboard,' says the mother. 'Wait, I'll lift you up there, because you are too small.' Mother lifts him up. Maxi puts the chocolate into the blue cupboard. [A toy chocolate is put into the blue matchbox.] Maxi remembers exactly where he put the chocolate so that he could come back and get some later. He loves chocolate. Then he leaves for the playground. [The boy doll is removed]. Mother starts to prepare the cake and takes the chocolate out of the blue cupboard. She grates a bit into the dough and then she does not put it back into the blue but into the green cupboard. [Toy chocolate is thereby transferred from the blue to the green matchbox.] Now she realizes that she forgot to buy eggs. So she goes to her neighbor for some eggs. There comes Maxi back from the playground, hungry, and he wants to get some chocolate. [Boy-doll reappears.] He still remembers where he had put the chocolate."
["BELIEF"-question] "Where will Maxi look for the chocolate?"
[Subject has to indicate one of the boxes.]

Source: Wimmer and Perner (1983).

stories (Wimmer and Perner, 1983), correctly assess the character's mistaken belief itself (Perner, Leekam, and Wimmer, 1987), and even know what the target character should say if he wishes to communicate truthfully his (false) belief to another or wishes to deceive the other by falsely communicating his belief (and paradoxically telling the truth) (Wimmer, Gruber, and Perner, 1984; Perner and Wimmer, 1987). Anyone who reads these many clever studies will be persuaded as to the proficiency achieved at belief-desire reasoning generally, and false-belief reasoning specifically, in the years from three to six.

Conclusions

At the start of this chapter I noted that there are substantial agreements underlying the often diverging positions among researchers interested in the young child's understanding of mind. Figure 9.2 is my attempt to provide a schematic depiction of the agreements and disagreements among several of us, at least as I understood them in early 1989. The depiction requires discussion.

First, unlike Piaget, most contemporary researchers believe that it is incorrect to describe young children as childhood realists, that is, as externalizing and physicalizing mental phenomena. The research in chapter 2 shows why. Indeed, the pendulum has swung so far in the other direction that a philosopher of mind (Fodor, 1987) has suggested that the human "species is born knowing its own mind" (p. 133), indeed with an innate belief-desire psychology. This is a minority opinion, however; most researchers in the area believe that knowledge of the mind is acquired developmentally. If so, it becomes reasonable to ask if and when children achieve a theory of mind. There are a variety of answers to this question depending on the researcher's interpretation of the phrase "theory of mind" and their appraisal of young children's abilities.

The concept "mind" is an everyday one. It is not a technical concept but a concept entrenched in commonsense psychology itself. It is a useful concept, providing an important means of construing and parsing other everyday concepts and everyday observations. When researchers use the concept, however (for example, when they ask whether children have an understanding of mind), they must fine-tune the concept for their more precise purposes. Part of the disagreements depicted in figure 9.2 simply depict differences in this process of conceptual refinement. For example, given the everyday notion of mind, it seems that such psychological states as emotions, pains, and desires are correctly termed mental states. When two-year-olds evidence an understanding of such mental states as emotion and desire, they can be said to have an understanding of mind. In essence this is how Bretherton proceeds (Bretherton and Beeghley, 1982). I am therefore in agreement with much of her description of two-year-olds' understanding. However, I take the phrase "theory of mind" in a rather precise way, a way I have described as requiring understanding of mental representational states of belief as well as mental dispositional states of desire and, indeed, as requiring adoption of a rather rich belief-desire psychology. In this sense I believe that two-year-olds have not yet attained a theory of mind, although I can see what Bretherton means when she says that they have.

My more precise claim is that a theory of mind is demonstrably in place by age three. This is a claim disputed by many other current researchers, with the prominent exception of Chandler, but one that I have tried to make convincing throughout this book. In one sense, the dispute concerns "mere" timing, specifically whether three-year-olds or four-year-olds achieve an understanding of belief and relatedly of mental representations, and hence a theory of mind. In other respects, however, the dispute is not simply about timing; it involves important issues as to what certain conceptions entail and how they unfold. In this arena I see the position I have been articulating in this book as having several distinct advantages. First, I see my position as

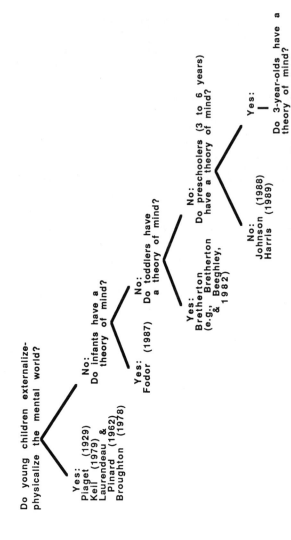

Do young children externalize-
physicalize the mental world?

Yes:
Piaget (1929)
Keil (1979)
Laurendeau &
Pinard (1962)
Broughton (1978)

No:
Do infants have a
theory of mind?

Yes:
Fodor (1987)

No:
Do toddlers have
a theory of mind?

Yes:
Bretherton
(e.g., Bretherton
& Beeghley,
1982)

No:
Do preschoolers (3 to 6 years)
have a theory of mind?

No:
Johnson (1988)
Harris (1989)

Yes:
Do 3-year-olds have a
theory of mind?

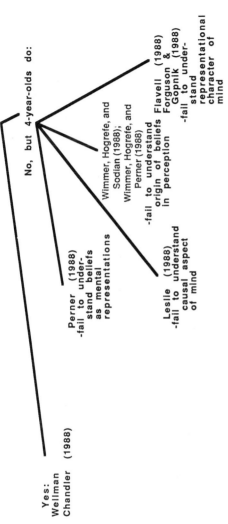

Figure 9.2
Diagram of various investigators' positions concerning the early development of a theory of mind.

straightening out some prevalent conceptual unclarities (about theories, simple desires, representations). Moreover, I see my position as depicting two important theory changes in the years from two to six, theory changes that have both been overlooked and misportrayed until now.

The first theory change is from a desire to a belief-desire psychology. The notion of simple desire psychology captures both the successes and the failures of very young children, two-year-olds. In the past we have been mostly unaware that such young children achieve any notable success in this realm. Characterizing an early desire psychology is also important because simple desire psychology constitutes an "initial" state for a theory of mind. That is, an initial belief-desire understanding of mind apparent in three-year-olds arises out of the legacy of successes and failures of simple desire psychology.

The second theory change (of equal magnitude to the first) is from an initial belief-desire psychology to a later belief-desire psychology. Specifically, it is a change from a copy-container theory of mind to an interpretive-homuncular theory. The fact that three-year-olds do achieve an initial belief-desire theory of mind becomes obvious if we carefully characterize that theory and carefully separate it from the latter belief-desire theory. Hence, properly characterizing the three-year-old's intermediate level of understanding, neither underestimating nor overestimating it, is essential to characterizing the entire progression. (That is why I spend so much of this book on that task.)

Figure 9.2 portrays a substantial agreement on the part of a sizable number of researchers. And since positions are constantly changing on these topics, I believe that agreements are increasing. The main agreement is that a theory of mind is now regarded as being well in hand during, if not at the start of, the preschool years. By five or six years of age, we agree, young children clearly understand mental entities to be ontologically distinct from physical ones, they clearly understand that mental entities such as beliefs are representational entities, and hence they understand the hypothetical and causal aspects of mind—for example, that beliefs are internal mental states but states directed toward a depiction of reality and hence controlling of actions. Furthermore, preschoolers begin to understand some of the interpretive aspects of mental representations as mere, faulty, individualized construals of the world. And hence they begin to achieve an understanding of mind itself as an active agent in cognition. These agreements are important; they are sizable recent advances in our understanding of young children.

Chapter 10

From Three to Six: Other Implications

If the new consensual view outlined in chapter 9 is true—grossly, that preschool children achieve a rich theory of mind—then this also encompasses several aspects of children's behavior and conception that I have slighted until now. For example, what about children's understanding of intention? Belief-desire psychology encompasses and indeed defines our understanding of intention and intentional behavior. As another example, there is a prevalent opinion that young children are afraid of dreams and of fictional characters like goblins and monsters and that they fear such things because they are unable to distinguish fantasy from reality. To them, dreamed-of monsters are real and dangerous. But if preschoolers sensibly distinguish between real entities and imaginings, then the explanation of such fears must be different, and such fears might be expected to be rare.

In this chapter I take up several topics of this sort, in three sections. I have reserved these topics until now not because they are less important or peripheral but because the scope of our everyday theory of mind is such that I cannot discuss it all at once. In this chapter, I am not trying to do comprehensive justice to each topic, for example, to explicate children's fears of dreams fully. This is fortunate because in many cases the relevant research is preliminary and sketchy. Even in cases where large literatures exist, I do not intend to offer comprehensive reviews. I only wish to probe each topic for a few insights, which though sketchy and promissory are relevant to children's understanding of mind. My main endeavor is to broaden the scope of discussion and thus elaborate and underwrite the characterization of children's theories of mind achieved thus far.

I have another interest in these topics and another reason for tackling them together here. There exists a sort of traditional wisdom that preschoolers are seriously ignorant or confused about several topics that are within the sphere of influence of a theory of mind—intention, lies, deception, fantasy. No one probably subscribes to this traditional view in its entirety, and developmental psychologists for the last 10 years or so have been dismantling it piece by piece as part of a general reappraisal of the skills and cognitions of preschoolers. Nevertheless, it has a certain lingering force. This traditional wisdom continues to exert a force because it rests on a cogent larger picture of young children that has yet to be replaced. I think that an accurate understanding of young children's first belief-desire psychology provides an alternative view, capable of and worthy of replacing the traditional wisdom.

The traditional view has two sources of strength. First, it is well grounded in Piaget's theory, partaking of the understandability and face validity of such constructs as animism, childhood realism, egocentricism, and moral realism. In addition, it seems to receive confirmation in the organized intuitions of workers with children. For example, at a recent meeting of the National Association for the Education of Young Children there was a presentation titled, "You can't help me until you know what I can't do" (Hodgins, 1987). The speaker presented a list of things that preschoolers cannot do, such as "I can't tell the difference between real and fantasy."

These two sources reinforce one another; aspects of the Piagetian picture are instrumental in organizing such clinical observations, but conversely the currency of certain observations seems to underwrite the Piagetian picture. If children are childhood realists as Piaget describes them, then it makes sense that they would fail to distinguish imaginary goblins from true scary beasts. If children are moral realists, it makes sense that they would fail to distinguish when someone did something (knocked over their block tower, for example) intentionally versus by accident. Therefore, it is of some interest that educators believe that preschoolers fail to react appropriately to intended versus accidental transgressions and thus fail to understand or to make appropriate apologies.

Suppose, however, that the new view is right: young children are sensible, if not proficient, belief-desire psychologists. If that new view captures an important part of childhood thought, as claimed, then there should be deep cracks in the traditional picture, and at some point we should be able to offer a new characterization of the young child more attractive and more serviceable to those who work with them. I believe the description of young children as novice belief-desire psychologists provides the needed alternative. Therefore, it seems that renewed, clearer scrutiny of children's understanding of lies, deception, intentional behavior, and fantasy fears should reveal the clear imprint of the child's belief-desire psychology. Conversely, children's understandings in these areas ought to help elaborate the core picture in some serviceable fashions.

Quite young children, three-year-olds, have an initial belief-desire theory of mind, but this initial theory changes significantly toward an active, interpretive theory in the years three to six. Thus, my tactic in these next sections has two parts. First, I attempt to show that three- and four-year-olds have some competencies unsuspected or ignored by the traditional view and undiscovered in research until recently. Second, I attempt to show that these first capabilities are still limited, whereas the skills of five- and six-year-olds are expanded in ways consistent with the proposal that children's theories move from a passive, copyist conception to an active, constructive one.

Deception and Lies

The traditional wisdom is that young children are mystified by or uncomprehending of deception. Thus, young children truly may be afraid of a familiar teacher who dons a Halloween mask. Similarly, young children fail to understand the nature of lies and thus often speak untruths.

The story with respect to deception goes something like this. Children do not separate a world of reality and a world of the mind, a world of reality and potentially false appearances. Thus, they cannot set themselves the task of engendering in someone a belief contrary to reality, and they invest even false appearances with reality. Young children, for example, fail at games like hide and seek—they hide in plain sight or call out "I'm here"—because they do not comprehend the game's deceptive nature. They are also charmingly frank about their own improper acts, failing to conceal them even when they know that punishment will result and wish to avoid it.

The story with respect to lies is similar. Young children experience their own desires and wishes, but they fail to distinguish such internal experiences from external realities. Thus they tell frequent untruths. But these are not lies in an adult sense; they are not intended verbal misrepresentations. In fact, the notion of an intentional misrepresentation is foreign to them, and children therefore judge that unintended mistaken statements by others are lies equal to intended deceptive statements. Both are bad exactly to the extent that they are objectively false, regardless of the speaker's intent. Piagetian notions of realism (1929) and research on the morality of lies (1932), as well as clinical lore about normal children, contribute to these related stories.

What if young children are instead as I describe them: ontological dualists and novice but dedicated belief-desire psychologists? In that case they should be able to grasp something of the essence of lies and deception. For example, according to belief-desire psychology, a person with a false belief is a person who is deceived, and to tell a lie is to attempt to engender a false belief in the listener. Young children therefore could be expected to become passably proficient at telling lies and understanding deception by about four years of age. Let me be clear. I am not claiming that the traditional wisdom is completely wrong; children do have confusions here. But the nature and pervasiveness of these confusions are different than is commonly believed. Most important, perhaps, even quite young children evidence understanding of deception and lies.

What about deception? In chapter 9 I described Chandler, Fritz, and Hala's (1989) research on very young children's deception. I believe this research has demonstrated young children to be impressively deceptive within the terms of simple desire psychology. They can thwart a competitor's desire by sending him away—by laying false trails, for example. Such activities are not aimed at creating in the competitor deceptive beliefs, however. Early deceptive behaviors of this sort may in fact create misrepresentations in the other, but they are not convincingly attempts to misrepresent intentionally in the sense of intending to create a false belief.

I do believe, however, that with the onset of an understanding of false beliefs, at just about four-years, children are able to create genuinely deceptive beliefs in others too. Using simple tasks, several researchers have shown that preschoolers can engage in attempts to create false expectations by about age five, if not younger. For example, in a study by Gordon and Flavell (1977), children were shown four to-be-hidden target pictures (a cowboy, mailman, doctor, fireman) and four clues (for example, for the doctor, a Band-Aid; for the fireman, a fire hat). Three and a half- and five-year-olds first correctly identified the intended target-clue pairings. Then an adult searcher was introduced, and children were asked to deceive the searcher. The searcher closed her eyes, and the children were to place clues so as to fool the searcher. I do not think that placing false clues in this task can be seen as simply attempts to steer the competitor away. In this task, for example, the searcher will find everything no matter what. But she could be fooled by finding things in unexpected locations. Twenty-three of 24 five-year-olds correctly placed all four clues on the wrong targets, and 16 of 24 said the searcher would look for the items in accordance with the false clues. Only 12 of 24 three and a half-year-olds placed all four clues on the wrong targets. Another 11 made some correct (that is, deceptive) placements, but some of these were probably simple errors and confusions, not purposeful deceptions. Indeed, in concert with the literature on children's failure to predict actions on the basis of false beliefs, 15 of the 24 three and a half-year-olds went on to say that the searcher would search for the targets where they really were rather than under their proper (but deceptive) clues. In short, older preschoolers but probably not younger ones can engage in deceptive actions specifically intended to create false beliefs.

Everyday experience with young children also suggests that this is probably true. For example, Abe, the child whose natural language conversations (among others) we studied in Shatz et al. (1983), produced these conversations when he was just four years old:

Child: I'm gonna drink my hot chocolate . . . poop, poop, I pooped in my hot chocolate. (laughs) I was teasing.
Mother: What a relief.
Child: I was teasing you. I was pretending 'cept you didn't know that.

Child: I don't wanna go . . . they would think I'm not there.
Mother: What?
Child: They would think you had not a kid.
Mother: Why would they think that if you come.
Child: No they would think that if I didn't come.

If young children do understand deception, this raises several practical questions. For example, if young children understand deception, why do they fail at deceiving others in most game situations? Even four-year-olds have failed in most prior attempts to study deception that have employed various rule-governed competitive games (De-Vries, 1970; Shultz, 1980). Playing rule-governed games and understanding the ins and outs of competition is not a particularly compelling concern to young children. Chandler, Fritz, and Hala's (1989) task is attractive in this regard in that it avoids some of these inessential extras. Still, why do children fail at everyday hide and seek? Hide and seek is more a form of social play rather than a rule-governed game, and it is a type of play that young children like and request. Why do children fail to hide themselves properly in everyday hide and seek unless it is from an inability to understand and create deception?

I think that it is exactly the social aspect of the everyday hide and seek game, where one person hides and another seeks, that takes precedence for young children. To an organism like the young child, one strongly interested in social interaction and uninterested in separation, the social isolation of hiding is to be avoided. To an organism interested in movement, keeping still is difficult. To an organism interested in shared social pleasure, the joy of reunion is much more important than the pleasure of imagining the other as deceived. In hide and seek, to hide effectively is to cut yourself off from the others, even from viewing them and their efforts to find you. That is not the fun of the game for young children. The fun is the shared excitement, available in finding and reunion rather than separation and hiding. All in all, hide and seek is a delightful game for young children, but its rewards do not lie in successful deception.

Beyond an early understanding of deception apparent in three- and four-year olds, I think that we will find in future research that there is a change later in the preschool years and beyond to an expanded understanding of deception, consistent with a shift from an early copy-container theory of mind to a later active-homunculus conception. For example, younger preschoolers should prove unable to deceive someone when the task requires letting that person actually look at the object. They should fail to be able to create a false appearance for a visible object. In hit-or-miss terms, if the object is in sight, it can be hit and thus represented. Thus I would expect young children to be unable to leave the object in sight but falsify its appearance, and young preschoolers should not understand the purpose of camouflage (which allows the viewer to see the object but not know that it is there), or how intentionally to "hide something in plain sight" where the object is to be seen but still cognitively overlooked. As another example, at age three, my son went through a stage where he continually said things like, "Close your eyes, Dad; I want to do something you won't like." To adults this is transparent, but at a hit-or-miss copy level of understanding, this could be thought of as an effective deceit: If Dad doesn't see it, he won't know.

What about lies, which to adults are verbal misrepresentations intended to create false beliefs? Piaget's data (1932) and those of others suggest that young children consistently misunderstand lies. That is, unintended verbal mistakes are lies in their eyes. To them, the objective fact—falsity—not the subjective one—intended misrepresentation—is all that matters. Do such demonstrations mean that young children fail to understand appropriately the nature of verbal misrepresentation—that is, truly fail to distinguish between intended and unintended untruths? Or do they perhaps fails to understand appropriately the term *lie*? Wimmer, Gruber, and Perner (1984) have shown convincingly that from four years on at any rate, children understand lies but misuse the term *lie*. In the most complete of their studies (experiment 6) four-, five-, and six-year-olds were given two critical stories. In one (truthful intention, false message), a character who intends to tell the truth unintentionally conveys a false message. In the other (deceptive intent, truthful message), a character who intends to deceive unknowingly communicates a true message. These stories, albeit a bit complex, create exactly the needed contrast between lying or not (intending to create a false belief verbally) and objective truth and falsity. Children were asked both whether the target character was lying and whether the target character should be rewarded, that is, should receive (from one to three) gold stars "because he was nice" or receive (from one to three) black marks "because he was nasty."

Four-year-old children consistently distinguished between the two characters in their rewards. On the average, they approved the speaker with truthful intent (awarding roughly one and a half gold stars) and disapproved of the speaker with deceptive intent (giving him roughly one black point). At the same time, however, there was no difference in their judgments of whether the characters lied. Four-year-olds said that both characters were lying. Only 1 of 15 four-year-olds distinguished between the characters in their judgments of whether they had lied, whereas 10 of 14 six-year-olds correctly did so. Young children therefore did not evidence ontological realism—because they distinguished deception from objective fact—or moral realism—because they properly rewarded deceptive versus truthful intent. However, four-year-olds did evidence what Wimmer et al. termed *lexical realism*—using the lexical term *lie* to describe objective, not subjective, aspects of the actor's speech.

Note some of the complexity here. Other studies have shown that young children judge a person who lies, as *they* use that term (that is who speaks an untruth, intentionally or not), to be much naughtier and deserving of punishment than one who does not (Piaget, 1932; Boehm and Nass, 1962; Weiner and Peter, 1973). Thus even the first character above (truthful intention, false message) is likely to be judged as considerably naughtier than a character who intentionally tells the truth. Similarly, both a character who intentionally says an untruth and one who accidentally says an untruth would be judged as liars by young children, and lying is an offense. Thus (as Wimmer et al. point out), Stern and Stern (1931) describe an instance where their five-year-old told someone that he wished to be a doctor and then, when he later changed his mind about this, seriously accused himself of having lied.

This is perplexing. How can children understand the nature of intentional verbal misrepresentation yet see unintended verbal untruths as lies and as serious wrong doing? Wimmer et al. (1986) speculate, as did Stern and Stern (1931) before them, that parents unintentionally miscommunicate the nature of lying to children when they say things like, "You should tell the truth; don't lie." That is, in their everyday proscriptions adults tacitly equate lying with untruthfulness. Beyond that, it seems likely that parents are often concerned that children learn to report things accurately, avoiding mistakes as well as lies. Mistakes, too (such as misreporting an assignment from school), often have serious consequences, consequences to be avoided and even punished. From this children might well misunderstand what lies are and have a punitive attitude even to mistakes. In short, for children, it might well seem to be the objective fact of falsity that makes a lie and that deserves punishment. Nonetheless, young children could, and apparently do, conceptually understand the distinction between intended misrepresentations and mistakes. While both are lies to them, they are certainly not identical. Thus when they are not using the term *lie*, preschoolers often communicate sensibly about lies as adults understand them, saying things like:

Mother: If someone said, "your name's Goofy," would they think your name was Goofy?
Child: No, they would be tricking me. They would say, "Hi, Abe; we tricked you."

(Child says he threw spear through a wall).
Father: Wow! Will Mommy be mad!
Child: It really didn't go through a wall. Let's really trick her. OK? And don't tell her I'm tricking. OK? But, Dad, tell Mommy my spear went through the wall.
Father: How come you want me to tell Mommy that?
Child: Because she won't believe me.

In total, young children do understand something of the nature of deception, and a little later they understand about deceptive beliefs and about the difference between lies and mistakes. That children understand these things is a manifestation of their understanding of differences between desires and outcomes and between beliefs and facts and thus a manifestation of their deeper, burgeoning theory of mind.

Fantasy Fears

The traditional view is that young children seriously fear fantasy entities because they think such things are real. For example, they fear bad dreams because they think dream experiences are real. A complex set of issues knots together here. Several possibilities exist:

1. Children understand the distinction between dreams and fantasy characters, such as goblins, versus reality and thus are not afraid of those things.
2. Children understand goblins and dreams as well as adults but are still afraid; they are afraid but no more or less than adults.
3. Children understand the basic distinction but make mistakes about specific experiences. In this case, they would have the same sort of fears as adults but more of them.
4. Children's fears of goblins and dream characters arise because they see them as real; hence they have "real" fantasy fears.

I admit right off that children have fantasy fears. Thus (1) is wrong. My claim, however, is that children's fantasy fears are no different in kind from adults'. That is, children show no essential conceptual difficulty with reality and fantasy. Nonetheless, children' fantasy fears are different in prevalence and in resolution in comparison to adults'. Thus, something like (3) represents the true state of affairs.

The traditional view, in contrast, claims something like (4), but it does so on the basis of a false dichotomy, construing the choice to be either (1) or (4). In that case, since children do have fantasy fears, they must have "real" fantasy fears. At a minimum, this false dichotomy ignores the reality expressed in (2)—that adults also have such fears. Adults wake up in the night with true fears caused by a dream. They wake up and their heart is racing, their body tensed; they are experiencing real fears, and they do so even after they know full well that the object of their fear was "just a dream." The same is true for fictional entities. It is quite possible for adults to be truly frightened by a good ghost story, knowing full well that ghosts are not real. Or consider horror movies. Part of the fun is experiencing real fright while still knowing "it's only a movie."

Thus, the presence of fantasy fears does not necessarily signal a failure to distinguish fantasy from reality. That is, the choice is not between (1) and (4) but among (2), (3), and (4).

I favor something like option 3 whereby children's fantasy fears are seen as no different in kind from adults' but are still admitted to be more prevalent. Here we must distinguish two levels of competence:

understanding the basic distinction between reality and fantasy versus correctly judging for specific instances whether that entity is real or fantastical. Children appreciate the same basic distinction that adults do but still make mistakes on specific judgments. Again, consider this first from an adult's perspective. Let's say that Joe knows full well the distinction involved between dreams and real events. Still, when Joe wakes up in the dark, in the afterglow of a vivid dream, he must decide whether that experience was real or dream. Even for adults this decision is not always foolproof; errors are made. Children presumably make more errors still, in spite of completely adequate notions about the basic distinction involved.

Childhood errors at classifying specific instances into well-understood general categories must be even more likely in the case of fantasy characters such as goblins. Consider the difference between dragons and dinosaurs (Morison and Gardner, 1978). Children have no direct experience of either dragons or dinosaurs, though they may see pictures and replicas of both. Surely it is not surprising that they might erroneously think dinosaurs are fantasy, not fact, or mistakenly think that dragons are fact, not fantasy. Similarly, children could be confused about goblins and witches, erroneously believing such things exist somewhere. Children can believe witches to be real and worthy of fear, albeit suffering no general fantasy-reality confusion. I think children make more classification errors of these sorts than do adults, and hence children's fears are more prevalent than adults'. However, this signals a yet-to-be-developed specific knowledge about the proper classification of instances, not a yet-to-be-developed knowledge of the basic classes themselves.

Recently Harris, Marriot, and Whittall (1988) provided some experimental evidence relevant to this discussion. Inspired by our findings in Wellman and Estes (1986) and in chapter 2, they asked whether and why children are afraid of witches and goblins. In their first study, they showed that four- and six-year-olds understood that a thought about a witch or a goblin (specifically, a mental image of such a thing) was not real, was immaterial, and was mental in the same way that a thought about a dog is. In a second study, they showed that even if such fantasy thoughts were made more vivid and mildly frightening (by asking children to imagine a monster wagging its tail and coming to chase them), children still understood them to be mental, imaginary, and not real. This was true even on items where children judged that they had indeed been really frightened (and not just pretend frightened) by the thought or image. In a third experiment, Harris et al. asked four- and six-year-olds about the reality of monsters, witches, and ghosts themselves rather than the reality of a thought about a monster or an image of a witch. Here four-year-old children differentiated in their judgments between clearly real entities (a dog that wags its tail), monster and witches (a monster that wags its tail), and clearly fantasy entities (an airplane that wags its tail). They consistently judged clearly real entities to be real and clearly fantasy entities to be not real. At the same time, they were more likely to think that monsters were real than clear fantasy entities were, but they were less likely to think that monsters were real than clearly real entities were. In short, four-year-old were often confused as to whether there actually are such things as real witches and real monsters.

In total, children experience real fears about fantasy entities; so do adults. Moreover, children fear some entities that adults do not because children mistakenly think they are real. Adults make this same sort of error, but the error is probably considerably more prevalent in young children than in adults. Young children, after all, are only in the process of acquiring the conventional wisdom about these things.

Beyond this there is a further reason that young children's fantasy fears seem more "realistic" to adults who work and live with them: children's fears are less under conceptual control than adults' fears. When I as an adult wake up from a vivid dream afraid—sweating, my heart racing, ready to flee—part of how I calm myself is to tell myself, "Whew, it was just a dream." This conceptual distinction provides real leverage for me on my fear. This leverage is less available to and less effective for preschoolers. Their strategies for emotional control are less developed than ours (Harris, 1989), and conceptual clarity affords much less comfort to them. Saying "it's not real" does not aid preschoolers very much when they are already in the grip of a strong emotional reaction. This is at times true for adults too; horror movies really scare me, no matter how much I tell myself, "It's just a movie." Still, lack of such conceptual control over emotions is more prevalent for preschoolers. The same reasoning applies to scary deceptions. A four-year-old can know full well that that is his teacher wearing a Halloween mask. Yet the mask and experience can still be scary. And telling the child "it is just a mask" may do little to calm him.

In total, the traditional wisdom that fantasy fears are more prevalent and less susceptible to conceptual resolution in childhood is correct, but these observations do not indicate, and they are not the result of, a deeper conceptual confusion between classes of mental or fictional versus real phenomena.

Intentions

At the end of chapter 4, by comparing figures 4.1 and 4.3, I offered three general sorts of suggestions as to how the first theory of mind of three-year-olds would differ from that of adults. One suggestion concerned the larger notion of mind and the generic notion of "thinking" that frame a more specific concept of belief. The discussion in chapter 9 elaborates on that early suggestion. Two other suggestions were that there would be changes in the child's understanding of intentions and changes in the child's understanding of character traits. In this section, I address changes in children's understanding of intention in the years three to six. I discuss the acquisition of a notion of character traits in chapter 11 because I think this occurs in the years beyond six.

I proposed that at some point there is a change from the child's understanding of acts as being intended (in the sense of having been produced because of relevant desires and beliefs) to, additionally, the adult's separated notion of intention. This separated notion of intention is especially obvious in consideration of future intentions and planning—thinking about and formulating an extended agenda for action to be executed in the future. The two aspects of an adult understanding of intention—whether an act was done intentionally versus a conception of intentional thinking about the future—are similar to Bratman's (1984) "two faces" of intention. My proposal was that children understand one face first.

At this point, I can also point out that a conception of people as internally formulating hypothetical plans for action is congenial with a larger conception of people as possessing active, constructive minds. But such a conception is difficult to derive from a passive, containerlike conception of mind. Thus, by my thinking, three-year-olds should have a sense of intentional versus accidental or mistaken acts but not a firm sense of planful future intentions. By five or six years children should be more aware of persons as planning devices.

What of the first part of this picture—that three-year-olds understand the intentional, on-purpose quality of voluntary acts? Until recently the traditional wisdom was that they did not. However, this perspective came primarily from studies on children's understanding of morality. Of course, to adults whether an action is intended is an important factor in our moral judgments; unintended accidental transgressions are less reprehensible than are intended transgressions. Thus when early studies of moral judgments seemed to show that preschoolers ignored intention in their moral judgments (Piaget, 1932), it was not nonsensical to conclude that young children had no understanding of intentional action. But if children do not parse their moral judgments on the basis of the actor's intentions, this might mean that they do not understand the difference between intended acts and accidents, or it might mean that they do understand such a difference but have yet to appreciate its relevance to moral culpability. For this reason (and others), early studies of moral judgment do not clearly inform us as to children's conceptions of intentionality (see Keasey, 1978).

One central feature of any belief-desire psychology, even the rudimentary one depicted in figure 4.1, is that it depends on, indeed defines, what it means to act intentionally. Intended acts are those committed because the actor wanted to and acted knowingly; they are caused and shaped by relevant desires and beliefs. Mistakes, in contrast, do not actualize the actor's desires and beliefs. Mistakes are undesired, unforeseen aspects of an act. There is evidence that even three-year-olds differentiate between intended acts and unintended mistakes in this fashion.

Shultz (1980), for example, demonstrated that three-year-olds differentiate between acts and unintended mistakes on several different tasks. In his penny task children saw two pennies, a shiny one and a dull one, and were told to point to the shiny one. In one condition, the intended condition, they simply viewed the pennies and executed the instruction. In the other, the mistake condition, they wore displacing prismatic glasses so that when trying to point to the shiny penny, they actually pointed to the dull penny instead. Children saw other children acting in these ways and participated in the two conditions themselves. In each case they were asked, "Did you [he] mean to do that?" Even three-year-olds judged that intended acts were "meant" and mistaken acts were not "meant." In this case "meant to" straightforwardly means something like "wanted to."

For adults, appropriate use of terms like "meant to" and "on purpose" requires an understanding of the difference between intention and mistake in the relevant sense, that is, the difference between acts that correspond to one's beliefs and desires (one's intentional acts) and those that do not. However, there are other ways to reveal comprehension of this basic distinction. Consider that since actors are generally happy or pleased when successful, then an understanding of intention can be evident in happiness judgments as well. To judge that a person who wants X is pleased if she accomplishes X but displeased if she accomplishes Y provides evidence of understanding the difference between intended and unintended acts.

Yuil (1984) presented preschoolers with match (wants to do X and does) and mismatch (wants to do X but does Y) scenarios and found that even three-year-olds differentiated between them by rating the actors as pleased with matches and displeased with mismatches. In Yuil's study, match and mismatch scenarios were presented by depicting the character's intention in a thought balloon and by describing the characters as verbally wanting a specified outcome. If we focus on this simple sense of wanting as equaling intending, then Stein and Levine's (1986) study, described in chapter 6, also reveals knowledge of intentions. In that study characters were said to want or not want something and then to get or not get it. Three-year-olds successfully differentiated between wants-gets matches and mismatches by appropriately rating the actors as happy, sad, or angry.

In belief-desire psychology a proper understanding of desire encompasses a simple but basic sense of intending to do something. Thus these data reinforce my prior discussion of children's understanding of desire. Such an understanding encompasses a basic understanding of intended (desired) and unintended (undesired) acts. Three-year-olds have such a basic conception of intentional action. Indeed, this sort of understanding of a character's intention in terms of simple desires is compatible with a simple desire psychology alone. And in chapter 8 I showed that even two-year-olds differentiate intended outcomes (he wants a dog and finds a dog) from unintended outcomes (he wants a dog and finds nothing or finds a rabbit). They did so by appropriately rating the actor's happiness or sadness. In short, quite young children understand a very simple sense of intention—wanting to do something—and differentiate between wanted and unwanted acts. Even two-year-old simple desire psychologists do so.

What about the more sophisticated conception depicted in figure 4.2, which revolves around an additional understanding of future intentions and planning? One simple instance of a plan to act would be a person sitting immobile but thinking that she will do something later. Recently Astington (1988) tried to capture children's understanding of this aspect of intention. She presented three-, four-, and five-year-olds with pairs of pictures, such as a girl standing in front of paints (but not painting) and a girl actually painting. Then she asked questions such as "Which girl is painting?" and "Which girl thinks she'll paint?" She found that three-year-olds and even most four-year-olds identified the girl who is painting for both questions. Most five-year-olds, however, identified the girl not painting when asked, "Which girl thinks she'll paint?"

This research program is in its early stages, but these sorts of data suggest an increasing propensity in the years three to six in conceiving of people as internally, mentally, formulating an intention separate from intentionally acting itself. Care is needed here because by my analysis even two- and three-year-olds understand that wanting is not just acting; for example, they understand that one can want and not get and also that one can want and not act (as in wishing you could hit your brother). Thus it would be improper to conclude that only at about five or six years do children begin to conceive of causal mental states prior to and separate from action. Some such conception is part of the initial belief-desire psychology of three-year-olds and in a limited sense should be part of simple desire psychology as well. Indeed, two-year-olds begin to state their desires separate from and in advance of their action. Thus Brown (1973) observed that at about two years of age children begin sensibly to use such semiauxiliaries as *gonna* and *wanna*. Brown states that such young children begin to use such expressions to state their intentions, in the sense of naming actions that they are just about to perform, such as *I gonna run* or *I wanna jump*.

Thus, at an early age children understand that desires can precede acts. Still, this is different from separating out a conception of someone mentally formulating plans for action and actively planning out agendas and coordinations of future actions. It is this sense of planning that develops in the years three to six and that I take Astington's data as suggesting.

The story on children's developing understanding of intention is complex and far from written yet. I do not claim to have marshaled even the extant research on it here. I am not intending to write that story but only to suggest that that story is constrained by children's larger understanding of mind, their developing belief-desire psychology. If I am right, then young children understand intention in one limited sense, but their understanding is significantly evolving in the years three to six because their naive psychology is evolving. Everyday psychology is at heart a psychology of intentional action. Thus the two are in many ways identical—a developing belief-desire psychology and a developing understanding of intentional action.

One important aspect of this identity concerns children's sense of the scope of belief-desire psychology, that is, the scope of intentional explanation. Belief-desire psychology is designed to explain intentional behavior; indeed it provides a basic definition of intentional actions. But some things fall outside its scope. For example, biological "behaviors" (fever chills) and object-like behavior (being bumped by a car) do not have belief-desire explanations. Such behaviors are outside naive psychology, or, alternately, such behaviors are not intentional. The years three to six see significant developments in children's understanding of the scope of intentional explanation. Apparently children begin by thinking that belief-desire explanation is appropriate to almost all human behavior. In the years three to six they begin to rein in this overextended theory, and this reining-in process continues in the years beyond six as well.

This was Carey's main point in her description of children's initial misunderstanding of biology (1985a). According to Carey, children in the preschool years have no naive biology; they generate everyday psychological explanations for phenomena adults explain biologically. It now appears that Carey may have underestimated five- and six-year-old's errors here (Hatano and Inagaki, 1987; Springer and Keil, 1989), but the general point stands; early in the preschool years children overextend the scope and domain of intentional belief-desire psychology. They fail, for example, to distinguish autonomic reflexes (such as the femoral or knee jerk reflex) from voluntary acts (intentionally lifting one's knee) (Shultz 1980). And even at four years of age children are only beginning to see that objectlike behaviors are unintended (Smith, 1978). Smith showed that four-year-olds did distinguish between a character's voluntarily raising her arm, say, and having it jerked upward by a hooked implement. At the same time, however, they tended to say that such objectlike acts were intended. They also tended to say that persons "tried to" sneeze, to yawn, and to say "ow" when poked by a stick.

In short, as the child's theory of mind develops and changes in the years three to six, so does her understanding of intention. At a young age children understand intended and unintended behavior in the sense of understanding the difference between acts caused by and matching one's desires versus those not. In the succeeding years, more and more acts become viewed as unintended—not only mistakes, acts that lie within the scope of belief-desire psychology, but acts outside the scope of everyday psychological explanations and within the scope of physical and biological explanations instead. Furthermore, children become increasingly aware of intention in the sense of deliberate internal formulation of extended organized plans for future actions. This latter development seems intimately related to the young child's change from a copy-container theory of mind (within an initial belief-desire psychology) to the older child's active, constructive homuncular theory of mind (within an expanded belief-desire psychology).

Conclusions

We do well to acknowledge that young children's lives are different from our own, that they need special help in managing fears, interpreting behavior, and understanding deception. Young children need aid in seeing how certain conceptual distinctions apply to day-to-day situations—such distinctions as that between appearance and reality, fact and fiction, lies and truth, intentions and accidents. However, these facts about young children do not mean that they live in a world radically different from our own, that they have no inkling of these distinctions. Their world is very much like our own in honoring these distinctions. There is commensurability, albeit not identity, in the framework theories of adults and children that speak to these issues. Framework theories do not dictate practices or specific theories, just as physics does not dictate engineering. Theories can engender such practices, but that is a process that takes time and creativity. Childhood acquisition of the full implications of a theory of mind also requires time and creativity. Young children require socialization, help, and comfort in their efforts because some of these theory applications are difficult for them, on the cutting edge of their conceptual abilities.

The copy-container belief-desire psychology of three-year-olds must undergo sizable changes to become the interpretive-homuncular belief-desire psychology of older children and adults. Still there is rich common ground. This is fortunate. The traditional wisdom also suggests that young children are susceptible to instruction ("he didn't do it on purpose; it was an accident"; "it's just a dream; don't worry"; "now remember this is a surprise; don't tell"). If adults and children had the sort of radically incommensurate views sometimes attributed to us, how could communication and instruction even get off the ground? It is because we share some quite basic agreements that adults can helpfully intervene in the child's world at all. A major source of these basic agreements comes from children's naive belief-desire psychology. Properly understood, that belief-desire psychology helps clarify the mystery of how children are so different from yet so familiar to adults. An important part of the answer is that their framework theory of mind, albeit different from that of adults, is still understandable in the terms of our adult theory of mind.

Chapter 11
Beyond Six

The years beyond six see several different developments in the child's belief-desire psychology and concomitant theory of mind. I will only outline a few of them here, to round off the prior discussion. My sketchy treatment of these developments does not indicate that they are insignificant or of any less importance than their predecessors. It simply means that I have concentrated in this book on the question of early development—how children's theories of mind originate and first establish themselves.

Specific Theories

Children develop not only a framework theory of mind but, within that framework, develop more specific conceptual structures including conceptual entities that can be called specific theories. The years beyond six see the development of several such specific theories and a larger array still of theory fragments, rules of thumb, and partial explanations housed under a framework theory of mind. In this section I discuss the development of three specific theories.

Self-Theory

In describing commonsense theories I mentioned that one sort of specific theory housed under belief-desire psychology was idiographic theory, detailed theories of the minds and actions of specific individuals. An important example of such an idiographic enterprise concerns our developing understanding of ourselves. Some researchers working in the area of self conception explicitly label our organized conceptions of ourselves self-theories (Epstein, 1973). I am in sympathy with this move, because our understanding of ourselves partakes of and is limited by our framework belief-desire psychology, but it provides a detailed instantiation of the framework theory in a specific self-story, an autobiography. Self theories constitute specific theories framed by the dictates of naive framework psychology—a specific coherent construal of one's own beliefs, desires, traits, history of perceptions, and memories.

Consider the following outline of how an individual might come to some specific self-conception, say, the notion "I'm a good athlete":

1. The self-conceiver begins with an awareness of certain basic person concepts. His or her conceptual repertoire includes some descriptions, states, and dimensions that can usefully characterize people: "athletic prowess," "preferences," "intelligence," and so on.

2. From among these concepts the person might become very interested in the potential relevance of some of these characterizations for self-definition. The person would then be especially receptive to information about self on this dimension. Over time this could lead to self-definition in respect to this concept: "I have good athletic skills, my athletic abilities are important to me, I win at sports, I find lots of physical games easy." In short, to use Hazel Markus's (1977) term, athletic ability (or some other attribution) becomes self-schematic for the person; it becomes particularly self-relevant.

3. The person would, at some point, then propose and generate further information about self in keeping with this conception—use it to predict future dispositions, compare self to others on this basis, use it to explain his or her past behavior. In short, the person would incorporate this self-conception into a self-theory, a theory with certain explanatory resources and capable even of distorting relevant experiences to make data fit theory, that is, to maintain or rationalize a certain self-image.

I do not propose that this outline be thought of as anything like a processing model; I do not think this is a valid specification of how self concepts unfold in time. I only wish to decompose self-conception a bit to show the potential impact of belief-desire psychology.

Most obviously belief-desire psychology plays a role at step 1, with respect to the thinker's basic repertoire of categories for person- and self-conception. Thoughts, desires, basic emotions, actions, perceptions and so on, as specified by belief-desire psychology, are the basic categories that frame specific person concepts. Everyday theory of mind provides the infrastructure for self-conception. In fact, it does so not only at step 1 but also at step 3. When the thinker has begun to see himself in a particular fashion (as athletic perhaps), how does he utilize this specific self-concept in his further thinking? He does so by building an increasingly coherent story, indeed an idiographic theory, to explain and predict his own acts and thoughts. This theory is not built completely from the ground up; it rests on a general infrastructure provided by a framework theory. Self-conception is dependent on a framework theory for basic terms, ontology, and causal-explanatory mechanisms; self-theory is dependent in this fashion on everyday theory of mind.

Because of this dependency, developments in children's belief-desire psychology should be reflected in self- and person-conception. I think that one major development of this sort occurs in the years beyond six. This development is so major that some researchers have concluded that before age six children's self-concepts are crude and deficient, unworthy of being considered self-conceptions at all. This development has to do with children's increasing understanding and use of trait explanations for behavior.

Recall that in our study of children's explanations of behavior (chapter 6) one exception to the basic commonality evident in adults' and young children's explanations involved the use of trait explanations. Adults often referred to explanatory character traits; three- and four-year-olds essentially never did. Other research focusing on children's understanding of people suggests that there is substantial developmental change in the use of trait explanations. For example, Barenboim (1981) studied the use of psychological constructs such as personality characteristics ("he's real stubborn"; "she's so kind"; "she's selfish"; "he's shy") in children's descriptions of people they knew well. His data showed large increases in the use of such trait descriptions after age seven or so. Thus he notes that "one of the most replicated findings in the developmental study of person perception is the large increase in use of psychological constructs" between the preschool years and adulthood (p. 129). I am in agreement with this conclusion, if allowed a significant reinterpretation.

Data from person perception studies are often interpreted as demonstrating young children's behavioral, nonpsychological understanding of persons and action. "In short, there is a major shift from a highly concrete level . . . to a more inferential level in which more covert aspects such as values, beliefs and so on are described" (Shantz, 1983, p. 506). This interpretation is applied to children's construal of others' actions (Flapan, 1968; Lively and Bromley, 1973; Peevers and Secord, 1973) and to self. Thus, Montemayor and Eisen (1977) conclude that children see themselves "in terms of concrete objective categories such as their address, physical appearance, possessions and play activities while adolescents used more abstract and subjective descriptions such as personal beliefs, motivational and interpersonal characteristics" (p. 317). These conclusions and research simultaneously contrast the self- and person-conceptions of young children and adults in two respects: their internal-psychological status and their trait-likeness. Adult construals simultaneously refer to internal psychological constructs, such as beliefs and desires, and also emphasize trait regularities, such as shyness or selfishness. Young children's conceptions, it is claimed, encompass neither of these features: persons are not seen in mentalistic-psychological or in traitlike fashions. This conclusion with respect to young children confounds two different capabilities. In contrast, my reinterpretation is that young children's appreciation of persons, including self, and their actions is generally mentalistic although not trait dependent. The data throughout this book firmly support the first point—they document the psychological-mentalistic construal of personal action by quite young children. However, as suggested in chapter 4 and depicted in the comparison of figures 4.1 and 4.3, I believe that early naive psychological conception does not extend itself to an incorporation of trait constructs. Thus, I am in substantial agreement with the person perception literature, properly understood, that trait explanations develop subsequent to the preschool years. With the onset of such trait characterizations, children's self-conceptions become substantially more adultlike. Indeed in the years beyond six children come to achieve a self-theory based on notions of self-relevant stable characteristics that organize one's sense of oneself.

There are other more subtle relations between children's framework theories of mind and their understanding of the self that deserve some mention as well. There is, in adult conception, something peculiarly self-relevant about the mind. The mind houses all my thoughts and memories, my autobiographical information and experiences. If I had no mind, it would seem quite strange to speak of my "self." When do children see it this way? To answer this question Johnson (in press) has conducted several "transplant" studies with children—asking them what would happen if different parts of themselves were transplanted into another body. Clearly from the adult point of view, a brain or mind transplant would be peculiarly self-relevant. According to Johnson's data, younger school-aged children (first graders) are only beginning to have any ideas about this. First graders correctly assessed the self-implications of a brain swap between themselves and a quite different animal (such as a pig) but not between themselves and another person. Later, in middle childhood (by fifth grade), children's adultlike performances on such transplant tasks were robust. At that point children clearly and consistently realized that if their brain or mind was put into another body, they themselves would also have been shifted; their self would be in the other place.

Most research on self- and person-perception has been conducted by personality and social psychologists whose primary interests often concern such trait characterizations as "shy," "aggressive," "depressed." However, consider characterizations like quick, brainy, witty, perceptive, slow, retarded, dumb, clever, egghead, intellectual, under- and over-achiever, and so on. The child's developing theory of mind provides the infrastructure for a host of basic categories that could become self-relevant, those related to cognition as well as conation. In the next section I pursue one such category further—that related to "intelligence."

I have not reserved discussion of self conception until this chapter because children are without self-concepts before six. That is false; even young children think about themselves. Nonetheless, children's self-conception takes a notable leap forward in the school years. Indeed, right about six years seems 'o be the time when children first begin to formulate a specific self-theory; they do so within the confines of their framework belief-desire psychology.

Theories of Intelligence

A framework belief-desire psychology and its concomitant theory of mind helps frame not only specific idiographic theories but specific topic theories as well. In the next two sections, I will take up two of these topics: intelligence and memory.

In recent years several studies have appeared investigating children's naive notions of intelligence. Yussen and Kane (1985) probed elementary school children's notions about such things as the signs of intelligence (how do you spot intelligent or smart people?), the characterization of intelligence (in what ways do smart people differ from others?), the constancy of intelligence (whether a person's intelligence changes or stays constant throughout life) and so on. Similarly, Sternberg, Conway, Ketron, and Bernstein (1981) have explored people's conceptions of intelligence. In this section, however, I will concentrate on and briefly describe Dweck's research on children's conceptions of intelligence because Dweck sees children's understanding of intelligence as more than an accumulating collection of ideas on the topic; instead, she claims children have a theory. Consequently, she has attempted to characterize the nature of children's theories rather than simply cataloging their beliefs. She has shown that a number of children's beliefs are organized coherently by an underlying theory, something on the order of a specific theory of intelligence, in my terms. It is also of interest that Dweck finds that children typically come to one of two possible theories and that which theory they come to has great import for the child's academic self-concept. Thus, Dweck's research ties the current topic into some of the concerns raised in the preceding section.

Dweck (Dweck and Bempechat, 1983; Dweck and Leggett, 1988) posits that children hold one of two naive theories of intelligence. One is an "entity" theory, based on the belief that intelligence is a stable, fixed entity. The opposing "instrumental-incremental" 'theory rests on the belief that intelligence consists of a set of skills and information that can be expanded through learning:

> Our research has indicated that children hold two functional or operating theories of intelligence. The one they tend to emphasize is the one that appears to guide their behavior in novel achievement settings. . . . The first theory, which we have called an "entity" theory, involves the belief that intelligence is a rather stable, global trait. Children favoring this theory tend to subscribe to the idea that they possess a specific, fixed amount of intelligence, that this intelligence is displayed through performance, and that the outcomes or judgments indicate whether they are or are not intelligent. The second theory, which we call an "instrumental-incremental" theory, involves the belief that intelligence consists of an ever-expanding repertoire of skills and knowledge, one that is increased through one's own instrumental behavior. By middle to late grade school, children understand aspects of both theories, but tend to focus on one in thinking about intelligence. That is, although instrumental theorists realize that individuals may differ in the rate at which they acquire skills, they focus on the idea that anyone can become smarter (more skillful and more knowledgeable) by investing effort. Entity theorists also realize that virtually everyone can increase their skills or knowledge, but they do not believe that people can become smarter. . . . We find striking individual differences in which theory children tend to endorse and use as a guide for their behavior. (Dweck and Bempechat, 1981, pp. 244–245)

Dweck demonstrates that these theories are established and then extensively utilized in the years beyond six. The fact that children come to two contrasting theories is helpful for my characterization of these as specific theories. Both specific theories recruit their terms and basic explanatory schemes from framework belief-desire psychology. But by emphasizing different things, providing different details, two specific theories are achieved quite different from each other, albeit both offspring of the larger global theory. Both skills and stable traits are belief-desire constructs generally, but those notions are selectively developed in the formulation of the two specific theories. That these specific theories are quite different becomes clear when Dweck outlines their differential implications for their holders when faced with learning situations:

> The view of intelligence as a judgable entity orients children toward competence judgments (toward looking smart, or, "performance" goals), whereas the view of intelligence as a quality that grows orients children toward competence building (toward getting smarter, or, "learning" goals). Further, we suggest it is the former view that renders children vulnerable to debilitation in the face of obstacles, and the latter view that spurs persistence even when children believe themselves to be unskilled at the task at hand. (Dweck and Bempechat, 1981, pp. 239–240)

In a series of studies Dweck has shown that in many tasks entity theorists do indeed tend to pursue performance goals (achieving good scores by avoiding errors even to the extent of choosing easy, noninstructive tasks) whereas incremental theorists tend to choose learning goals (choosing tasks where errors are likely because of their instructive value).

Metamemory or Memory Theory?

Children's understanding of their memory, that and how the mind stores and retrieves information and experiences, has been well studied in the last fifteen years. These studies are termed studies of metamemory (Flavell, 1971b). And there are sizable increases in the amount and organization of children's understanding of memory in the years beyond six (see Flavell and Wellman, 1977; Schneider, 1985). I briefly consider this developing knowledge and return to my concern as to whether and when everyday specific knowledge structures can be said to constitute specific naive theories. The question is, Does children's metamemory constitute a specific naive theory of memory, or is it a looser, less organized sort of conceptual structure? I am unsure. I am sure, however, that children's knowledge of memory, however organized, is housed under and constrained by their framework theory of mind. Memory, after all, is to be understood as a faculty of the mind, for children (Johnson and Wellman, 1982) as well as for adults.

Whether children develop a naive memory theory or not, it seems abundantly clear that they do acquire a useful collection of conventional lore ("use a rhyme"), rules of thumb ("verbatim recall is harder than gist recall"), and isolated self-relevant concepts ("I'm bad at remembering names but good at remembering poems") as part of their increasing knowledge of memory. Memory beliefs of this sort need not be tightly integrated into a coherent theory of memory; they can exist as a body of specific conceptions loosely anchored to a framework theory of mind instead. This leaves as an unresolved question whether, in addition, children achieve a coherent specific theory about memory. In spite of some mention of the question (Wellman, 1983), no research really tackles this issue. Research on metamemory typically investigates only a discrete set of memory knowledge; for example, it might address children's knowledge about memory cues (Gordon and Flavell, 1977; Fabricius and Wellman, 1983; Beal, 1985). Even studies that investigate a host of memory beliefs at once probe a collection of taxonomically related facts but offer no picture of a possible naive theory of memory underlying people's discrete memory beliefs (Kreutzer, Leonard, and Flavell, 1975; Herrmann, 1982). Indeed, from a naive point of view, memory covers such an assortment of phenomena (memory for pictures versus memory for names, autobiographical memories of past events versus storage of information for classroom tests) that people may simply not integrate such different abilities into a single theory of memory, although cognitive scientists do. Our naive knowledge of memory at its best may represent a family of theory fragments.

On the other hand, it seems that naive adults, cognitive scientists, and school-aged children are all prone to think of remembering information on analogy to storing and retrieving objects. Consider one elaborated instantiation of this—for example, a description of our memory as rather like an internal librarian acquiring new memories (books), sorting and organizing them, storing acquisitions, retrieving and utilizing them. The librarian's acquisitions are selective, her shelves limited, her retrieval sometimes faulty, and acquisitions can get lost or destroyed. A metaphor such as this may well form the basis of a specific coherent naive theory of memory adopted during the school years and elaborated thereafter. At this point we do not know.

Regardless, our metamemories do show the imprint of naive theorizing. They are still specific conceptual structures, within a framework theory of mind, even if they do not cohere into a specific theory. As such, metamemory should be constrained in part by the nature of the global theory and metamemory development constrained by developments in children's theories of mind. I want to sketch one way in which I think this happens.

The classic supposition in the study of metamemory is that knowledge of one's memory influences one's selection of memory strategies and hence one's memory performance. In short, knowledge of memory includes and influences one's attempts to amplify and utilize one's memory. My belief is that theories exert little immediate direction here. Theories, recall, are on the order of maps, not specific route itineraries. Still theories, especially naive framework theories, frame one's worldview and hence can shape one's general approach to a topic or endeavor. They do so not by dictating a certain approach, by dictating a specific itinerary, but by allowing consideration of limited alternatives. You are unlikely to chart a route not on your map. That is, one need not discover the practical implications of one's theory, but one is unlikely to make discoveries that lie outside one's theory or are contradicted by it. In this way theories constrain discovery.

In this fashion, the child's theory of mind should set some broad limits on children's attempts to use the mind. And one of our most frequent attempts to use the mind concerns our use of memory strategies, deliberate attempts to remember, that is, to store and retrieve information in the mind. Our theories of mind therefore should set some quite general limits on our discovery and assimilation of memory strategies. Of course, this is not hard and fast. A child could stumble onto or be told of a memory trick that works well and then simply continue to use it on the basis of its empirical success. Such empirical success stories need not conform to the dictates of one's theory of mind. Still, theory should make a discernible imprint. I think it does. I think there is an imprint on children's acquisition of memory strategies of the child's shift from a passive copy-container theory of mind to an active processing theory of mind late in the preschool years.

In the 1970s the generally accepted view of memory development was that increases in memory performance from about age six on were largely due to the older child's increasing propensity to employ deliberate memory strategies to aid both storage and retrieval. Conversely, children younger than this were thought to be nonstrategic in memory endeavors. This characterization of the young child received direct and indirect support from four sources. Soviet theory and research described the memory activities of young children as involuntary, not voluntary (Smirnov and Zinchenko, 1969). In North America, young children were similarly described as production deficient (Flavell, 1970b). Direct data on the presence of memory strategies were abundant for older children but absent for preschoolers (Appel, Cooper, McCarrell, Sims-Knight, Yussen, and Flavell, 1972). And finally, that memory strategies first appeared at around school age fit well with cross-cultural research on schooling itself. In this research (Wagner, 1978), it seemed that the increased memory demands placed on Western children entering into formal educational arrangements provoked strategic attempts to remember.

Starting in the mid-1970s, however, demonstrations of the employment of certain memory strategies by quite young children began to appear (see Wellman, 1977). By now the existence and utilization of such strategies in preschool children seems irrefutable (Wellman, 1988b). A large part of the earlier confusion, and the new clarity, concerns differences in the sort of strategies used by children before and after age six. To most experimental psychologists, the prototypic memory strategies are those of verbal rehearsal, categorical clustering and organization, and imaginal and verbal elaboration. There is still little, if any, evidence of the use by preschoolers of these strategies. Preschoolers use other strategies, essentially those of trying, attending, and using external reminders. Even to adults these are genuine memory strategies, things to do to enhance one's remembering, even if they also seem simple and obvious (see Wellman, 1988b, for a larger discussion).

When confronted with memory tasks—for example, the need to remember the location of a target toy hiding in an array of hiding locations—preschoolers try. They exert more effort and they evidence an intention to remember that is not evident if they are set nonmemory tasks such as to look at, play with, or count the same materials (see Somerville, Wellman, and Cultice, 1983; Baker-Ward, Ornstein, and Holden, 1984). The best way to demonstrate children's efforts here, however, is to discuss certain specific strategies that they use. Since these strategies require deliberate effort, when children employ them, they simultaneously demonstrate an intention to remember and use a specific strategy. One strategy that preschoolers employ is that they carefully visually attend to the to-be-remembered target or materials (DeLoache, Cassidy and Brown, 1985; Yussen, 1974; Wellman, Ritter, and Flavell, 1975). For example, in the Yussen (1974) study, preschoolers who were instructed to remember a model's picture selections deliberately attended to the model (and avoided watching an attractive distraction). Children given alternative nonmemory instructions rarely did so. Similarly, preschool children will set up external cues to help themselves remember a target's location (Wellman et al., 1975; Ritter, 1978). For example, when needing to remember a hidden object's location in one of a number of identical hiding containers, preschoolers make the correct container distinctive, for example, by tagging it with a marker (Ritter, 1978). Children also at times verbally name the to-be-remembered item during a memory delay, although they do not actively engage in rehearsal until about age six or seven (Baker-Ward, Ornstein, and Holden, 1984).

These early stages are, I now think, strategies within the scope of a copy theory of mind, whereas rehearsal, elaboration, and clustering require an active interpretive outlook. Here is my analysis. (I am indebted to discussions with Bill Fabricius for helping me formulate these ideas.)

I will credit young children with an awareness of the general possibility of forgetting, an awareness that memory is faulty. That awareness fuels the need to engage in strategies at all—that is, to attempt to avoid forgetting. But beyond that, I credit young preschoolers with an initial belief-desire psychology, including only a copy notion of knowledge uptake. What sorts of strategies fall within the scope of such a theory? Trying, that is, intentionally doing something to achieve what one wants, is certainly a notion well within initial belief-desire psychology. Intentional action is a cornerstone of even the most basic belief-desire understanding. Moreover, as depicted in figure 9.1, initial belief-desire psychology includes the knowledge that mental contents arise from seeing (and also hearing, smelling, and so forth), but ignorance arises from not seeing. Therefore, young children could certainly appreciate the need to attend visually to a target if they want to remember it. Thus, the most rudimentary copy notions could engender trying and attending as memory strategies.

Suppose we also grant to young children some understanding that forgetting occurs—for example, that as a delay continues, one's mental copy of reality can fade. This seems a striking phenomenal fact about remembering, a basic experiential aspect of mind of the sort that Johnson (1988) argues should be apparent to even very young children. That one additional awareness seems sufficient to encompass within a copy understanding of mind the practical idea that reminders are helpful. From a copy perspective, the most direct sort of reminder conceivable would be reexposure to the target. Since perception leads directly to representing, in a copy theory, there could be no more obvious way to update, refresh, reestablish a fading copy-representation than to reexperience it. And indeed this is one of the most prevalent strategies of young children. It is most obvious in two and a half- and three-year-olds' deliberate attempts to re-present the to-be-remembered target (Wellman et al., 1975; DeLoache et al., 1985), but it also occurs at a somewhat later age in renamings of the target during a delay (Baker-Ward et al., 1984).

Finally, consider the use of external reminders. Young children's use of external reminders has occurred essentially in situations where an object is hidden in one of several locations and children mark the target location to make it distinctive (Wellman et al., 1985; Ritter, 1978) or deliberately place the object in a distinctive location such as an end or corner of the array (Heisel and Ritter, 1981). In such a situation the child is faced with the problem of ignorance (as depicted in figure 9.1); in the course of the delay, the child can forget, that is, become ignorant of the correct alternative. A marker simply and directly marks the correct alternative; it staves off ignorance.

To summarize, an early copy-container theory of mind and mental representation encompasses certain hit-or-miss limits on the uptake of information. That is, it encompasses some but not other understandings about the production of reality-oriented mental representations. Concomitantly such a copy theory suggests only some strategies for ensuring that a reality-oriented mental representation is produced and maintained. Fittingly these strategies seem to be the memory strategies generated by preschoolers up until the age of five or six years.

In the years beyond six the child's increasingly active interpretive theory of mind should expand his or her sights with respect to memory strategies. Strategies should move beyond simple attempts simply to hit the representational target or to remind oneself of the target during a delay. This theory expansion does not dictate the acquisition of new memory strategies, but it allows for them. Consider imaginal or verbal elaboration as a memory strategy. Imaginal elaboration is an attempt to augment the memorability of pictured items rather than simply an attempt to hit them perceptually in the first place. That is, a strategy of elaboration rests on some understanding of the constructed character of mental representations beyond simple copy notions. Similarly, engaging in meaningful elaborations of verbal materials seems to rest on a realization that such materials are not sufficiently memorable to begin with. From a copy perspective, however, if the targets are perceivable, they are memorable. Attempts to enhance memorability beyond this seem to require a constructive view of mind. The same sort of argument holds for attempts to reorganize incoming information in order to remember it better. From this perspective, even systematic attempts at verbal rehearsal seem to require an active, not passive, theory of mind. Active, subvocal, in-the-head rehearsal as an attempt to ensure memorability is a step beyond simple re-presentation of the initial copied stimulus. It is no surprise therefore that rehearsal, elaboration, and organization make their appearances as memory strategies in the years beyond six (Wellman, 1988b).

This explanation for early- versus late-appearing memory strategies is admittedly post hoc. Still, it seems reasonable, and I believe we will find in future research that young preschoolers' passive copyist view of the mind constrains their thinking about memory and their creation and utilization of memory strategies. Similarly, older children's increasingly active-homuncular theory of mind affords them the opportunity to create and acquire a different, additional set of mnemonic techniques.

Natural Epistemology

In chapter 9 I credit old preschoolers (four- and five-year-olds) with a beginning grasp of an active, interpretive understanding of mind. At times I refer to this as a constructive view of mind. By this I mean a beginning understanding that errors of cognition can result from misconstrual beyond just hit-or-miss representation. Thus children begin at this time to replace a passive container view of the mind with an active homuncular view, where the mind interprets information and constructive processes influence representation.

It is important to distinguish my attribution of a constructive, interpretive view of mind from attribution of a constructivist view of epistemology. An interesting literature exists on children's and adolescents' changing epistemic assumptions in which a constructivist epistemology is typically seen as a development of adolescence or adulthood (Broughton, 1978; Chandler, 1987; Kuhn and Phelps, 1982; Mansfield and Clinchy, 1985a, 1985b; Perry, 1970). This literature focuses on person's natural epistemology (Broughton, 1978; Mansfield and Clinchy, 1985) in the sense of their understanding of when personal beliefs are justified, true, and legitimate and what sorts of evidence can count in justifying and legitimizing one's beliefs. The general developmental scenario here is one of movement from absolutism to multiplism (Perry, 1970) or objectivist to constructivist epistemologies (Chandler, 1987). Crudely put, absolutist or objectivist epistemologies rest on a notion of there being one single truth, one objective way in which the world really is. Multiplistic, constructivist, relativistic epistemologies admit that truth itself may be relative, "the possibility that persons may find *legitimately* different meanings in what are ostensibly the same facts" (Chandler, 1987, p. 135).

I want to clarify that children can have an active homuncular and hence interpretive view of the mind in the way I have described it without having a constructivist epistemology. Indeed, I believe this is an apt characterization of the thinking of older preschoolers and early school-aged children. As an example it seems clear that I could understand that beliefs are the products of an active mind that processes and interprets information, without thinking that truth itself is relative. I could believe that there is a single true set of facts, although our access to those facts is mediated by our active, interpreting mind.

According to this view, processes of construal do exist leading to mis-construals, but such misconstruals are simply errors. They are errors because there is, in this view, always an objective truth against which construals can be evaluated. Seeing the mind as an active interpreter therefore does not dictate seeing truth as relative. Seeing the mind as active does put me in a position so that eventually I may come to suspect that "truth" itself is a constructed impression or a subjective stance with respect to experience, and hence from such a position I might eventually come to develop a constructivist epistemology. But such an epistemology is not necessarily encompassed by an active-interpretative conception of mind of the sort described in chapter 9.

Development of a constructivist natural epistemology is, I believe, a development beyond six. The literature on this topic, although divided on many issues, is unanimous in agreeing that constructivist epistemology begins to be appreciated only beyond six: by school-aged children (Mansfield and Clinchy, 1985a) or adolescents (Chandler, 1987; Broughton, 1975) or even older persons (Perry, 1970).

Flavell (1989) has recently shown that even three-year-olds under-stand that different persons may have different preferences or tastes—value-beliefs, he terms them. Thus, Ellie may think that cookie is yucky, whereas I think it is yummy and delicious. This is, of course, an important awareness, an early insight into the possibil-ity of mentalistic, or perhaps even representational, diversity. This insight does not mean, however, that the young child believes, even for preferences, that truth is relative, that the cookie truly is both yummy and yucky in some sense. In fact, Mansfield and Clinchy (1985a) seem to have shown that preschoolers are absolutists about this issue. They told three-, four-, seven-, and ten-year-olds about two people eating soup, one who liked the soup and one who did not. They then asked if the child thought one protagonist was right, whether one had to be right or one wrong, and whether we could ever find out for sure who was right. The preschoolers consistently answered that one person would have to be wrong because the other was right.

Beyond this early absolutist position Mansfield and Clinchy (1985a) and Chandler (1987), following Perry (1970), speculate that develop-ment proceeds next to a position of objective multiplism. From a per-spective of objective multiplism, disputants may disagree because they are referring to "different aspects of the same phenomena, and that either one answer or the other would apply, depending on where and when one looked" (Mansfield and Clinchy, 1985a, p. 12). "These children accommodate to the reality of different opinions but still maintained their belief in absolute empirically derived truth. The protagonists had different experiences, not because of any subjective factors, but because the outside world is fluctuating or multifaceted" (p. 13). Only later still do children adopt subjective multiplism (Mansfield and Clinchy, 1985a), generic doubt (Chandler, 1987), and perhaps postskeptical rationalism (Chandler, 1987).

I do not intend to propose a developmental story for children's natural epistemology. The literature and issues are complex, and I am not confident or knowledgeable about these later developments; instead I recommend such reviews as Chandler's (1987). Still, I do propose the more obvious but still important claim that constructivist epistemology is a development beyond six but one built on an earlier appreciation of the active-interpretive quality of mind.

Additional Developments, Briefly

One sort of additional change in the years beyond six concerns further increases in proficiency in children's belief-desire reasoning and concomitant theory of mind. Children achieve a beginning grasp of an interpretive view of representation and an active-homuncular theory of mind before six; in the years after six children elaborate and consolidate these notions. For example, during this time personification of the mind becomes prevalent (Wellman and Johnson, 1982). And in the years beyond six, children's discussion of appearance-reality phenomena and the role of misinterpretation in visual representations becomes increasingly explicit and sophisticated (Flavell et al., 1986). Belief-desire reasoning itself—children's proficiency at predicting and explaining others' actions on the basis of their beliefs and desires, and abilities at diagnosing others' beliefs and desires—increases. An informative example of this sort of advance is that children get progressively better at considering another's thinking in the years beyond six. They become able to deal with someone's thinking about thinking or similarly their beliefs about beliefs. Perner and Wimmer (1985) have termed this advance in children's conception the acquisition of second-order beliefs, and Miller, Kessel, and Flavell (1970) have termed it thinking about thinking about thinking. Both sets of investigators have documented children's increasing facility and understanding in the years beyond six with the recursive notion that not only do you have your thoughts but that these can include thoughts about my thoughts.

A quite different sort of change in the years after six concerns the decreasing scope of belief-desire psychology. Belief-desire psychology takes as its domain of explanation voluntary actions and thoughts. Children and adults believe that most human behavior constitutes belief-desire dependent actions, but in the years after six, children achieve sizable increases in awareness that this is not the only game in town; belief-desire explanations retreat somewhat in the face of a variety of competitors. Some of these competitors have theory status in their own right; for example, children develop a naive framework biology, and this has implications for the explanation of some behaviors. Naive framework biology is the primary explanatory system (at least in Western European cultures) for explanations of sickness, death, reproduction, certain bodily functions (such as urination), and autonomic behaviors (such as reflex blinking). In the years beyond six, children decreasingly give psychological explanations for such bodily activities and increasingly give biological ones (Carey, 1985a).

Even within the realm of psychology proper, belief-desire psychology makes room for an assortment of other psychological explanations. Primary examples are unconscious and subcognitive, or mindless, explanations for behavior. By unconscious explanations, I mean explanations that appeal to everyday versions of things like displacement or denial. In at least piecemeal and fragmented ways, naive adults understand that people at times act from such underground, nonconscious, irrational processes, processes hard to fit within the cognitive rational machinery of belief-desire psychology. In the years beyond six, children also become aware of this (Whiteman, 1967). One way in which belief-desire psychology makes room for such explanations, without being overcome by them, I think, is by further exploitation of a homunculus metaphor. As children increasingly come to view the mind as an active agent in its own right, in personified terms; it becomes possible to see the mind as a deceptive agent hiding some of its own workings even from the person whose mind it is.

In the years beyond six, children also come to realize the existence of subcognitive influences on behavior. It is not an uncommon adult explanation to talk of "mindless" behavior. For example, I get in the car to go to the airport and begin thinking of other things and mindlessly drive to my office instead. How do I explain how I perceived, acted, and made certain decisions in order to get to the office? My actions to go to the airport fall nicely under belief-desire psychology. However, to explain how I got to the office instead requires some appeal to mindless processes as well. Other sorts of mindless behavior, like addictions and behavior under hypnosis, also require subcognitive explanations at least partly outside the scope of typical belief-desire psychology. In the years beyond six, children become increasingly aware that mindless mentation goes on and accounts for some of these nonstandard acts.

In short, in the years beyond six, there is a resurveying of the behavioral terrain wherein belief-desire psychology ends up with less of the real estate and gives way in certain locales to neighboring explanatory systems or system fragments. Beyond this, the child's theory of mind, on its own home turf, must come to an accommodation with the body in the form of an increased understanding of the brain. In a series of studies, Carl Johnson and I asked children about both the mind and the brain (Johnson and Wellman, 1982). We asked questions such as, "Do you need your brain/mind to sleep/think/yawn?" and "Where is your brain/mind"? Preschoolers identified the brain with the mind; both were terms for the same mental entity, a mind that dreams and thinks and that exists inside the head. In the school years, children progressively differentiated the two concepts: mind retaining its mentalistic status, brain becoming an increasingly biological organ, entrenched in the body, housing the mind but separate from it. In these years, children increasingly realized the brain's neurological role in all activity, even in biological acts such as breathing and blinking. In short, beyond six, children distinguish brain from mind as part of the process of distinguishing biology from psychology and then struggle with how to reintegrate the two notions since the brain houses the mind.

Conclusions

I have barely skimmed the surface with regard to developments in theory of mind beyond age six. But my goal has been to be suggestive, not comprehensive, to extend the discussions of prior chapters in some concrete fashions. By my account, advances in belief-desire psychology, in theory of mind, beyond six should lead to advances in specific conceptual structures beyond six. And advances beyond six build on achievements before six. I have not tried to detail these extensions and developments but simply to outline a scarce few in order to elaborate the earlier work a bit and to point to future horizons.

Chapter 12
Conclusions

Summary of Results

The results I have presented are analytic and empirical; I have provided conceptual analyses and research findings. These go hand in hand. The conceptual analyses underpin and frame the empirical research; the findings serve to articulate the framework as much as to confirm it. My summary therefore is not confined to replicated findings but provides a recapitulation of children's theories of mind as I see them.

"Care must be taken not to endow the child with a systematic theory" (Piaget, 1929, p. 100). In contrast to this admonition from Piaget, I have taken pains in this book to endow the young child with a systematic theory, an everyday belief-desire psychology. I justify doing so both by articulating a notion of everyday theory and by empirically demonstrating the systematicity and depth of children's thinking. I have stressed two things. First, I tackled an everyday framework theory; at this level of analysis, talk about everyday theories makes great sense. Second, I have concentrated on three-year-olds because this is the approximate age at which a first theory of mind develops. But theory change is also important and apparent. Therefore, I have described both change to an initial theory of mind (the transition from simple desire psychology to belief-desire psychology) and change from an initial copy-container theory of mind to a later interpretive-homuncular theory.

Because of their place within this three-part progression, I have devoted much energy to three-year-olds, to characterizing correctly three-year-olds' everyday psychology and concomitant theory of mind. Three-year-olds occupy the middle ground, evidencing a first belief-desire psychology but one considerably different from children only a few years older and indeed from our own. For this reason three-year-olds' theory is a curious mix—both commensurate with adult thinking but also foreign to it. It is all too easy to overestimate and to underestimate three-year-olds' first theory of mind, to dismiss it falsely as not a theory of mind at all or to embrace it falsely as the adult theory. Neither of these reactions is appropriate, as becomes clear when the theory is properly characterized and carefully compared to its predecessor and successor. In comparison to simple desire psychology alone, initial belief-desire psychology is a momentous advance, achieving for three-year-olds a worldview not unlike our own in character and significance. In comparison to later interpretive notions, however, the passive copy-container theory of mind entrenched in three-year-olds' mentalism seems radically limited, so limited that several researchers have unwittingly overlooked it altogether.

Why am I so certain that three-year-olds have a belief-desire psychology and a theory of mind?

1. They evidence understanding of the basic ontological distinction between mind and world (chapter 2). In doing so, they evidence understanding of the hypothetical aspect of mind.
2. They evidence understanding of the existence and nature of beliefs as well as desires (chapter 3). In doing so, they evidence understanding of the causal nature of mind in general and the convictional nature of beliefs specifically.
3. They understand much, if not all, of the coherent causal-explanatory scheme evident in figure 4.1 (see chapter 6) including:
    a. The difference between beliefs and desires.
    b. The interaction of beliefs and desires to cause action.
    c. The intentional—that is, belief-desire dependent—nature of human action.
    d. The nature of belief-desire-dependent emotional reactions.
    e. At least something of the origination of beliefs in perception as well as the origination of fantastical ideas in imagination.
4. They understand, in an early copy-container sense, the representational nature of mind (chapter 9).

Together these understandings constitute an impressive adherence to a belief-desire psychology in which mind is a central construct. Three-year-olds have achieved an initial understanding that people live their lives not simply with respect to an external world of objects but also with respect to an internal world of imaginings and beliefs, which complement, cause, and explain their actions. The earlier simple desire psychology does not qualify as a theory of mind in this essential fashion, although it does respect some mentalisms. Development of a simple desire psychology is itself important, however, both because it constitutes a naive psychology of some explanatory power and because it lays the groundwork for development of the initial belief-desire theory. That two-year-olds possess such a theory is also significant in that it allows some important communication between two-year-olds and adults (after all, simple desires are not alien to adult everyday psychology).

As impressive as it is, three-year-olds' initial belief-desire theory is still far from that of adults because of its copy understanding of belief, hit-or-miss view of misrepresentation, and container-view of mind. All in all, it fails to honor an immensely important aspect of an adult theory of mind: the inimitable interpretive aspects of mind and hence the constructive relation between all minds and reality.

Crafting this story has required considerable preparatory conceptual-analytic work with respect to characterizing belief-desire psychology, distinguishing framework from specific theories, distinguishing ontological from epistemological realism, distinguishing beliefs from desires and from simple desires, and separating an initial (copyist) view of reality-oriented representation from a later (interpretive) view. When these conceptual pieces are properly analyzed and in place, the description of children's early theory articulated in this book becomes compelling.

At many places throughout this book I have contrasted my findings and interpretations to those of Piaget. I do so not because Piaget's position is so obviously deficient but rather because it is so persuasive. The research reported in this book represents a return to the intriguing questions Piaget raised long ago and a return to the spirit of his early research in which he explored the content of children's thinking, that is, how children make sense of the substantive nature of their worlds. If, as I argue, everyday thought is constrained by framework theories and theories are irreducibly content dependent, then we must return to the job of understanding children's substantive knowledge. If we choose our topics appropriately, this is a task of immense value. Children's theory of mind is an appropriate, perhaps inspired, topic, and I am indebted to Piaget for his research and inspiration.

Theory Changes

At several places in this book and in the preceding summary I describe children's theory of mind as changing "substantially" or "qualitatively," albeit earlier and later versions are described as "commensurate" and "recognizable." Additionally, I have described later ideas and conceptions as "developing out of" or "stemming from" earlier ones. What exactly do I mean? What sorts of changes occur, and how are they to be characterized? These are hard questions, and I have no comprehensive answers, but I can discuss my approach a bit further.

My approach to these questions has been more specific and descriptive than general and definitive. This seems to have been a helpful strategy in the philosophy of science; philosophers' ideas about theory change have been informed by detailed case studies of how various conceptions and theories have actually changed in the history of scientific ideas (Cantor, 1970–71; Hacking, 1981; Kitcher, 1985). I offer the current research as a detailed case study of how conceptions of mind change in the ontogenesis of everyday ideas. However, I have acknowledged often in this book that observation and description are theory laden; it is impossible to conduct a descriptive case study without some commitment to a framework for description. It behooves me to make my commitments more explicit.

One such commitment concerns a perspective on the general mechanisms of cognitive change. In recent years, we have witnessed a renewed interest in the mechanisms of cognitive development—the processes underlying developmental change (Sternberg, 1984). Much of this discussion has stemmed from one or the other of two complementary approaches. One is an information-processing approach. From this stance, investigators have hypothesized that changes in the basic processing parameters of the human cognitive system, or changes in the basic representational format of the system, drive many more obvious developmental changes in thinking and reasoning. Some possibilities of this sort focus on changes in memory span (Case, Kurland, and Goldberg, 1982), speed of processing (Chi, 1977), changes from enactive to iconic to propositional representations (Bruner et al., 1967), or changes from representational to metarepresentational capacities (Leslie, 1987). The second approach emphasizes what I call the socialization of cognition. Here investigators have hypothesized that social interactions sponsor crucial changes in the child's thinking and reasoning (Rogoff and Wertsch, 1984; Wertsch, 1984; Wertsch, 1979). Investigators from this perspective tend to cite Vygotsky (1978) as emphasizing that advances in intrapsychic processes stem from previously experienced interpersonal processes.

A perspective on cognitive development as representing theory development focuses attention on a third sort of process determining cognitive change. I have termed this a process of conceptual engendering (Wellman and Gelman, 1988). In this process, an early achieved concept or distinction engenders or makes possible later conceptual progeny. It certainly seems that in the history of science, the formation of some new distinction or conception has often led to important further developments. For example, distinguishing between heat and temperature was pivotal in the formation of the modern caloric theory of heat (Wiser and Carey, 1983). Similarly, a conception of zero led to basic changes in our understanding of number and mathematics (Kline, 1972). The basic idea here is simple: new ideas come from old ones; new concepts come from transformations of existing ones. Concepts have ancestors, parents, and descendants, and tracing such conceptual family trees provides insight into and a starting point for eventually answering deeper questions about how ideas produce and reproduce other ideas. In short, I believe there is a history of ideas to be traced and understood in cognitive development as well as in intellectual history and that conceptual change in this sense is an important part of the story of cognitive development.

This perspective on cognitive development and on theory change inevitably confronts two related issues: how to conceive of and analyze conceptual continuity in development and how to conceive of and analyze conceptual change or discontinuity. Let me consider discontinuity first. Some philosophers of science, for example, Feyerabend (1962; and possibly Kuhn, 1962, but not Kuhn, 1983), hold that scientific change has yielded new theories that are radically incommensurate with their predecessors. In essence, since the meanings of terms, even observation terms, are determined by the theory that frames them, and since such theories change, then adherents to different theories speak radically different languages and cannot communicate with one another.

When in this book I have claimed, for example, that three-year-olds' theory of mind is commensurate with our own, I mean we do not face this sort of radical incommensurability between our theory and theirs. Our theory and theirs are not as discrepant, for example, as cognitive psychology and behaviorism. If children were behaviorists, parsing the domain of human action solely into externally observable behaviors and their contingent relations to objectively described antecedent and consequent stimuli, I do not think that we and they could talk sensibly at all. Additionally, our theories and children's are not as discrepant as Piaget's description of childhood realism and precausal animism suggests. Again, such a worldview seems radically incommensurate with ordinary belief-desire psychology. In contrast, three-year-olds' belief-desire psychology and even two-year-olds' simple desire psychology seems substantially more recognizable and interpretable in adult terms; we can and do talk sensibly with our children about human actions, beliefs, and desires.

Kuhn (1983) and Kitcher (1988) make the point that radical incommensurability is rare or nonexistent in the history of science. Less severe, more local forms of incommensurability obtain. Further, even when two locally incommensurable theories refer to different phenomena-in-the-world, scientific adherents to the theories can still talk to and understand one another. Here these philosophers distinguish between whether theories are intertranslatable or communicable. Two theories, one a predecessor and one a successor, can differ substantially so that it is not possible to translate certain expressions from one theory into expressions in the other, but adherents of one theory can still make sense of the other and communicate about it. How? As Carey puts it, "What one does in this process is not *translation* but rather *interpretation* and *language learning*" (1988, p. 178). If two theories are not intertranslatable they are substantially different. When theories are substantially different yet not radically incommensurate, their adherents can communicate sensibly about specific instances by identifying core agreements and referring to phenomena indirectly by extensive glosses of disputed or conflicting theory terms.

How does all this apply to cognitive development? Imprecisely, perhaps. But I mean something along these lines when I claim, for example, that three-year-olds' belief-desire psychology is qualitatively different from our own but recognizable and familiar. We can interpret three-year-olds' communication about psychological aspects of persons, although their explanations and communications often seem peculiar to us, requiring considerable effort at interpretation. Three-year-olds can gloss many of our terms although often imperfectly. And we constantly engage in attempts to teach children our theory; that is, we engage in language instruction in our adult theory.

To descend to the descriptive and specific again, I think I have charted two different theory changes in our developing theories of mind that are substantial in the above sense. These two changes also differ in their specific characterization and these differences are worth noting. One theory change concerns that from a simple desire psychology to a belief-desire psychology. It is difficult for adults even to imagine and make sense of a theory of human action that includes no conception of belief or representational mental states. The complexity and length of my attempt to characterize simple desire psychology attest to the difficulties. Still, with considerable interpretation and language adjustment, it is possible to see in our terms what such a theory must mean. Intertranslation is not possible; the later theory contains a concept—belief—not represented in the former one at all. Acquisition of this concept and the acquisition of belief-desire psychology thus constitutes a "substantial" change, resulting in a theory with an additional core concept unrecognizable in the terms of the first theory. Such a change is substantial along the lines outlined because the later theory cannot be construed as just another way of talking about the same things. We are not just talking about the same things, because simple desire psychology presents us belief-desire psychologists with more than just alternative descriptions and terms; it presents us with anomalies and contradictions, from our point of view.

A second theory change is that from a copy-container theory of mind, evident in three-year-olds, to the homuncular-interpretive theory of older children and adults. Again the change is substantial but in an interestingly different manner. It is not obvious that the theory change involves addition of an essential new core concept (such as belief). Instead, as I have characterized it, the root metaphors of the two theories change. Three-year-olds and adults are talking about the same things, in large part, but the metaphors that ground this talk have changed. Consequently the concepts and terms "fall into new relations with one another" (Kuhn, 1962, p. 149).

I am unable to answer very general questions about theory change as yet, questions such as the one that Carey (1985a) poses: "Do theory changes in cognitive development represent weak restructuring or strong restructuring?" In fact we know little enough about the nature of conceptual engendering that that may not even be the proper question. Still a descriptive level of analysis is available that captures several sorts of identifiable theory changes that do happen in the course of development. A comprehensive understanding of everyday theory change requires insights garnered from the study of actual theory change.

Universality?

What of children who grow up in a different culture? Do they too develop an initial belief-desire psychology along the lines suggested here? It would be grand to be able to answer this question. It is related to the intriguing question of how our basic knowledge of the world is socialized, and it is part and parcel of the question of whether any of our most basic theories are universal. But I cannot answer the question definitively, and I find myself in two minds about it.

First Mind

Most often I believe that some basic aspects of initial belief-desire psychology must be universal. These aspects include the fundamental distinction between mind and world, the basic difference within the mind between the two generic categories of beliefs and desires (between thoughts and ideas versus wants, longings, and simple intentions), and the causal combination of beliefs and desires to produce actions. When I think that these may well be universal acquisitions, it is not because I believe them to be simply innate (Fodor 1987) but more because I suspect that these are very real qualities of mind itself. If the mind is indeed like this, then all cultural theories of mind that have survived the test of time will probably honor these distinctions in some fashion. When I am thinking in this way, I do not think that the details of belief-desire psychology will be replicated in every human culture. My description in chapter 4 is too inevitably bound up in the specifics of our own Western European construal to capture such universality. But still I feel that that description rests on some quite basic distinctions, such as the three just mentioned, that must be honored in some form by any viable theory of mind. For example, I think to myself, there just is a difference between (our experience of) the mental world and (our experience of) the real world. Ideas are not physical things, and no viable society's ontological understanding can afford to confuse the two. Of course, I do not mean that all cultures would judge ideas and dreams as "not-real" and physical objects as "real" as we do. Some other cultures might think that ideas, or better yet dreams, are real in some very profound sense (beyond our understanding that they are "real" dreams). Still, I tell myself, those cultures could not fail to honor some deep distinction in the reality status between these two sorts of phenomena, just because they are so different. In this way I find myself working toward a minimalist but still firmly universalist position. Some deep truths are captured in our theory of mind, and these truths must be seriously encompassed in some form by all commonsense theories of mind. In this way there may well be something about our naive belief-desire theory of mind that binds all human cultures together. (See also D'Andrade, 1987, for this sort of cross-cultural story.)

Second Mind

At other times I pull myself back from this line of thought and consider another view. I note, for example, how the belief-desire theory characterized in chapter 4 is, at its deepest level, one that concerns itself primarily with the issue of individual human agency. It is the inner mental world of individual humans that accounts for their intentional acts. Such an initial concern with individual agency seems so in tune with a modern Western concern with individualism that I begin to think it is tainted at the start with our cultural worldview. Surely there are other cultures of thought where social interaction and unity, for example, rather than individual agency form the basic building blocks for a theory of human action. If so, such a cultural-intellectual tradition may well encompass a theory of mind so different in initial form from our individualistic one that it truly constitutes an alternative theory radically unlike our own. There are claims in anthropology as to the existence of nonindividualistic worldviews and speculations as to the radical differences that such social systems imply for basic ways of thinking (see Rosaldo, 1982). There are claims in modern history that we are moving toward a postmodern era where social systems rather than individuals will represent the fundamental unit of analysis (see Sampson, 1989 for a review). Certainly systems of faith and belief do exist that are so different from contemporary Western rationalistic ones that they suggest that our core notion of "belief," seemingly central to a belief-desire psychology, may be irrelevant in certain alternative worldviews.

The First Mind Again

It is premature to attempt to decide between these two different positions; however, I favor the first. I find it hard to imagine, for example, that even a culture whose views of persons and mind are fundamentally social (rather than individual) can avoid altogether the grips of a framework theory of individual action. And I read contemporary work on infant cognition as confirming that at an early age infants parse the world into individuated objects and vigorously explore how such objects move and change (Harris, 1983; Spelke, 1988). People too are individual objects in this sense, and the infant, however culturally situated, must possess a fundamental concern with the actions and agency of individual persons. If so, it seems to my first mind that something like a belief-desire psychology may indeed represent a universal commonsense achievement propelled to begin with by a universal infant cognition.

I repeat, however, that the answer to questions as to the universality versus culture-boundness of our theory of mind, and hence as to the universality of the sort of developmental story I have told, are at present beyond me. These are intriguing questions to unravel in the future. Even posing these questions, however, underwrites the importance of studying everyday theory of mind and, as a first step, properly characterizing the nature and development of our own.

Eliminative Materialism

Throughout this book I have avoided taking a stand on whether our everyday belief-desire psychology and theory of mind are right or true: "We must deal with commonsense psychology regardless of whether its assumptions and principles prove valid under scientific scrutiny. If a person believes the lines in his palm foretell his future, this belief must be taken into account in explaining certain of his expectations and actions" (Heider, 1958, p. 5). Everyday psychology profoundly influences us even if it should prove completely wide of the mark. It is self-fulfilling in this way. To the extent that we construe and treat ourselves and others as belief-desire organisms, then this constitutes a personal-social world that is quite real, even if it proves erroneous as a scientific psychology. I have tried to investigate and understand the construction of this everyday reality.

Recently, however, it has become a matter of contention among philosophers whether belief-desire psychology, or the propositional attitudes, are approximately true. "Eliminative materialism is the thesis that our commonsense conception of psychological phenomena constitutes a radically false theory, a theory so fundamentally defective that both the principles and the ontology of that theory will eventually be displaced, rather than smoothly reduced, by completed neuroscience" (Churchland, 1981, p. 67). The primary issue under contention here concerns whether belief-desire psychology provides a valid starting point for the development of a cognitive science. If belief-desire psychology captures some profound truths about the mind, then it deserves pursuit. Cognitive science can advance in part by refining and distilling its truths and extending its explanatory successes. On the other hand, if belief-desire psychology is radically false, then cognitive science faces the task of eliminating the propositional attitudes in the process of achieving a true science of mind. I raise this issue not to join the debate. Regardless of where the truth lies and how this debate is resolved, no parties to it seriously deny the profound importance of belief-desire psychology to our everyday lives. That is the point that drives my research, and it continues unharmed in the midst of the fray.

Still, there are some implications in this debate relevant to my concerns and vice-versa. Importantly, this philosophical debate about elimination has contributed indirectly to a characterization of what everyday psychology is. I wish to make a few comments here because to my mind some mischaracterizations have been advanced. These mischaracterizations are not so serious for the conduct of the philosophical debate, but they become serious for my aim. To investigate acquisition of the theory, we must begin with some apt sense of its nature, and thus it is important to refine and undo mischaracterizations.

For my purposes, one sort of mischaracterization is that everyday psychology is "a loose knit network of largely tacit principles, platitudes, and paradigms which constitute a sort of folk theory" (Stitch, 1983, p. 1). "We could assemble the relevant folk theory by simply collecting platitudes" of the sort "toothache is a kind of pain" (Stitch, 1983, p. 20). "There is no escaping the fact that for a theory-theorist, most of our folk platitudes must be true if any attribution of a mental state is true" (Stitch, 1983, p. 21).

Folk platitudes are allowed by an everyday framework theory of mind. But platitudes of the sort described by Stitch are too specific and local to capture the heart of the theory, just as scientific statements like "the sun is a kind of star" do not capture a scientific theory such as celestial mechanics. Statements of this sort are the wrong level of description; they are by-products of a theory, not constitutive of it. A theory is not a "loose knit network" of such statements; it is an interwoven theoretical scheme that frames such statements. Something like the depth and coherence alluded to in chapter 4 is necessary to characterize everyday psychology.

A second issue of some importance concerns the successes and failures of everyday belief-desire psychology. To eliminative materialists:

> When one centers one's attention not on what FP [folk psychology] can explain, but on what it cannot explain or fails even to address, one discovers that there is a very great deal. As examples of central and important mental phenomena that remain largely or wholly mysterious within the framework of FP, consider the nature and dynamics of mental illness, the faculty of creative imagination, or the ground of intelligence differences between individuals. Consider our utter ignorance of the nature and psychological functions of sleep, that curious state in which a third of one's life is spent. . . . FP sheds negligible light. One particularly outstanding mystery is the nature of the learning processes itself. . . .
>
> Failures on such a large scale do not (yet) show that FP is a false theory, but they do move that prospect well into the range of real possibility, and they do show decisively that FP is at best a highly superficial theory, a partial and unpenetrating gloss on a deeper and more complex reality. . . .
>
> A look at the history of FP does little to allay such fears, once raised. The story is one of retreat, infertility, and decadence. . . .

Both the content and the success of FP have not advanced sensibly in two or three thousand years. The FP of the Greeks is essentially the FP we use today, and we are negligibly better at explaining human behavior in its terms than was Sophocles. (Churchland, 1981, p. 73–74)

This gloomy portrayal, by association, may create the impression that the theory is demonstrably erroneous, that it is a reasoning mechanism leading to straightforward wrong predictions about action. If so, one wonders why people would subscribe to the theory and, for my purposes, why children would ever adopt it. It is important to note, therefore, that the failures listed concern the theory's failure to progress scientifically. This picture ignores the theory's everyday explanatory successes, successes sufficient to motivate its adoption and use.

Dennett describes the theory's everyday success story. He addresses what he terms the intentional stance: the central strategy in folk psychology of treating people as intentional belief-desire organisms and predicting-explaining their behavior accordingly:

Do people actually use this strategy? Yes, all the time. There may someday be other strategies for attributing belief and desire and for predicting behavior, but this is the only one we all know now. And when does it work? It works with people almost all the time. . . .

Once the intentional strategy is in place, it is an extraordinarily powerful tool in prediction—a fact that is largely concealed by our typical concentration on the cases in which it yields dubious or unreliable results. Consider, for instance, predicting moves in a chess game. What makes chess an interesting game, one can see, is the unpredictablity of one's opponent's moves, except in those cases where moves are "forced"—where there is clearly one best move—typically the least of the available evils. But this unpredictability is put in context when one recognizes that in the typical chess situation there are very many perfectly legal and hence available moves, but only a few—perhaps half a dozen— with anything to be said for them, hence only a few high-probability moves according to the intentional strategy. Even when the intentional strategy fails to distinguish a single move with a highest probability, it can dramatically reduce the number of live options. . . .

Suppose the US Secretary of State were to announce he was a paid agent of the KGB. What an unparalleled event! How unpredictable its consequences! Yet in fact we can predict dozens of not terribly interesting but perfectly salient consequences, and consequences of consequences. The President would confer with the rest of the cabinet, which would support his decision to relieve the secretary of state of his duties pending the results of various investigations, psychiatric and political, and all this would be reported at a news conference to people who would write stories that would be commented upon in editorials that would be read by people who would write letters to the editors, and so forth. None of that is daring prognostication, but note that it describes an arc of causation in space-time that could not be predicted under any description by any imaginable practical extension of physics or biology. (Dennett, 1987, pp. 21–25)

The debate in philosophy also tends to lose sight of another of the theory's successes. Note that the theory is a framework theory; its viability and development depends on the success of specific theories it inspires. In this regard the framework theory has inspired numerous specific idiographic theories of some repute. Cogent, insightful biographies, for example, count as successful theory developments in this view. Biographers, novelists, and dramatists, perhaps, rather than cognitive psychologists are the most expert practitioners of the theory.

Eliminative materialists have significantly advanced our understanding of belief-desire psychology in one important regard: a general characterization of that everyday body of thought as a theory. They have been principal proponents of a theory-theory, the contention that everyday understanding of mind is a theory; indeed it is part and parcel of our naive psychology. It is true that their motive in this is to disparage the enterprise as a troubled, faulty theory, unworthy of scientific allegiance. But they have persuasively characterized the domain nonetheless.

My thinking about the mind has gained considerably from this philosophical discussion, and I am grateful for it. At the same time, however, the results and findings reported in this book stand outside the arena of that debate. Still, they may be of some relevance. After all, there are two sides to the debate. There are many cognitive scientists and some philosophers who do consider everyday psychology as providing some insight for cognitive science. Those scholars presumably will be interested to know how the naive theory is acquired, where its basic constructs come from, and how they are forged in the crucible of development.

Why Is Achievement of a Theory of Mind Important?

Let me end this book where I began, with the question: Why write it? Why take such pains to describe this naive theory and its development? I hope that the answers to such a question are clear by now. Belief-desire psychology is our framework theory of persons. As a framework theory it dictates our basic ontology, our parsing of personal action and thought into its most basic categories. And it dictates our causal-explanatory infrastructure, our basic grasp of how to go about making sense of ourselves and others. In short, belief-desire psychology frames our worldview. Piaget was right in suggesting that a creature with a different set of conceptions would live in an alien, fundamentally different world. Note in this regard that all the scholarly disciplines of the humanities and social sciences, as well as our everyday notions of morality, social interaction, personhood, and self-definition, are anchored in this framework naive psychology. We live our lives in this arena. Of course, since this is a framework theory, it is compatible with a large variety of specific theories, positions, confusions, and personal stances as to our nature and lives. Adherence to the global framework by no means answers all questions or ensures that we all think alike. Nonetheless, there is an important theoretical hegemony here, with the framework theory influencing this rich, derivative conceptual activity and debate.

It is helpful at this point to take up that persistent and intriguing thought experiment once again: What would an organism without this theory be like? Would it be like normal three- and four-year-olds? No! The data in this book contradict such a claim. Instead, and this more vividly shows the fundamental importance of acquiring the theory at all, recent research suggests that a good model for an organism without a grasp of belief-desire psychology is the autistic child.

Autism is characterized by profound deficiencies in social interaction and skill; it is fair to say that we cannot communicate to or cooperate with autistic children in the negotiation of a common social world. Our approaches and conceptions are alien. Research by Baron-Cohen, Leslie, Frith and colleagues (Baron-Cohen et al., 1985; Leslie and Frith, 1987) has begun to show that an understanding of mind, along the lines of that documented for normal three- and four-year-olds in this book, is beyond the grasp of autistic children, even those with mental ages much higher than three or four years. An understanding of mind, however, is within the grasp of mentally retarded individuals and language-delayed individuals with mental age of three or four years. Of course, the deficit in autism may be broader than acquisition of a theory of mind. Nonetheless, the research on this topic stands as an informative thought experiment as to how profoundly important an initial theory of mind is to our everyday functioning and social discourse.

For organisms that do acquire a theory of mind, once the theory is initially in place, it makes its importance felt in a number of fashions. I outlined its influence in several areas of thought in chapters 10 and 11 and now suggest some further, more subtle influences.

First, much human conceptual understanding is built on the shoulders of earlier understandings. We strive to comprehend novel, problematic phenomena on analogy to more well-understood phenomena. This is a powerful tactic in science (Gentner, 1982) and in everyday thought (Lakoff and Johnson, 1980; Gick and Holyoak, 1980). Since belief-desire psychology is an early and important conceptual conquest, it often is recruited to fill this role, to serve as analogical ground for further conceptual gains. Consider, for example, our everyday understanding of germs and the body's immune system. A typical and useful first analogical understanding here is to view this biological process on analogy to human conflict. Similarly, consider our understanding of the supernatural in the personification of a god. Recall as well the discussion in chapter 9 about the homuncular theory of mind, which itself depends on a metaphorical personification of mind. This particular analogical strategy for understanding is continued in scientific efforts to model mental functioning as something like an aggregation of demons or an aggregation of experts pooling knowledge at a committee meeting (Hayes-Roth and Hayes-Roth, 1979). Deliberate personification is a cognitive strategy we use often in many domains. At its heart it is an attempt to understand complex phenomena on analogy to our belief-desire understanding of human action and thought. This strategy is available to us and to children because of the conceptual potency of everyday theory of mind.

This discussion throws new light on an old complementary phenomenon, children's putative animism. Recent research has shown that young children are not animists in the way Piaget developed that term (Carey, 1985a; Gelman, Spelke, and Meck, 1983). However, once again there is a key truth in Piaget's early observations: young children do personify physical and biological phenomena. This can be viewed as use of the very potent strategy of explanation by analogy, of applying concepts from a better-understood domain to attempt to achieve insight into an ill-understood one (Inagaki and Hatano, 1987). Children, like adults, engage in this process, and this further demonstrates the importance of belief-desire thinking in our everyday cognition.

Belief-desire psychology is fundamental to our thinking about people and the world, and it is instrumental to our interaction with others. Belief-desire psychology and its concomitant theory of mind represent a basic and persuasive aspect of adult thought. Understanding the childhood development of this way of thinking is important. Capturing childhood thought in this domain helps us to understand how we have become ourselves, and it helps us to understand, guide, and interact with our children.

Notes

Chapter 2

1. The data for this one child were collected by Stan Kuczaj (Kuczaj and Maratsos, 1975). I thank Stan for his generosity in lending me his transcripts.
2. The questions were always asked in the order presented, but the 18 items were presented in two randomly determined orders.

Chapter 3

1. Within each type of story, certain procedural controls were instituted. Within the explicit false-belief stories, the order of the belief information (Sam thinks the puppy is in the garage) and the reality information (the puppy is really under the porch) were counterbalanced, as was the order of the two questions ("Where will he or she look?" and "Where is it really?"). In the inferred belief stories, the order of the two phrases ("saw the kitten in the playroom" and "not in the kitchen") were alternated ("didn't see the kitten in the playroom but did see the kitten in the kitchen"). In the inferred belief-control stories, the same precaution was taken in addition to an alternation of the order of the two questions ("Where will he or she look?" and "Is there a kitten in the kitchen, too?").
2. Across children, the location believed correct by the character was counterbalanced ("thinks bananas are in cupboard" versus "thinks bananas are in refrigerator"). In each story, the belief statement had two parts; the character, for example, (1) "thinks there are only bananas in the cupboard" and (2) "doesn't think there are any bananas in the refrigerator." The order of mention of these "thinks" and "doesn't think" parts was counterbalanced across stories and children so that each appeared equally often in last (and first) place. Thus, children could not be correct simply by predicting the last-mentioned location.

Chapter 4

1. Much of what I outline here is not new; it is composed from a variety of bits and pieces scattered among several writers. As important as the bits and pieces, however, is understanding the bigger picture. In this endeavor my thinking was initially aided by reading Morton (1980) and Willensky (1983). When I had roughed out an initial version of this chapter, I encountered an article by D'Andrade (1987) where he undertakes the same descriptive task, characterizing everyday psychology. His description helped me complete my own.

Chapter 5

1. One area of difference concerns what to term such theories: naive, folk, commonsense, lay, or everyday theories. In part these different names overlap; they are different but parallel attempts to capture the idea that such theories are held and developed by everyday persons, not scientists, and emerge out of commonsense or unrefined cognition rather than scientific methods. For this reason I use each of the terms at some point or another in this book. And the labels provide some needed different emphases. *Folk theory* or *ethnotheory*, for example, is often used by anthropologists concerned with the different everyday theories derived by different folk or cultures. In part, however, these different terms connote different evaluative stances. The term *naive theory* often conveys a disparagement of everyday knowledge and naiveté in comparison to the sophisticated edifices of modern science. The term *folk theory* is used by Churchland (1981) and Stitch (1983), both of whom believe that folk psychology will be replaced by cognitive science in the way that suspect folk remedies have been replaced by pharmacology. Such negative characterizations seem premature to me, and so I prefer the terms *everyday, lay,* or *commonsense psychology* and, analogously, *everyday* or *commonsense theories.*
2. In earlier versions of this chapter I contrasted specific theories with global theories. Pat Kitcher convinced me that a better terminology was that of framework theories because the issue of most concern to me is that these megatheories set the theoretical framework for our specific attempts to understand and theorize about phenomena. I thank Pat for, and have gratefully adopted, her suggestion.
3. Much of what I say on this topic owes an obvious debt to Sue Carey's recent work and writing (Carey 1985a).

Chapter 6

1. Analyses of variance (age × story type) performed on each of the nested explanation types shown in figure 6.1 (psychological explanations, belief-desire explanations, and relevant belief-desire explanations) yielded no effects of age.

Chapter 7

1. Kelli, as is true for many blind individuals, was not completely bereft of visual input; she had some ability to detect a minimal amount of light-dark contrast. This does not undermine my argument, however, because this marginal visual experience was not sufficient for her to apprehend objects, to see through barriers, in short to experience an articulated visual world. Yet she attributed just these sorts of visual experiences to others.

Chapter 9

1. This is something quite akin to Flavell's Level-1 versus Level-2 differences (see Flavell, 1988).
2. I claim that children younger than five or so understand something about imagining but have a passive-container understanding of mind. How does this work? Isn't imagining—thinking up something fictional—an active process? It works like this, I think. Young children understand people as active, that is, as inde-

pendent actors. Early belief-desire psychology explains just this fact. But they do not understand the mind as active. For the three-year-old, imaginings are something people do with the mind, not something minds do. An analogy to fictional drawings is again helpful. When making a fictional drawing, it is not the pencil or the paper that is active, it is the person. Similarly, for three-year-olds, in the case of imaginings, it is the person who is. An early understanding of imaginings, however, may be a breeding ground for a later active understanding of mind itself.

References

Anderson, E. (1960). A semi-graphical method for the analysis of complex problems. *Technometrics, 2*, 387–392.

Anscombe, G. E. M. (1957). *Intention*. Oxford: Oxford University Press.

Appel, L. F., Cooper, R. G., McCarrell, N., Sims-Knight, J., Yussen, S. R., and Flavell, J. H. (1972). The development of the distinction between perceiving and memorizing. *Child Development, 43*, 1365–1381.

Arnheim, R. (1974). On the nature of photography. *Critical Inquiry, 1*, 149–161.

Astington, J. W. (1988). Young children's understanding of the distinction between intention and action. Unpublished study, Ontario Institute for Studies in Education.

Astington, J. W., Harris, P. L., and Olson, D. R. (1988). *Developing theories of mind*. New York: Cambridge University Press.

Baker-Ward, L., Ornstein, P. A., and Holden, D. J. (1984). The expression of memorization in early childhood. *Journal of Experimental Child Psychology, 37*, 558–575.

Barenboim, C. (1981). The development of person perception in childhood and adolescence: From behavioral comparisons to psychological constructs to psychological comparisons. *Child Development, 52*, 129–144.

Baron-Cohen, S., Leslie, A. M., and Frith, U. (1985). Does the autistic child have a "theory of mind"? *Cognition, 21*, 37–46.

Bartsch, K., and Wellman, H. M. (1989). Young children's attribution of action to beliefs and desires. *Child Development, 60*, 946–964.

Beal, C. R. (1985). Development of knowledge about the use of cues to aid prospective retrieval. *Child Development, 56*, 631–642.

Beilen, H. (1971). The training and acquisition of logical operations. In M. Rosskopf, L. Steffe, and S. Taback (eds.), *Piagetian cognitive-developmental research and mathematical education*. Washington, DC: National Council of Teachers of Mathematics.

Boehm, L., and Nass, M. L. (1962). Social class differences in conscience development. *Child Development, 33*, 565–569.

Boyd, R. (1981). Scientific realism and naturalistic epistemology. *PSA, 2*, 613–662.

Brainerd, C. J. (1974). Neo-Piagetian training experiments revisited. *Cognition, 2*, 349–370.

Brainerd, C. J. (1978). The stage question in cognitive-developmental theory. *Behavioral and Brain Sciences, 2*, 173–213.

Bratman, M. (1984). Two faces of intention. *Philosophical Review, 93*, 375–405.

Bratman, M. (1985). Five grades of intention involvement: Demystifying commitment. Unpublished paper, Stanford University.

Bratman, M. (1987). *Intention, plans, and practical reason*. Cambridge, MA: Harvard University Press.

Brentano, F. (1874/1973). *Psychology from an Empirical Standpoint*. Translated by A. C. Rancurello, D. B. Terrell, and L. L. McAlister. London: Routledge & Kegan Paul.

Bretherton, I., and Beeghley, M. (1982). Talking about internal states: The acquisition of an explicit theory of mind. *Developmental Psychology, 18*, 906–921.

Bretherton, I., McNew, S., and Beeghley-Smith, M. (1981). Early person knowledge as expressed in gestural and verbal communication: When do infants acquire a "theory of mind"? In M. Lamb and L. Sherrod (eds.), *Social cognition in infancy*. Hillsdale, NJ: Erlbaum.

Broughton, J. (1978). Development of concepts of self, mind, reality and knowledge. In W. Damon (ed.), *Social Cognition* (pp. 75–100). *New directions for child development*. San Francisco: Jossey-Bass.

Brown, R. (1973). *A first language: The early stages*. Cambridge, MA: Harvard University Press.

Bruner, J., Olver, R. R., and Greenfield, P. M. (1967). *Studies in cognitive growth*. New York: Wiley.

Bryant, P. E. (1973). What the young child has to learn about logic. In R. Hinde and J. Stevenson-Hinde (eds.), *Constraints on learning* (pp. 417–425). New York: Academic Press.

Bullock, M., Gelman, R., and Baillargeon, R. (1982). The development of causal reasoning. In W. J. Friedman (ed.), *The developmental psychology of time*. New York: Academic Press.

Bullock, M., and Russell, J. A. (1984). Preschool children's interpretation of facial expressions of emotion. *International Journal of Behavioral Development, 1*, 193–214.

Cantor, G. (1970–71). The changing role of Young's ether. *British Journal of the History of Science, 5*, 44–58.

Carey, S. (1985a). *Conceptual change in childhood*. Cambridge, MA: The MIT Press. A Brandford book.

Carey, S. (1985b). Are children fundamentally different kinds of thinkers and learners than adults? In S. F. Chipman, J. W. Segal, and E. R. Glaser (eds.), *Thinking and learning skills*. Hillsdale, NJ: Erlbaum.

Carey, S. (1988). Conceptual differences between children and adults. *Mind and Language, 3*, 167–181.

Cartwright, N. (1983). *How the laws of physics lie*. Oxford: Clarendon.

Case, R., Kurland, D. M., and Goldberg, J. (1982). Operational efficiency and the growth of short-term memory span. *Journal of Experimental Child Psychology, 33*, 386–404.

Cavanaugh, J. C., and Perlmutter, M. (1982). Metamemory: A critical examination. *Child Development, 53*, 11–28.

Champagne, A. B., Klopfer, L. E. and Gunstone, R. F. (1982). Cognitive research and the design of science instruction. *Educational Psychologist, 17*, 31–53.

Chandler, M. (1987). The Othello effect: Essay on the emergence and eclipse of skeptical doubt. *Human Development, 30*, 137–159.

Chandler, M. (1988). Doubt and developing theories of mind. In J. Astington, P. Harris, and D. Olson (eds.), *Developing theories of mind*. New York: Cambridge University Press.

Chandler, M. (1989). Fledgling theories of mind: Social cognitive development from infancy to adolescence. Paper given at the Society for Research in Child Development, Kansas City, MO.

Chandler, M., and Boyes, M. (1982). Social-cognitive development. In B. Wolman (ed.), *Handbook of developmental psychology*. Englewood Cliffs, NJ: Prentice-Hall.

Chandler, M., Fritz, A. S., and Hala, S. (1989). Small scale deceit: Deception as a marker of 2-, 3- and 4-year-olds' early theories of mind. *Child Development, 60*, 1263–1277.

Chandler, M., and Helm, D. (1984). Developmental changes in contribution of shared experience to social role taking competence. *International Journal of Behavioral Development, 1*, 145–156.

Cheng, P. W., and Holyoak, K. J. (1985). Pragmatic reasoning schemas. *Cognitive Psychology, 17*, 391–416.

Chi, M. T. H. (1977). Age difference in the speed of processing: A critique. *Developmental Psychology, 13*, 543–544.

Chi, M. T. H.,, and Koeske, R. D. (1983). Network representation of a child's dinosaur knowledge. *Developmental Psychology, 19*, 29–39.

Churchland, P. M. (1981). Eliminative materialism and propositional attitudes. *Journal of Philosophy, 78*, 67–90.

Churchland, P. M. (1984). *Matter and consciousness*. Cambridge, MA: The MIT Press. A Bradford book.

Churchland, P. M., and Hooker, C. A. (1985). *Images of science*. Chicago: University of Chicago Press.

Clement, J. J. (1983). A conceptual model discussed by Galileo and used intuitively by physics students. In P. Gentner and A. Stevens (eds.), *Mental models* (pp. 325–339). Hillsdale, NJ: Erlbaum.

D'Andrade, R. (1987). A folk model of the mind. In D. Holland and N. Quinn (eds.), *Cultural models in language and thought*. Cambridge: Cambridge University Press.

Davidson, D. (1963). Actions, reasons, and causes. *Journal of Philosophy, 60*, 685–700.

Davidson, D. (1974). Psychology as philosophy. In S. Brown (ed.), *Philosophy of psychology*. London: Macmillan.

Davidson, D. (1980). *Essays on actions and events*. London: Oxford University Press.

DeLoache, J. S., Cassidy, D. J., and Brown, A. L. (1985). Precursors of mnemonic strategies in very young children's memory for the location of hidden objects. *Child Development, 56*, 125–137.

Dennett, D. C. (1978). Beliefs about beliefs. *Behavioral and Brain Sciences, 4*, 568–570.

Dennett, D. C. (1979). *Brainstorms: Philosophical essays on mind and psychology*. Cambridge, MA: The MIT Press. A Bradford book.

Dennett, D. C. (1987). *The intentional stance*. Cambridge, MA: The MIT Press.

DeVries, R. (1970). The development of role-taking as reflected by the behavior of bright, average, and retarded children in a social guessing game. *Child Development, 41*, 759–770.

di Sessa, A. (1982). Unlearning Aristotelian physics: A study of knowledge-based learning. *Cognitive Science, 6*, 37–75.

di Sessa, A. (1985). Learning about knowing. *New Directions for Child Development, 28*, 97–124.

Dretske, F. (1969). *Seeing and knowing*. Chicago: University of Chicago Press.

Dweck, C. S., and Bempechat, J. (1983). Children's theories of intelligence. In S. Paris, G. Olson, and H. Stevenson (eds.), *Learning and motivation in the classroom* (pp. 239–256) Hillsdale, NJ: Erlbaum.

Dweck, C. S., and Leggett, E. L. (1988). A social-cognitive approach to motivation and personality. *Psychological Review, 95*, 256–273.

Epstein, S. (1973). The self-concept revisited, or a theory of a theory. *American Psychologist*, 28, 404–416.

Estes, D., Wellman, H. M., and Woolley, J. D. (1989). Children's understanding of mental phenomena. In H. Reese (ed.), *Advances in child development and behavior*. New York: Academic Press.

Evans, J. St. B. T. (1982). *The psychology of deductive reasoning*. London: Routledge & Kegan Paul.

Fabricius, W. V., Sophian, C., and Wellman, H. M. (1987). Young children's sensitivity to logical necessity in their inferential search behavior. *Child Development*, 58, 409–423.

Fabricius, W. V., and Wellman, H. M. (1983). Children's understanding of retrieval cue utilization. *Developmental Psychology*, 19, 15–21.

Feyerabend, P. (1962). Explanation, reduction, and empiricism. In H. Feigl and G. Maxwell (eds.), *Minnesota studies in the philosophy of science* (vol. 3). Minneapolis: University of Minnesota Press.

Fischer, K. W. (1980). A theory of cognitive development: The control and construction of hierarchies of skills. *Psychological Review*, 87, 477–531.

Flapan, D. (1968). *Children's understanding of social interactions*. New York: Teachers College Press.

Flavell, J. H. (1970a). Cognitive development. In P. H. Mussen (ed.), *Carmichael's manual of child psychology* (vol. 1). New York: Wiley.

Flavell, J. H. (1970b). Developmental studies of mediated memory. In H. Reese and L. Lipsitt (eds.), *Advances in child development and behavior*. New York: Academic Press.

Flavell, J. H. (1971a). Stage-related properties of cognitive development. *Cognitive Psychology*, 2, 421–453.

Flavell, J. H. (1971b). First discussant's comments: What is memory development the development of? *Human Development*, 14, 272–278.

Flavell, H. H. (1978). The development of knowledge about visual perception. In C. G. Keasey (eds.), *Nebraska symposium on motivation, 1977*. Lincoln: University of Nebraska Press.

Flavell, J. H. (1988). The development of children's knowledge about the mind: From cognitive connections to mental representations. In J. Astington, P. Harris, and D. Olson (eds.), *Developing theories of mind*. New York: Cambridge University Press.

Flavell, J. H. (1989). Three-year-olds' understanding of fact beliefs versus value beliefs. Paper presented at the Society for Research in Child Development, Kansas City, MO.

Flavell, J. H., Green, F. L., and Flavell, E. R. (1986). Development of knowledge about the appearance-reality distinction. *Monographs of the Society for Research in Child Development*, 51, Serial No. 212.

Flavell, J. H., and Wellman, H. M. (1977). Metamemory. In R. Kail and J. Hagen (eds.), *Perspectives on the development of memory and cognition*. Hillsdale, NJ: Erlbaum.

Fodor, J. A. (1987). *Psychosemantics: The problem of meaning in the philosophy of mind*. Cambridge, MA: The MIT Press. A Bradford book.

Forguson, L., and Gopnik, A. (1988). The ontogeny of commonsense. In J. Astington, P. Harris, and D. Olson (eds.), *Developing theories of mind* (pp. 226–243). New York: Cambridge University Press.

Freeman, N. H. (1980). *Strategies of representation in young children: Analysis of spatial skills and drawing processes*. London: Academic Press.

Gelman, R., and Baillargeon, R. (1983). A review of some Piagetian concepts. In J. H. Flavell and E. M. Markman (eds.), *Handbook of child psychology*, vol. 3: *Cognitive development*. New York: Wiley.

Gelman, R., and Gallistel, C. R. (1978). *The child's understanding of number*. Cambridge, MA: Harvard University Press.

Gelman, R., Spelke, E. S., and Meck, E. (1983). What preschoolers know about animate and inanimate objects. In D. Rogers and J. A. Sloboda (eds.), *The acquisition of symbolic skills*. New York: Plenum Publishing.

Gentner, D. (1982). Are scientific analogies metaphors? In D. Miall (ed.), *Metaphor: Problems and perspectives*. Brighton, England: Harvester Press.

Gibson, J. J. (1979). *The ecological approach to visual perception*. Boston: Houghton Mifflin.

Gick, M. L., and Holyoak, K. J. (1980). Analogical problem solving. *Cognitive Psychology*, *12*, 306–355.

Giere, R. N. (1985). Constructive realism. In P. M. Churchland and C. A. Hooker (eds.), *Images of science: Essays on realism and empiricism* (pp. 75–98). Chicago: University of Chicago Press.

Golinkoff, R. M. (1975). Semantic development in infants: The concepts of agent and recipient. *Merrill-Palmer Quarterly*, *21*, 191–193.

Golinkoff, R. M. (1983). The preverbal negotiation of failed messages. In R. Golinkoff (ed.), *The transition from prelinguistic to linguistic communication*. Hillsdale, NJ: Erlbaum.

Golinkoff, R. M. (1986). "I beg your pardon": The preverbal negotiation of failed messages. *Journal of Child Language*, *13*, 455–476.

Golinkoff, R. M., and Kerr, J. L. (1978). Infants' perception of semantically defined action role changes in filmed events. *Merrill-Palmer Quarterly*, *24*, 53–62.

Gombrick, E. H. (1976). *Art and illusion: A study in the psychology of pictorial perception*. New York: Pantheon Books.

Goodman, N. (1976). *Language of art: An approach to a theory of symbols*. Indianapolis: Hackett Publishing.

Gopnik, A., and Astington, J.W. (1988). Children's understanding of representational change and its relation to the understanding of false belief and the appearance-reality distinction. *Child Development*, *59*, 26–37.

Gordon, F. R., and Flavell, J. H. (1977). The development of intuitions about cognitive cueing. *Child Development*, *48*, 1027–1033.

Grice, H. P. (1975). Logic and conversation. In P. Cole and J. L. Morgan (eds.), *Syntax and semantics*, vol. 3: *Speech acts*. New York: Academic Press.

Hacking, I. (1981). Do we see through a microscope? *Pacific Philosophical Quarterly*, *62*, 305–322.

Harris, P. L. (1983). Infant Cognition. In M. Haith and J. Campos (eds.), *Handbook of child psychology*, vol. 2: *Infancy and developmental psychobiology* (pp. 689–782). New York: Wiley.

Harris, P. L. (1989). *Children and emotion*. Oxford: Basil Blackwell.

Harris, P. L., Marriot, J. C., and Whittall, S. (1988). Monsters, ghosts and witches: Testing the limits of the fantasy-reality distinction in young children. Unpublished ms., University of Oxford.

Hatano, G., and Inagaki, K. (1987). Everyday biology and school biology: How do they interact? *Quarterly Newsletter of the Laboratory of Comparative Human Cognition*, *9*, 120–128.

Hayes-Roth, B., and Hayes-Roth, F. (1979). A cognitive model of planning. *Cognitive Science*, *3*, 275–310.

Heider, F. (1958). *The psychology of interpersonal relations*. New York: Wiley.

Heisel, B. E., and Ritter, K. (1981). Young children's storage behavior in a memory-for-location task. *Journal of Experimental Child Psychology, 31*, 350–364.

Herrmann, D. J. (1982). Know thy memory: The use of questionnaires to assess and study memory. *Psychological Bulletin, 92*, 434–452.

Hodgins, D. (1987). You can't help me until you know what I can't do. Paper presented at the meetings of the National Association for the Education of Young Children, Chicago.

Hogrefe, G., Wimmer, H., and Perner, J. (1986). Ignorance versus false belief: A developmental lag in attribution of epistemic states. *Child Development, 57*, 567–582.

Holland, J. H., Holyoak, K. J., Nisbett, R. E., and Thagard, P. R. (1987). *Induction: Processes of inference, learning and discovery*. Cambridge, MA: The MIT Press.

Hood, L., and Bloom, L. (1979). What, when, and how about why: A longitudinal study of early expressions of causality. *Monographs of the Society for Research in Child Development*, Serial No. 181.

Hopman, M., and Maratsos, M. P. (1978). A developmental study of factivity and negation in complex sentences. *Journal of Child Language, 5*, 293–309.

Horton, F. (1979). Ritual man in Africa. In W. A. Lessa and E. Z. Vogt (eds.), *Reader in comparative religion*. New York: Harper & Row.

Huttonlocher, J., and Smiley, P. (1987). Emerging notions of persons. Paper presented at the conference on Psychological and Biological Processes in the Development of Emotion, Harris Center for Developmental Studies, Chicago, September 1986.

Huttonlocher, J., Smiley, P., and Charney, R. (1983). Emergence of action categories in the child: Evidence from verb meanings. *Psychological Review, 90*, 72–93.

Inagaki, K., and Hatano, G. (1987). Young children's spontaneous personification as analogy. *Child Development, 58*, 1013–1020.

Inhelder, B., and Piaget, J. (1958). *The growth of logical thinking: From childhood to adolescence*. London: Routledge & Kegan Paul.

James, W. (1890/1900). *The principles of psychology*. New York: Dover Publications.

Johnson, C. N. (1986). The structure of conscious experience. Paper presented at the Workshop on Children's Early Concept of Mind, Oxford, England.

Johnson, C. N. (1988). Theory of mind and the structure of conscious experience. In J. Astington, P. Harris, and D. Olson (eds.), *Developing theories of mind*. New York: Cambridge University Press.

Johnson, C. N. (in press). If you had my brain, where would I be? Children's understanding of brain, mind, and identity. *Child Development*.

Johnson, C. N., and Wellman, H. M. (1980). Children's developing understanding of mental verbs: Remember, know, and guess. *Child Development, 51*, 1095–1102.

Johnson, C. N., and Wellman, H. M. (1982). Children's developing conceptions of the mind and brain. *Child Development, 53*, 222–234.

Johnson-Laird, P. N. (1983). *Mental models*. Cambridge, MA: Harvard University Press.

Keasey, C. B. (1978). Children's developing awareness and usage of intentionally and motives. In C. Keasey (ed.), *Nebraska symposium on motivation* (vol. 25). Lincoln: University of Nebraska Press.

Keil, F. C. (1979). *Semantic and conceptual development*. Cambridge, MA: Harvard University Press.

Keil, F. C. (1989). *Concepts, word meanings, and cognitive development*. Cambridge, MA: The MIT Press. A Bradford book.

Kitcher, P. (1985). Darwin's achievement. In N. Rescher (ed.), *Reason and rationality in science* (pp. 127–189). Washington, DC: University Press of America.

Kitcher, P. (1988). The child as parent of the scientist. *Mind and Language, 3,* 215–228.

Kline, M. (1972). *Mathematical thought from ancient to modern times*. New York: Oxford University Press.

Kohlberg, L. (1969). Stage and sequence: The cognitive-developmental approach to socialization. In D. A. Goslin (ed.), *Handbook of socialization theory and research*. New York: Rand McNally.

Kreutzer, M. A., Leonard, C., and Flavell, J. H. (1975). An interview study of children's knowledge about memory. *Monograph of the Society for Research in Child Development, 40* (1, Serial No. 159).

Kuczaj, S. A., and Maratsos, M. P. (1975). What children *can* say before they *will*. *Merrill-Palmer Quarterly, 21,* 89–111.

Kuhn, D. (1972). Mechanisms of change in the development of cognitive structures. *Child Development, 43,* 833–844.

Kuhn, D., and Brannock, J. (1977). Development of the isolation of variables scheme in experimental and "natural experiment" contexts. *Developmental Psychology, 13,* 9–14.

Kuhn, D., and Phelps, E. (1982). The development of problem-solving strategies. In H. Reese (ed.), *Advances in child development and behavior*, vol. 17 (pp. 1–49). New York: Academic Press.

Kuhn, T. S. (1962). *The structure of scientific revolutions*. Chicago: University of Chicago Press.

Kuhn, T. S. (1983). Commensurability, comparability, and communicability. In P. Asquith and T. Nicles (eds.), *PSA 1982*. East Lansing, MI: Philosophy of Science Association.

Lakatos, I. (1970). Falsification and the methodology of scientific research programmes. In I. Lakatos and A. Musgrave (eds.), *Criticism and the growth of knowledge*. Cambridge: Cambridge University Press.

Lakoff, G., and Johnson, M. (1980). *Metaphors we live by*. Chicago: University of Chicago Press.

Landau, B., and Gleitman, L. R. (1985). *Language and experience: Evidence from the blind child*. Cambridge, MA: Harvard University Press.

Larkin, J. H., and Simon, H. A. (1987). Why a diagram is (sometimes) worth ten thousand words. *Cognitive Science, 11,* 65–100.

Laudan, L. (1977). *Progress and its problems: Towards a theory of scientific growth*. Berkeley: University of California Press.

Laurendeau, M., and Pinard, A. (1962). *Causal thinking in the child*. New York: International Universities Press.

Leslie, A. M. (1984). Infant perception of a manual pick-up event. *British Journal of Developmental Psychology, 2,* 19–32.

Leslie, A. M. (1987). Pretense and representation: The origins of "theory of mind." *Psychological Review, 94,* 412–426.

Leslie, A. M. (1988). Some implications for mechanisms underlying the child's theory of mind. In J. Astington, P. Harris, and D. Olson (eds.), *Developing theories of mind* (pp. 19–46). New York: Cambridge University Press.

Leslie, A. M., and Frith, U. (1987). Metarepresentation and autism: How not to lose one's marbles. *Cognition, 27,* 291–294.

Lewis, D. (1972). Psychophysical and theoretical identifications. *Australian Journal of Philosophy, 50,* 249–258.

Limber, J. (1973). The genesis of complex sentences. In T. E. Moore (ed.), *Cognitive development and the acquisition of language.* New York: Academic Press.

Lively, W. J., and Bromley, D. B. (1973). *Person perception in childhood and adolescence.* London: Wiley.

McCloskey, M. (1983). Naive theories of motion. In D. Gentner and A. L. Stevens (eds.), *Mental models* (pp. 299–324). Hillsdale, NJ: Erlbaum.

MacNamara, J., Govitrikar, V. P., and Doan, B. (1988). Actions, laws, and scientific psychology. *Cognition, 29,* 1–27.

Mandler, J. M., and Johnson, N. S. (1977). Remembrance of things parsed: Story structure and recall. *Cognitive Psychology, 9,* 111–151.

Mansfield, A. F., and Clinchy, B. M. (1985a). The early growth of multiplism in the child. Paper presented at the Jean Piaget Society, Philadelphia.

Mansfield, A. F., and Clinchy, B. M. (1985b). A developmental study of natural epistemology. Paper presented at the Society for Research in Child Development, Toronto.

Markman, E. M. (1976). Children's difficulty with word-referent differentiation. *Child Development, 47,* 742–749.

Markus, H. (1977). Self-schemata and processing information about the self. *Journal of Personality and Social Psychology, 35,* 63–78.

Marvin, R. S., Greenberg, M. T., and Mossler, D. G. (1976). The early development of conceptual perspective taking: Distinguishing among multiple perspectives. *Child Development, 47,* 511–514.

Miller, P. H., Kessel, F., and Flavell, J. H. (1970). Thinking about people thinking about . . . A study of social cognitive development. *Child Development, 41,* 613–623.

Misciones, J. L., Marvin, R. S., O'Brien, R. G., and Greenburg, M. T. (1978). A developmental study of preschool children's understanding of the words "know" and "guess." *Child Development, 49,* 1107–1113.

Montemayer, R., and Eisen, M. (1977). The development of self-conceptions from childhood to adolescence. *Developmental Psychology, 13,* 314–319.

Morison, P., and Gardner, H. (1978). Dragons and dinosaurs: The child's capacity to differentiate fantasy from reality. *Child Development, 49,* 642–648.

Morton, A. (1980). *Frames of mind.* Oxford: Clarendon Press.

Moses, L. J., and Flavell, J. H. (1989). Inferring false beliefs from actions and reactions. Unpublished ms., Stanford University.

Mossler, D. G., Marvin, R. S., and Greenberg, M. T. (1976). Conceptual perspective taking in 2- to 6-year-old children. *Developmental Psychology, 12,* 85–86.

Murphy, G. L., and Medin, D. L. (1985). The role of theories in conceptual coherence. *Psychological Review, 92,* 284–316.

Nezworski, T., Stein, N. L., and Trabasso, T. (1982). Story structure versus content in children's recall. *Journal of Memory and Language, 21,* 196–206.

Nisbett, R. E., and Ross, L. (1980). *Human inference: Strategies and short-comings of social judgment.* Englewood Cliffs, NJ: Prentice-Hall.

O'Connor, J., Beilin, H., and Kose, G. (1981). Children's belief in photographic fidelity. *Developmental Psychology, 17,* 859–865.

Olson, D. R., Astington, J. W., and Harris, P. L. (1988). Introduction. In J. Astington, P. Harris, and D. Olson (eds.), *Developing theories of mind* (pp. 1–15). New York: Cambridge University Press.

Omanson, R. C. (1982). The relation between centrality and story category variation. *Journal of Verbal Learning and Verbal Behavior, 21,* 326–337.

Peevers, B. H., and Secord, P. C. (1973). Developmental changes in attribution of descriptive concepts to children. *Journal of Personality and Social Psychology, 27,* 120–128.

Perner, J. (1988). Developing semantics for theories of mind: From propositional attitudes to mental representations. In J. Astington, P. Harris, and D. Olson (eds.), *Developing theories of mind.* New York: Cambridge University Press.

Perner, J. (1989). Is "thinking" belief? Reply to Wellman and Bartsch. *Cognition, 33,* 315–320.

Perner, J. (in press). On representing that: The asymmetry between belief and desire in children's theory of mind. In C. Moore and D. Frye (eds.), *Children's theories of mind.* Hillsdale, NJ: Erlbaum.

Perner, J., and Hadwin, J. (1989). Children's cognitive theory of emotion. Paper presented at the Society for Research in Child Development, Kansas City.

Perner, J., Leekam, S. R., and Wimmer, H. (1987). Three-year-olds' difficulty with false belief. *British Journal of Developmental Psychology, 5,* 125–137.

Perner, J., and Wimmer, H. (1985). John thinks that Mary thinks that . . . Attribution of second-order beliefs by 5- to 10-year-old children. *Journal of Experimental Child Psychology, 39,* 437–471.

Perner, J., and Wimmer, J. (1987). Young children's understanding of belief and communicative intention. *Pakistan Journal of Psychological Research, 2,* 12–40.

Perry, W. (1970). *Forms of intellectual and ethical development in the college years.* New York: Holt, Rinehart, and Winston.

Piaget, J. (1926). *The language and thought of the child.* New York: Harcourt, Brace.

Piaget, J. (1929). *The child's conception of the world.* London: Routledge & Kegan Paul.

Piaget, J. (1930). *The child's conception of physical causality.* London: Routledge & Kegan Paul.

Piaget, J. (1932). *The moral judgment of the child.* London: Kegan Paul.

Piaget, J. (1953). *The origins of intelligence in the child.* London: Routledge & Kegan Paul.

Pillow, B. H. (1989). Early understanding of perception as a source of knowledge. *Journal of Experimental Child Psychology, 47,* 116–129.

Poulin-Dubois, D., and Shultz, T. R.(1988). The development of the understanding of human behavior: From agency to intentionality. In J. Astington, P. Harris, and D. Olson (eds.), *Developing theories of mind* (pp. 109–125). New York: Cambridge University Press.

Pratt, C., and Bryant, P. E. (1988). Young children understand that looking leads to knowing. Unpublished ms., Oxford University.

Premack, D., and Woodruff, G. (1978). Does the chimpanzee have a theory of mind? *Behavioral and Brain Sciences, 1,* 515–526.

Putnam, H. (1975). *Mind, language, and reality.* Cambridge: Cambridge University Press.

Rips, L. J. (in press). Mental muddles. In M. Brand and R. M. Harnish (eds.) *Problems in the representation of knowledge and belief.* Tucson: University of Arizona Press.

Ritter, K. (1978). The development of knowledge of an external retrieval cue strategy. *Child Development, 49,* 1227–1230.

Rogoff, B., and Wertsch, J. V. (1984). *Children's learning in the zone of proximal development.* San Francisco: Jossey-Bass.

Rosaldo, M. Z. (1982). The things we do with words: Ilongot speech acts and speech act theory in philosophy. *Language and Society, 11*, 203–237.

Rumelhart, D. E. (1975). Notes on a schema for stories. In D. Bobrow and A. Collins (eds.), *Representation and understanding.* New York: Academic Press.

Russell, J. A., and Bullock, M. (1986). On the dimensions preschoolers use to interpret facial expressions of emotion. *Developmental Psychology, 22*, 97–102.

Salatas, H., and Flavell, J. H. (1976). Behavioral and metamnemonic indicators of strategic behaviors under remember in first grade. *Child Development, 47*, 81–89.

Salmon, W. C. (1984). *Scientific explanation and the causal structure of the world.* Princeton, NJ: Princeton University Press.

Sampson, E. (1989). The challenge of social change for psychology: Globalization and psychology's theory of the person. *American Psychologist, 44*, 914–921.

Scheffler, I. (1967). *Science and subjectivity.* Indianapolis: Bobbs-Merrill.

Schneider, W. (1985). Developmental trends in the metamemory-memory behavior relationship: An integrative review. In D. L. Forrest-Pressley, G. E. MacKinnon, and T. G. Waller (eds.), *Cognition, metacognition and performance.* New York: Academic Press.

Searle, J. R. (1983). *Intentionality.* Cambridge: Cambridge University Press.

Shantz, C. U. (1983). Social cognition. In J. H. Flavell and E. M. Markman (eds.), *The Handbook of child psychology,* vol. 3: *Cognitive development.* New York: Wiley.

Shatz, M. (1983). Communication. In J. Flavell and E. M. Markman (eds.), *The handbook of child psychology,* vol. 3: *Cognitive development.* New York: Wiley.

Shatz, M., Wellman, H. M., and Silber, S. (1983). The acquisition of mental verbs: A systematic investigation of first references to mental state. *Cognition, 14*, 301–321.

Sheppard, R. N. (1984). Ecological constraints on internal representation: Resonant kinematics of perceiving, imagining, thinking, and dreaming. *Psychological Review, 91*, 417–447.

Shultz, T. R. (1980). Development of the concept of intention. In W. A. Collins (ed.), *The Minne Sofa Symposium on Child Psychology* (vol. 13). Hillsdale, NJ: Erlbaum.

Shultz, T. R. (1982). Rules of causal attribution. *Monographs of the Society for Research in Child Development.* Serial no. 194.

Siegler, R. S. (1976). Three aspects of cognitive development. *Cognitive Psychology, 8*, 481–520.

Siegler, R. S. (1978). The origins of scientific reasoning. In R. Siegler (ed.), *Children's thinking: What develops?* Hillsdale, NJ: Erlbaum.

Siegler, R. S., and Liebert, R. M. (1975). Acquisition of formal scientific reasoning by 10- and 13-year-olds: Designing a factorial experiment. *Developmental Psychology, 11*, 401–402.

Smiley, P., and Huttenlocher, J. (in press). Young children's acquisition of emotion concepts. In C. Saarni and P. Harris (eds.), *Children understanding of emotion.* New York: Cambridge University Press.

Smith, M. C. (1978). Cognizing the behavior stream: The recognition of intentional action. *Child Development, 49*, 736–743.

Smirnov, A. A., and Zinchenko, P. I. (1969). Problems in the psychology of memory. In M. Cole and I. Maltzman (eds.), *A handbook of contemporary Soviet psychology.* New York: Basic Books.

Sodian, B., and Wimmer, H. (1987). Children's understanding of inference as a source of knowledge. *Child Development, 58*, 424–433.

Somerville, S. C., and Wellman, H. M. (1987). Where it is and where it isn't: Children's use of possibilities and probabilities to guide search. In N. Eisenberg (ed.), *Contemporary topics in developmental psychology*. New York: Wiley.

Somerville, S. C., Wellman, H. M., and Cultice, J. C. (1983). Young children's deliberate reminding. *Journal of Genetic Psychology, 43*, 87–96.

Spelke, E. (1988). The origins of physical knowledge. In L. Weiskrantz (ed.), *Thought without language*. New York: Oxford University Press.

Springer, K., and Keil, F. C. (1989). On the development of biologically specific beliefs: The case of inheritance. *Child Development, 60*, 637–648.

Stein, N. L., and Glenn, C. G. (1977). An analysis of story comprehension in elementary school children. In R. Freedle (ed.), *Advances in discourse processes* (vol. 2). Norwood, NJ: Ablex.

Stein, N. L., and Levine, L. (1986). Causal organization of emotion knowledge. Paper presented at the Psychonomic Society Meetings, New Orleans.

Stein, N. L., and Levine, L. J. (in press). Thinking about feelings: The development and organization of emotional knowledge. In R. Snow and M. Farr (eds.), *Aptitude, learning and instruction*, vol. 3: *Cognition, conation and affect*. Hillsdale, NJ: Erlbaum.

Stein, N., and Trabasso, T. (1982). Children's understanding of stories: A basis for moral judgment and dilemma resolution. In C. Brainerd and M. Pressley (eds.), *Verbal processes in children: Progress in cognitive development*. New York: Springer.

Stephany, U. (1986). Modality. In P. Fletcher and M. Garman (eds.), *Language acquisition*, 2d ed. (pp. 375–400). Cambridge: Cambridge University Press.

Stern, D. N. (1985). *The interpersonal world of the infant*. New York: Basic Books.

Stern, C., and Stern, W. (1931). *Monographien uber die seelishe Entwicklung des Kindes*. Leipzig: Barth.

Sternberg, R. (1984). *Mechanisms of cognitive development*. New York: W. H. Freeman.

Sternberg, R. J., Conway, B. E., Ketron, J. L., and Bernstein, M. (1981). People's conception of intelligence. *Journal of Personality and Social Psychology, 41*, 37–55.

Stiles-Davis, J., Kritchevsky, M., and Bellugi, U. (1988). *Spatial cognition: Brain bases and development*. Hillsdale, NJ: Erlbaum.

Stitch, S. (1983). *From folk psychology to cognitive science*. Cambridge, MA: The MIT Press. A Bradford book.

Suppe, F. (1974). *Structure of scientific theories*. Urbana: University of Illinois Press.

Tagg, J. (1988). *The burden of representation*. Amherst: University of Massachusetts Press.

Tagiuri, R. (1969). Person perception. In G. Lindzey and E. Aronson (eds.), *The handbook of social psychology* (vol. 3). Reading, MA: Addison-Wesley.

Taylor, M. (1988). Conceptual perspective talking: Children's ability to distinguish what they know from what they see. *Child Development, 59*, 703–718.

Tenney, Y. J. (1975). The child's conception of organization and recall. *Journal of Experimental Child Psychology, 19*, 100–114.

Toulmin, S. (1967). *The philosophy of science*. London: Hutchinson & Co.

Toussaint, N. A. (1974). An analysis of synchrony between concrete-operational tasks in terms of structural and performance demands. *Child Development, 45*, 992–1001.

Trabasso, T., and Sperry, L. L. (1985). The causal basis for deciding importance of story events. *Journal of Memory and Language, 24*.

Trabasso, T., Stein, N. L., and Johnson, L. R. (1981). Children's knowledge of events: A causal analysis of story structure. In G. H. Bower (ed.), *Learning and motivation* (vol. 15). New York: Academic Press.

Trabasso, T., and van den Broek, P. (1985). Causal thinking and the representation of narrative events. *Journal of Memory and Language, 24.*

Turiel, E. (1969). Developmental processes in children's moral thinking. In P. Mussen, J. Langer, and M. Covington (eds.), *Trends and issues in developmental psychology.* New York: Holt, Rinehart, & Winston.

van Fraassen, B. C. (1980). *The scientific image.* Oxford: University of Oxford Press.

Vosniadou, S., and Brewer, W. F. (1987). Theories of knowledge restructuring in development. *Review of Educational Research, 57,* 51–67.

Vygotsky, L. S. (1978). *Mind in society.* Cambridge, MA: Harvard University Press.

Wagner, D. A. (1978). Memories of Morocco: The influence of age, schooling, and environment on memory. *Cognitive Psychology, 10,* 1–28.

Weiner, B., and Peter, N. (1973). A cognitive developmental analysis of achievement and moral judgments. *Developmental Psychology, 9,* 290–309.

Wellman, H. M. (1977). The early development of intentional memory development. *Human Development, 22,* 86–101.

Wellman, H. M. (1983). Metamemory revisited. In M. T. H. Chi (ed.), *Trends in memory development.* Basel, Switzerland: S. Karger.

Wellman, H. M. (1985a). The child's theory of mind: The development of conceptions of cognition. In S. R. Yussen (ed.), *The growth of reflection* (pp. 169–206). New York: Academic Press.

Wellman, H. M. (1985b). The origins of metacognition. In D. Forrest, G. MacKinnon, and T. Walker (eds.), *Metacognition, cognition, and human performance.* New York: Academic Press.

Wellman, H. M. (1988a). First steps in the child's theorizing about the mind. In J. Astington, P. Harris, and D. Olson (eds.), *Developing theories of mind* (pp. 64–92). New York: Cambridge University Press.

Wellman, H. M. (1988b). The early development of memory strategies. In F. Weinert and M. Perlmutter (eds.), *Memory development: Universal changes and individual differences.* Hillsdale, NJ: Erlbaum.

Wellman, H. M., and Banerjee, M. (1989). Mind and emotion: Children's understanding of the emotional consequences of beliefs and desires. Unpublished ms., University of Michigan.

Wellman, H. M., and Bartsch, K. (1988). Young children's reasoning about beliefs. *Cognition, 30,* 239–277.

Wellman, H. M., and Estes, D. (1986). Early understanding of mental entities: A reexamination of childhood realism. *Child Development, 57,* 910–923.

Wellman, H. M., and Gelman, S. A. (1988). Children's understanding of the nonobvious. In R. Sternberg (ed.), *Advances in the psychology of intelligence* (vol. 4). Hillsdale, NJ: Erlbaum.

Wellman, H. M., and Johnson, C. N. (1979). Understanding mental processes: A developmental study of *remember* and *forget. Child Development, 50,* 79–88.

Wellman, H. M., and Miller, K. F. (1986). Thinking about nothing: Development of concepts of zero. *British Journal of Developmental Psychology, 4,* 31–42.

Wellman, H. M., Ritter, K., and Flavell, J. H. (1975). Deliberate memory behavior in the delayed reactions in very young children. *Developmental Psychology, 11,* 780–787.

Wellman, H. M., and Woolley, J. D. (in press). From simple desires to ordinary beliefs: The early development of everyday psychology. *Cognition.*

Wertsch, J. V. (1979). From social to higher psychological processes. *Human Development, 22,* 1–22.

White, B. Y. (1983). Sources of difficulty in understanding Newtonian dynamics. *Cognitive Sciences, 1*, 41–65.

Whiteman, M. (1967). Children's conceptions of psychological causality. *Child Development, 38*, 143–155.

Willensky, R. (1983). *Planning and understanding.* Reading, MA: Addison-Wesley.

Wimmer, H., Gruber, S., and Perner, J. (1984). Young children's conception of lying: Lexical realism-moral subjectivism. *Journal of Experimental Child Psychology, 37*, 1–30.

Wimmer, H., Hogrefe, J., and Perner, J. (1988). Children's understanding of informational access as source of knowledge. *Child Development, 59*, 386–396.

Wimmer, H., Hogrefe, J., and Sodian, B. (1988). A second stage in children's conceptions of mental life: Understanding sources of information. In J. Astington, P. Harris, and D. Olson (eds.), *Developing theories of mind.* New York: Cambridge University Press.

Wimmer, H., and Perner, J. (1983). Beliefs about beliefs: Representation and constraining function of wrong beliefs in young children's understanding of deception. *Cognition, 13*, 103–128.

Wimmer, H., and Tornquist, K. (1980). The role of metamemory and metamemory activation in the development of mnemonic performance. *International Journal of Behavioral Development, 3*, 71–81.

Wiser, M., and Carey, S. (1983). When heat and temperature were one. In D. Gentner and A. Stevens (eds.) *Mental models.* Hillsdale, NJ: Erlbaum.

Yaniv, I., and Shatz, M. (1988). Children's understanding of perceptibility. In J. Astington, P. Harris, and D. Olson (eds.), *Developing theories of mind.* (pp. 93–108). New York: Cambridge University Press.

Yuil, N. (1984). Young children's coordination of motive and outcome in judgments of satisfaction and morality. *British Journal of Developmental Psychology, 2*, 73–81.

Yussen, S. R. (1974). Determinants of visual attention and recall in observation learning by preschoolers and second graders. *Developmental Psychology, 10*, 93–100.

Yussen, S. R., and Kane, P. T. (1985). Children's conception of intelligence. In S. Yussen (ed.), *The growth of reflection in children.* New York: Academic Press.

Zaitchick, D. (in press). When representations conflict with reality: The preschooler's problem with false beliefs and "false" photographs. *Cognition.*

Index